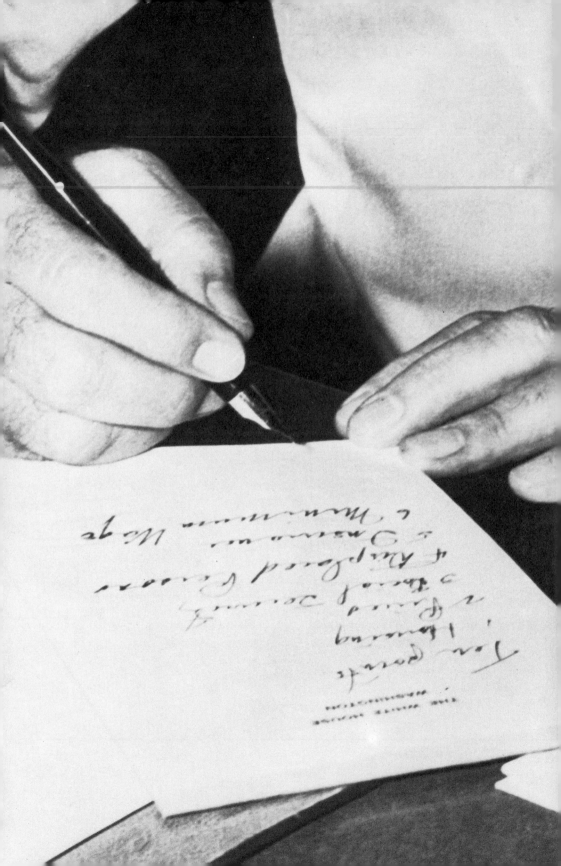

The Truman Persuasions

ROBERT UNDERHILL

The Iowa State University Press / Ames

For three girls, women, and ladies—Marge, Sue, and Sandy

ROBERT UNDERHILL was born in Van Buren, Indiana. He served as an air force officer in both World War II and the Korean War. He holds the B.A. from Manchester College and the M.A. and the Ph.D. from Northwestern University. In 1947 he joined the Department of English and Speech at Iowa State University, where he now is Professor of Speech. He initiated and presented a series of television shows entitled ''Mr. Speaker'' over WOI in Ames, Iowa. He has lectured to many business groups and has conducted seminars on various aspects of persuasion. His teaching record includes courses in persuasion, rhetorical criticism, American public address, and semantics. His scholarly articles have dealt with individual speakers in American history, propaganda practices, and the language of metaphors.

Portrait of Harry S. Truman.   TRUMAN LIBRARY

FRONTISPIECE: *President Truman with his memorandum of topics to be covered in his acceptance speech at the Democratic national convention in Philadelphia, July 1948.*   UPI

© 1981 The Iowa State University Press. All rights reserved

Composed and printed by The Iowa State University Press, Ames, Iowa 50010

Library of Congress Cataloging in Publication Data

Underhill, Robert, 1920–
    The Truman persuasions.

    Includes bibliographical references and index.
    1. Truman, Harry S., Pres. U.S., 1884–1972. 2. United States—Politics and government—1945–1953. 3. Presidents—United States—Biography. I. Title.
E814.U43   973.918′092′4   [B]   80–28803
ISBN 0–8138–1640–8

Contents

Foreword

AS a member of President Truman's White House staff throughout his first term and most of his second, I had unusual opportunities to see him exercise his talents of persuasion, to use Professor Underhill's aptly chosen word for one of the principal tasks of a president of the United States. President Truman excelled in face-to-face explanation of his convictions.

The Truman staff had none of the policymaking role that has come to characterize White House staff in recent years. We were aides, helping provide the president with information he needed for his dealings with the Congress, for press conferences, in preparing public addresses, or for meetings with government officials and the endless stream of visitors who trooped through the Oval Office. We were seekers of information, clarifiers of positions, and simplifiers of documents. In all this, we were adherents to the Truman philosophy that the best way to persuade is to present the facts and let the facts speak for themselves.

Truman had an appetite for facts, plain and unvarnished, and lots of them. He studied documents late at night and early in the morning, and it was a rare day when White House staff members failed to start the morning with a note or two from "the Boss" asking for more information on matters he had been poring over since the official close of business the evening before. Harry Truman seemed convinced that he could prove a case if only he had enough facts.

In retrospect I feel there may have been too much reliance on this simple doctrine of letting the facts speak for themselves. As Professor Underhill notes, we who helped him in the preparation of his speeches hewed so closely to his emphasis upon facts that there is little or nothing that may be termed eloquence in many of the most important pronouncements of the Truman Administration. Style was less important than substance. However, language that is too terse or too direct and unequivocal may close the door to negotiation or accommodation of conflicting views. A little ambiguity in political matters, domestic and foreign alike, can be useful. Truman's brusque terseness at a famous press conference in December 1950 misled allies into thinking that General MacArthur had authority to use atomic weapons at his discretion. This is one example that is well discussed by Professor Underhill. Others will come readily to mind when reading this volume.

President Truman's sources of information were extensive, and Professor Underhill correctly emphasizes the importance he placed on maintaining close personal relationships with Republican and Democratic congressional leaders. I observed the respect, for example, that he had for such Republican stalwarts as senators Taft and Vandenberg. No matter how sharp the differences in political philosophy might be on many issues, he benefited greatly from his private discussions with them and learned from such meetings how to state his own case better in the Congress and to the public.

In the Truman White House a sense of personal ethics prevailed that astounded all who initially had perceived him as no more than a Pendergast product. Once after a presidential meeting with congressional leaders in the Cabinet Room when the MacArthur issue was developing, an aide picked up a manila envelope left behind in error. It was clear from annotations on the face that it not only belonged to a Republican senator but that the contents dealt with Republican congressional strategy. The envelope was promptly carried into the Oval Office. Did the President want to see it? The response was as emphatic as Henry Stimson's had been when as Herbert Hoover's secretary of state he had closed down the department's cryptographic unit with the statement, "Gentlemen do not read other men's mail." Truman's sentiments were the same, more earthily expressed, and the envelope was returned unread to the Capitol by messenger.

A final word on President Truman: his persuasions were as effective as they were because they were a reflection of his personal convictions. No ghostwriter ever put words into his mouth that did not reflect deep-seated beliefs. No president persuades successfully on all issues. Truman had his share of failures, but his successes were numerous and are increasingly recognized. We are indebted to Professor Underhill in helping us understand some of the sources of those successes.

GEORGE M. ELSEY

Washington, D.C.
February, 1981

Preface

ONE night in October of 1963 I sat, along with 4000 other closely packed listeners, in a gymnasium at Grinnell College. We were there to hear a speech by former President Harry Truman, who had come to that campus to serve as "statesman-in-residence." In many ways, the evening typified Truman's career. The program began awkwardly and developed erratically, but through it all Truman persevered and by the time the evening ended he had captured the crowd's admiration.

The ceremony was opened by a male quartet who appeared on stage to sing "The Star Spangled Banner." The audience dutifully arose but was unsure—was it expected to join the singing? Some people did; others just stood in respectful silence. While the anthem was being sung, a large American flag slowly descended from rollers on the wall in back of the quartet. Unfortunately, the rollers jammed, and when the anthem ended the flag had unfurled only partially. The leader looked around, sized up the situation, and gamely started the anthem again. Then with a sudden thud the rest of the flag dropped down. The quartet was startled but finished the song for a second time. The singers retired; the audience sat down; and the professor who had conceived the idea of inviting President Truman to Grinnell came out and made a short speech of tribute. The listeners expected him to present President Truman, but instead he introduced the president of the college. That dignitary then came on stage and made a slightly longer speech of introduction for Truman. Most of us were mildly disappointed by the delay but accepted the idea that it was only fitting for the highest official of the college to present a former president. We expected that the person we had come to hear would next appear from the wings. However, after his praise of Truman, the college president abruptly said, "Now I want to present to you the Governor of the State of Iowa." So Governor Harold Hughes next strode onto the stage. He too made a speech introducing President Truman. At last, Truman himself came out to applause from the standing crowd. After a proper period of acknowledgement, he approached the lectern and began, "Ladies and Gentlemen—," whereupon the professor jumped up and interrupted, "Just a minute, Mr. President." The professor again praised Truman and then presented him with an appropriately inscribed "chair," which was brought onto the stage. After these delays, Truman stepped cautiously to the lectern and with his familiar grin asked impishly, "Now, Professor, may I speak?" His question delighted the crowd.

In his speech, Truman offered no new or momentous ideas, but he showed a warm and likable personality that seldom was apparent over radio or in newsreels. His speech that night in Grinnell was but one of many experiences that helped reinforce my growing bias in his favor. As a student and teacher of public address, my background has demanded studying and even on occasion memorizing passages from such oratorical giants as Webster, Hayne, Lincoln, Wilson, and Franklin Roosevelt. In their biographies, the bridge between eloquence and leadership is evident and incontrovertible. Harry Truman, on the contrary, was a person no one ever called eloquent, and few observers even considered him a strong public speaker.

It is a truism that in our democracy the president must speak often and effectively. Nor can there be much doubt that President Truman led our country through one of its most critical eras. This book is the result of my attempt to explain the paradox between his lack of traditional eloquence and his successes in public persuasions.

Whatever its worth, the book would not have been possible without the help of many persons. I appreciate the encouragement given me by President Robert Parks and Vice-President George Christensen of Iowa State University, whose farsighted administration made possible a faculty leave that permitted more concentrated research into Truman's career.

I want also to acknowledge appreciation for the ever courteous and always helpful assistance of officials at the Harry S. Truman Library in Independence, Missouri, particularly archivists Dennis Bilger, Irwin Mueller, Warren Ohrvall, and librarians Elizabeth Safly and Pauline Testerman.

My special thanks go to my longtime friend and colleague at Iowa State, Professor Keith Huntress, whose career and writing provide constant stimulation.

And finally, my thanks go to my family who have waited more or less patiently for this publication but who often must have wondered why I spent so much time in libraries.

WRU

The Truman Persuasions

1

Eloquence and Presidents

THE speaker was nervous; everyone could see that. His voice, naturally thin and somewhat nasal, now was strained and higher pitched than usual. His hands shook; his normally ruddy complexion had paled; and small beads of sweat were popping out on his forehead. The audience although small by most standards appeared to him as a huge sea of white faces all staring curiously, expecting him either to fall down or say something brilliant. He did neither, but he clearly had a bad case of stage fright—that bugaboo of so many public speakers.

The man was thirty-eight years old and giving his first bona fide public speech. He had been a farmer, a soldier who had fought bravely in some of the bloodiest battles of World War I, and then a businessman in Kansas City. Yet he later would remark about this early platform ordeal:

> That first meeting was a flop for me. I was scared worse than I was when I first came under fire in 1918.[1]

The man had decided to run for public office and was giving his talk in the little community known as Oak Grove, Missouri. Today Oak Grove is a mere cluster of homes lying alongside the busy interstate highway that runs east out of Independence—a town which in turn is so close to Kansas City that only an alert motorist will notice the sign marking the line between the city proper and suburban Independence. However in 1922 Oak Grove was more rustic, and at a picnic there on a sweltering day in July a nervous but aspiring politician mounted a platform to give his speech. More than two score years later this same man spoke to a crowd only twelve miles to the west on the steps of the Harry S. Truman Library. The number of years between the two occasions could

3

be numbered, but the experiences encountered by the man in that span of time were immeasurable by any standard.

On the first occasion in 1922, Candidate Harry S. Truman was running for judge of the Eastern Division of the Jackson County Court. The day saw him launch his first political campaign, and it also was the day on which he took his first airplane ride. He had initiated a promotion stunt by getting a military buddy from World War I, Ed McKim, to swing a deal with a former army pilot to fly over the crowd and drop circulars. The pilot, Clarence England, and Truman went up in an old jenny plane "held together with baling wire" and dropped the leaflets somewhat as planned. In later years, McKim recounted the episode:

> Well, we got them started off and got the leaflets loaded in; they took off from the pasture, and circled around this picnic in Oak Grove. Then they were to come down in a pasture right next to the picnic grounds. They came down all right, but Clarence [the pilot] had a little trouble stopping the plane, and it ended up about three feet from a barbed wire fence. Our candidate got out and gave forth with a lot of things I know he didn't eat. He was as green as grass. I think it was his first flight, but he mounted the rostrum and made a speech.[2]

The second event occurred on July 5, 1965, when an eighty-one-year-old man, poised and assured after having received the highest accolades his country could bestow, spoke on the lawn of the national library named in his honor. More than a thousand friends, townspeople, and tourists had come to Independence to visit the Truman Memorial Library and to hear the aged former president deliver an old-fashioned history lesson. This time Harry Truman was neither an aspiring politician nor a frightened speaker. Flashing his broadest smile, he exuded self-confidence as he acknowledged greetings, cheers, and good wishes from the crowd. On this occasion he stuck closely to his prepared speech and offered no wisecracks. He read from a small white tablet, pausing occasionally when the glinting sun blinded his vision, and remarking once with a wry grin, "I can't read my own writing." The crowd chuckled delightedly, for they were with him all the way, right from the first, when he peered over his glasses and said with a schoolteacher's look, "I'm going to talk to you a little bit about the Fourth of July."[3]

The history lesson he gave spanned all 189 years of his country's record, from the day in July of 1776, when the Continental Congress passed its momentous resolutions, through the year that saw the admission of Alaska and Hawaii as the forty-ninth and fiftieth states. Although he lived seven more years, it was quite fitting that in his last public speech President Truman talked about American history, a subject especially dear to him. He closed his final public address by summing up:

When those 13 little colonies started this whole thing they didn't think the
United States would amount to anything. But it's still the greatest country
in the world.[4]

When Harry Truman delivered his final public address he already had
secured a place among our nation's leaders. Most citizens believe they know
what personal characteristics had been responsible for his successes or failures.
Over the years, however, there has been controversy regarding the relative importance of personal leadership as opposed to social forces in the shaping of
history. During the nineteenth century a number of writers, notably Thomas
Carlyle, emphasized the forceful personality. "History," he wrote, "is the
essence of innumerable biographies." The American essayist, Ralph Waldo
Emerson, offered a similar observation: "There is properly no History, only
Biography." In his random but passionate study of history, Harry Truman was
always intrigued by the lives and remarks of famous men and women.

A different interpretation is offered by some writers who believe that great
historical movements are inevitable and that leaders have only limited power in
deciding which directions these movements will take. These scholars see history
as being determined mainly by social forces, and believe that conditions making it possible for acceptance of what may appear to be bold, new programs are
already in existence when a leader appears on the scene. They argue that the
"great man" is more or less an accidental expression of the spirit of his times or
the values of his culture. Proponents of the latter theory of history point out
that in 1932, when Franklin Delano Roosevelt came into office, the country was
in a severe depression and ready for nearly anyone representing change.

Most people do agree that a leader in democratic society must be one
whose judgments and feelings are accepted by the citizenry. Perhaps that leader
does not always initiate the arguments that trigger opinion, but he must
crystallize public opinion and direct it into a specific program. This means that
he is a persuader who can articulate his convictions, rationalizations, and opinions. When issues under discussion are clearly important to us or if the
American president is talking, the communication is more than a routine happening. The president's arguments and phrases are picked up by writers and
radio and television commentators. His ideas and expressions soon find their
way into the thoughts and vocabularies of secretaries and professors, auto
workers and salesmen, writers, bartenders, farmers, merchants, bankers—citizens from every walk of life.

No matter who he is, the president is the real Voice of America. Whenever
he speaks he is expected to set the tone, lead the way, or make some dramatic
announcement. He speaks with more authority than any other person in the
country, perhaps in the world. *New York Times* columnist James Reston once
called him the Number One Voice:

When he speaks, he speaks for America. . . . The President, consequently more than any other member of his administration or any political competitor, because of the pre-eminence of his office and the competition of the various news gathering agencies, can be assured of getting his views before the public whenever he likes. He is in part symbol, part executive, part actor, part "graven image." No man in history ever had such an opportunity to reach so many people so quickly and so often, with the assurance of an attentive audience.[5]

The goal of any persuader, including presidents, is to create favorable images in the minds of viewers and listeners, for it is the image the viewer forms of the speaker and his message that determines whether or not the persuader is successful. His words must be filtered through each listener's mind, and what is left after this filtering process is what determines action. As the history of the Truman administration began to unfold, it seemed clear that the Peppery Persuader from Missouri had won on the biggest issues he chose to champion. If his persuasive efforts were to be judged by the resulting programs and legislation, he was eminently successful.

What were the primary forces that led Harry Truman to his fundamental beliefs and values? And what were the real connections between his achievements and his skills of persuasion? The answers to those questions are neither simple nor ready.

Establishing causal linkages between a persuader and subsequent happenings is complicated by the difficulty the average voter has in knowing the real character and talent of official spokesmen. True, in our mobile society and through our electronic marvels we can now see and hear our chosen leaders more than ever before, but to what extent are public appearances and utterances faithful reflections of character and leadership? Is the charisma of a strong candidate the best qualification for public office? Is the best public speaker necessarily the best leader? What effect does theatrical ability have on the voters? The spoken words of high officials are widely reported, and these words may be perceived by ordinary citizens as being the "real" person. The perceptions become common images perpetuated through family talk, schools, radio, television, books, and recorded history. Kenneth E. Boulding has said that "a nation is the creation of its historians, formal and informal."[6] Other observers have argued that comprehension of complex issues cannot be achieved through the mass media and that increased public exposure of national leaders establishes a cult of personality.

In this age of organized persuasion we like to think that the person talking to us from the television screen in our home is speaking freely and without planning or motive. We are apt to forget the careful writing and attention to detail that may have gone into the public statements and appearance of our favorite candidate. The historian Henry Steele Commager opined that some of our nation's best presidents might have been defeated if they had been forced to appear on television and contrasted with a more glamorous but less able opponent.

In the two hundred years of our nation's history there have been presidents who were unusually gifted in their ability to use the spoken word. Through it they were able to capture public attention, to combat fears of war and panic, or to override feelings of defeatism and complacency. Fifteen presidents have served the nation during the twentieth century, and most were persuasive at certain times and on specific issues; otherwise they could not have been elected. Among these fifteen presidents three, Woodrow Wilson, Franklin Roosevelt, and John F. Kennedy, would have to be judged eloquent by almost any standards. In contrast and on any scale of eloquence, Truman would be weighed and found wanting.

Eloquence is not the only factor in persuasion, and perhaps Harry Truman was too blunt to ever be called eloquent. He lacked the ability to dramatize his ideals as Wilson had done through his speeches. Truman admired Wilson's record and the ideas he had so forcefully expressed from the platform, but there is no evidence that Harry Truman ever shared Wilson's ambition to become a great speaker. From his earliest youth the latter had longed to be a leader, and he viewed the effective use of language as a handmaiden to leadership. Since the leaders he admired most were orators, he determined to become one.[7]

If judged by the usual standards of eloquence, Harry Truman also suffered in comparison with the rhetoric of his immediate predecessor. After Woodrow Wilson there was a dearth of eloquence coming from the U.S. presidency. Presidents Harding, Coolidge, and Hoover made speeches, of course, but their addresses were neither long remembered nor stimulative of much public action. Not until 1932 did vivid discourse return to the White House.

No previous American president placed so much faith and importance in the spoken word as did Franklin Delano Roosevelt. Like Wilson, Roosevelt succeeded in putting his arguments on a high moral plane, and whenever a new issue or event took place he talked to the people. One of America's most quotable historians, Charles E. Beard, attached great significance to Roosevelt's speeches. The historian praised Roosevelt for speaking "with courage and great appeal," and he closed his book with tributes to Roosevelt's rhetoric.[8]

It would be impossible to appraise Franklin Roosevelt's presidency without paying attention to his public addresses. He gave thousands of speeches throughout his thirteen years as president; his fireside chats especially became noted for their informality, and his other radio addresses were often cited as models of eloquence. In the period immediately following Franklin Roosevelt's death there were many accounts and reviews of selected episodes from his life. Among the recollections, Bob Trout, a veteran newscaster whose duties had placed him in frequent contact with Roosevelt, noted one effect of his speaking:

> The President [Franklin Roosevelt] was known as an exceptionally able broadcaster. . . . He was the first statesman to use the radio as a vital instrument of social power. He used it in a personalized fashion. He saw, clearly the power of radio, before many men in government had seen it. . . . Now it is the custom for the heads of the greatest nations to make their most important pronouncements to all the world at once, by radio.[9]

Harry S. Truman followed this charismatic orator. After Truman himself left the White House and while historians and other citizens were still trying to place his presidency in perspective, there came John F. Kennedy, an orator in the tradition of Wilson and Roosevelt. The televised debates of 1960 afforded many American voters their first chance to see and hear John F. Kennedy. On four different occasions the two presidential candidates appeared together on programs which were broadcast over all radio and television networks. These joint appearances dominated all other news media and provided an unusual opportunity for the electorate to compare the persuasiveness of two aggressive aspirants. The 1960 debates were supposed to be in the spirit of the Lincoln-Douglas debates of 1858, but those confrontations a century earlier, important as they proved to be, had been attended by a total of no more than 75,000 people. In contrast, more than 85,000,000 persons heard at least one of the encounters between Richard Nixon and John Kennedy. Thanks to the marvels of our electronic age, a television viewer 2500 miles from the studio had a better close-up on his screen than did a person in the front row at Freeport, Illinois, in 1858.

The young, articulate Kennedy was never more eloquent than in his inaugural address, and yet like most eloquence these passages did not come easily. Theodore Sorensen, his chief speech writer, close confidant, and biographer, reported that no other Kennedy speech ever underwent so many drafts.[10] Work on the speech had begun immediately after the election in November. Kennedy told Sorensen that he wanted suggestions from everyone; he wanted the talk short; he wanted it to focus on foreign policy; and he did not want it to sound partisan, pessimistic, or critical of his predecessor. He solicited paragraphs and even complete drafts from advisers, newsmen, and friends. The final address contained many phrases that had been shortened, reworked, and polished. For instance, the "ask not" sentence was refined from earlier campaign utterances. In a former televised talk Kennedy had declared, "We do not campaign stressing what our country is going to do for us as a people. We stress what we can do for the country, all of us." A similar statement had been made in Detroit, but most Americans would note and remember the easy flow and balance of the final phrasing in the inaugural: "And so, my fellow Americans, ask not what your country can do for you; ask what you can do for your country."

Kennedy was a speaker who like Lincoln could speak the most sublime thoughts phrased in the simplest style. Any speech as delivered is necessarily distinct from the words that appear on a manuscript. Those who listen to a speech or watch a speaker are seeing communication that is never static. It must be seen and heard, perceived by eye and ear. The manuscripts submitted to Kennedy did not become speeches until he gave voice to them, and his ability to read them in a moving, inspirational manner won him praise for eloquence.

Harry Truman was a different kind of persuader. He was a winning speaker but one who never achieved eloquence. His genuine accomplishments have assured him of a significant place in our nation's history, and each year formal and informal historians are inclined to move him up a peg higher in the presidential rankings. No single speech he made ever matched the benevolent idealism of Woodrow Wilson, the dramatic utterances of Franklin Roosevelt, or the inspiration of John Kennedy. Yet Truman seemed to win the important arguments. The issues on which he spoke were as grave as ever faced any American leader, and his forthrightness in discourse compensated for what his addresses may have lacked in other rhetorical aspects. He was clear without being radiant, serious without being theatrical, and articulate without being inspiring.

Harry Truman was to become one of the most widely quoted of all American presidents. The quotations frequently are from phrases that were not original with him but instead were aphorisms, axioms, and common expressions well known to many persons, but he was able to give old phrases larger dimensions and newer applications.

It has become a truism that language affects thought and action. We like to boast that "we speak what we think," but often we end by "thinking what we speak." In this sense the words *language* and *speech* can be used almost interchangeably. The way a person uses language, therefore, is much more than a question of style; it is a reflection of the substance of one's thoughts and the quality of one's mind. Language, far from being merely a tool for exchanging ideas, may actually shape the ideas themselves.

Language is a powerful force, but it is only one of many forces making up the complex we call persuasion. To many persons the term persuasion means simply the influencing of beliefs or actions in other individuals. This simple definition may be adequate for casual discourse, but it says nothing about the logical, emotional, and ethical forces that bring about successful persuasion. Nor does it seem to recognize the role played by habit and impulse in human behavior. Actually, there can be no satisfactory, all-inclusive definition of persuasion, for the term is used in several different contexts.

Often persuasion does refer to the effort or attempt involved in influencing the belief of others. This usage is shown in a sentence such as: "He tried to *persuade* his friend to enter the race." The emphasis in this context is on the effort or attempt to induce persuasion. At other times, the word persuasion calls our attention to various stimuli which combine to determine human behavior or action. This usage is presented in a textbook definition of *Persuasion* as "discourse, written or oral, that is designed to win belief or stimulate action by employing all the factors that determine human behavior."[11] Frequently, the word persuasion is used in a third sense, that is, as a term referring to attitudes, inner drives, habits, and beliefs which may propel an individual to act in a certain way. Thus we might hear it said, "He didn't attend that church because he belonged to a different *persuasion.*"

All these kinds of persuasions enter into the life of every human being. To study the speech of an individual, therefore, is to study the sources of that individual's beliefs, his values, and his character. To examine the speech of Harry S. Truman is to examine more than just what he said. One must be ready to explore his early life and family influences, his education and adult experiences, his lifelong reading habits and informal writing patterns, his everyday talk and favorite expressions, his formal pronouncements and messages. These factors are the milieu that created the discourses of a leader who, if not eloquent, was eminently successful in persuasion—Harry S. Truman.

2

Young Truman in Missouri

Missouri has produced three notorious characters—Mark Twain, Jesse James, and me.

HARRY S. TRUMAN

HAD Harry Truman died before 1945—the year in which he reached his sixty-first birthday and became the thirty-second president of the United States—it is unlikely that a single syllable of his utterances would be remembered. He served the nation well, and when he died on December 26, 1972 he was eulogized as a common man who rose to uncommon stature. Interest in his life grows greater each year as more and more persons probe history hoping to find clues that will help explain his remarkable career. Behind the tributes lie eighty-eight years filled with episodes and experiences each of which in some measure helped shape his thoughts and actions.

The pages of history never contain an entire description of any single situation, person, or event, and no one, no matter how careful the effort, can recount every occurrence of one day, of one year, or of any one life. Certain events—possibly very influential ones—may be overlooked. Some happenings, of course, are remembered and passed from one generation to another, but in any period there will be omissions of instances which, if known, and reported, would be relevant to later situations.

How can one hope to recapture every significant circumstance of any man's boyhood? How persuasive are family and friends in shaping an individual's outlook and beliefs? How strong a chain can be forged between episodes in a man's youth and his actions in maturity? The answers to such questions are obvious. The best one can do is to recount a few events or situations and then infer their probable impact on the person's attitudes and decisions.

Harry Truman's Boyhood Era

In May the Missouri countryside is at its best, and it was in the spring in 1884 that Harry S. Truman was born. His parents, John and Martha Ellen

Truman, were living in Lamar, Missouri, a pretty little village which lies among the rolling hills of this midwestern state. In such hamlets life then seemed to spread outward from the post office or the grocery store where farmers and town folk gathered to discuss crops, cracker-barrel politics, funerals, and births. The arrival of Harry Truman did not receive much attention except among members of the family and a few close friends and neighbors.

Beyond the village limits of Lamar, Missouri, a great deal was happening in the year of Truman's birth. In Harrow, England, Winston Churchill, a speaker Harry Truman would introduce in Fulton, Missouri, more than half a century later, was only ten years old and having trouble with schoolwork. In Berlin that year the prefect of police received letters threatening to blow up the Parliament Chambers if Chancellor Bismarck appeared there again. Adolph Hitler was not yet born; he would enter this world five years later in a little town on the boundary line between Germany and Austria. That year Austrian anarchists demanded laws prohibiting further emigrations. In Rome the Pope issued an encyclical letter critical of Freemasonry, an association that would loom large throughout Harry Truman's political career.

The year 1884 was the third one for Chester Alan Arthur in the White House. During its twelve calendar months more than 800,000 additional immigrants would land on American shores. In eastern cities learned societies began to emerge; the Knights of Labor began yielding to a new organization that would be named the American Federation of Labor. The Brooklyn Bridge was officially opened and the Statue of Liberty was presented to the U.S. In the midwest the Granger movement, established first in boom times as a social association, now faced poverty and shrinking membership. It was a year that brought hard times to many and unprecedented wealth to a few. It was a year of change and contrasts, of complacency and unrest.

By this year 1884 a measure of the fierce sectionalism aroused by the Civil War had faded and was beginning to be replaced by other attitudes and opinions. There were pockets of old loyalties and antagonisms, and Truman's parents were among those who could not easily forget former animosities. Yet there was no doubt the young nation was changing fast.

The impact of writers and speakers contributed to rapid change. Charles Darwin's *On the Origin of Species* was picked out by some who applied his biological theory to political and economic matters. Most Americans accepted Mark Hopkins's earlier pronouncement that men who had strong desires for property had done the most to build the country; the venerable poet Walt Whitman fell into the mood of industrial growth and accepted "the extreme business energy" as an indispensable part of progress. The credo was expressed most simply in the writings of Horatio Alger, Jr. Dubbed "Holy Horatio" by his classmates at Harvard Divinity School, his first book, *Ragged Dick,* was rewritten more than thirty times under similar titles and identical plots. The theme was always the same: a poor boy who is honest, works hard, and has courage can overcome every difficulty. There was enough evidence to support Alger's thesis because the country had such an abundance of resources that enterprising individuals sometimes did find that success came from new ventures and hard work. The story line would later appear trite to sophisticated readers, but it dramatized the American dream and sold more than thirty million copies. It was literature that stirred imaginations and hopes in boys like the young Harry Truman.

American public opinion at the time was conducive to the gathering of great wealth, and a few industrial moguls were becoming famous. From the panic of 1873 emerged John D. Rockefeller leading the huge Standard Oil Company. In Chicago were Cyrus McCormick and Philip Armour. In Pittsburgh was Andrew Carnegie; from California came stories about the growing financial power of Leland Stanford.

There was beginning to be, however, an ever widening gap between the titans of finance and the average citizen. The breach was evident when one visited the hamlets, the farms, or the outer reaches of the growing nation. The gap was evident, too, in such remarks as one made by the aging William H. Vanderbilt, who, when asked why his trains did not run for the public benefit, replied crustily, "The public be damned!" The Commodore meant to run the New York Central Railroad for the benefit of its stockholders.

Voices of protest came mainly from the Midwest—voices that later would be called Populist. A decade later Hamlin Garland gave graphic descriptions of the hard, toilsome life of the average family voicing the protests—descriptions of disillusionment in the lives of men and women who hopelessly and cheerlessly helped make the wealth that enriched the financier but often impoverished the producer.

> The *Main-Travelled Road* in the West (as in everywhere) is hot and dusty in summer, and desolate and drear with mud in fall and spring, and in winter the winds sweep the snow across it; but it does sometimes cross a rich meadow where the songs of the larks and bobolinks and blackbirds are tangled. Follow it far enough, it may lead past a bend in the river where the water laughs eternally over its shallows.

> Mainly it is long and wearyful, and has a dull little town at one end and a home of toil at the other. Like the main-travelled road of life it is traversed by many classes of people, but the poor and the weary predominate.[1]

Truman's parents and grandparents knew firsthand the frustrations and disappointments that stimulated the Populist movement. Young Harry heard family members exchange stories of hard luck with crops, unpredictable prices, and extremes of weather. These chronic complaints were not readily grasped by easterners, city folk, and those who controlled the money, but they were standard topics for the Truman families.

Harry Truman was a thorough midwestern creation. The region with its culture and mores created attitudes that neither years nor public office would erase. His career can be fully understood only within the context of the geography and history of Missouri, particularly the Kansas City area. The Missouri Territory had been admitted to the new Union in 1821, but in many respects it still was a frontier state in 1884 even though it had two of the nation's greatest river ports—St. Louis on the east and Kansas City on the west.

Most big cities credit their origin to the importance of transportation in one form or another, and Kansas City is no exception. The first white settlements of any permanence near the present-day Kansas City had followed closely the purchase in 1803 of the Louisiana Territory. A trading post established by Francois Chouteau on the bank of the Missouri River about three miles downstream from the municipal dock in modern Kansas City, gave early traders a convenient market. From this post the trader had access by water to the entire valleys of the Kaw, Missouri, and Platte rivers and their tributaries. At this post, too, steamboats from St. Louis, four hundred miles away by river channel, discharged their cargoes. Traders and settlers were spared the long overland haul from St. Louis.

In 1826 by an act of the state's general assembly Jackson County was organized and named after the seventh president of the United States. In the period before railroads spanned the country the town of Independence, Missouri, was the jumping off point for both the Santa Fe and Oregon trails. It was the outfitting station and point of exchange of freight from steamboat to wagon trains bound for the western trade.

In sixty years the town of Independence and nearby Kansas City had shown staggering expansion, but living patterns in 1884 still were shaped by the river and weather. The daily newspaper then was not a regular commodity enjoyed by every family, and even if newspapers had been more common it is unlikely that the birth of a baby boy named Harry S. Truman would have warranted much attention locally let alone in the metropolitan papers of the East. In Missouri it might be several days before citizens would learn of events that had made headlines in the papers of the big cities. Only later would midwesterners learn that the front page news in the East for that day of May 8 reported the sinking of the steamship *State of Florida.* That vessel had collided in midocean with the bark *Pomona,* and one hundred and thirty-five persons were believed to have perished in the accident. Survivors with their grim tales of heroism and escape were just arriving in Quebec.[2]

In New York City where the leading newspapers, the *New York Herald* and the *New York Times,* each sold for two cents per copy, a small item noted: "woman suffrage received its annual defeat in the Assembly."[3]

In Washington, D.C., a bill establishing eight hours as the legal working day had been introduced but was lost in the Senate. In that body, the day's debate centered on a bill to place Ulysses S. Grant on the retired list of the army. Advocates of the bill stressed the financial losses incurred by the failure of the firm in which Grant was a member. The bill would secure to him the pay of a general ($14,500) and emoluments amounting to about $19,000 annually.[4]

Sixty-eight years intervened between the presidencies of Ulysses S. Grant and Harry S. Truman. The latter's grandparents on both sides of the family had emigrated from Virginia and Kentucky during the decade of the forties. Truman's grandfather on his mother's side was Solomon Young, a man who had driven cattle and wagon trains across western plains and through mountain passes in the years between 1840 and 1870. Later he set up a business outfitting other pioneers who planned to trek westward, and he farmed successfully near the small community of Hickman's Mill in Jackson County.

Hickman's Mill had once been a leading town of the region, but it had also been a center of activity for both Union and Confederate soldiers during the Civil War. When Order No. 11 issued by Brigadier General Thomas Ewing in August of 1863 compelled all citizens, except those who could prove loyalty to the Union and who resided within one mile of specified towns, to vacate their property, the population of Hickman's Mill grew to beyond the town's capacity. A year later the destitute and harassed Confederate army of General Sterling Price pillaged the town. Hickman's Mill never recovered from this direct involvement in the war.

Solomon Young's daughter, Martha Ellen—destined to become Harry Truman's mother—was eleven and twelve years old when these events around Hickman's Mill occurred. They were events she would never forget, and they helped fix many of her strong attitudes and opinions.

Solomon Young seems to have had considerable influence on his young grandson, Harry, and frequently took the lad to neighboring fairs and for buggy rides. Many years later when campaigning, President Truman's pride in his maternal grandfather would show itself in extemporaneous remarks:

> I left Salt Lake City the next morning after breakfast . . . and arrived in Kansas City, Missouri, in exactly three hours and a half. My grandfather made that trip time and time again from 1846 to 1854, and again from 1864 to 1870, and when he made that trip it took him exactly three months to go, and three months to come back.[5]

Harry Truman's paternal grandfather, Anderson Shippe Truman, also was a farmer in Jackson County, Missouri. He seems to have been a mild-mannered man, proud of his southern heritage and of his marriage to the daughter of John Tyler's brother. Later in life and as president, Harry Truman often referred to this relationship and attributed to it his own streak of stubbornness. He sometimes fabricated details by insisting that Grandfather Anderson Shippe Truman had run off with President John Tyler's niece to the consternation of the entire Tyler family and that years later it had been necessary for

Margaret Truman to visit Shelbyville, Kentucky, just to see if her great-grandparents had been legally married.[6]

In his *Memoirs,* Harry Truman wrote: "My grandfather Truman lived with my father wherever he went, and I remember him very well. He was a dignified, pleasant man, particularly with Vivian and me."[7] The child probably had little chance to know this grandfather, however, even though the latter did move in to live with Harry's parents in 1887. Harry was then only three years old, and Anderson Shippe Truman died in that same year.[8]

Harry Truman's father, John Anderson Truman, was born in Jackson County in December of 1851. Most of his adult life was spent as a farmer and livestock trader although his avocation of Democratic politics kept him almost equally occupied. He was a short man both in stature and temper, and he was known locally as "Peanuts." His granddaughter, Margaret, puzzled by the fact that in the few pictures taken of him he was always sitting while his wife was standing, estimates that he was about five feet four inches in height.[9]

In 1881 John Anderson Truman married Martha Ellen Young, and the couple set up housekeeping in a small white cottage in Lamar, a village some distance south of Jackson County and one hundred and twenty-three miles due south of Kansas City. The town was named after Mirabeau Buonaparte Lamar, second president of the independent Republic of Texas, who in the closing years of his life reversed his earler position and advocated annexation of Texas by the United States on the frank ground that such a measure was necessary for the preservation of slavery and the safety of the South. The naming of the town suggests its sectional loyalties during the "irrepressible conflict." On the line between free and slave state, the entire locality suffered from the border war of 1859–1860, the Civil War, and the depredations of bands of outlaws who came later.

On the day of Harry Truman's birth the news in Missouri reflected the violence and emotions of an outlying state. In Richmond, Missouri, Charles Ford, who with his brother Bob were the acknowledged slayers of Jesse James, shot himself. It was commonly said, however, "But little, if any, sympathy is manifested by the people, who look upon his removal by his own hand as one of the wise decrees of Providence."[10] At Hatton, a small village in the northwestern part of Callaway County, a black man named Ham Patterson was taken from his bed and killed by a mob. Patterson and his brother supposedly had circulated "scandalous reports" about many of the ladies in the neighborhood, and the town's more "reputable" citizens decided to take the matter in their own hands. Blacks in the vicinity were reported to be outraged over the incidents and were said to be making threats of vengeance against the whites.[11] In Kansas City the sensation of the day was a story about a presumably insane shoemaker, John Gill, who had fatally shot a young man passing his shop. The young man's father, first restrained by a crowd, was then released and having a shotgun of his own, "filled Gill's face full of small shot, putting out both his eyes."[12]

Stories of violence and destruction were not entirely new to the Trumans at the time. Most of the Truman kin were Confederate Democrats by conviction and were outspoken in their loyalties. Harry Truman's father, John Anderson Truman, had been too young to enlist in the military during the Civil War, but an uncle had served as a foot soldier in the Confederate army under the command of General Sterling Price. Missouri had sent 109,111 men into Union armies, and another 30,000 wore the gray. In spite of numerical superiority, the Union side never gained complete control of the state, and in 1884 there were still plenty of oldsters around whose lively minds and rich vocabularies could recreate various versions of the pillaging and the guerrilla engagements.

Martha Ellen Truman, Harry's mother, remained a Confederate sympathizer all her life. Without doubt, she was the person most responsible for channeling Harry Truman's early energies and in shaping his outlook on life. Even if she failed to convince him entirely that all Yankees were devils in disguise, he always remembered her persuasive maxims and colorful descriptions. She often would retell stories of that morning in 1861 when she was a young girl and Jim Lane, leader of a band of Union-sympathizing Kansas "Red Legs," rode into the yard and ordered her mother, Harriet Young, to be quick in making biscuits for his troop. While Harry's grandmother was in the kitchen baking the biscuits, the raiders went through the barns killing all the livestock. The invaders butchered more than four hundred hogs, ate the biscuits, slung the raw hams across the saddles, set the barns on fire, and then rode away.

Martha Ellen and John Truman were childhood sweethearts and grew up together on the families' neighboring farms at Grandview. John was fairly successful by local standards in his business of trading horses and mules. His barn was a natural gathering place for farm folk who wanted to gossip, talk Democratic politics, or "swing a deal." John himself had a sense of humor, quick pride, and a temper ever ready in the firing position.

Small and vivacious Martha Ellen (Young) Truman had in her character the tough-fibered determination often found in pioneers. She was a strong-willed person to whom frankness was a virtue, and evasions were sinful. Good and evil, heaven and hell, salvation and damnation—these were the eternal truths set forth in her Bible and rules enough for proper conduct. She described herself as a "lightfoot Baptist," which meant that she did not frown on dancing and other worldly diversions. Gaiety and dignity, fun and work could be blended by her moral code. This daughter of Solomon Young gave unusually strong direction to the lives of her children. Her influence on Harry was profound, and the son never attempted to deny it.

Martha Ellen Truman was thirty-two years old and had been married for two and a half years when her first son arrived. He was named Harry after her brother, Harrison, and was given the simple middle initial S. The initial by itself could have been in honor of either grandfather, Solomon Young or Anderson Shippe Truman.

> Dad owed the middle initial in his name to both grandparents. To placate their touchy elders, his parents added an S, but studiously refrained from deciding whether it stood for Solomon or Shippe.[13]

In keeping with local custom, John Truman proudly nailed a mule shoe over the door of his low, white frame home to celebrate the birth of his first son. Later that year he had further cause to rejoice when he won a seventy-five-dollar election bet. Always a loyal Democrat, he had wagered against strong odds that the Democrat Grover Cleveland would defeat his rival James Blaine. In the closing days of the campaign a delegation of Protestant ministers called on Blaine in New York City, and their spokesman referred to Democrats as the party of "rum, Romanism, and rebellion." Soon Democrats were spreading the news through New York and other eastern cities that Blaine had countenanced a slander on the Catholic church. His denial came too late to counteract the charge, and the incident helped swing New York State to the Democrats. That state turned out to be a pivotal one in the extremely close election.

Both by temperament and economic situations, John Truman found it hard to stay in one place for very long. While Harry was still an infant John moved his family from Lamar to a farm just southeast of the village of Belton in Cass County, and here another boy, Vivian, was born in 1886.

A year later the family moved in with Solomon Young on his farm at Grandview. It was named Grandview because it was situated on the highest point of land in the vicinity. Six miles north of it lay the village of Belton, and eighteen miles farther north was Kansas City.

One reason for this latter move might have been that Solomon Young needed help. His son, Harrison, was an indifferent farmer, and Solomon must have been about sixty-two years old at the time even though he was proud that he could "snap as much corn as any other two men in the field." As an inducement to John and Martha Ellen, Solomon sold them forty acres from his own farm, and they acquired another eighty that were nearby.

The couple farmed here for three years, and their daughter, Mary Jane, was born at the Young homestead in 1889. Harry's parents farmed at Grandview long enough and returned to visit it so often that it gave him a real sense of rural beginnings. It also was the source for many fond remembrances:

> We had the whole 440 acres to play over and 160 acres west across the road for the same purpose. Some of my happiest and most pleasant recollections are of the years we spent on the Young farm when I was between the ages of three and six.[14]

In 1890, when Harry was six years old, his father had amassed enough money to buy a house in Independence—a town which then must have seemed quite large to the boy because 6000 people lived there. The move meant that John Truman could better follow his interest in buying and selling mules, and it also meant more convenient schooling for the children. In fact, many years later Margaret Truman asserted that better schooling was the prime reason for the family's move into town:

> Mamma Truman [Martha Ellen] was the moving spirit behind the family decision to set up housekeeping in Independence. They had been living on the Young farm for three or four years, but the country schools in nearby Grandview were decidedly inadequate, compared to those in Independence.[15]

Truman's Early Education and Schooling

For practical purposes Independence today is a suburb of Kansas City, but in 1890 its separation from the nearby population center was more evident. Harry Truman had a happy childhood there. There were new friends to be made, animals to ride, and plenty of room for play, hiking, or short explorations. His mother, Martha Ellen, had attended a Baptist "female academy" near Lexington, Missouri, and had developed a taste for literature and the piano. She taught the basics of the instrument to her young son, and at the age of thirteen he began taking regular music lessons from a teacher in Independence. These lessons continued twice weekly until Harry was seventeen years old, and especially in the early years he was conscientious in his daily practice.

In addition to his interest in music, there was the town's small library. Harry's general education came mostly from his extensive but unsystematic reading. For many years the Independence Public Library had no more faithful patron than this quiet, studious little boy dressed not in the common overalls but in knickers and with a clean shirt and tie. He had begun wearing glasses when he was eight. His observant mother had noticed the trouble he was having in making out objects he should be seeing and the difficulty he had in reading fine print. Alarmed she had taken him to an oculist in Kansas City who discovered that the boy's eyeballs were so flat that he was severely shortsighted. The eye doctor warned him about the danger of breaking the glasses and injuring his eyes, so he did not try to play ball or join rough games with other boys his age. No matter whether it was natural inclination or compensation for his sight impairment, Harry Truman began developing reading habits which would last throughout his life.

His favorite reading seemed to come from history. At home there was the red-backed four-volume set of biographies edited by Charles F. Horne, *Great*

Men and Famous Women.[16] This set is extremely modest in size and detail when compared with modern collections, but the young Harry must have read each of the biographies many times. It was literature aimed to impress the young with the virtues of the great and good, but according to the editor the object of the works was:

> to furnish readers with a series of about 275 biographical sketches of eminent men and women who have greatly distinguished themselves in some department of human activity, no matter where or when. These sketches are midway, in extent and elaboration, between the short articles to be found in biographical dictionaries, and the long treatises which apportion a small volume to each subject.[17]

A "question book" accompanied the volumes, and listed after each question was the page where the appropriate answer could be found, The editor went further to promise:

> By being familiar with this work one can discuss almost any subject broached, for the world is what the great men and women of history have made it, and by being familiar with their lives, one knows nearly all that is worth knowing.[18]

The impact these abbreviated biographies had on the young boy can be inferred partly by the number of references Harry Truman made to episodes and lives contained in the volumes. For instance, in *Plain Speaking: An Oral Biography of Harry S. Truman*,[19] Merle Miller recounts interviews he held with President Truman after the latter left office. An examination of the conversations with President Truman reported throughout Miller's book reveals that Truman referred one or more times by name to the following persons included in the Horne collection:

John Adams	Alfred, Lord Tennyson
Alexander the Great	George Washington
Julius Caesar	Daniel Webster
Cicero	Benjamin Franklin
Grover Cleveland	Sir Francis Bacon
Gen. Ulysses S. Grant	Robert Burns
Oliver W. Holmes	Horace Greeley
Andrew Jackson	Alexander Hamilton
Thomas Jefferson	Stonewall Jackson
Gen. Robert E. Lee	Abraham Lincoln
Plato	Plutarch
Gen. Winfield Scott	James Madison
Shakespeare	William McKinley
Gen. William T. Sherman	Napoleon
Horace	William Henry Seward[20]

Another book always within easy reach in the Truman home was the family Bible. The Bible was relevant to his regular Sunday school lessons; it was the subject of frequent family discussions, and he liked the large type in which such Bibles were printed. On several occasions in later life, President Truman stated that by the time he was thirteen or fourteen years old he had read "our big old family Bible three times through."

Much has been written about young Harry's predilection for reading while other boys his age were playing and following other youthful pleasures. Truman himself was not immodest about the extent of his reading habits, and in his *Memoirs* he wrote:

> My time was spent in reading, and by the time I was thirteen or fourteen
> years old I had read all the books in the Independence Public Library.[21]

There may be pardonable exaggeration in this statement, however, if one remembers it was made by an elderly man looking years backward into his boyhood. The Independence Public Library then had about 3000 books in its catalog. The Trumans moved to Independence in December of 1890, and Harry had only eight years until he was fourteen. If his assertion were literally true he would have read on an average of 375 books a year or more than one book every day for eight years. Nevertheless, his biographers agree that he did read far more widely than the average youth, and he seemed able to remember what he read.

The accounts of Harry Truman's formal schooling are meager and consist mainly of scattered recollections given years later by his former teachers and classmates. The high school building in Independence burned to the ground in 1938 and all the early records were lost. It is known that he was a punctual, dutiful student who was graduated in the class of 1901 when he was seventeen years old. He was one of eleven boys in the class of forty, and although well up in the class standing he did not capture any special academic honors; those went to his tall, lank friend, Charles G. Ross.

Harry Truman was fortunate enough to have teachers who encouraged him in his reading, and two of them, Miss Margaret Phelps in history and Miss Tillie Brown in English, received his praise on several later occasions. On April 20, 1945 shortly after he became president, Harry Truman chose his former classmate, Charlie Ross, then chief of the editorial page for the *St. Louis Post Dispatch,* as his presidential press secretary. On that day when the appointment was announced, Ross placed from the president's desk phone a call to Miss Tillie Brown in Independence. The two students talked to their former teacher who said she was very proud of both of them.

Notwithstanding Truman's assertion that he had never had a "bad teacher," his reading and study were largely self-motivated. In high school he was introduced to *Plutarch's Lives,* but often at home he and his father would read together from their old red edition of this famous collection. In it the essayist, who took evident pride in Greek culture and the greatness of its men, presented biographical sketches which if not always accurate in facts were real enough to leave indelible impressions on the young reader's mind.

It cannot be said that Harry Truman's schooling was as thorough as that of Franklin Roosevelt or indeed as complete as that of many other statesmen with whom he would associate. While Truman was studying high school Latin in Independence, Roosevelt, whose entrance to the academy had been delayed two years because of tutoring and overseas traveling, was at Groton pursuing a curriculum that stressed Latin, Greek, English literature, and composition. Truman's exposure to the classics stayed with him throughout his life, and years later when interviewers asked him about his training for public speaking he recalled his Latin study.

QUESTION: *Would you care to mention any speaker, living or dead, as being especially worthy of emulation?*

ANSWER: I believe an audience approves of Cicero's method, which was to state his case and then prove it. That is what I always tried to do. Charlie Ross and I used to translate Cicero's orations from the Latin. I guess I have read almost all of his speeches. They are models of clarity and simplicity. I wish I could do half as well.[22]

The reference to Cicero's "method" was surprisingly accurate considering the lapse of time since Harry Truman's high school study. No one knows whether or not he had been briefed just prior to this interview in 1953, but the Roman author in his classic text indeed had written:

Next comes the statement of the case, a section in which the precise point at issue must be envisaged; and then the case must be supported by proofs, which is effected by conjointly demolishing your opponent's arguments and establishing your own.[23]

Whenever asked about his education for public speaking, President Truman always denied that he ever had any such particular training. Perhaps like many persons he put a narrow definition on what is meant by public speaking, and the phrase automatically stirred up in him a mental image of an impassioned orator addressing a huge throng.

Harry Truman's reading begun in his youth and maintained throughout his life constituted an indirect but very important preparation for the role he was destined to play. His reading habits shaped his speech habits—both those in everyday usage and in formal addresses. For him reading was not merely a pastime, but a source of inspiration and knowledge. He said reading was the one great influence that nourished and sustained his interest in government and public service. Emerson, too, had testified on the value of books in the gaining of knowledge:

> I would not be hurried by any love of system, by any exaggeration of instincts, to underrate the Book. We all know, that as the human body can be nourished on any food, though it were boiled grass and the broth of shoes, so the human mind can be fed by any knowledge. And great and heroic men have existed who had almost no other information than by the printed page. I only say that it needs a strong head to bear that diet. One must be an inventor to read well.[24]

Rhetoricians throughout all ages have agreed that effective speaking grows out of effective thinking, and in turn thinking depends on knowledge. The starting point in the education of a speaker, therefore, is the acquisition of knowledge. Obtaining knowledge should not be confused with "getting an education," and speakers need knowledge regardless where and how it is acquired. Speech without it is what Sinclair Lewis satirized when he had George Babbit exclaim:

> It certainly is a fine thing to be able to orate. I've sometimes thought that I had a little talent that way myself, and I know darn well that one reason why a four-flushing old back number like Chann Mott can get away with it in real estate is just because he can make a good talk, even when he hasn't got a doggone thing to say.[25]

Harry Truman said he did not believe that what he called "oratorical trimmings" were necessary for public persuasion. He insisted that listeners wanted only plain and simple facts. It was enough if a speaker knew his subject and knew it well.

World War I and Early Jobs

When Harry Truman graduated from high school he hoped briefly for an appointment to West Point, but he soon realized that because of his eyesight he could not meet the rigorous admissions standards then in effect. Like many other young boys in small towns he started by taking part-time jobs wherever he could find them. While still in high school he had begun working at the Clinton Drug Store. His specific tasks there included mopping floors, sweeping the sidewalk, dusting bottles and shelves, and generally being available for any chores the owner assigned him.

His first full-time work began late in the summer of 1901 when he accepted a job as timekeeper for the L. J. Smith Construction Company. That company had been awarded a contract to grade the main track levels for the Atchison, Topeka, and Santa Fe Railroad in a section close to Independence. For his work he received a salary of thirty-five dollars a month and board. Being timekeeper for a construction crew gave the young boy a down-to-earth education quite different from what he had encountered in books. It meant signing checks and paying off the men every Saturday night, often in one of the local saloons. He learned something about these workers' hopes, habits, and frustrations. He picked up some of their attitudes and expressions. Their speech was flavored with vernacular phrases and idioms. Many of them spoke a Missouri dialect suggestive of the Ozarks just a little farther south. Some said "hit" for it, "poke" for bag, and "evenin'" for afternoon. Similes fell easily: "slow as a pond," "high as a pine," or "sorry as gully dirt." Exaggeration in statement was permitted and enjoyed, for it was a region where a man had been known to "shingle the roof with a bullhide and use the tail for a lightning rod." No place for the timid or dainty, it was a tougher talking crew than Truman ever saw again until he took command of his artillery battery in France. He once said that it was while he worked with this construction crew that he learned "all the cuss words in the English language—not by ear but by note."[26]

The construction contract was finished in the spring of 1902, and with it went Harry's job as timekeeper. He worked briefly in the mailing room of the *Kansas City Star* for a salary of seven dollars a week, but stayed there only six months. Then he became a clerk at the National Bank of Commerce in Kansas City. He and his brother, Vivian, worked in what was called "the zoo," a part of the bank that served as clearing house for transit checks drawn on other banks. A short time later Harry again changed employers and went to work for the Union National Bank as a bookkeeper. A better salary was the main reason for this move because his pay increased from forty to sixty dollars a month.

During most of his sojourn in the banking business, Harry Truman lived in a rooming house at 1314 Troost Avenue in Kansas City where he paid five dollars a week for room and board, a charge which included breakfast and dinner. Arthur Eisenhower, an older brother to the man who succeeded Truman in the presidency, also roomed at this boarding house during the same period.

In the evenings, Harry sometimes would play the piano for the group of boarders gathered in the living room, and there were other diversions. He had given up his ambition of becoming a concert pianist, but he tried to see most of the musicians and actors who came to the city to present their specialties. Nearly every Saturday afternoon found him attending one of the vaudeville shows then popular. "Between the time I was about sixteen to twenty I used to go to every vaudeville show that came to Kansas City at the Old Orpheum and at the Grand Theater." Comedy was the most popular bill, but he would remember the actress Eva Tanguay in her roles or George M. Cohan's appearances stressing national loyalty with the American flag as a standard stage prop. The latter shows with their unbridled appeals to patriotism kindled the natural pugnacity of the young Truman.

In 1905 his father moved back to Grandview, and a year later Harry gave up his short career in banking to join his parents and grandmother there. He helped run the farm for the next ten years. They were years of hard physical labor—years in which he and his father working together did all of the farm toil that raised honest sweat and sent them in from the fields at sunset with their overalls grimed and caked by dust, grease, and dirt. On the six hundred acres they raised corn, wheat, oats, and clover, and always fed numerous hogs.

Harry learned to bang his banjo No. 12 scoop against the corncrib and yell ''whoo—eeee'' to call hogs from a quarter mile away; he knew the sounds of the first streams of milk rattling into a tin pail; he wore a straw hat in the summer and a felt one in the winter. His mother claimed that he could ''plow as straight a furrow as could be found in all Missouri.'' Decades later amid political hustings, Harry Truman, remembering such language, often talked about how he learned to plow a straight furrow; usually he would add something like, ''It had to be straight. If it wasn't, I heard about it from my father for the next year.''

He liked to ride the gangplow and watch the earth curl in a black, sweetly fresh ribbon away from the shining steel moldboard. He watched the weather so that he would know when the wind meant rain or when it would be safe to mow the hay. Veterinarians were scarce, and most farmers themselves learned enough rudimentary surgery to ring a bull or castrate the pigs. He reputedly became so expert at the latter the neighbors joked, ''When Harry sharpens his knife the pigs run out to pasture.''[27]

As a young farmer, Truman acquired the habit of rising early in the morning, 4:30 in the summers and 6:30 in the winters, long before the sun had climbed clear and warm over the lush Missouri cropland. The pattern of early rising never left him nor did some other habits formed during this period of his life.

Most persons when old look back fondly on their young adult years, and Harry Truman was no exception. He often reminisced that the ten years he spent farming with his father at Grandview were extremely happy ones, marred only by the latter's death in 1915. More than just a happy interlude, however, it was a period in which a future politician learned something about the art of talking with farm people. The Populist movement was not so intense as it had been ten years earlier when such orators as the female firebrand from Kansas, Mary B. Lease, urged her listeners ''to raise less corn and more hell.'' Populist arguments were far from silenced, however, for their echoes were heard wherever and whenever farmers gathered. Moreover, the arguments were real enough to endure even after the Populist movement itself became history. Similar themes could be clothed in slightly different vocabulary and used for other occasions in later years. Thus Truman would find that Populist lines of attack and defense were practical tools for persuading voters throughout the Great Depression as well as in the years following the Second World War.

Harry Truman was only twelve years old in 1896 when William Jennings Bryan captured the Democratic nomination for president with his dramatic Cross of Gold speech delivered to the Chicago convention. Four years later when the Democrats convened in Kansas City, young Harry was a convention page who watched the party select Bryan for the second time. Truman described the convention and his ideas on the Great Commoner:

> He [Bryan] was one of my heroes. I remember that there were seventeen thousand people in the old convention hall in Kansas City when Bryan spoke. There were no loudspeakers, and a man had to have a real carrying voice to be heard in that hall. . . . Bryan took charge. But so great was the enthusiasm of the delegates for the great orator that he was nominated at once—by acclamation. His appeal that day was like nothing else I have ever heard. He had a bell-like voice that carried well and he knew how to use it.[28]

But it was not only hero worship that influenced Truman at the turn of the century. He believed in what he heard and saw. The persuasive ideas that came from Populist speakers and their immediate successors were ones Truman himself would copy and use. The vicarious arguments fitted neatly into the experiences he gained during his decade of farming. These years provided him first-hand acquaintance with the worry, independence, and pride so often found on an American farm. He developed a litany which throughout his career helped identify him as a farmer. He picked up common expressions for animals, types of work, and equipment, and he enjoyed barnyard humor and homely wisdom. When he went into Grandview or nearby Belton there was always talk of local politics—Democratic politics centering around crops, prices, mortgages, and weather. He would not forget these subjects, the expressions, or the attitudes which gave rise to them.

These formative years on the farm contributed elements of practical persuasion that surfaced in Truman's surprising victory at the polls in 1948. During that campaign when he went after votes in the Midwest he gave his listeners an image of a man who shared their problems. He talked their language. He could inspect plowing and tractor equipment, compliment ladies for their prizewinning cakes, and talk knowledgeably about the differences between mules and machines. One survey team when analyzing voting patterns in the election of that year underscored the importance of the image Truman created through his language:

> about one person out of five spoke of Truman in words that carry a flavor of personal affection or admiration—'honest,' 'sincere,' 'spunky,' 'down-to-earth.'[29]

After about eight years at Grandview, however, Truman began spreading his interests beyond the actual operation of the farm. In 1915 when his father died, Harry Truman was thirty years old. He was doing reasonably well if judged by the economic standards of Jackson County, but his career so far was local. Alben Barkley, who would be his vice-presidential running mate in 1948, was completing his first term as a congressman from Kentucky; Franklin Roosevelt was assistant secretary of the navy; Douglas MacArthur already had served as aide to President Theodore Roosevelt and was assigned to the army general staff in Washington; Henry A. Wallace had graduated from Iowa State College and was associate editor of *Wallace's Farmer;* Dwight D. Eisenhower had just graduated from West Point.

In 1909 Truman made a decision that would bring political dividends throughout his public life; he joined the Masonic Lodge at Belton. Beliefs and commitments he gained from Shriner associations would play important roles in various stages of his political career. By 1916 he was investing on a small scale in zinc mining and oil drilling. His economic interests ranged into Kansas, Oklahoma, and Texas. In partnership with five or six others, he had helped form the Morgan Oil and Refining Company. Through business contacts he was becoming familiar with zoning laws and municipal government. Rather than being a young man come to town with mud on his boots and a wheat straw dangling from his lips, he dressed nattily and was seen frequently in the best entertainment and eating spots the city had to offer. He bought second hand a four-cylinder Stafford automobile for about six hundred dollars at a time when owning an auto was considered a mark of affluence.

Another persuasive influence on Harry Truman during these formative years came from his army contacts. It was to be expected that his interest in the military somehow would surface and lead him into a soldier's role. While a bank clerk in 1905 he had attended his first encampment. It was a great experience for him; he liked the excitement, the camaraderie, and the hard work. Thereafter he attended summer camps regularly.

Missouri might seem a long way from Europe, but when Woodrow Wilson in 1917 announced a state of war between the United States and Germany, Truman already was involved. His involvement was entirely voluntary. He had plenty to do on the farm; his oil company could be a full-time job if he chose to make it so, and his eyesight was as defective as it had been when it kept him from trying for an appointment to the military academy.

He teamed up with Major John L. Miles and others in recruiting men from the Missouri National Guard to build a field artillery regiment. The regiment became the 129th Field Artillery, and Harry S. Truman was made a first lieutenant.

In August of 1917 the new regiment left Kansas City for further training at Camp Doniphan near Fort Sill, Oklahoma. Because of Truman's banking experience, the commanding colonel put him in charge of the regimental canteen, a business venture of considerable importance. Lieutenant Truman at once sought help from a sergeant and friend, Eddie Jacobson. The latter knew a little more about merchandising because he had been a shirt salesman in Kansas City. Jacobson understood the ways of buying low and selling profitably, so he actually ran the canteen while Truman acted as accountant and chief policymaker. They began by collecting two dollars from each of the 1100 men in the regiment. After six months each man received back not only his two dollars, but Truman and Jacobson declared dividends of $15,000 on the original $2200 investment.

In March of 1918 Truman along with about one hundred other men constituting an advance force sailed for France on the *George Washington*. Two weeks later the ship docked at Brest. During the summer the rest of the regiment arrived, and in July Truman was put in charge of Battery D of the 129th Field Artillery. The battery consisted of 188 men and 167 horses. The unit fired its first barrage on September 6, and thereafter saw some of the heaviest fighting of the war. It participated in the St. Mihiel drive, the Meuse-Argonne attack, the Verdun front, and was moving toward Metz when the war ended.

In October Harry Truman was promoted to captain, and with that rank came new challenges. He was a fair but firm commanding officer, for Battery D was no milk and water outfit. Captain Truman filled the guardhouse when necessary. He slept in the same mud, faced the same dangers as all the others, and he could match the profanity of any man in the outfit. He was an officer who expected his orders to be obeyed by every man, but also he was ready to drink cognac, vin rouge, or vin blanc with any or all of them.

He had learned something about cards before he left Missouri, but in France, particularly after the armistice had been signed and the fighting stopped, the days and nights fused into one continuous poker game. His favorite was seven-card stud, a choice that stayed with him throughout most of his political career. During his years in the Senate he often played poker with other senators, who were joined by Vice-President John Nance Garner. "Cactus Jack" Garner from Texas was dubbed by John L. Lewis, the mine workers' union head, as "a poker-playing, whiskey-drinking, labor-hating, evil old man." In truth Cactus Jack was fond of poker and proud of his winnings. Once Truman confided gleefully to a reporter friend, Bill Helms, "I nicked the Vice President last night." Apparently Truman had been "nicked" frequently enough that he relished the revenge.[30]

Early in 1918 Truman and a number of his fellow officers were granted leave to visit Paris. While there he witnessed the tumultuous welcome French citizens gave Woodrow Wilson. Many years later President Truman recalled that he never again saw such a reception. But in 1918 Harry Truman from Missouri meant to take in all the sights he could while on his short furlough. He went to Nice; he visited the Casino in Monte Carlo; in Paris he attended two operas and then perhaps as counterbalance went to the Folies-Bergere. His reactions to these diversions were not recorded at the time, but when he wrote his *Memoirs*—a work displaying his political acumen and perhaps with subtle persuasion of voters in mind—he saw fit to describe the Folies as "a disgusting performance."[31]

In April of 1919 Truman's outfit came back to America, but it was May before he was discharged to return to the Blue Ridge farm in Missouri. He was always proud of his World War I record, and even in old age he regularly wore that war's service pin in his lapel. He liked to reminisce about persons he had met or about episodes he had lived through. His talk was peppered with military expressions, quotations, and anecdotes gleaned from that war. When the Second World War broke out, he was a U.S. senator and fifty-seven years old. Nevertheless, he went to General George C. Marshall, then chief of staff, and volunteered his services. He said he wanted, if possible, to command an artillery battery. General Marshall appreciated the offer but advised:

> Senator Truman, you've got a big job to do right up there at the Capitol, with your Investigating Committee. Besides, Senator, this is a young man's war. We don't need any old stiffs like you.[32]

The last remark seems to have been an affectionate one, and Truman protested, "I'm younger than you are, General Marshall." The general, who indeed was three years Truman's senior, answered:

> But I'm a general and you'd only be a colonel. You stay right where you are.[33]

This exchange ended the discussion.

A great many stories have come out of Harry Truman's World War I experiences, and after he became famous it sometimes seemed as if nearly every veteran who went overseas in that war had in some way or another "served with Harry Truman." Friendships formed then proved intense and lasting; many of his wartime friends and buddies later became trusted associates working with him in various Washington posts. He once said, "My whole political career is based upon my war service and associates."

He was a soldier who saw the worst of war; he also was a young man at the time who enjoyed some of its freedoms, its conviviality, its travel, and its excitement. Truman's military record, like his schooling and years on the farm, left indelible imprints on his speech, character, and outlooks. Throughout his public life he would recall experiences from schooling, reading, farming, or the army—experiences that might aid him in resolving a problem, guide him toward a difficult decision, or help convince himself and others that the course he had decided on was a proper one. The persuasive impact of his early years in Missouri would never leave him.

3

The Truman Women

Cleopatra's nose, had it been shorter, the whole face of the world would have been changed.

BLAISE PASCAL

THE president, no matter who he is, is a product of home, school, associates, friends, family, and earlier experiences that mold his speech, personality, and capacities. Not that such a person is the complete product of each environment, but these formative influences must be considered in accounting for later speech characteristics. Lincoln's speech, for example, was typical of southern Indiana and Illinois during the first half of the nineteenth century. John F. Kennedy spoke the language of Boston in spite of his years away from that particular area.

In the Truman family, Harry, of course, was the visible persuader. His name was on the ballots; he showed up at the hustings and gave the talks. Behind his public appearances and utterances, however, were persuasions radiating from family members who were especially dear to him—persuasions that propelled him toward an action and in some instances urged more caution. The public was seldom aware of specific pressures from his family, but their influences were constant and compelling.

There is no evidence that politics was in Truman's mind when he came back to Missouri after World War I. He was so glad to return to America that when he landed in New York, he resolved, "If old lady Liberty in New York harbor wanted to see me again she'd have to turn around."

He was aware that in Paris the "Big Four" of the peace conference were struggling to reconcile the hostility among countries devastated by war. The conference did not include representatives from the new Bolshevik government, and the deliberations were tinged with an urgency born of starvation and fear of communism. Already some treaties and practices of the new Soviets had been disclosed, and the disclosures set off alarms because they seemed to run counter to ideals Woodrow Wilson had so eloquently expressed.

In 1919 Harry Truman's attention was not focused on these world problems; his opinions were much like those of most other veterans. The nation's sense of pride bordered on arrogance—hadn't Truman helped his fellow Americans clean up the mess in Europe? Now he wanted to return to normal living. There was the matter of earning a livelihood, and even more on his mind was marrying the girl who had promised to wait for him.

In Truman's career there were four women he loved, sometimes heeded, and always protected: his mother, his sister, his wife, and his daughter. He admired women, thought most of them deserved special protection, and believed they were all cast in the same mold as the four he knew and loved. Around most women Harry Truman was uncharacteristically shy; his knowledge of them was bounded by what he knew of his mother, his sister, his wife, and his daughter. Even in France, amid the fracturing of habits and loyalties brought on by war, it is unlikely that he ever met other women. He had the same opportunities as most soldiers, but there has never been a scintilla of evidence suggesting that then or later was he ever involved in any way with women outside his immediate family.

Harry Truman's Mother, Martha Ellen Truman

The influence of Harry Truman's mother was an enduring one, and his attitude toward women in general was shaped in part by his love and respect for her. In an interview after he left the presidency he expressed his opinion of any man who did not live up to the teachings of his mother or was unfaithful to his wife or family:

> Three things ruin a man if you want to know what I believe. One's power, one's money, and one's women. . . . And a man who is not loyal to his family, to his wife and his mother and his sisters can be ruined if he has a complex in that direction. If he has the right woman as a partner, he never has any trouble. But if he has the wrong one or if he's mixed up with a bunch of whores, why, then he's in a hell of a fix. And I can name them to you, the ones that got mixed up in that way.[1]

These statements were more than mere political posturing by Truman. Like many of his sayings, the blunt expression of the effects of power, money, and women takes on the shades of a maxim. It is the kind of advice a boy might receive from a plain-spoken mother.

His mother, Martha Ellen Truman, was said to be witty and known for her terse, pungent remarks. While the processes involved in the acquisition of language are still not entirely understood, the best scholars in the field today do agree that speech itself must be learned. The learning comes from imitation of speech and language patterns a person most frequently encounters. John Locke, the seventeenth-century English philosopher, believed that at birth the human mind is a *tabula rasa,* or clean slate, waiting for impressions and experiences to make their recordings there. Modern authorities believe most language habits are fixed by imitation during early childhood, and that by the time of adolescence the language-learning processes decrease tremendously. If this generalization is accurate, Harry Truman's language and expressions understandably would echo the positive style and substance of remarks made by his mother. As might be expected of one from her generation and pioneer stock, her pronouncements often were opinionated and undiluted. She showed strong affection for all her children, but there seems little doubt that as a child, Harry was her favorite.

He was the oldest of the children, followed by his brother Vivian, two years younger, and then his sister, Mary Jane. She was five years younger than Harry, and during their childhood both he and Vivian were taught to be protective of their little sister. Brother Vivian easily fell in with his father's habits and temperament because he liked farming and outdoor life. He early gained a reputation of being "a born horse trader." Harry was inclined toward bookishness, perhaps in part because of his weak eyesight. He developed a special attachment for his mother and sister. He learned to fix the latter's hair—an assignment that most boys his age would consider sissy. He helped with household chores, did not seem to mind working in the kitchen, and enjoyed practicing the piano. On that matter his brother Vivian stoutly declared: "Mamma wanted me to take piano lessons, too, but she couldn't get a lasso big enough."

Margaret Truman protested that her father was not really the "mamma's boy" some writers have pictured him:

> Any boy who spent a lot of time with a mother like Martha Ellen Truman could only emerge from the experience the very opposite of a conventional mamma's boy. This is one among many reasons why my father always bridled when a writer or reporter tried to pin this image on him. The rest of the family, knowing Mamma Truman, simply guffawed at the notion.[2]

Was Harry a "mamma's boy?" No one can be sure, and arguments today over the question serve no real purpose. Certainly, he cherished his mother, and after fame came to him he zealously protected her from the press and public. He retained an unusually tender relationship with her throughout his public life. Problems were never so big nor the week ever too busy for him to write or telephone her. During his tenure in the Senate and his first two years as president he seemed to write or phone her whenever crises or major events occurred. The spontaneous vocabulary he used freely in these exchanges set an intimate tone and reveal much of his private thinking and attitude.

On the day of President Roosevelt's death, Vice-President Truman was presiding over the U.S. Senate while he wrote his mother and sister back in Independence about "a windy Senator" who was making a speech "on a subject with which he is in no way familiar."[3] The following Monday, only four days after he had taken the presidential oath of office, Harry Truman again wrote his mother. This second letter was penned before he finished what had been a very arduous day, for it was the one during which he had addressed the combined Houses of Congress for the first time. He rose early that morning, looked over his speech and penciled in some changes. Then he read a few reports, scanned the morning papers, and had breakfast.

He arrived at his new office in the White House at 8:00 A.M. and met first with the secretary of state and then with Admiral William D. Leahy. At ten o'clock British Foreign Secretary Anthony Eden and British Ambassador Lord Halifax, called on him. Following this conference he wrote a long message about its substance to the American ambassador in Moscow, Averell Harriman. After a quick lunch he addressed Congress and then returned to the White House to tackle more correspondence and office conferences. That same day Mrs. Truman with her mother, Mrs. David Wallace, and Margaret were moving out of the apartment on Connecticut Avenue and into Blair House, which had been readied for them.

Early in the evening the new president walked across the street from his office to Blair House, but that night before his hectic day was ended, he wrote to his mother and sister a chatty account of his introduction to the presidency:

> Well, I have had the most momentous, and the most trying time anyone could possibly have, since Thursday, April 12th. Maybe you'd like to know just what happened. We'd had a long drawn out debate in the Senate and finally came to an agreement for a recess at 5 P.M. until Friday, April 13th.
>
> When I went back to my office, a call from Sam Rayburn, Speaker of the House, was awaiting me. Sam wanted me to come over to the House side of the Capitol and talk to him about policy and procedure and, as Alice in Wonderland would say, "shoes and ships and sealing wax and things." . . .
>
> But—as soon as I came into the room Sam told me that Steve Early, the President's confidential press secretary wanted to talk to me. I called the White House, and Steve told me to come to the White House "as quickly and as *quietly*" as I could. Well I told Sam I had to go to the White House on a special call and that he should say nothing about it.
>
> I ran all the way to my office in the Senate by way of the unfrequented corridors in the Capitol, told my office force that I'd been summoned to the White House and to say nothing about it . . .
>
> When I arrived at the Pennsylvania entrance to the most famous

house in America, a couple of ushers met me . . . and then took me up to Mrs. Roosevelt's study on the second floor.

She and Mrs. Boettiger, her daughter and her husband the Lt. Col., and Steve Early were there. Mrs. Roosevelt put her arm on my shoulder and said, "Harry, the President is dead."

It was the only time in my life, I think, that I ever felt as if I'd had a real shock. I had hurried to the White House to see the President, and when I arrived, I found I was the President. No one in the history of our country ever had it happen to him just that way.

We waited for Bess and Margaret to arrive. We then had to scurry around and find a Bible for me to put my hand upon to take the oath. They finally found one. If I'd known what was afoot, I'd have used Grandpa Truman's Bible, which was in my office bookcase.

You of course know from the papers what happened and what has happened since.

Saturday afternoon, the White House funeral; Sunday morning the burial at Hyde Park, today my speech to Congress.

This afternoon we moved to this house, diagonally across the street (Penn. Ave.) from the White House, until the Roosevelts have had time to move out of the White House. We tried staying at the apartment, but it wouldn't work. I can't move without at least ten Secret Service men and twenty policemen. People who lived in our apartment couldn't get in and out without a pass. So—we moved out with suitcases. Our furniture is still there and will be for some time. . . . But I've paid the rent for this month and will pay for another month if they don't get the old White House redecorated by that time.

My greatest trial was today when I addressed the Congress. It seemed to go over all right, from the ovation I received. Things have gone so well that I'm almost as scared as I was Thursday when Mrs. R. told me what had happened. Maybe it will come out all right.

Soon as we get settled in the White House you'll both be here to visit us. Lots of love from your very much worried son and bro.[4]

Regular letters and phone calls were a routine that was set when Harry Truman first went to Washington in 1935 as the junior senator from Missouri. When days of triumph or celebration came around he usually saw fit to write or call the folks in Independence. For example, on that snowy Saturday in January of 1945 when he was inaugurated as vice-president, he slipped away from a postinaugural luncheon at the White House with President Roosevelt, went back to Capitol Hill, and immediately telephoned his mother. She told him she had heard the ceremony on the radio and warned, "Now you behave yourself."

Even though he had written Martha Ellen Truman on Thursday, April 12, 1945, and four days later on April 16, he wrote her again two days later on April 18. Three days afterwards, on April 21, he penned another letter. A week later he again wrote and complained mildly about the "nuisance of being kin to the President," and advised: "Don't let the pests [reporters] get you down."[5] Thus, in slightly more than two weeks, the new president wrote his mother four separate letters in addition to phone calls he had made to her.

On May 8, 1945, he had a major announcement to broadcast, for on that day the German surrender went into effect. To celebrate the end of the war in Europe, and also because it happened to be his sixty-first birthday, he wrote his mother telling her about some of the informal telephoning that had been necessary so that the Americans, the British, and the Russians could make simultaneous announcements of the surrender.

Later that month, his mother and his sister Mary Jane visited Washington. By this time the living quarters in the White House had been repainted, and the Trumans had moved from Blair House into the president's official home. Then in June, after Martha Ellen and Mary Jane had returned to Independence, President Truman resumed his habit of writing. Although major events and work crowded his daily schedule he wrote them on June 13, June 16, June 19, and June 22. In one of these letters he shared his plans for a party at which he was to entertain "Eisenhower, a real man."[6] At the time he seemed awed by the thought of hobnobbing with one of America's most popular generals, but in later years that awe would turn sour.

The letters President Truman wrote his mother expose his private attitudes and opinions better than his public statements issued at the time, because expressions sent home were unguarded and untreated by advisers or ghost writers. There are instances where the son apparently was still trying hard to please his mother. For example, filial love and political experience may have prompted this kind of compliment:

> Well, the *Washington Post* had your pictures yesterday morning and the finest kind of statements from both you and Vivian. My Press Staff said that the smartest press agent in the world could not have written any better ones. I told them that my family all told the truth all the time and that they did not need a press agent.[7]

When writing to Independence President Truman readily slipped into the vernacular and homely metaphors he enjoyed so much and knew Martha Ellen would understand. Some examples might include:

> They gave me a pretty *hefty* fifteen minutes. . . . This day has been a *dinger* too [italics supplied].[8]

> I am getting ready to go see Stalin & Churchill, and it is a chore. I have to take my tuxedo, tails . . . *preacher coat, high hat, low hat* and *hard hat* as well as sundry other things.[9]

> Stalin gave his state dinner night before last, and it was a *wow*.[10]

> Mr. Churchill began calling me at daylight to know if we shouldn't make an immediate release without considering the Russians. He was refused and then he kept pushing me to talk to Stalin. He finally had to stick to the agreed plan—but he was *mad as a wet hen*.[11]

Epithets and contemptuous terms when used by the president of the United States make news. President Truman reserved most name-calling for his special angers and domestic targets; even then he was often careful in making public statements about colleagues, diplomats, and dignitaries. There were no such restraints when he wrote his mother, and he said freely that "in a country as big as this one there are necessarily a lot of nuts and people with peculiar ideas."[12] Another time he offered his opinion of one of Hitler's generals:

> Three generals came in to see me yesterday and General Patch gave me Herr Goering's baton. I always get those dirty Nazis mixed up but it makes no difference. Anyway it's the fat Marshal's insignia of office. It is about a foot and a half long, made of ivory inlaid with gold eagles and iron crosses with diamond studded end caps and platinum rings around it for engraving. Must have cost several thousand dollars—maybe forty—to make. Can you imagine a fat pig like that strutting around with a forty thousand dollar bauble—at the poor taxpayer's expense and making 'em like it?[13]

While attending the important conference at Potsdam, he wrote:

> You never saw such pig-headed people as are the Russians. I hope I never have to hold another conference with them—but, of course, I will.[14]

When these letters were arriving in Independence Martha Ellen Truman was in her nineties but still keen and alert mentally. It was no longer a case of a young son seeking advice and support from his mother but that of a mature person, whose emotions were ever near the surface, mindful of his love and a lifetime habit of exchanging confidences.

In the spring of 1947, Martha Ellen Truman fell and broke her right hip; it was an accident from which she would never fully recover. In July, the gravity of her illness became apparent, and at last on July 26, 1947, the mother who had seen her son evolve from Missouri farm boy to world leader quietly passed away.

Bess Wallace Truman

When he was thrust into the presidency, Harry Truman had been in public life for twenty-three years, and understandably during this time his wife was the person to whom he turned most often. The Constitution says nothing about the duties and privileges of the first lady; indeed the law eliminates her from the administration of government. Who would be so reckless, however, to deny the influence a wife may have on her husband's judgment, actions, and decisions? The role of first lady epitomizes the prominence that can be gained through marriage.

The president's wife can never escape the focus of national scrutiny, homage, and sometimes vilification. Abigail Adams was a forceful and witty figure in her own right. Mary Todd Lincoln was criticized by what she called the "vampyre press" for her political meddling. Eleanor Roosevelt learned from experience that a president's wife faces double jeopardy—she is without legal authority but is expected to show leadership in some way. When she dares to assert leadership, it may be resented and resisted; if she offers nothing, officials try to anticipate what she believes or wants. While she was first lady, Mrs. Roosevelt garnered her own massive constituency—as well as widespread criticism—as she exhorted women to join and support trade unions, set up consumer groups, enter politics, and lead in the New Deal moves for social justice.

Bess Truman's influence was not always so visible as that of some of her predecessors. By design and inclination, she stayed clear of the limelight, but her husband often boasted: "She is my chief adviser. I never write a speech without going over it with her."

Upon Truman's elevation to the presidency, Mrs. Truman, hitherto little publicized, suddenly found herself sought by avid reporters and interviewers. Journalists soon agreed that "she was a hard person to write about." Helen Wiegel Brown described her for *Liberty* readers as the average American woman, little different from the "big businessman's wife who manages a household staff, shares in community activities, and completes the circle of her husband's social and business life."[15]

Harry Truman was six years old when he first met Elizabeth Virginia Wallace. Everyone called her Bess, and so did Harry, except years later when he would refer to her formally as "Mrs. Truman" or jocularly as "the Boss." With members of the family and intimate friends, he might call her "the madam" in pretense that she was forever attempting to control his reckless deeds and utterances.

Early in his presidency, Truman was irked by attacks on his close associates from several newspapers, and suggestions that he fire certain officials. At a dinner one night he exploded: "Everyone is telling me who I should have on my staff and in my Cabinet. No s.o.b. is going to dictate to me who I'm going to have." When he got home that night, Bess is supposed to have given him a severe lecture on the need for dignity in his new office. Several days later, while the controversy over his uncensored words still raged, an aide told him the rector of a large Washington church had remarked that under similar provocation he, too, might have said the same thing. The president grinned ruefully, and said, "I just wish that the rector would go talk to my wife." This kind of story may have been greatly exaggerated, for Harry Truman liked to promote the myth of his wife's prudery. Bess accepted it as part of the family banter.

The first meeting of Bess and Harry most likely was in Sunday school. The year was 1890, and John Truman had just moved his family into a house on South Chrisler Street in Independence. ("Chrisler" is the spelling used in *The*

Truman Memoirs; Margaret's book, *Harry S. Truman,* uses the spelling "Chrysler.") Harry's parents were Baptists, but the pastor of the Presbyterian church was exceptionally friendly to new arrivals, and the Truman family started attending services there. The Wallace family lived at 610 Delaware, not far from Chrisler Street. In 1895 John Truman moved to another home on Waldo Street at River Boulevard; Harry then was only two blocks from the Wallace home.

Bess and Harry went to school together from the fifth grade through graduation in 1901. They were in the same classes, and when he went twice a week to his Aunt Ella Noland's house to study Latin, everyone understood that the trips were caused by more than an interest in early Romans. Ella Noland's house was just across the street from the home of Bess's grandfather, and Bess usually managed to come across the street and join the Noland girls whenever Harry came over.

Bess belonged to one of the leading industrial families in Independence. Her maternal grandfather, George Porterfield Gates, was founder of the milling company making "Queen of the Pantry" flour—a brand that became famous throughout the South and Midwest. According to her grandfather's will on file in the Jackson County courthouse, his fortune amounted to slightly under half a million dollars. Bess inherited from this grandfather his sense of thrift and a large portion of his money. The George P. Gates residence, known locally then as the Gates Mansion, was situated at 219 North Delaware. This is the home accepted today as the Truman residence in Independence and made famous as the Summer White House during the Truman presidency.

The "Truman Home" was built in 1865. It was impressive then and stands today as a charming attraction for visitors to Independence. The buildings are surrounded by stately maples and elms, and the house is distinguished by its many gables, its several porches, and its stained glass windows. Inside its rambling, clapboard Victorian structure are an old-fashioned parlor, a music room, a large dining room, kitchen, and seven bedrooms. There are three fireplaces with marbled mantels, and outside in the rear is a former coach house now serving as a multicar garage. After the home became famous and souvenir hunters began chipping off bits of the house itself, a high iron fence enclosing the entire lot was erected.

Bess Truman was born on February 13, 1885, the daughter of Madge (Gates) Wallace and David Willock Wallace. Stories persist that the Wallaces represented "aristocracy" more than did the Trumans during those days in Independence. Actually, there seems to have been little class distinction among citizens of that midwestern community. Perhaps Bess's mother did picture herself as the daughter of one of the town's leading and richest citizens. In 1883 she had married David Willock Wallace, a personable and promising young man who everyone agreed was quite a catch. He was a convivial civic leader—he was Eminent Commander of the Knights Templar of Missouri and could always be counted on for public services and events. For a time he served as a deputy county recorder, and he later worked in the Kansas City customs office.

Many observers and writers have commented on Bess Truman's obvious distaste for publicity. It is not unreasonable to infer that her desire to avoid public attention might have begun with a natural reserve and was reinforced by two very unhappy incidents that occurred during her formative years. Both incidents were local sensations and involved violent deaths.

The first tragedy happened within her immediate family. She was only a little beyond eighteen when her civic-minded father began drinking heavily. The more he drank the more despondent he became, and early one morning he committed suicide. He left no message to indicate a reason for his act, but he was known to have been distressed over his financial affairs. One newspaper at the time of his suicide gave the following account:

> Mr. Wallace retired early. At 5 o'clock this morning without disturbing Mrs. Wallace, he left his bed and went to a writing desk in the same room, where there was a revolver. This he took to the bath room in the rear of the house. From the position of the body, Mr. Wallace evidently stood in the center of the bath room floor, placed the muzzle of the revolver back of the left ear and fired. . . . The family and neighbors were aroused by the report. Mr. Wallace was found by his wife lying on his back.[16]

Mrs. Wallace had returned two days earlier from a visit to Pittsburgh, and the suddenness of her husband's death must have devastated her as well as Bess and three younger sons. The shocked widow never recovered from the effects of her husband's suicide, and for the rest of her life she led a very secluded existence. Bess likewise grew ever more concerned about privacy.

The second shock in Bess's young life did not involve anyone in her immediate family, but it was a bizarre series of events that penetrated her circle of intimate friends and captured great public attention.

Bess Wallace was a member of a small, tightly knit group of young people who frequently intermingled at dances, parties, picnics, and meetings of all sorts. In the group was Chrisman Swope, a nephew of Colonel Thomas H. Swope. Chrisman was six years older than Bess, and the exact depth of their friendship is not known. It is known that Bess was an especially close friend of his younger sister, Lucy Lee, and some people at the time thought of Chrisman Swope as one of Bess Wallace's beaux.

Only a few blocks from her home in Independence lay the expansive Swope residence. Colonel Thomas H. Swope, one of the wealthiest men in the entire Midwest, had come into the Kansas City area in 1855 when the city listed a population of only 442 people. He was smart enough to realize that because the Missouri River lay to the north, the town must necessarily expand to the south. Acting on this belief he bought a rugged farm for $7500 immediately south of the levee district. As the population grew, Colonel Swope divided his purchase into lots, and soon the farm had become million-dollar acres of steel and concrete. Among his many benefactions is Swope Park, located today within the Kansas City metropolis. When people later complimented him for his foresight, he scoffed:

> Me smart? I owned all of downtown almost, and I sold it off for a few hundred dollars an acre. . . . There were two of these lots I couldn't sell. One was a hole in the ground, and the other was an ugly clay hill. Nobody would give me anything for them; nobody thought they were worth anything, so I kept them—and they made me rich.[17]

The two lots to which Swope referred later became sites for office buildings, and at the time of his death each was paying him a ground rental of more than $50,000 a year!

In his later years, the eccentric bachelor millionaire moved in with his brother's widow and her seven children in their brick Gothic castle on Pleasant Street in Independence. The year 1906—the year in which Bess turned twenty-one—marked the beginning of what came to be known as the Swope-Hyde murder case. It happened in Independence, and Bess's friend, Chrisman, was one of the victims.

The Swope family loved to entertain, and Bess rarely missed any of their parties. In 1906 Mrs. Logan Swope gave a reception for her oldest daughter, Frances, who, against her mother's wishes, had married a doctor named Bennett Clark Hyde. The reception was the social highlight of the year, and Bess was there with her blond hair piled high in a pompadour. One of her most attentive partners was Chrisman Swope.

Three years later, Colonel Swope's cousin and estate manager, who also lived in the Swope residence, died of what was first thought to be a stroke of apoplexy. His physician was Dr. Hyde, the husband of Colonel Swope's niece and the guest of honor at the ball mentioned earlier. Then the colonel himself was suddenly stricken with a fatal illness. He too had been attended by Dr. Hyde. The third victim was Bess Wallace's beau, Chrisman Swope. The latter was first thought to have succumbed quickly to a freak case of typhoid diagnosed and treated by Dr. Hyde, but there were no other known cases of typhoid in the vicinity.

The bodies of the two Swope victims were exhumed and sent to Chicago for examination. Reports from there provided enough evidence to support the growing suspicions, and in the spring of 1910, after three weeks of inquiry into the mysteries of the Swope deaths, a grand jury handed down eleven indictments against Dr. Hyde.

The charges and the ensuing trials rocked the entire community, and although the doctor was tried only for the alleged murder of Thomas Swope, the indictments included:[18]

First Degree Murder—For the death of Col. Thomas H. Swope, October 3, 1909

First Degree Murder—For the death of Chrisman Swope, December 6, 1909

Manslaughter—For negligently killing Col. Moss Hunton [the estate manager]

Poisoning—Three counts in one indictment, charging that three attempts were made on the life of Margaret Swope

Poisoning with Typhoid Germs—Lucy Lee Swope

Poisoning with Typhoid Germs—Mildred Fox

Poisoning with Typhoid Germs—Sarah Swope

Poisoning with Typhoid Germs—Stella Swope

Poisoning with Typhoid Germs—Georgie Comptonn

Poisoning with Typhoid Germs—Nora Belle Dickson

Poisoning with Typhoid Germs—Leonora Copridge

In the subsequent trials evidence was produced to show that Dr. Hyde indeed had purchased enough cyanide and typhoid culture to wipe out the entire population of Independence, let alone the Swope family—the family that stood between him and Colonel Swope's fortune. Hyde was judged guilty at the first trial. An appeal resulted in a mistrial when one man on the jury, fretting against enforced confinement, jumped out a window and went home. A third trial ended in acquittal.

After his third trial, Dr. Hyde moved to Lexington, Missouri, and lived there until his death in 1934. The widespread exposures of lives of people she knew well weighed heavily on Bess Wallace's temperament, and repercussions from the sensationalizing of the events undoubtedly gave her increased reason to dread public attention.

Bess and her mother moved into the big, fashionable Gates mansion shortly after her father's death. As the years went by, her mother would be variously described as aloof, queenly, aristocratic, very particular, dictatorial, and certainly ultraconservative. Under her close supervision Bess herself grew less lively, more sedate and guarded.

As a young girl Bess had been considered something of a tomboy. She liked competition, was athletic herself, and was popular with friends of both sexes. From her father she got her warm friendliness and sense of humor. After graduation from high school she began attending the Barstow School for Girls in nearby Kansas City—a school taught by two Wellesley College graduates who had come to mid-America in order to teach grace and gentility to young women. Her favorite academic subjects were literature and language. Years later when she was first lady, Bess visited the Barstow School and with pride told the teachers there that for two years she got up every morning at 6:30 to catch the trolley from Independence to Kansas City—a distance of nine miles.[19]

There was a time when the paths of Harry Truman and Bess Wallace seemed to be going in different directions. Harry was successively a bank clerk in Kansas City and then a farmer at Grandview. They saw each other occasionally, but not too much is known about their relationship during the period between 1903 and 1913. And it is impossible to determine the exact date their courtship began. As is often the case with persons who gain fame, certain stories crop up, without authentication, and become accepted on the strength of mere repetition. One story found in several biographies is that Bess's mother was strongly opposed to Harry's courtship. She looked on him as a dirt farmer without a college education, a totally unpromising prospect as husband to George Gates's granddaughter. In those days Bess was conspicuous among the young social set in Independence. Her grandfather had the first Studebaker in town, and she drove it. She dressed conservatively but wore the richest tweeds, and she was frequently seen walking her two greyhounds—a gift from her affluent grandfather.

One day after Bess had finished her schooling in Kansas City and was spending her full time in Independence, Harry came to town to see his Aunt Ella Noland. That morning, Mrs. Wallace, Bess's mother, had sent over a cake to the Nolands, and Aunt Ella asked her daughter to return the cake plate. Instead Harry insisted that he would do it, seized the plate, and rushed out. Two hours later he returned grinning foolishly and announced, "Well, I got to see her."[20]

This episode or some event similar to it must have intensified their old friendship. Usually he came into Independence by train or streetcar, but in 1913 he was able to scrape up enough money to buy his secondhand Stafford. The automobile, a really grand machine for the time, made him slightly more acceptable in the Wallace home. Not only did Harry start seeing Bess more often, he launched a voluminous correspondence with her. Exchanging letters became a habit he continued whenever he was away at military camps or later overseas. From France he wrote her nearly every day—a fact vouched for by Eddie Jacobson, Harry's sergeant and later business partner, who often mailed the letters. Another anecdote, equally impossible to document, has grown from this voluminous correspondence.

> One day, after he had become President, Truman discovered his wife on her knees, burning a yellowed pile of papers in the fireplace. He asked what she was doing. "I'm burning your letters to me," she said, hastily shoveling in the rest. "Bess, you oughtn't to do that," Truman protested. "Why not? I've read them several times," she said.
> "But think of history."
> "I have," replied Mrs. Truman.[21]

Harry and Bess Wallace Truman on their wedding day, June 28, 1919, in Independence, Missouri.

Although Harry and Bess were considered to be "going steady" after about 1913, it was not until shortly before Harry was shipped overseas in World War I that they announced their engagement. At that time Bess gave him her picture and inscribed on its back, "Dear Harry, May this photograph bring you safely home again from France—Bess." Harry carried the picture in his mind, heart, and pocket during the weeks of training in Oklahoma and while his battery survived mud and dangers on the Western Front. The picture occupied a prominent place on his desk in the White House and can be seen today on his restored desk at the Truman Library in Independence.

Truman's World War I service ended on May 6, 1919, when he was released from active duty and given the rank of major in the army reserves. Six weeks later he and Bess were married at Trinity Episcopal Church in Independence; he was thirty-five and she was thirty-four. After a brief honeymoon, the newlyweds moved into the Gates house, already occupied by the bride's mother, her grandmother, and her youngest brother. The home was roomy enough and was kept immaculate by the fastidious Mrs. Wallace. The residence then really belonged to her, but if Truman ever resented the living arrangements he never said so publicly. This house was to be his and Bess's home—their haven of quiet and privacy—for more than fifty years. When their only child, Margaret, was born there on February 17, 1924, four generations for a time lived within its spacious interior.

Some writers have speculated that Harry's successful political career can be traced to his determination to show his mother-in-law that he could amount to something. He was always the dutiful son-in-law; never mind the wags in Independence who, during the run for election in the 1948 campaign, announced: "Harry is sure he will be elected President; Mrs. Wallace has her doubts!" If Mrs. David Wallace was the adversary in his house as she often was pictured, he never allowed that opposition to become public knowledge. When the Trumans moved into the White House, Mrs. Wallace went there to live with them. Bess insisted on caring for her mother even though such living arrangements at times complicated her own life. When her brothers in Independence repeatedly offered to have the aging Mrs. Wallace live with them, Bess always replied, "It's a daughter's duty to look after her mother."

One cannot hope to understand the character of Harry Truman without taking into consideration his lasting affection for his wife. Few presidential couples ever displayed such closeness and total dependence on each other as did the Trumans. More than mere posturing to promote the all-American story of a poor country boy who married his childhood sweetheart and went on to become president, their lives are a record of enduring love and cooperation. Bess persistently played down her role, but her influence on Harry was ever present. She was the one person who, on occasion, might persuade him to ignore an attack or soften a statement. Her natural inclinations, strengthened by her unusually close association with her mother, were toward dignity, conservatism, and restraint—three traits in sharp contrast with the ebullience of her husband.

Harry and Bess at their Washington, D.C.,
apartment in 1944.

Her determination to remain in the background should not lead one to think that Bess was a weak person. At the outset of her marriage she seems to have decided that her role would be one of assistance, guidance, and subtle direction. When Harry Truman was in the haberdashery business in Kansas City, she helped in planning the advertising signs, taking inventory, and going over the books at night. When he went to Congress in 1934 she took care of the household, drafted much of his correspondence, and helped with his speeches and research. When there was criticism of her receiving $4500 salary annually as his secretary, Senator Truman vehemently defended her. One of his critics, arch-Republican Roy Roberts, managing editor of the *Kansas City Star,* agreed, ''She earns every cent of it.''

So little was known about Bess Truman when her husband inherited the presidency that a mimeographed biography of her was put out by the Women's Division of the Democratic National Committee, and it erroneously reported that she had been a schoolteacher at one time. The mistake was quickly caught, and a second communique was issued denying that she had ever taught school.

When President Franklin Roosevelt died, the Trumans were living in a five-room apartment. Bess took care of it and did the cooking with only occasional aid from daughter Margaret, just turned twenty-one. Harry usually dried the dinner dishes. Unlike many of his presidential predecessors, he had no extra income and could not afford domestic help. He was still paying off debts from his defunct haberdashery.

Bess Truman valued her privacy so much that it prevented the public from learning much about her that was interesting and revealing. One sign of her determination surfaced soon after Roosevelt's death when she announced that she was not going to emulate Eleanor Roosevelt's weekly press conferences. The newspaperwomen in Washington were thunderstruck, chagrined, and angry. They protested to no avail, and some vowed to bring her down. Bess Truman praised Mrs. Roosevelt as a warm, gracious, likable person, and she quietly arranged for her two press secretaries to discuss the White House social calendar twice a week. But she herself adamantly refused to be interviewed.

As first lady, Bess Truman became guest of honor at innumerable teas, luncheons, and social occasions of many different types. Sometimes it seemed as if every organization wanted her to serve as its honorary chairman. Most of these requests she accepted graciously and without fanfare. Her Washington friends described her as a considerate person and found her small talk entertaining but guarded. She carefully refrained from making public statements on any political matters. She continued to read widely and told a reporter from the *New York Herald Tribune* that she preferred Dickens and Scott to modern authors, most of whom she considered a waste of time. Not a musical performer herself, she enjoyed music and helped amass the large collection of records the Trumans owned.

She evoked considerable criticism when she attended a tea given for her by the Daughters of the American Revolution, because that organization had refused to allow Hazel Scott, black pianist, to perform in the DAR-owned Constitution Hall. Mrs. Truman offered a forthright statement: "I deplore any action which denies artistic talent an opportunity to express itself because of prejudice against race or origin." Having accepted the invitation to attend the event before the action against Miss Scott was taken, however, it was not in her code of manners that there could be any "idea other than to complete this engagement."

President Truman could not avoid all the repercussions from this incident, for Hazel Scott was the wife of New York Congressman Adam Clayton Powell.

Enraged by the insult to his wife, Powell charged that Mrs. Truman ought to be called not the first lady but the "last lady" of the land. Others joined in the criticism and maintained that because she came from Missouri, Bess Truman must be steeped in southern tradition and prejudice.

As a result of Powell's outburst, Truman retaliated by refusing to invite him to the White House, even for the annual reception given for all members of Congress. Others, like Congresswoman Claire Boothe Luce, who attacked members of his family received similar treatment. President Truman explained to the latter's husband, publisher Henry Luce:

> I have been in politics for thirty-five years and everything that could be said about a human being has been said about me. But my wife has never been in politics, and she has always conducted herself in a circumspect manner. No one has the right to make derogatory remarks about Mrs. Truman. Your wife has said many unkind and untrue things about her. And as long as I am in residence here, she'll never be a guest in the White House.[22]

President Truman's zealous protection for members of his immediate family soon became so well known as to be a target for wags and critics. At one time his sensitivity pushed him close to an international incident. It happened in January of 1946 on the afternoon of his first annual diplomatic dinner—an event to which all the chiefs of missions, their deputies, and their wives were invited, together with their American counterparts, to an evening in the White House. On the afternoon of this scheduled dinner, Chief of Protocol Stanley Woodward received a phone call and a female voice informed him that Soviet Ambassador Nikolai V. Novikov and his counsellor had been taken ill; they regretted that they would not be able to dine with the president. Just to be sure that the phone call was authentic, the State Department put through a call to Ambassador Novikov in New York, and found him to be cheerful and in good health. The reason for the cancellation was diplomatic rather than physical. The State Department had thoughtlessly invited to the same dinner envoys from the USSR and Lithuania, a small country which, along with Latvia and Estonia, had been swallowed up by the Soviet Union. The United States had continued to recognize the three former states as sovereign nations, however.

The next morning Secretary of State Dean Acheson and Woodward were summoned to the president's office. They were flabbergasted to learn that he was planning to tell the Soviet ambassador to leave the country because he had been "inexcusably rude" to Mrs. Truman. The dismayed Acheson and Woodward pointed out that such action would be regarded as rash and might have serious consequences abroad even among America's best friends. The president remained adamant until Matt Connelly, his appointment secretary, came in and handed him the telephone, saying, "Mrs. Truman." After listening for a few moments and saying only, "I'm talking with him now. He agrees with you," Truman gave the receiver to Acheson, who later recounted his conversation with Mrs. Truman:

> I must not, Mrs. Truman said, let the President go through with his plan. I agreed in the objective, but asked for operating instructions. Mrs. Truman thought delay while the President's temper cooled the best procedure. She added that if he went ahead his critics would have a field day. This gave me an idea. While she talked I murmured in horror pretending to be repeating phrases that she never uttered, such as ". . . above himself . . . delusions of grandeur . . . too big for his britches. . . ."
>
> The President took the receiver away from me, "All right, all right," he said. "When you gang up on me I know I'm licked. Let's forget all about it.[23]

A few moments later Truman was smiling and seemed in better humor, but he picked up the old-fashioned photograph of Bess as a young lady and handed it to Acheson, saying, "I guess you think I'm an old fool, and I probably am. Look on the back." Most accounts of the incident report that Truman added: "Any s.o.b. who is rude to that girl is in trouble with me." In his writings, Acheson has omitted this particular sentence but did remember that as he and Woodward left the office the still unmollified president called out to them, "Tell *Old Novocaine* we didn't miss him!"[24]

In retrospect this incident seems small and might even evoke grudging admiration for a husband so protective of his wife. It also has its comic overtones, but it shows that on occasion Bess did curb rash actions or words of her peppery husband.

When her husband became president, Bess Truman did not change her attitudes. She had always conducted herself as she thought a proper lady should, and she had no intention or desire to play the part of grande dame. Acquaintances and friends from Missouri could not always visit the Trumans in Washington, but Bess kept in touch with many of them. When there was illness or trouble back home she thoughtfully would send gifts or notes. In April of 1946 she invited ten members of her long-time Independence Bridge Club to visit the White House. One of them, Mrs. J. C. Noel, said in advance of the visit, "At our club meetings we never play much bridge. It's mostly talk. We play bridge for awhile, then we talk. That's what we'll probably do in Washington."[25] While this group was in Washington, Mrs. Truman took them to a Shriners circus. A circus clown eager to amuse the party stood in front of her box and began cutting up. Mrs. Truman did not like it, and when he familiarly put his hand on her shoulder, she blazed, "That's enough!" Just as she said this, a photographer snapped her picture.[26]

Her close friends understood that Bess chose to build her life around her husband, her daughter, and her home. Guarding her husband's health and reputation was her chief concern. His favorite foods were fried chicken, roast turkey, chili, and for dessert, strawberries. She had to watch his diet as well as his exuberance in language. In public she usually kept quiet about politics, but her husband acknowledged that behind the scenes she might pencil in some comments on a forthcoming speech or urge him to use more moderate wording. Servants around the White House recalled that one of her most frequent comments was, "You didn't have to say it that way!"

During the 1948 camgaign two of the Truman women—Bess and Margaret—were very much in the public eye. They joined the president as he crossed the country drawing standing crowds from the Mississippi to the Golden Gate Bridge. The appearances came to follow a well-set pattern. First, President Truman would make a few extemporaneous remarks from the rear of the train, and then smilingly he would say something like, "Now I'd like to introduce my family. Here comes the boss." That line was the cue for Bess to step out. After a proper recognition from the crowd, President Truman then would say, "Now the one who bosses her." Margaret would then appear, wearing a gracious smile, and usually draw a few whistles from the young men in the crowd.

As a campaigner, Bess never lost her poise. At one stop when her husband tried to pin a red carnation on her right lapel, she nonchalantly shifted it to the left one. In Iowa she frowned slightly when he launched into a mother-in-law story. On that occasion he said:

> I feel like the man who was going to his wife's funeral. The undertaker tells him her mother is going to ride out to the cemetery with them. "OK," he says, "but it is going to spoil my whole day."[27]

Mrs Truman did not think that story was funny, and it was dropped from Truman's collection of anecdotes.

Some observers of that campaign called Bess Truman a one-woman Gallup Poll. She was constantly watching the crowd for its immediate reactions to her husband's appeals and arguments. Lines that drew favorable responses were used again; lines that seemed to leave the listeners unmoved might be dropped. If her husband showed signs of strain she prompted him to rest. If his voice began to sound hoarse she quickly called in his physician, Brigadier General Wallace Graham.

She never let the headiness of campaigning or her position in Washington destroy her open friendliness. She did not like the Secret Service following her on shopping trips, particularly when she went back home to Independence. There she would climb one flight of stairs in the Battery Building to Pearl Wood's beauty parlor, a typical neighborhood hairdressing salon with washbasins lined up on one side and hair driers on the opposite. Pearl Wood handled Mrs. Truman's appointment just as she did other customers'. Bess always ordered an ordinary shampoo and set; after that would come a quick comb without much fussing and she would be done. In Washington Bess followed much the same practice.

Bess's modesty was anything but a handicap to her husband's career. The Trumans were friendly with a Washington hostess, Perle Mesta, and the story is told that once Bess joined columnist Leonard Lyons and Mesta to attend a Broadway musical, *Call Me Madam.* The play itself was based on the life of the popular hostess, and when this particular trio of patrons marched down the aisle to take their seats, the theater audience began to clap in recognition. The applause continued after they were seated, so Perle Mesta arose and took a bow. That did not stop the applause, so the modest Bess urged, "Stand up, Perle, they want you again."

Though Bess preserved her common touch, she was ever the lady. She was poised but had no exalted notions about her status. Standing by her husband's side she represented stability and careful judgment. Her devotion to him and to his well-being was unshakeable. Once an old friend asked her what she considered the most memorable aspect of her life, and she replied:

> Harry and I have been sweethearts and married for more than forty years—
> and no matter where I was, when I put out my hand Harry's was there to
> grasp it.[28]

Throughout their long marriage, Bess Truman served as Harry's most valuable single listener. It was not simply that he wanted his persuasions to please her; he knew that if he failed to convince her of the soundness of his argument or the propriety of his position, a great many other practical-minded persons would be unmoved.

Harry Truman's Daughter, Margaret

Margaret Truman was twenty years old when her father became president. He had been in politics since two years before her birth, and his general attitudes and convictions had crystallized and become well known. There was not much chance that his daughter could change many of his basic beliefs or alter his pronouncements. Nevertheless, he was extremely sensitive to Margaret's feelings and aspirations, and as his only child she was a beloved figure for him to protect.

Just as his own mother had encouraged a move from the farm into town so that her children might have a better education, Harry Truman was ever concerned about his daughter's home life and her schooling. In his early political posts he had worried lest she be kidnapped, and as more and more prominence came to him this fear grew. In private letters to his mother he might chafe a little about the Secret Service and all the guards assigned, but he was aware of the need for them and thankful for the protection they gave.

> A guard has to go with Bess and Margaret everywhere they go—and they don't like it. They both spend a lot of time figuring out how to beat the game, but it just can't be done.[29]

There is no evidence that Margaret ever was asked for advice on forthcoming speeches or remarks. However, she contributed to the total persuasive picture Truman presented to the American electorate, and she played her definite role in the 1948 presidential campaign. Just by joining her father and mother on the rear platform of a train or on an improvised stage, she helped complete a picture of the wholesome American family—the kind of family that would be an asset to any candidate. The appearance of the three together during this campaign appealed to the people. The presentations had dignity, warmth, and put the nation's first family on a comfortable footing with voters.

Unusually poised, perhaps because of earlier exposures in political circles as well as her own appearances as a vocalist, Margaret was a stage asset. She learned to laugh at the right cues; she gladly signed autographs, and voters remembered her. During the campaign she rejected all requests to sing, and seemed content to bask in the attention given her father. A farmer in shirt sleeves allowed that Margaret was "just like one of us." At another time a hospital veteran in a wheelchair called out, "What are you doing tonight?" It was all part of the show, and the Trumans accepted and even encouraged the badinage.

The president enjoyed the banter as long as there was no suggestion of criticism of his family or any of his closest friends. Anyone who stepped across that line risked Truman's displeasure and would soon learn of it through either oral comment or written remonstrance. He was particularly sensitive to slights or innuendoes about the female members of his family. Among President Truman's blasts at those who dared criticize a member of his family was the real humdinger sent to Paul Hume, music critic for the *Washington Post*. Hume's review of daughter Margaret's singing detonated the president's anger through his shortest fuse, protection of his family. Margaret aspired toward an operatic career, and as might be expected because she was the president's daughter, each of her public appearances attracted attention. At a concert in Constitution Hall during early December of 1950, President and Mrs. Truman together with their guests, British Prime Minister Clement Attlee, British Ambassador Sir Oliver Franks, and Lady Franks were among those who came to hear Margaret sing. The next day the following review by journalist Paul Hume appeared in the *Post:*

> Margaret Truman, soprano, sang in Constitution Hall last night.
>
> It was not her first recital there, and it was probably not her last. Miss Truman is a unique American phenomenon with a pleasant voice of little size and fair quality.
>
> She is extremely attractive on the stage. Her program is usually light in nature, designed to attract those who like the singing of Jeanette Mac-Donald and Nelson Eddy. Yet Miss Truman cannot sing very well.
>
> She is flat a good deal of the time—more last night than at any time we have heard her in past years. There are few moments during her recital when one can relax and feel confident that she will make her goal, which is the end of the song.
>
> Miss Truman has not improved in the years we have heard her. She has learned about her diaphragm and its importance to her singing. She has learned that she must work in order to make something of her voice. But she still cannot sing with anything approaching professional finish.
>
> She communicates almost nothing of the music she presents. Schumann, Schubert, and Mozart were on her program last night. Yet the performance of music by these composers was no more than a caricature of what it would be if sung by any one of a dozen artists today.
>
> And still the public goes and pays the same price it would for the world's finest singers.
>
> It was wise and very sensible of this young American to open her program with three songs by Francis Hopkinson. For Hopkinson not only is numbered among the signers of the Declaration of Independence, but he is also counted as our first native composer.
>
> A Waltz Song by Edward German was not worth resurrecting, nor were Besley and Spross songs in the final group.
>
> It is [an] extremely unpleasant duty to record such unhappy facts about so honestly appealing a person. But as long as Miss Truman sings as she has for three years, and does so today, we seem to have no recourse unless it is to omit comment on her programs altogether.
>
> Herman Allison gave fine accompaniments, but played two solos and an encore quite badly. Miss Truman's first encores were by Popper and Delibes, from whom she sang songs arranged from instrumental works. Her final encores were Grieg's My Johann, and Sweethearts, by Romberg.[30]

The morning after this review appeared, Mr. Truman went to his office and in longhand wrote a letter to Paul Hume. He then called in a messenger to deliver the note. Hume at first refused to believe in its authenticity, for the letter was signed only with the initials "H.S.T.," and Hume thought it might be some kind of practical joke. He called his counterpart on the *Washington Daily News,* and the two met in a coffee shop to discuss the matter. Two days later the *Daily News* carried the story, and then on December 9, the *Washington Post* quoted its competitor:

NOTE SIGNED H.S.T. THREATENS
CRITIC OF MISS TRUMAN'S SINGING

The *Washington Daily News* carried the following story Friday afternoon:

H. for Hello

S. for Sweet

T. for Thing

Margaret Truman sang here the other day.

Paul Hume, The *Washington Post*'s music critic, panned her unmercifully.

He is now showing around a letter which goes like this: "I have just read your lousy review buried in the back pages. You sound like a frustrated old man who never made a success, an eight-ulcer man on a four-ulcer job, and all four ulcers working."

"I never met you, but if I do you'll need a new nose and plenty of beefsteak and perhaps a supporter below. Westbrook Pegler, a guttersnipe, is a gentleman compared to you. You can take that as more of an insult than as a reflection on your ancestry."

The letter was initialed H.S.T. and Mr. Hume, who once wanted a career as a singer himself, is wondering whether the initials stand for whom he thinks they might stand for.[31]

It was a perfect example of a journalistic bank shot—played with restraint but not missing the essential news value. Hume himself made no charges but issued the following statement:

The day after my review of Margaret Truman's concert I received a note on White House stationery signed "H.S.T." It was similar to but not identical with the quotation above. The letter was seen by my office associates and by my editors, but I did not desire to publish it. I can only say that a man suffering the loss of a close friend[32] and carrying the terrible burden of the present world crisis ought to be indulged in an occasional outburst of temper.[33]

Later White House officials confirmed that Mr. Truman indeed had written Mr. Hume, and one source said the published version sounded like what Mr. Truman wrote. The episode did not end there, of course. Margaret had left for a concert in Nashville, Tennessee. When contacted there she at first termed the reported letter "ridiculous," and added:

I am absolutely positive my father wouldn't use language like that. In the first place, he wouldn't write a letter to Mr. Hume. My father wouldn't have time to write a letter. I don't know why anyone would do anything like that and sign my father's name. That is ghastly. It is very easy to get a hold of White House stationery.

Mr. Hume is a very fine critic. He has a right to write as he pleases.[34]

In the biography she later wrote of her father Margaret insisted that he had discussed the letter with his aides and was annoyed to find that all of them thought it was a mistake. She wrote that he had summed up his stand and entered it on his office calendar-diary:

December 9, 1950

Margie held a concert here in D.C. on December 5th. It was a good one. She was well accompanied by a young pianist named Allison, whose father is a preacher in Augusta, Georgia. Young Allison played two pieces after the intermission, one of which was the great A Flat Chopin Waltz, Opus 42. He did it as well as it could be done and I've heard Paderewski, Moritz Rosenthal and Josef Lhevinne play it.

A frustrated critic on the *Washington Post* wrote a lousy review. The only thing, General Marshall said, he didn't criticize was the varnish on the piano. He put my baby as low as he could and he made the young accompanist look like a dub.

It upset me and I wrote him what I thought of him. I told him he was lower than Mr. X and that was intended to be an insult worse than the reflection on his ancestry. I would never reflect on a man's mother, because mothers are not to be attacked, although mine was.

I've been accused of putting my baby, who is the apple of my eye, in a bad position. I don't think that is so. She doesn't either—thank the Almighty.[35]

The fires kindled by President Truman's letter on this occasion burned for several weeks, and editors were not reluctant to print the incendiary letters most of them received on the subject. Some of the responses were highly critical of the president for his attack, and many defended the right of Hume to express his judgments. Mr. Truman tried to rationalize that he had a right to be two persons—the president of the United States and Harry S. Truman, father of Margaret and husband of Bess—but many found his concept in this instance incompatible with his usual high concern for the image of the presidency and the person holding that office. He kept insisting that most fathers of daughters would have reacted in the same way: "The trouble with you guys [advisers who did not agree with him on the propriety of his letter] is you just don't understand human nature."[36]

As years passed, some of the strong feelings aroused by the incident began to weaken, but in retrospect it is hard to imagine how the episode added much to President Truman's luster. Later, dramatized versions of the exchange shown in the stage presentation, *Give 'Em Hell, Harry*, or the television offering based on Merle Miller's biography, *Plain Speaking*, tried to elicit good-natured support for the idea of a loving father merely defending his daughter from unfair critics.

President Truman's quick and emotional outburst at music critic Hume was consistent with his protective pride toward members of his family, particularly its female members. To him, women were "ladies" and warranted special consideration. No real gentleman would criticize them or treat them with anything but extreme courtesy. His intemperate language might sometimes offend, but it is doubtful that he ever swore or uttered an obscenity in the presence of what he called "mixed company." Such behavior would be unchivalrous and contrary to his ideas on womanhood.

4

Grassroots Politician

This party comes from the grass roots. It has grown from
the sod of the people's hard necessities.

SENATOR ALBERT J. BEVERIDGE
Bull Moose Convention, 1912

A growing cult pictures Harry Truman as a decisive leader, who, overcoming
handicaps of a rural background and a lack of formal college education, rose
suddenly as the champion of the people—the man who in times of crisis won
signal victories for democracy against the forces of totalitarianism wherever he
encountered them. The concept contains elements of truth but ignores many
essential facts.

In the first place, Harry Truman had been an active and successful politician for nearly a quarter of a century before he stepped into the presidency.
Among the important American leaders of 1944, his name was not unknown.
Perhaps it was because military reports from distant battlefields captured public
attention; at any rate domestic politics then did not always receive comparable
newspaper coverage. Moreover, Truman's advancement had been steady rather
than brilliant or rapid.

Second, while biographers have fondly related stories of Truman's humble
start in life, more careful studies disclose that by no means did the Truman
family live in straitened circumstances when measured by the regional standards of his boyhood. True, he did not attend college, and as a result his education although intense was not as broad as it might have been. But in place of
formal curricula were his compulsive drives, his thirst for facts, his retentive
memory, and a thorough grounding in practical politics.

There was considerable truth to the jest Harry Truman often made when
he returned home: "I can't be President of the United States in Jackson County." The welcome given him by old friends there always touched him; their
recognition, he said, made him swell up "like a pizened pup." Back home his

personality was well known; his insights, biases, and prejudices also were discernible. When he became more famous, his words and deeds would become blurred by image-makers and public relations counselors.

Voters in Jackson County learned early of Harry Truman's abundant energy, his urge to act decisively, his insistence on precise facts, and his gregarious, affable personality whenever things were going his way. Character strengths and weaknesses dot his highly visible trails through the politics of his home county. Moreover, tactics and patterns of campaigning during those early years in Jackson County emerge clearly, and analysis of them provides clues to his later behavior and decisions.

Jackson County Politics

Harry Truman's early interest in politics was stimulated by his penchant for American history and was nurtured through discussions with his father. The latter, who unashamedly favored the Democratic party and opposed the Republican, took his son to hear William Jennings Bryan when the famed orator ran for the presidency in 1900. At that convention young Harry was only sixteen, and he sat with his father in the sweltering heat of a quickly built Kansas City auditorium. Twelve years later when the free silver advocate ran for the third time and the convention was held in Baltimore, Harry waited at the telegraph office in Grandview so that he could carry news of the convention home to his anxious father.

In Jackson County, politics demanded unswerving party loyalty. Identity with a party was an allegiance not unlike a church affiliation—an act of faith that might be followed by whole families. Much of it had started with the events of the Civil War, and the traditions continued well into the twentieth century. To John Truman, Harry's father, local politics as well as national events were compelling subjects and seldom far from his mind and talk. He had been appointed by the county court—the court over which his son was destined to preside—as an overseer of roads. Not a high paying job, it was recognized patronage, and after his death in 1914 some of the patronage descended to the shoulders of his elder son.

Democrats in Jackson County then were divided into two main factions: the "Goats" and the "Rabbits." Harry, like his father before him, belonged to the Goat branch. The original use of the two labels, Goats and Rabbits, is not entirely clear, but most people believe that "Goats" came about because that group, led by Tom and Mike Pendergast, lived mainly in the West Bluff region of Kansas City, an area having a large Irish population that kept a sizable number of goats grazing near their homes. The other contingent, led by Joe Shannon, dwelled mostly in the southeast section of town close to creek bottoms where rabbits were numerous.[1]

Even before 1914 Harry had gained some community recognition as a hard working, dependable farmer. He had succeeded his father in the road overseer's job four years before the latter's death, and in 1915 served for slightly more than six months as postmaster at Grandview. The Farm Bureau was just beginning to get organized there, and the new county agent advised its members to select town representatives who combined qualities of a "progressive farmer and one who would also have some political support with the County Court of Jackson County." He thought Harry Truman of Grandview was just such a candidate.[2]

At the outset of his political career Harry Truman's support stemmed from three overlapping but identifiable groups: the Masons, veterans, and relatives or friends. Members of Masonic lodges around Kansas City played a key role in helping Truman launch his political career and in his numerous campaigns for elective office. He enjoyed the fraternal associations, and they were rewarding to him. His dedication to the principles of Freemasonry was unswerving, and he took into his grave the Masonic mementos he loved best—his pin, apron, and his Thirty-third Degree Scottish Rite Ring.

In his early twenties he had been left a Masonic emblem as a keepsake,[3] and in his *Memoirs* he wrote:

> One day in late 1908 a cousin of my mother came to the farm to look at some stock. I noticed a Masonic pin on his coat and told him I had always wanted to be a member. A few days later he brought me an application.[4]

Once accepted in the Masons, Truman advanced rapidly through the various ranks. Within a month he became a Third Degree Mason. He expanded his studies and began accompanying the Grand Lecturer in visits to lodges as far north as St. Joseph. It was during this period and while he worked the horses and mules on the farm that he practiced aloud his speeches on Masonic principles:

> In January 1909 I put in an application for membership in Belton Lodge 450 A.F. and A.M. They voted me in, and I took the First Degree in February, and in March finished up with the Third. That spring and summer I spent teaching the plow horses all the Masonic lectures.[5]

As he acquired knowledge and skill in the various rituals he went on a tour of all lodges in the thirty-fourth Masonic district. He traveled to St. Louis and successfully presented to the Grand Master there a petition for a new lodge at Grandview. When that chapter was established, it did him the singular honor of appointing him Worshipful Master. He was one of the youngest Masters ever appointed to such a post.[6]

By 1916 his Masonic involvements competed with his growing obligations in the national guard. Then his overseas service in World War I forced a two-year hiatus in lodge participation. After the armistice and his return to Missouri, however, he quickly resumed his Masonic activities. He liked the color and pageantry, and he came to be known as an expert on rituals and ceremonies. Because of this expertness, when he visited other lodges—which he did frequently—he usually was called on to carry out some function.[7] He was thus a highly visible person, and because lodge members often were leaders in their home communities, Truman was building a base of influential support which later would be very helpful to him.

In addition to his Masonic associations, Truman could count on another bastion for political support—his reservoir of friends and acquaintances from the army. The record he and Jacobson had made with the operation of the canteen at the military camp near Fort Sill was well known to many citizens around Kansas City and had helped in his advancement as an officer. The canteen experience also became an impetus for his ill-fated excursion into haberdashery.

In 1919 when Truman returned from the war he was not certain what he wanted to do. He and Jacobson, who had been discharged about the same time, met and reminisced about army times and their mutually satisfying work at the canteen. They began planning another venture—this time a men's clothing store in the downtown district of Kansas City. In the fall of that year they opened their establishment on Twelfth Street just across from the Muehlebach Hotel.

Wholesale prices were very high following the war, and it took all the capital Truman could scrape up just to stock the store. Jacobson served as buyer because he had had more merchandising experience. Truman's affable manner made him the logical one to sell the shirts, neckties, belts, socks, and hats. He and his wife, Bess, also kept the books. After a short run of initial success, the store started losing money. It was caught in the same financial grip as most of the country. Farm prices fell more than 40 percent in one year's time, and nearly 10 percent of the farms in the state were lost through foreclosures or were held only through the leniency of creditors. By 1922 the inventory that Truman and Jacobson had bought at high prices was not moving for cash at any price. As early as January of 1922 it was clear the store was in deep trouble, but it did not close until April—two and a half years after it had opened. Truman refused to take bankruptcy, and for the next ten years he worked to settle any and all claims on the best basis he could get. Years afterwards he estimated that he lost $28,000 on the whole affair.[8]

Truman's First Campaign (1922)

The circumstances prompting Truman to become a candidate for county judge grew from the attraction politics had always held for him, the realization that his business was going under, and the assurances of support from the Pendergasts, who were the undisputed leaders of the dominant Democrats. In Missouri a county "judge" was not a judiciary official in the usual sense; rather the term was applied to administrators who in other sections of the country might be called commissioners of one sort or another. In 1915 Truman had begun attending party meetings at the Kansas City Tenth Ward Democratic Club—the home base of Mike Pendergast. Mike was a brother to Tom, who was the kingpin in Kansas City politics.

Just as a wartime friendship had been an impetus for starting his clothing business, Truman's unique ties with Battery D helped launch him into local politics. Not then or later did he ever hesitate to proclaim himself partisan when it came to matters dealing with veterans. He expected and received their steadfast endorsements in return. Typical of the early loyalty he drew from his army comrades was the support of Tom Murphy, a veteran of Battery D and a Kansas City attorney. Murphy had been a sergeant serving under Truman's command, and he later became an active, promising prizefighter. He recalled his role in an early political rally held for Truman:

> I fought in Boston in 1920 and won the national AAU boxing championship. And in 1922, when Harry first ran for office, I was still boxing, and I helped him open his campaign out at Lee's Summit. I went out there with a boxing partner and gave an exhibition to help draw a crowd. A lot of men in the outfit helped him in the campaign. They'd go out in cars and tack up campaign posters for him, and we'd go to the rallies and cheer and applaud. We'd do whatever was necessary to help Harry. We were that loyal to him.[9]

Truman's opening shot at politics must have resembled a veterans' reunion almost as much as a political rally, for he himself stressed the part another veteran played on that occasion:

> I opened my campaign in Lee's Summit with Colonel (Now Major General) E. M. Stayton making the principal address. The Colonel had been in Command of the 110th Engineers in the 35th Division. He knew my war record, what there was of it and he made the most of it.[10]

Through a fortuitous combination of politics and the military, Jim Pendergast, son of Mike and nephew of Tom, had been a second lieutenant in Truman's army battalion. The fact that Truman was picked by the Pendergasts is attested by several sources, but the versions differ somewhat.[11] His name as a possible candidate had begun appearing in January of 1922, and soon thereafter, as one biographer reported, Mike Pendergast came into the failing haberdashery store and told Truman that if he wanted to be county judge, he could "have it."[12] Eddie Jacobson remembered that the two politicians had come into the store and offered his partner the nomination if he wanted it.[13]

Truman's version of the circumstances surrounding his entry into Jackson County politics indicate that he did not meet Tom Pendergast until some time later:

> Mr. Wm. Southern, editor and publisher of the *Independence Examiner*, the most widely read paper in Jackson County outside of Kansas City, suggested to some of the Eastern Jackson County politicians, that if they wanted a candidate for Eastern Judge who could win they should take an ex-soldier of the late war. He suggested Harry Truman. I knew nothing of this until a delegation of men from the County came into my store on 12th Street and asked me to run. My father having been road overseer, and both of us having always been interested in politics to some extent, I knew all the men in the delegation personally. They told me about Mr. Southern's suggestion to the "Goat" faction of the Democrats and urged me to go. . . . They told me that the Eastern Jackson County "Goat" faction would back me tooth and nail, and that if I won the nomination the "Rabbits" had agreed to support me.[14]

When the primary contest began, the presiding judge of the county court was Eliju Hayes, a judge openly identified with the Rabbits—those Democrats opposed to Pendergast and his supporters. The other judge was H. F. McElroy, who was supposed to have a "newspaper complex" and was very friendly to the *Kansas City Star*. Truman considered McElroy to be the *Star*'s man on the court and said:

> He [McElroy] was also a close friend of T. J. Pendergast. In fact he introduced me to T. J. Pendergast the first time I ever saw him.[15]

In that year of 1922 it was conceded by even the most ardent Republicans around Kansas City that the fall election would show a Democratic sweep, particularly in the county offices. As might be expected, therefore, the Democratic primary drew several candidates and was intensely waged. Five Democrats were vying for the available judgeship: Emmet Montgomery, a banker from nearby Blue Springs who was backed by the Shannon-led Rabbits; Tom Parent, a road overseer; two independents who had Ku Klux Klan backing; and Harry Truman, the Pendergast candidate. It was the first time that women had been permitted to vote for county candidates in Missouri, and the impact these new voters would have on the election was unknown. Moreover, prohibition was a volatile issue lying just below the surface of most public pronouncements. The wets were neither organized nor ready to fight on the issue, but in general the rural population and those living in the smaller towns were ready to sink any candidate from Kansas City or Independence who wavered toward the wet position on the liquor question. The editor of the local newspaper described the locale and the mood of many of the voters:

Saturday night now is quite different from Saturday night when the open saloon was an important feature and was the loafing place for the male of the species. Where a dozen or more saloons with their swing doors used to stand on the square sending forth their odor of booze and a drunken crowd of men, many businesses of a respectable nature grace these one-time black spots of our town. In the days before prohibition, a woman hardly dared to pass along this line of liquor-selling stores but now it is safe for the smallest child. Today a drunken person is a curiosity on the streets of Independence.

On a Saturday night thousands of people come to town. The square and the streets leading from the square for more than four blocks in every direction are lined with cars ranging from Fords to Packards. This shows that the town is prosperous.

Anyone not used to the town and its Saturday night crowd would think a circus had come in, for there is laughing and merriment on every hand. The street cars clang and the automobiles honk, young girls laugh as the vast crowd moves slowly but surely around the square. Part is going in one direction and part in another.

There are country boys and country girls, with city boys and city girls, older folks and little children in this great Saturday night crowd. The older folks buy groceries and clothes while the younger people patronize the confectionaries and places of amusement. Of course the shows and ice cream parlors also get a large per cent of the married couples as well as the other variety.

Dad smokes a good cigar while mother talks clothes with a friend when she isn't chasing the baby in order to keep from losing the little fellow in the big crowd. Here comes a happy couple, they can't see a thing except each other. Others look, laugh, and repeat aloud or to themselves, "Love is blind."

Much window shopping is done, and many an event of interest to the parties concerned is told and retold with variation when little groups get together in the drug store or on the street corner. The police are out in their bright new uniforms but they are not needed except now and then to straighten out the heavy traffic at the intersection of the streets, because the Independence Saturday crowd is a law abiding, home-loving, amusement-seeking group. They are filled with the joy of living and with the interest of Independence, first, last, and always.[16]

Early in the campaign it had seemed that Emmet Montgomery, the banker, was the leading contender. He was a capable speaker, and he saw the campaign through his banker lenses—to him the issue was to get the county out of debt. Truman defined the main issue as providing better services to the people for each dollar spent. He tried to show how every individual citizen would be helped if the county had more miles of oiled roads within its borders. The other candidates stressed their own successful business backgrounds, which were evident and undeniable, but their emphases may have been thinly veiled attacks on Truman's disastrous haberdashery venture.

On July 12 in the final weeks of the primary race, a large Democratic rally was held in nearby Oak Grove, where an estimated crowd of four thousand came to hear the five contenders. The *Independence Examiner* had offered free space for statements from each candidate, and Harry Truman used his speech on the occasion as a statement of his principles and goals. The rally provided him with a setting for what must have been one of his earliest public speeches, and as noted elsewhere he was not at his physical best.[17]

What later would be called the "Truman style" was evident even in this seminal speech given twenty-three years before he became president. His pattern of simple organization and his direct language were easily discernible; he liked to concentrate on hard, factual data. Never a spellbinder, his approach was candid and more specific than paths taken by his opponents. In straightforward language that would become his trademark, he said:

> I am not in favor of spending the county's money for waterbound macadam roads. They will not stand up under the heavy traffic of the present day. They were a success some twenty or thirty years ago under steel tires and two-ton loads moving at three miles per hour, but under five-ton and ten-ton loads moving at twelve to twenty miles per hour they are not a success and money spent on them is wasted. It costs from $15,000.00 to $30,000.00 per mile to construct a waterbound macadam road and if this money were used for grading and oiling dirt roads it will put anywhere from forty to sixty miles of road in better condition and will benefit from ten to twenty times the number of people that one mile of rock road will benefit. If properly cared for oiled dirt roads will stand up as well as a Kansas City boulevard.[18]

By unequivocally stating his preference for oiled roads and the greater economy they represented, Truman revealed his characteristic lack of ambiguity. He promised to bring order and predictability to county finances, and insisted that the affairs of government at all levels ought to be run "just as if it was a big business corporation."

At the close of his Oak Grove speech Truman made a strong bid for support from the many veterans of the recent war. The other candidates in the primary were veterans also, but Truman was more successful in presenting himself as the one who was most understanding on matters affecting veterans. He capitalized on the deep devotion and loyalties developed by former comrades-in-arms, and the implication was plain—if he supported veterans seeking jobs and economic advancement, they should support him at the polls. Party loyalty was another commitment not to be readily forgotten, and usually he did not forget it. In one instance, however, he had crossed party lines and endorsed a Republican running for county marshal. Some Democrats subsequently had charged him with being unfaithful to party principles. He turned the charge to his advantage by meeting it head on and thereby strengthening his appeal to veterans.

You have heard it said that I voted for John Miles for County Marshal. I'll have to plead guilty to that charge along with some 5,000 other ex-soldiers. I was closer to John Miles than a brother. I have seen him in places that would make hell look like a playground. I have seen him stick to his guns when Frenchmen were falling back. I have seen him hold the American line when only John Miles and his three batteries were between the Germans and a successful counter-attack. He was of the right stuff and a man who didn't vote for his comrade under circumstances such as these would be untrue to himself and his country. My record has been searched and this is all my political opponents can say about me and you knowing the facts can appreciate my position. I know that every soldier understands it. I have no apology to make for it. John Miles and my comrades in arms are closer than brother[s] to me; there is no way to describe the feeling. But my friend John is the only Republican I ever voted for and I don't think that counts against me.[19]

After the Oak Grove event, primary campaigning intensified. Perhaps the other candidates had peaked too soon. At any rate the balance seemed to swing in Truman's favor, and he became the candidate to beat. The allegiance he drew from Masons and army buddies was welded to his sizable clan of relatives in the county. His first name was so widely used that one wag announced: "Everyone around here thinks Harry will get it, but there is some talk of a man named Truman!"

Truman's advertisements stressed that he was a native son, a veteran, a farmer, and a businessman. The opposing factions, mainly the Rabbits, tried to attack him as a "busted merchant" and chorused that all the contenders had served the nation during its late war.

It could not be said that Truman's oratory was responsible for his improved standing with the voters. At outdoor rallies other persons with louder, better-carrying voices were asked to make introductions or short speeches, but he was always on the program. His presentations, although factual, were not particularly impressive. Even his most loyal supporters remembered him as a poor speaker at the time. In commenting on his platform skills, one long-time friend said:

I will never forget the first speech he made—that I ever heard him make—was down at Sugar Creek one night. Bess and my wife and I were sitting there—it was outdoors—sitting on a kind of bank in the park there. Boy, it was about the poorest effort of a speech I ever heard in my life; I suffered for him.[20]

Even his friend McKim admitted: "I didn't think he had any [ability as a speaker]. He was a very poor speaker but he developed."[21]

Notwithstanding his shortcomings on the platform, when the primary votes were counted he led the field. The crowded slate of nominees unquestionably helped him secure this first victory, and perhaps the number of contenders was an early example of the Truman "luck." He received 4230 votes, 35.6 percent of those cast. His nearest rival was Montgomery with 3951, or 33.3 percent.[22] Harry Truman had won his first political race, and like most of the races that were to follow, it had not been an easy one. At the outset his chances had appeared slim, but he had worked harder and had out-hustled his opponents. In four months of campaigning during the primary, he had spent $524, the second highest expenditure among the five contenders.

Winning a Democratic nomination in Jackson County, Missouri, in 1922 was tantamount to winning the office. In the subsequent general election, public interest switched from the primary contenders to the issue of prohibition and to the race for the U.S. Senate. A high tariff enacted by Republicans at the national level irked many Missourians, and throughout the state it was called simply "the robber tariff."

After his primary victory, Truman developed and began using a set speech. For the first time in his life he was able to release his pent-up bias against the Republican party and what he claimed it stood for. He charged that within the county the Republicans were wasting money and were extravagant in their spending.[23] Because persons attending most of the rallies where he spoke were already committed to his party, Truman undoubtedly felt safe in exposing his strong partisan bias. He believed that such an attack would help weld even deeper Democratic party loyalty; moreover, then as in later years he seemed to enjoy assaulting the Republicans. His speeches were usually very short and promised to run county affairs along realistic but economical guidelines. At one early gathering, the Democratic candidate for the U.S. House of Representatives spoke for nearly two hours; Truman spoke but a few minutes from the same platform.

Truman inherited a liability in this early county race because of the endorsement he received from the Pendergast brothers. Even though he was a southern Baptist and came from Kentucky hill folk by way of Missouri, it soon became known that he was the preferred candidate of Irish Catholic Tom Pendergast. That liability became more serious because of the growing strength of the Ku Klux Klan in Jackson County. The Klan was never as strong there, or indeed any place in Missouri, as it was in states like Indiana or Ohio, but in 1922 it was a political reality to be reckoned with, nevertheless. At one meeting in Kansas City, members were vociferous in their assaults on Pendergast and on Joe Shannon, leader of the Rabbit faction. Klansmen saw these two as "puppets of the Papacy." The robed speakers insisted that voters should defeat not only every Irish candidate but also any candidate endorsed and supported by the "Catholic machine." One group kept singing a lilting protest:

> Goodbye Tom and goodbye Joe;
> You and Reed will have to go.
> You may not know what it's all about,
>   But we bet, by Gosh, you'll soon find out.
> The town is full of KKK
>   And the only thing we have to say,
> Is goodbye Tom and goodbye Joe,
>   The crooked gang has got to go.[24]

The Sunday before the general election, klansmen stood at the doors of several local churches and handed out sample ballots. On these ballots and following Harry Truman's name was the notation, "Church affiliation Protestant, endorsed by Tom and Joe." A footnote on the sample ballot then explained, "The Tom and Joe referred to are two Roman Catholic political bosses who dominate and control political affairs and the government of Kansas City and Jackson County."[25]

The campaign, whetted by such tasteless tactics as those of the klansmen, grew more rancorous, but they were not the only speakers who used hyperbole. One Republican candidate likened the Democratic organization in Jackson County to Lenin's stranglehold in the Soviet Union:

> A Soviet government has Jackson County by the throat in a stranglehold as absolute as that of the Soviet government of the great Russian Empire.[26]

Truman's strategy seemed to be aimed toward getting out a big vote in the general election. He concentrated his efforts on the county's pockets of highest population density, and he carefully selected areas that already had the greatest number of committed Democrats. He put forth little effort in trying to win the independent voter.

On the day before the election, one of Truman's friends, who was editor of the *Independence Examiner,* gave him a ringing endorsement and complimented him on running a "clean campaign." When the votes began coming in, it was quickly apparent that the Democrats would sweep the county offices. Truman won handily over his Republican opponent by 2749 votes. Truman's number of total votes was higher than any other Jackson County candidate; he even ran ahead of U.S. Senator Reed and Henry L. Jost, the candidate for the U.S. House of Representatives.[27]

Thus Harry Truman, a man who eight months earlier had been forced to close his failing business, became the county judge for the Eastern District of Jackson County. His campaign performance had been excellent. Especially noteworthy was his insistence on exact data, his specificity of language when talking about the county's roads, and his open avowal of friends and party faith. His total campaign performance was considerably better than his early platform behavior had implied, and it would be naive to think that Tom

Pendergast, as he went over the election returns, would fail to appreciate the political strength and new vigor that Harry Truman had brought into the Goat faction of his party.

Soon after the election and Truman's installation as county judge, however, the precarious balance of political trade-offs between Rabbits and Goats was destroyed. The voting pattern of the court was clearly established along the lines of two Goats and one Rabbit. Patronage was the name of the game and Truman became the target for acrid attacks, not only from opposing Republicans, but more particularly from disgruntled Rabbits within his own Democratic party.

He was not without supporters, however, and because he was by far the most aggressive of the three-member court, Truman soon captured control of it. Under his leadership and because of his talents as a peacemaker, the court began working together more than it had done previously. He gained other plaudits because he kept his campaign pledges. Moreover, his actions made good news copy, and his personality won the imagination of local editors. Voters saw him as a person who got the job done. When he closed his first year in office even a newspaper which had strongly supported his chief rival in the primary, Emmet Montgomery, praised the court and its record of road improvement:

> Under the circumstances the County Court which took charge January 1, has made a remarkable record in County road work this year.[28]

The Losing Race (1924)

As Truman approached the end of his two-year term, the forces opposed to him stepped up their efforts. Soon after he had announced for reelection the dissatisfied Rabbit faction chose him as its primary target. The Pendergast forces, however, had won notable victories in Kansas City proper and now thought they saw a chance to kill off their Rabbit opponents once and for all. Harry Truman was to be caught in the crossfire between the Pendergast Goats and the Shannon Rabbits.

Truman's speeches continued to lack any quality that could be called stirring, but they were unequivocal. He talked repeatedly about economy in government even though there was no real evidence that he had helped shave down the number of county employees. He concentrated on precise figures and assaulted his listeners with explanations of the amounts of money spent, the dollars saved through obtaining lower interest rates, and the improved conditions of specific roads in the county.

In the summer of 1924 the Kansas City Chamber of Commerce, which usually was accepted as a bipartisan group, broke precedent and passed a resolution praising the operation of the Jackson County Court. This was no small endorsement inasmuch as the real issue in the forthcoming election had to be the way the court had operated. Shortly after the endorsement by the chamber of commerce, the *Kansas City Times,* a newspaper which had a strong record of opposition to the Pendergasts, printed a complimentary editorial on the court and singled out Judges McElroy and Truman as giving "the kind of service needed not only in this community but everywhere."[29] Such endorsements helped deflate some of the attacks made on Truman by his rivals. Moreover, his personality and strong court record encouraged many of his friends and associates to step forward and speak for him. Again, Masonic friends and army buddies were in the vanguard of his supporters.

In 1924 the Ku Klux Klan exploded into national attention, and shock waves from this explosion reverberated into Jackson County. The Democratic National Convention in New York had voted by only a slight margin not to condemn the Klan by name in the party platform, but the acrimony engendered by the debate engulfed most parts of the nation. In Jackson County, Missouri, the Klansmen chose to aim their venom at Harry Truman. While it is problematical how much they were able to help Truman's opponent, it is certain that the Missouri Klan was more powerful than it had been two years earlier.

The enmity was gradual rather than immediate, however, and one bit of evidence indicates that Truman once even considered joining the burgeoning group. His friend, Edgar Hinde reported on his brief flirtation:

> So I talked to him [Truman] and he said: "All right." So I took $10 and went down to this organizer, and he took it. And then he wanted to have a meeting with him in Kansas City at the Hotel Baltimore. There was a fellow by the name of Jones, who was an organizer; he wanted to talk to Truman and see what his intentions were. . . . When he went over there this fellow Jones wanted him to agree that he wouldn't give a Catholic a job if he was elected; and Harry told him no, he wouldn't do that. He said that he commanded a battery of artillery that was about 90% Catholic and if any of his boys wanted a job—needed a job—and he could give it to them he was going to give it to them. "Well, we can't be for you." So that was it, and he gave me the ten dollars back.[30]

Truman's hope to enlarge his political base had run smack into his loyalty to veterans, and there was no question which commitment would prove stronger. Then and throughout his political life Harry Truman would feel free to appoint veterans, friends, and acquaintances to patronage positions. His political opponents were quick to capitalize on the charge, and they were fortified also by the Klan, who seemed bent on humbling the man who had rejected them.[31]

When the primary ended, it showed a disaster for Truman's opponents; he swept the district by 1599 votes. The voting pattern showed clearly his growing popularity among all Democrats in the Eastern District of the county. His strength was no longer based solely in the outlying rural districts nor limited to a crowd of army buddies and close friends. He was gaining Democratic support from the suburban regions around Kansas City and Independence.

As Tom Pendergast explored new possibilities to expand his power base, the spreading support for Truman became a factor for him to consider. Truman had proved that he could be frank and honest with voters and if not a quid pro quo Pendergast man, at least he was not opposed to the Boss and his henchmen.

In those years Democratic candidates who won the primary elections around Kansas City had every reason to expect success in the general election. As November of 1924 approached, however, there were national circumstances beyond the control of the freshman judge in Jackson County and even the grip of Tom Pendergast. It was a presidential election year, and prosperity was in the saddle. Business was booming; prices were high, and new technologies captured public admiration. The Democratic party of Woodrow Wilson was in shambles, and the contest was complicated because Senator Robert La Follette entered it with a new third party. National support for Calvin Coolidge, who declared "the business of America is business," rose quickly and swept him into office. The Republican wave reached Jackson County, where a friendly harness maker, Henry Rummel, had been drafted as the Republican candidate to oppose Truman.

At first Rummel's candidacy was not taken very seriously:

> Everybody thought it was a joke when they filed this old man Rummel 'cause he'd never been in politics, and they tried to get him to withdraw after they filed him, and he wouldn't withdraw.[32]

Truman opponents argued that a harmless Rummel would be better than a Pendergast protege. This decision, when linked with the national Republican mood, spelled defeat for Truman, notwithstanding his record and energetic campaigning.

The November voting was exceedingly heavy, and almost as soon as the first returns began coming in, the trend was obvious. Republicans were going to sweep across the county just as Democrats had done two years earlier. The Republicans gained total control, and Henry Rummel was only the second Republican elected Eastern District county judge since the Civil War.[33]

Harry Truman again was unemployed, and he now had a new nine-month-old responsibility at home. Daughter Margaret had been born in the preceding February. Harry Truman, politician, had won a campaign, and he had lost a campaign. His style of campaigning would become refined by more experience and would be guided by an ever-growing body of advisers, but the pattern was clearly evident in the Jackson County campaigns. One careful student of this period in his life summarized:

> This [Truman's] style was tested first in the early 1920's and continued to surface and develop as he grew in political maturity. . . . Candidate Truman's rhetoric—his style of discourse—was anchored to the bedrock of cold, pure facts. In his 1922 campaign he relied upon a set speech consisting of dry, factual exposition. . . . He rested his entire appeal on impregnable, precise logical statements of fact. His overwhelming, probably excessive faith in the self-evident power of rightful data continued throughout his life. The almost mystical devotion to the potency of facts pervaded his tenure as County Court Judge.[34]

Although his emphasis on facts and figures undoubtedly won him some supporters, there is no evidence that Truman's performance on the platform had improved measurably over the previous campaign. His speeches continued to be dry and lacking the entertainment or bombast usually found in political rhetoric. His lackluster speaking though was not reason enough for his loss in 1924, and it is probable that he would have lost in that year no matter what his style or abilities. The momentum had been captured by another party. A euphoric haze had settled over the nation and had filtered down to local elections. Business was good, and prosperity was to last forever. The country needed little leadership and could run itself. Calvin Coolidge was in the White House, and according to satirist H. L. Mencken, he fitted nicely into the national mood:

> He [Coolidge] slept more than any other President, whether by day or night. Nero fiddled, but Coolidge only snored.[35]

Factors other than the national mood contributed to Truman's loss. The widened fissure within the Democrats made a victory for their party most unlikely. Moreover, Truman's public statements criticizing the Ku Klux Klan probably cost him at the time more votes than they won. It was the only public election he would ever lose, and the loss taught him a lot about campaigning. Without his realization he had practiced even then certain aggressive tactics which he would strengthen and use in the future.

Elected Presiding Judge (1926)

After his failure to win reelection in 1924, Truman made a connection with the Automobile Club of Kansas City, where he was given the task of increasing its membership. He spent a year and a half in this job, adding substantially to his income. He had tasted politics, however, and as the next elections approached he began scouting for another opportunity. His preference was to run for county collector because that office carried with it a respectable income. By this time he was quite friendly with Mike Pendergast, who agreed to take him to see his brother—the big chieftain, Tom Pendergast—so that they could discuss the matter. The latter told them he had promised to support someone else for the county collector's job. Nobody can be sure whether this was fact or whether the Boss of Kansas City politics preferred Truman in some other office. At any rate, Tom Pendergast encouraged Truman to run instead for presiding judge of the county.

Boss Tom Pendergast then was fifty-four years old, a huge, bearlike man with massive neck, shoulders, and hands. He was prone to violence, and stories said that he could knock a man out with a single punch from one of his giant fists. It was an era of crude, rough politics though, and fisticuffs were not unusual. In addition to his formidable physical strength, Tom Pendergast was a shrewd leader who had been building his political clout in Kansas City and its environs since 1900. Endorsement from this most powerful of all Missouri politicians in 1926 almost assured victory for a Democrat running for office in Jackson County.

Local Democrats had been startled by their losses two years earlier, and in 1926 the party drew together in order to back a winning candidate. With a more united party, with solid Pendergast support, and with good marks for his previous two-year term, Harry Truman had considerably bigger chips to toss into the game. That fall he was elected presiding judge of the Jackson County Court by 16,000 votes. He would never lose another public election, and he ascribed that one as the real beginning of his political career.

Immediately upon assuming leadership of the county court, "Judge" Truman renewed his efforts to improve the county's roads. About this time Kansas City itself was calling for a bond issue of $28 million to finance a great many metropolitan improvements. Boss Pendergast was pushing this city issue and was not overly enthusiastic about Truman's request for support of a $6.5 million proposal for an issue of bonds to be used for improving county and rural roads. Nevertheless, Truman was confident he could sell his bond issue to the voters by telling them precisely how the money was to be spent. Pendergast gave him the green light, and he carried his persuasion into every corner of the county. He proposed a bipartisan board of engineers to supervise the road building and explained that all contracts would be awarded on a competitive low-bid basis.

Whether the need was so evident or Truman's explanations so eminently persuasive, when the votes for the bond issue were counted they showed a favorable majority of three-fourths instead of the necessary two-thirds. The road-building projects were started almost immediately and were completed as promised despite some occasional grumblings from disgruntled members of the faithful who did not get the contracts or employment they thought they deserved.

There is no hard evidence that Pendergast ever directed the awarding of such contracts, even though he himself owned the Ready-Mixed Concrete Company—a firm which in the past had been used almost exclusively by contractors paving Jackson County roads. Truman gave his version of the extent of Pendergast's influence in this matter:

> When the first contracts were to be let, I got a telephone call from Tom Pendergast saying that he and some of his friends were very anxious to see me about those contracts. I knew very well what was in the wind, but I went to their meeting. I told them that I expected to let the contracts to the lowest bidders, just as I had promised the taxpayers I would do, and that I was setting up a bi-partisan board of engineers to see that specifications were carried out according to contract, or else the public would not pay for them.

> Pendergast turned to the contractors and said, "I told you he's the contrariest man in the state of Missouri." When the contractors had left, he said, "You carry out the agreement you made with the people of Jackson County."[36]

The political talks Truman gave during the time he was county judge were largely ones of explanation, description, or defense of the court's record. Just as county roads had been a frequent theme during his campaign, the subject also served as the main topic in many subsequent speeches. He liked to praise the road-building programs initiated and carried through during his ten years on the court. His favorite technique was to contrast the improvements with road conditions in 1923. He described those conditions as: "360 miles of oiled dirt roads, some 200 miles of old water bound, scandal built, dram shop fund, piecrust roads, and a few miles of state roads either under construction or to be built sometime."[37]

In the course of his career as a politician in Jackson County, Harry Truman learned more about the need of a speaker to adapt his remarks to the interests of listeners. Adaptation to veterans and to his fellow Masons came easily to him, and for general audiences he often referred to his farm background or expressed pride in his home area. The language was often trite, but it served his purpose.

> To me, Jackson County, Missouri, is the greatest County in the whole United States. It is almost in the geographical center of the country. It is the center of agricultural activities of the United States. It is the Heart of America, the cross roads of the Nation.[38]

It was his practice during this period to write his speeches in longhand before they were delivered. The drafts of these talks indicate that he wrote them in a manner similar to the way he spoke—rapidly, and often unmindful of the nuances of wording. The sentences were short and choppy, with little attention paid to niceties of conjunctives or transitions. There is little evidence that he ever gave the speeches much polish or editing, for seldom are his first words or phrases changed. The result was a pattern of speaking that was terse, dry, and lacking in much intellectual stimulation.

It was not unusual for high schools then to call on elected officials to deliver the commencement address, and Judge Truman gave several such talks. There is no evidence that his talks were remembered any longer than those given by others on such occasions. In one commencement address he acknowledged his shortcomings as a speaker:

> Young Ladies & Gentlemen:
> This is an honor that I appreciate and one I wish I could fulfil as it should be done. I am not the gifted orator you should have to talk to you on this occasion. Nevertheless, I have some things I want to say to you and I believe you'll be interested in them.[39]

When he gave this address Truman was not yet fifty years old, but he probably appeared ancient enough to the young graduates. He recalled that his own graduation was both a sad and a happy occasion for him. He said that during that earlier ceremony he had looked the boys over one by one and remembered all the good times and bad times they had shared. After adding that some of those boys remained his very good friends, he attempted a feeble jest:

> I didn't look the girls over so closely because I could only see one of them and I'm still looking at her because she's Mrs. Harry Truman.[40]

Judge Truman noted that it was customary for commencement speakers to hand out a lot of advice, but he insisted:

> I'm not going to do much of that [hand out advice]. I'm going to say to you that experience is better than all the advice that the wisest man in the world can give you and you'll heed it a lot more carefully.[41]

Although Judge Truman promised not to offer advice, he proceeded to do so and warned the young graduates that if they wished to succeed, the "first thing for you to do is to conquer yourself." He asserted that General Washington had started on his way to being the greatest American only when he overcame his violent temper and "made the Adam inherited evil in his giant body a slave to his great brain." Truman advised his listeners to study the lives of great men and to remember that the best rules "ever promulgated on this earth" are found in the twentieth chapter of Exodus and the fifth, sixth, and seventh chapters of the Gospel according to St. Matthew. Truman told his audience that good followers were as necessary as good leaders, and he admonished them to keep physically and mentally fit. They were not to eat too much or sleep too much or go to excess in anything. Truman's speech offered no startling revelations or insights and contained many of the cliches used on such occasions. In a peroration which he must have hoped would inspire his listeners, the judge said he had been told by General Harry E. Smith that

> some German scientist investigated some sixty odd thousand primroses and that he found one with nine petals, he found several with eight a number with seven quite a number with six, he found over sixty thousand with five petals which was the normal number and he found a large number with four petals a smaller number with three a few with two and only one with one petal. The General said that the human race ran the same way. Out of the wars of the French Revolution came one military genius, Napoleon. There were several great generals but the majority of the other four million engaged were just normal men.
>
> Most of us are just normal men and women and lets [sic] prepare to live normal honorable and proper lives as God intended we should and lets [sic] bear in mind we are living in the greatest age in the greatest country and that whatever we can add to that greatness we are in duty bound to do and then we can die happy and leave the next generation something to strive for.[42]

On many occasions Judge Truman liked to make personal references to his family, and he was particularly fond of comparing the travel of his day with traveling in the days of his grandfather. He would choose such comparisons in order to show the glories of the Midwest, to defend his road-building program, or to advocate that the state's 114 counties should be consolidated into thirty.

> These small counties were made to accommodate the people in oxcart days. My grandfather lived twenty miles from the county seat. It took him as long to come to Independence as it takes me today to ride from Independence to St. Louis. With 30 counties not a person need be over 25 miles from the county seat if the county seat is centrally located. Roads and modern transportation have shortened distances marvelously.[43]

Many times in the next thirty years Harry Truman would refer to his grandfather's travels. It was a reference that he used in order to help establish common ground with listeners wherever he found them, and it could be easily sandwiched into several different lines of argument. In his speeches he used personal references more than he did historical allusions, and when he did employ the latter they tended to be quick and superficial. There were no extended examples taken from the lives of his heroes but rather brief references or apt quotations.

He seldom tried to impress his listeners by dropping in bits of erudition, but one exception may have occurred when he talked to the Club Presidents'

Round Table. This was a prestigious group of thirty-six presidents of civic clubs around the Kansas City area. The group and their guests met weekly at the Muehlebach Hotel, and Presiding Judge Truman opened his talk to them by saying:

> The science of government has been the study of educated men since society has been organized. Some wonderful theories on the proper organization of a state have been written by the great men of ancient and modern civilizations. We have all read and studied Plato's Republic, Aristotle's Politics, Cicero's Orations, Bacon's Essays, and others including Fiske and Lord Brice [*sic*].[44]

Harry Truman was a joiner. It was not in his nature to be a passive member of any organization, and so his contacts helped give him more than local exposure. He belonged to the American Legion, the Veterans of Foreign Wars, was in the line of the Masonic Grand Lodge, and took a leading part in a statewide association of county judges. In 1934 he had served on the Jackson County Court since 1922, except for his two-year hiatus from 1924 to 1926. He had proved himself through his record on the court; now his ambition spurred him toward a political role at the state rather than at the county level.

Truman had shown himself and others that he could win public elections. His persuasive strength sprang not from eloquence but from his exemplification of the ordinary person. He was the common citizen who dared to reach a little further than other persons around him. The resultant public image was a persuasive asset that would follow him and grow firmer throughout his public career.

5

The Happiest Ten Years

Don't start out with an inferiority complex. For the first
six months you'll wonder how you got here, and after that
you'll wonder how the rest of us got here.

SENATOR HAM LEWIS *to Harry Truman, 1934*

IN 1933 the Missouri legislature redistricted the state. As a result of the redistricting, Jackson County obtained two districts from which to elect members to the state's house of representatives. Of the two new districts, the Fourth District was all that part of the county outside Kansas City except Washington Township, which lay south of the city, and three or four of the eastside city wards. The Fifth District was all the city proper except for the wards in the Fourth District and in Washington Township.

Truman had reason to believe that he could be elected representative from the newly created Fourth District:

> I helped arrange the 4th District because my ambition was to become a member of the House of Representatives. I believed I could go to the House from the new 4th District and stay as long as I chose to stay, but when the party caucus was held to decide on candidates in the 1934 election from Jackson County my good friend Judge C. Jasper Bell had talked T. J. Pendergast into endorsing him for Congressman from the 4th District and my plan to be a Congressman went out the window. I decided to go back to the farm and stay out of politics but that didn't happen either.[1]

His resolution to return to farming never was realized, for another political glow appeared on the horizon. In the spring of 1934 the state was scheduled to vote on a bond issue to enlarge some of its institutions—specifically, four or five hospitals and the state penitentiary. Because Truman was a gregarious politician with a growing reputation throughout the state, the governor asked him to join a bipartisan team touring several counties in an effort to promote support for the forthcoming issue. While he was on tour with this group, Truman received a phone call asking him to meet with the state Democratic party chairman and Jim Pendergast. The latter, it will be recalled, was a nephew of Boss Tom Pendergast and a friend whom Truman often described as "my war buddy." When Truman met with these two, he discovered they had been sent to encourage him to seek the nomination to the U.S. Senate.

> I told them I had no legislative experience, that I thought I was something of an executive and I'd rather wait two years and run for Governor. But they insisted that I owed it to the party to run, that Senator Clark was from the eastern side of the State and that Jackson County was entitled to one of the Senators.[2]

Campaign for Senate (1934)

In Missouri that year three candidates filed for the Democratic nomination to the U.S. Senate. Jacob Leroy Milligan filed in January, and for a few months it appeared that he would be the only candidate. However, in the middle of May, Harry Truman filed, and a week later John Joseph Cochran entered the race. Milligan was a lawyer, also a Mason, a decorated war hero and had served in the U.S. Congress for nearly thirteen years. John Cochran had only an eighth grade education but had become a lawyer by passing the bar examination, had served as a congressional secretary, and later as a member of Congress for eight years.

Although the other two candidates had substantial records, neither could match the support Truman received because of his endorsement by the Pendergast organization. Any consideration of Missouri politics during that period had to begin with the Pendergast organization around Kansas City. It was a depression era, and Tom Pendergast chose candidates who could help people with their day-by-day needs. Tariffs and war debts were not as compelling issues in his mind as paving a road, putting in a water main, ensuring better police protection, or a promise about taxation. In better times people might have been more concerned with honesty in government, but he wanted politicians who could get things done at the local level and without too much concern for the exactness of the law.

Tom Pendergast believed in loyalty to the party and to his organization; he kept his word and expected the same of others. The extent of his control can be seen in the fact that in the period between 1926 and 1928 only six Pendergast-backed candidates lost in state or national elections. Whenever the Kansas City slate did lose, it was because Boss Tom allowed personal friendship to becloud his political vision.

By 1934 some of the old wounds from the battles within the Democratic party around Kansas City had healed. Because of the resounding party victory two years earlier, and in large part because of the strengthened control of Tom Pendergast, Missouri Democrats were united as never before. Nevertheless, Truman and his supporters realized that if he were to capture the nomination they would have to battle a nominee from the St. Louis region, John Cochran. With two great metropolitan centers on opposite sides of the state it was inevitable that factions based on geography would divide the party. Democrats from the western edge of Missouri sent Joseph B. Shannon to do some "politicking" in the opponent's territory.

Although Shannon had been a leader of the rival Rabbits, formerly opposing Pendergast candidates, he was ready to work for the Kansas City faction and endorse his "friend, Judge Harry S. Truman." Shannon had been elected to Congress and had served there for two sessions with Cochran, whom he chose to call "ranting John." It is impossible to assess the impact of Shannon's speeches in behalf of Truman, but in one vitriolic attack on Cochran in the latter's home territory of St. Louis, Congressman Shannon charged that Cochran was only "pawing the air" and denouncing the other candidates. Shannon said that Judge Harry Truman had become "his [Cochran's] special target of abuse."[3]

John Cochran, notwithstanding Shannon's highly biased attack on him, was a formidable contender. He had been active in the planning of the early New Deal and had been voted by Washington reporters as one of the six most useful members of the House. He could count also on the organization within St. Louis—an organization which in 1932 had amassed majorities on only a slightly lower scale than those produced by the Pendergasts.

Congressman J. L. "Tuck" Milligan lacked the organizational support enjoyed by his two opponents, but he was acknowledged to be a strong campaigner in the crucial areas where Bennett Clark had won in 1932. The Pendergasts had refused to back Clark in the Senate race which he had won, and two years afterwards he meant to retaliate by throwing his influence to Milligan.

All three candidates declared themselves in line with New Deal programs, but Milligan suffered on this point because of Senator Clark's open opposition to the National Recovery Administration and the Agricultural Adjustment Act. Because Cochran and Milligan were well-known congressmen the initial prospects for the judge from Jackson County, despite Pendergast backing, did not

Campaigning in Missouri for a seat in the U.S. Senate, October 1934.

appear bright. And Cochran lost no chance to strike at Truman's Pendergast connections:

> If I am elected I will not have to telephone Kansas City or step across the aisle in the Senate to know how to vote.[4]

Truman concentrated his campaign in the environs of Kansas City, in the agricultural midstate counties, and he neglected St. Louis. The primary campaign reached its climax in the middle of a hot Missouri summer, and when the returns came in they showed that Judge Truman had won the senatorial nomination with a 40,745 plurality over second-running Cochran. The Pendergasts had more than offset the St. Louis organization in "getting out the vote." Kansas City gave 137,529 votes to Truman, 8912 to Milligan, and 1525 to Cochran; St. Louis had delivered 104,265 for Cochran, 6670 for Milligan, and 3742 for Truman.[5] Most of the newspapers cried "bossism," and it is probable that this 1934 primary campaign represented the zenith of Pendergast power. Although frequently besmirched because of his connections with the Pendergast machine, Truman had shown himself to be personally honest and not even his bitterest opponents accused him of malfeasance in office.

As a result of his primary victory, Harry Truman was in an advantageous position, for President Franklin Roosevelt and his party were at the height of popularity. Truman's Republican opponent for the Senate was the incumbent Roscoe C. Patterson, who had championed the conservative cause during his twelve years in the Senate. Patterson had a near perfect record of voting against the New Deal since its inception, and Truman lost no time in attacking that record. Because Truman earlier had been appointed by the governor to be state director of Reemployment Services—one of the many depression era agencies created by Roosevelt—he had become identified with the basic concepts of the New Deal.

The campaign against Patterson was dull in comparison with the intensity and efforts of the primary race. Patterson warned of the dangers of concentration of authority at the federal level and urged instead that relief programs be established at state and local levels. Truman unequivocally endorsed the leadership of Franklin Roosevelt and praised all the national relief programs. So solid was Truman's backing of the administration, it was said that he approved in advance all that the administration would thereafter do.[6]

During this period Truman received little help with his speeches, and they were phrased often in raw language and contained themes popular with the grassroots politicians. The country was in the depths of depression and Herbert Hoover's name had become an anathema to many who were out of work and without homes. The makeshift, crowded huts on the outskirts of cities were derisively called "Hoovervilles," and Truman in his attacks on Patterson was not above using appeals built on hatred of the former president:

Senator Roscoe C. Patterson, one of the more piteous bewailers against the New Deal, particularly the effort to feed and clothe the people and to furnish them work, would return at once to the days of Hoover for recovery. How many days of Hoover? The former President had slightly over three years under the rugged individualism scheme of government in which to break the back of the depression. He had in all that time Senator Patterson to help him. Now that Hoover is gone to return no more, what could Patterson do all by himself, either to help the people or to restore his rugged individualism? . . . I feel that they the people of Missouri know that a Senate full of Pattersons would have chased the golden dragon of rugged individualism while the people starved to death. It is hard to fool a people who within less than a year and half have had a sample of the cold and brutal philosophy of the Hoovers and the Pattersons and the benignant and generous belief of Roosevelt.[7]

In his lashing of Patterson, Truman charged him with being allied with men of great wealth—most of whom opposed Franklin Roosevelt and what he stood for:

On the other side, we see former President Hoover, Senator Patterson, Senator Fees, Ogden L. Mills, Andrew W. Mellon, Iranee du Pont [sic], the munition king and contributor to the campaign funds of all parties in the sacred name of his business of blood and slaughter, whose munitions has [sic] slain more liberty than the swords of all the Caesars; James W. Wadsworth, whose reactionary belief is so extreme that the New York Republicans refused him the nomination for governor; Nathan Miller, attorney for the steel trust, Arthur M. Curtis, Chairman of the Missouri State Republican Committee, and men of that ilk.[8]

The results of the general election in November were anticlimactic, and Truman captured a plurality of 262,000 votes. He later recalled that outcome:

The election in the fall of 1934 was a pushover for the Democrats, so I came to the United States Senate and went to work.[9]

To the voters in Missouri, the choice had seemed clear, and they went the same way as did voters in Pennsylvania, Indiana, and other states where established conservatives met and were defeated by comparative unknowns supporting Roosevelt and the New Deal.

Junior Senator from Missouri

The off-year election of 1934 was encouraging for the Roosevelt administration. Normally, in an off-year election the party in power would expect to lose some strength, but that year the Democrats counted an unprecedented gain of thirteen seats in the House. In the Senate they increased their margin by ten with the election or reelection of twenty-three Democrats.

Wearing a long frock coat, striped pants, and a gardenia boutonniere, Harry Truman joined eleven other newly elected senators in Washington for swearing-in ceremonies on January 3, 1935. The ceremonies began what he later called the happiest ten years of his life. Of these first-term senators, most had college degrees and four were college professors. Because he lacked a college degree and because he had entered a different world in Washington, Truman was genuinely humble as he began his first term in the Senate.

In his first year as a senator, Harry Truman remained almost anonymous. He made no speeches on the floor and introduced no major legislation. Actually he sat in the Senate nearly two and a half years before he made a speech; he told one reporter:

> Maybe in a year or so I will have something to say, but not now. I'm more interested in the welfare of Missouri than I am in oratory.[10]

His committee assignments were to Appropriations, District of Columbia, Interstate Commerce, Printing, and Public Buildings and Grounds. He had requested appointment to the Military Affairs Committee, but that appointment was not made during his first term. Most of his energies went into the Interstate Commerce Committee assignment because there he found an outlet for his long-standing interest in transportation. Although not active in the Senate debates of 1935, Truman did give several speeches aimed for a nationwide audience. One of these was a radio broadcast in March of 1935, urging new legislation to replace the Agricultural Adjustment Act. He argued for extension of farm subsidies and federal aid but rejected state relief for agriculture.[11] Shortly after this speech he gave an address over the National Broadcasting Company's network entitled, "Highways and the Regulation of Transportation."[12] He also continued his participation in Masonic affairs, and frequently when the Senate was in recess he would deliver talks to nearby lodges.[13]

Those who believed that Harry Truman was always laconic never heard him discourse on the subject of Masonry. It was not calculated political gain that he sought when talking on Masonry; he believed in its principles and dedicated himself to them. He usually kept the sentimental side of his nature reserved for members of his family, but when the subject was Masonry, Harry Truman became rhapsodic. He returned to Missouri in November of 1935 and addressed the Appleton City Lodge:

> I want you to know, my friends and brethren, that it has been genuinely inspirational to mingle in this gathering of Masons, and to again realize that such enthusiasm as we have seen evidenced here is now rampant all over this country—an absolute indication that our ancient and honorable

fraternity has again successfully ridden out a storm and once again has its prow pointed toward a program of even greater advancement. . . . What a real source of satisfaction it is to all of us to see Masonry continue to live up to the many traditions that have been established within its realm, from the days of our own King Solomon, right down through the ages to the present moment. What a pleasure it is to know that Masonry has again demonstrated the soundness of its spiritual and human structure by the way it has ridden out the terrific economic storm that came upon us six years ago—a storm my brethren that has left an appalling wreckage of human hopes, human ambitions, human accomplishments—yes—and of human hearts—strewn around on all sides of us. . . . It is a glorious testimony to the Craft we love that it has withstood the buffeting of economic disasters, devastating wars, of tyrannical persecutions and of every form of obstruction, for decade after decade, and emerged always victorious, in its very foundation stronger than ever; its valient [*sic*] membership taking a new lease on life and pushing on to greater accomplishments; its standing as the fraternity supreme unchanged and its determination to never for a single instant relax in the principles of Faith, Hope and Charity, stronger than ever.[14]

On another occasion, when the Grand Lodge of Missouri laid the cornerstone for the courthouse in Neosho, Missouri, Senator Truman was the featured speaker, and he extolled the glories of Freemasonry. In this address of about fifteen hundred words he praised the Masons for possibly being the organizers of the Boston Tea Party; he hailed Thomas Jefferson and Benjamin Franklin for their membership in the Lodge of Paris; and he suggested that Patrick Henry's inspiration for his ''Give me Liberty or give me Death'' speech stemmed from his Masonic education. Truman recounted that George Washington officiated at the laying of the cornerstone of the Capitol Building and that the trowel he used then was still in possession of the lodge in Virginia. Senator Truman marched down through the list of signers of the Declaration of Independence and asserted that twenty-three of the fifty-six signers of that document were Masons. He singled out John Hancock, James Madison, and James Monroe, and then went on to mention other Masons in the pantheon of American heroes: Andrew Jackson, John Tyler, James Polk, Zachary Taylor, Franklin Pierce, James Buchanan, Andrew Johnson, James Garfield, William H. Taft, and Warren Harding. ''Franklin Delano Roosevelt,'' he said, ''has had the distinction of giving to his sons their degrees as Master Masons.'' He closed his talk by linking the purposes of the courthouse, for which the cornerstone was being laid, with the enduring purposes embodied in the Masons' creed and in American principles.[15]

If he did not win senators to him through speeches on the floor during his first year in Washington, Harry Truman did make important contacts. His easy, gregarious nature soon got him into the poker-playing, cloakroom-chatting coterie that dominated the Senate in those years. He chose friends from both parties and came to be known as a hard worker ready to go down the line for Roosevelt programs. He found powerful friends in Vice-President John Nance Garner, Carl Hayden of Arizona, and Burton K. Wheeler of Montana. On the other side of the aisle he made acquaintance with Arthur Vandenberg of Michigan, Charles McNary of Oregon, and William Borah of Idaho.

Truman brought with him to the Senate an innate Populist suspicion toward business interests, and his daily language was peppered with phrases nurtured by that suspicion. He called railroad financiers "wrecking crews," Wall Street lawyers the "highest of high hats" who would pull "tricks that would make an ambulance chaser in a coroner's court blush with shame." His language was equally intemperate as far as Carnegie Libraries were concerned. He declared they were "steeped in the blood of Homestead steel workers." The Rockefeller Foundation was "founded on the dead miners of the Colorado Fuel and Iron Companies and a dozen other similar performances."

The first real test of Senator Truman's mettle came in connection with proposed regulation of public utilities. Sam Rayburn in the House and Burton Wheeler in the Senate introduced legislation aimed toward limiting the control being exercised by the huge financial structures that had been formed in the utilities field. The Public Utility Holding Company Act, as it was called, was intended to curb such abuses as excessive control by these companies, to reduce their exorbitant fees for management services, and to nullify the practice of using the mammoth holding companies in order to bypass the regulatory power of the states. Truman was in favor of the bill despite pressures put on him by interested parties in his home state.

The *Kansas City Journal Post*, which was the only major metropolitan newspaper friendly to Pendergast, strongly opposed the bill. Moreover, in this instance the *Kansas City Star* joined with the Pendergast newspaper in vigorously opposing any federal control of utilities. When Truman defied the pressures and voted for regulation, the wrath of the Kansas City press soon descended—charges bloomed that Senator Harry Truman was nothing but a stooge of the Roosevelt administration. Four months earlier the *Journal Post* had praised Harry Truman and Bennett Clark as the two best senators from Missouri in a generation. Now the *Kansas City Journal Post* began its denunciatory editorial by stating:

> Harry S. Truman . . . became United States Senator from Missouri by default, so to speak, getting the Democratic nomination in 1934 because there were no other takers.[16]

Actually, Truman was caught in a bind. In this case when he sided with the administration in favoring the Public Utility Holding Act he was labeled an "unthinking tool of the administration." If he disagreed with the administration he was accused of being unfaithful to his campaign promises and not a man of his word. On occasion he would have to prove independence from both the administration and Tom Pendergast.

The suspicion incurred by his affiliation with the Pendergasts continued to plague him throughout his first term in the Senate. Some Democratic leaders failed to receive the new "Senator from Pendergast" warmly, and this fact probably helped spur him toward greater effort and individual action. He admitted that Pendergast frequently did send him telegrams urging him to vote one way or another, but denied that he followed Pendergast's advice on legislation.

Senator Bennett Clark, having come to the Senate in 1933, had filled most of the federal patronage appointments before Truman arrived. Both district attorneys had been recommended by him as were all U.S. marshals and collectors of revenue for the Eastern and Western Districts of Missouri. When the terms of these men ended in 1937 Truman tried unsuccessfully to get his own recommendations approved:

> I recommended other men for their places. But the vote fraud scandal and Pendergast troubles were ripe about that time and the Administration didn't have the nerve to back up its friends in Missouri.[17]

After 1934 the efforts to uncover crime and bossism in Kansas City intensified to a very great extent. Two years later Pendergast helped elect Lloyd C. Stark as governor of the state, and it seemed that the regime was entrenched more firmly than ever. But the winds of reform were gathering and could not be stilled. Before that year ended a federal judge empaneled a grand jury to investigate vote frauds in the Kansas City elections. Maurice Milligan, an ambitious district attorney, had promised when he took office that he would prosecute crime vigorously, and he proceeded to do just that. He handled the vote fraud prosecution and directed the government's case against the Kansas City chieftain for income tax evasion. Milligan's efforts were so successful that, although the case dragged on for nearly three years, Boss Tom pleaded guilty in 1939 and was sentenced to prison.

Truman's awkward deference to Pendergast in regard to Maurice Milligan's reappointment as district attorney in the Kansas City region caused him considerable embarrassment. Four days after Senator Clark announced that he had recommended Milligan for reappointment, Senator Truman conferred with Pendergast in Kansas City. When that conference ended, the wily Boss told reporters:

> I have nothing to say. Whatever is said will be by Senator Truman on the floor of the Senate.[18]

It was Roosevelt's practice to confer with both senators when making such appointments, and he called Truman to explain that Milligan's appointment was "inevitable" because of the existing political situation in Missouri, namely, that it was not good politics to offend voters there by repudiating the man who had gained such a favorable reputation. The telephone exchange with the president was not enough to keep the freshman senator from making known his views on the appointment, however, and on February 15, 1938, Truman delivered what a friendly biographer, Jonathan Daniels, called "the most vigorous pro-Pendergast speech of his whole career in the Senate."[19] Truman insisted that Milligan was neither professionally nor morally qualified for the job, that the newspapers had created a hero out of him, and that government prosecutors had intimidated the defense attorneys and jurors chosen from nonresidents of Jackson County. He accused Milligan of having accepted fees for bankruptcy proceedings from the very court trying the vote fraud cases. He grew more intemperate and charged:

> I say to the Senate, Mr. President, that a Jackson County, Mo., Democrat has as much chance of a fair trial in the Federal District Court of Western Missouri as a Jew would have in a Hitler court or a Trotsky follower before Stalin.[20]

The Senate, by a voice vote, approved Milligan's confirmation, but Truman's attack on him set off a barrage of criticism back home. The speech was a real setback in his efforts to divorce himself from the Pendergast identity. The Lawyers Association in Kansas City passed a resolution calling his speech "unwarranted" and censured him for making such statements. Even the *Journal Post*, a newspaper usually favorable to him, conceded that the attack on Milligan "had done his [Truman's] cause no particular good." Edgar Bergen, a radio entertainer and ventriloquist very popular at the time, put on a skit for the Advertising Club in St. Louis. In the skit Bergen's wooden dummy, Charlie McCarthy, was asked, "What is Senator Truman's relationship to Tom Pendergast?" Charlie replied mischievously, "I'll give you the real lowdown if it kills me. You know my relationship to Edgar Bergen. Welllll—." A cartoon, with the caption "Charlie McTruman does his stuff," showed a McCarthy-type dummy on a knee and saying, "Milligan and those Judges are railroading the Democrats."[21]

If Truman's remarks about Milligan's fitness for office actually reflected his own opinion, he must have had cause to change that judgment in the next year and a half. At any rate, in September of 1940, after the discredited Pendergast had been sentenced and after Truman had defeated Milligan in the primary race for the Senate nomination, he warmly recommended Milligan to President Roosevelt:

September 14, 1940

Dear Mr. President:

There is a vacancy in the office of the District Attorney for the District of Western Missouri. I am suggesting that you reappoint Maurice Milligan to fill out the unexpired term.

Due to legislation passed in this Congress, it was necessary for Mr. Milligan to resign in order to make a Primary campaign for United States Senator. Had this legislation not been passed, Mr. Milligan could have made the race and still held his position.

He has made a good District Attorney, and I do not feel that he ought to be penalized by losing his job.[22]

Truman survived the derision over the Milligan affair and set himself to careful reading and study of important pending legislation. He did not speak often in the Senate, but away from it and while talking to the public he became voluble on national problems. Some of his topics were hardly controversial and his remarks could be phrased in language general enough to please nearly everyone. For instance, he talked over the National Broadcasting Company's network about highway safety and the regulation of transportation. In this kind of discussion he could engage in his favorite method of contrasting citizen mobility in earlier days with the ease of modern travel. In 1937 he spoke over another radio network, the Columbia Broadcasting System, about the growing death rate caused by automobile accidents. To industrial groups he talked about the value of industrial safety and described the costs borne by both laborer and manager whenever industrial accidents occurred. He talked to the Eagle Scouts of the Kansas City Council—a class of scouts named in his honor—about patriotism, citizenship, and duty to the flag. On St. Patrick's Day he went to Providence, Rhode Island, and praised the Irish for their contributions to the United States as well as to the formation of other governments. He called Ireland "a land of the most lovable, irascible, belligerent, kindly people on earth."

Harry Truman was too much the politician to neglect fences in need of mending back home. He returned to Missouri after the first session of the seventy-fourth Congress ended and addressed a capacity crowd in the ballroom of the Muehlebach Hotel. In his address he reviewed the work of Congress as he saw it, not omitting, of course, his own committee assignments and commitments to the administration's successes. He praised the social and economic measures that Congress, under goading from Roosevelt, had passed, including the Social Security Act, the Banking Act, the Federal Home Loan Act, the Reconstruction Finance Corporation, and the Utilities Holding Act. Because he had supported the Utilities Holding Act, Truman was well aware of smoldering criticism among some of his usually loyal supporters. He said that he had sat on the Senate committee listening to all the arguments pro and con, had read all the documents pertaining to the bill, and as a result was in a position to know something about the conditions the act aimed to overcome. Residue from the Populist credo was evident in his remarks as he declared:

> We found that there were successful operating companies supporting as many as five and six holding companies—companies intended to do nothing but a miling [*sic*] operation. Public utility operating companies are gold mines—oil wells—bonanzas, really, when it comes to making money, and like everything of that kind they attracted the pirates of finance to milk and get all out of them they could at the expense of the stock holders and the utility users. There have been financial pirates in our business set-up since the country was organized—land speculators and the United States Bank in Andrew Jackson's time—Jay Gould, Jim Fish, Harriman, in the railroad promotion days. Wild cat oil promoters in the development of the oil industry, and now Hopson, Insull et al. in the utility game. This holding company business was merely a dodge to avoid state regulations.[23]

In this speech Senator Truman praised the banking bill as another piece of progressive legislation and said that while it was being debated, bankers had raised "hell" about it; after its enactment the bankers came around to endorsing it. In language reflecting the times and his border state background he said:

> People are making investments now in a stock exchange controlled for investors and not a pit operated for gamblers and stock market niggers [*sic*].[24]

The word *nigger* was common parlance in Harry Truman's home region throughout most of his life. Perhaps he should not be judged too harshly for his use of a term which, as the years passed, was to become more insulting. Actually, Truman enjoyed more support from black people in and around Kansas City than did most of his opponents. C. A. Franklin, editor of *The Call*, a newspaper for blacks in Kansas City, endorsed his candidacies and maintained close relations with him. When times were hard and people everywhere were deprived of food, jobs, clothes, and housing, the black population suffered most. Because Truman spoke in specifics and addressed himself to these immediate problems, blacks identified with him and helped him in his numerous political victories.

In addition to solidifying his backing from Missouri voters, Truman repaired any possible ruptures with his Senate colleague, Bennett Clark. After all, both were Democrats and often voted together in support of New Deal measures. Some time in 1935, Lloyd Stark, who had been one of Truman's supporters in the primary fight of 1934, visited him in his Washington office. He told Truman that he wanted to be governor of Missouri but knew he could not win that office without the backing of the Kansas City Democratic organization. He asked for Truman's help in getting an endorsement from Pendergast. Stark was able to persuade the two senators from Missouri—Bennett Clark and Harry Truman—to go to New York and see the Big Boss who had returned from one of his frequent trips to Europe. Truman and Clark together called on Pendergast, and although Clark appears to have been less than enthusiastic about Stark, Truman told Pendergast that he thought Stark was an honorable man. Truman later regretted his judgment and opined:

> . . . which shows how easy it is to be fooled by your friends. Stark had neither honor nor loyalty. He should have been a member of the Spanish Inquisition or the Court of Louis XI of France.[25]

After being successful in his efforts to obtain Pendergast's backing, Stark was elected governor of Missouri in 1936, but Truman apparently became miffed because Stark came to see him only once after that event, although Stark did come to Washington several times. On those visits he would call on the president, the vice-president, or the secretary of war or navy. On one occasion he told Senator Truman's receptionist that there was no truth to the rumors that he [Stark] would run for the U.S. Senate in 1940. Truman was skeptical, however.

> I told the secretary that I'd bet my last dollar that Mr. Stark would try for my place in 1940.[26]

In keeping with his belief that the important work of Congress is done in committee meetings, Senator Truman worked diligently in his assignments. His long-standing interest in transportation was not unrelated to the state he represented, for the manufacture of transportation equipment constituted one of Missouri's major industries. From the earliest days of westward expansion, his state had been one of the nation's most active transportation centers. In the 1930s there were more than eleven thousand miles of railroad track within its borders, and many of the nation's railroads served parts or all of the state: St. Louis Southwestern; Gulf, Mobile and Ohio; Chicago, Milwaukee, St. Paul and Pacific; Kansas City Southern; Missouri, Kansas, Texas; Atchison, Topeka and Santa Fe; Chicago, Rock Island and Pacific; Wabash, Chicago, Burlington, and Quincy; St. Louis–San Francisco; and the Missouri Pacific. The economy of many localities was directly related to the railroads. If the nation's transportation system were to be improved the state of Missouri would benefit from stepped-up commercial and economic activity of many sorts.

Senator Truman's interest in transportation problems and his general knowledge of the field won him political support from the railroad brotherhoods throughout his state and the nation. Besides the railway unions themselves, he gained endorsements from most of the state's labor publications. His votes in the Senate were followed by the labor organizations, and his record showed consistent loyalty to labor's cause. He voted for the Wagner Act, the Social Security Act, the 1937 Wage-Hour Act, and the Fair Labor Standards Act.

Whenever he returned home to speak, Senator Truman stressed New Deal measures that aimed to invigorate the business community. He tried to present himself as friendly to business as long as it acted fairly and honestly. Some of his most steadfast supporters came from the business and commercial worlds. It was big business and gouging which he lambasted.

During his first term in the Senate, Truman did not address himself especially to the problems of agriculture. This did not mean that he was uninterested in farm problems but rather that his energies went toward transportation, finance, and regulation of corporate practices. He spoke over the National Broadcasting Company's network in 1936 and described the plight of the nation's farmers. Although that plight was generally well understood and it was the remedies that were so hotly debated, Senator Truman declared that the farmer's depression really had started in 1921 and that the farmer remained at the bottom of the financial pit until Franklin Roosevelt came to rescue him.[27] Despite his actual farming experiences and his ease in talking with rural groups, there is no evidence that Truman made any positive contribution to the formation of New Deal farm policies, except for his consistently favorable voting record.

When Truman did speak in the Senate during his first term, it was likely that the subject would deal with transportation. His maiden speech in Congress, given two and a half years after he had been seated, concerned transportation and railroad corporations. His speech grew mainly from what he had learned from membership on a special committee within the Interstate Commerce Committee, but there were also echoes from his Populist leanings:

> The Subcommittee of the Senate Interstate Commerce Committee investigating railroad finance has found that some of the country's greatest railroads have been deliberately looted by their financial agents. The committee has found that the laws of the United States have been deliberately evaded and in some instances actually broken by railroad holding companies and New York bankers acting for railroad management. . . .

> Speaking of the Rock Island Railroad reminds me that the first railroad robbery was committed on the Rock Island in 1873 just east of Council Bluffs, Iowa. The man who committed that robbery used a gun and a horse, and got up early in the morning. He and his gang took a chance of being killed, and eventually most of them were killed. The loot was $3,000. That railroad robber's name was Jesse James. The same Jesse James held up the Missouri Pacific in 1876 and took the paltry sum of

$17,000 from the express car. About 30 years after the Council Bluffs hold-up, the Rock Island went through a looting by some gentlemen known as the tin-plate millionaires. They used no gun, but they ruined the railroad and got away with $70,000,000 or more. They did it by means of holding companies. Senators can see what "pikers" Mr. James and his crowd were alongside of some real artists. . . .

I wish to say a word or two about the Chicago & Eastern Illinois Rail-road. . . . In 1930 the Van Sweringen octopus decided to buy the C. & E. I. from the Thomas Fortune Ryan estate. Manipulation immediately started. In one specific instance that stands out in the hearings before your committee the Van Sweringens caused the Midland Bank of Cleveland, in which they were interested, to lend the C. & E. I. $700,000 for the Chesapeake & Ohio Railroad through the Virginia Co., a wholly owned subsidiary of the Chesapeake & Ohio.[28]

Notwithstanding his occasional exuberance of language, the speeches Truman gave in the Senate during his first term do not read well. His explanations were thorough but so complete that they could be followed only by careful reading. As a result, most newspapers did not print his talks in detail but would extract only a few of his more colorful analogies or phrases. He made little or no attempt to state his arguments in a way that reporters and editors would find exciting. He sought clarity and understanding from Senate colleagues whom he approached as men of intelligence, capable of making rational decisions. In this regard, his speeches in the Senate were less fiery and more indirectly complimentary to his listeners than the talks he gave while campaigning.

Reelection to Senate (1940)

In 1939 Senator Truman made up his mind to run for reelection. By this time Pendergast had been convicted and Truman was not entirely free of stigma from his association with the former kingpin. Some of Truman's close friends feared that a tidal wave of opinion condemning Pendergast and his practices would drown Truman's chances for relection, and they encouraged him to seek an appointive federal position. The doughty Truman was not to be dissuaded, however, and insisted that he would stay in the campaign and win it.

Senator Truman was proved right in his prediction that Governor Lloyd Stark would seek the Democratic nomination to the Senate in 1940. The latter was the first candidate to announce and did so early in September of 1939. Notwithstanding the endorsement from Pendergast which he had sought so avidly four years earlier, Stark joined with those who denounced Boss Tom and his machine. In part because of this denunciation and in part because of his position as governor, Stark expected support and did receive it from most of the metropolitan newspapers.

Maurice Milligan, the embattled district attorney, resigned his position in April of 1940, so that he too could try for the Senate job. His brother, Jacob "Tuck" Milligan, had served several terms in Congress and had run against Truman in the 1934 primary. Even more important, as a result of the Pendergast investigations the name "Milligan" was familiar to many Missourians.

Both Stark and Milligan formally opened their campaigns six weeks before Truman did; however, the latter was very active in trying to line up his bases of influence. He wrote to twenty-five of the state's most influential Democrats asking for their support, but less than half of them showed up at a private rally arranged for him in St. Louis. Furthermore, the remnants of the once strong Kansas City organization appeared only lukewarm toward him. He knew his record in the Senate was sound, but he realized that the political situation in Missouri meant trouble.

In the spring of 1940 it was generally believed that Truman would announce for reelection. He approached the primary very gingerly and apparently wrote three drafts of an announcement he made from Washington. One of these drafts is on Pickwick Hotel stationery, and the second and third are on his Senate memorandum stationery. The first and second drafts are in his handwriting; the third is typed. He introduced his remarks by stating:

> I had not intended to make a political announcement until the Congress had adjourned, but so many rumors have been circulated regarding my future intentions that my interests and those of my friends must be protected by a statement of my position.[29]

The phrase "and of my friends" in this excerpt did not appear in the earlier drafts but does appear in Truman's handwriting as an insertion on the typed copy. Most of the changes in the various drafts are minor and involve insertions. For example, when stating that he had kept his promises, the first draft shows only:

> I have supported the the [sic] leadership of the Democratic Party in the Senate and have upheld the President in all matters of National Policy.[30]

The second draft reads:

> I have been faithful to my promises to veterans, to labor, to the Administration. I have supported the leadership of the Democratic Party in the Senate and have upheld the President in all matters of National Policy.[31]

In the third draft the wording was changed slightly:

> I have been faithful to my promises *of 1934* to veterans, to labor, *to the farmers,* to the Administration. I have supported the leadership of the Democratic Party in the Senate and have upheld the President in all matters of National Policy.[32]

The popular Roosevelt wore long coattails in 1940, and most Democrats grabbed eagerly at them. In this speech Truman remarked rather breezily:

> Just the other day I spent a very pleasant hour with the President at the White House, discussing various bills pending in Congress, and he expressed the hope that I would come back to the Senate next year.[33]

Truman felt that he deserved Roosevelt's backing because of his faithful New Deal voting record. Furthermore, he had praised Roosevelt on many occasions and had been particularly laudatory at the Missouri Democratic convention in 1936 where he characterized the president as the "Bonhomme Roosevelt." Truman was unsuccessful, however, in getting an endorsement from Roosevelt, who refused to be led into open avowal of any of the contenders.

Truman chose central Missouri (Sedalia) and June 15, 1940, to formally begin his reelection campaign. In the afternoon of that day several hundred supporters, including some from St. Louis and Kansas City, attended a reception held for him at his campaign headquarters there. That evening, speakers representing a spectrum of political, religious, and economic groups praised the Truman record. His close friend, Senator Lewis B. Schwellenbach from the state of Washington, lauded him for persistent and conscientious work in the Senate. Schwellenbach stressed Truman's participation in the subcommittee of the Senate Appropriations Committee and argued that Truman had become one of the Senate's most knowledgeable authorities in the matter of transportation.

When Truman's turn on the program came, he identified himself with the New Deal and acclaimed Roosevelt's programs for the farmer, laborer, and blacks. Near the end of his remarks he made a special and extended plea for support from the 240,000 Missouri blacks.[34]

Thereafter Truman campaigned in his usual intense way. For instance, he delivered fifteen speeches in the course of four days. During the hot months of July and August, he went into seventy-five counties. He addressed audiences in Cape Girardeau and Joplin in the extreme southeast and southwest corners of the state, and Maryville and Hannibal in the northwest and northeast. He went to Chicago where he talked to the National Colored Democratic Association and outlined the efforts New Deal Democrats had made to improve conditions among blacks. Black leaders throughout the state rallied to him, especially after *The Call* endorsed his candidacy.

Although Truman tried to give the appearance of confidence, he was apprehensive about the primary. Despite his feelings that Stark was a betrayer and that Milligan was a sensationalist, he knew that both were formidable opponents. Actually, the fact that there were two other contenders was another example of the Truman "luck." Some of Stark's supporters had hoped that Milligan would announce for governor rather than the Senate, for they felt that their man could easily win a two-way race with Truman. There is some evidence, too, that Truman backers rejoiced over the third entry, for they declared that Milligan and Governor Stark would "cut up the Bible belt."[35] Milligan's entry enhanced Truman's chances so much that throughout the primary, there were allegations that Truman's followers had conspired with Milligan to get him to run and thus split the anti-Pendergast vote which otherwise would go entirely to Stark. During the campaign, Truman denied such charges, and it was not until many years later that he admitted having anything to do with Milligan's entry into the race.[36]

Throughout the primary it seemed that Stark was the front runner. His name was known not only because he was governor, but Stark Brothers Nurseries and Orchards were so successful that the "Stark Delicious Apple" had become famous throughout the nation. Stark made several tactical errors, however, which caused some waning of enthusiasm for him. To many voters he seemed uncertain as to which office he really wanted. There had been early mention of his name as a possible presidential candidate in 1940, but he changed any such aspirations and sought the vice-presidential nomination instead. At the Democratic National Convention in Chicago he openly campaigned for the vice-presidency by providing each delegate with a small crate of "Stark Delicious Apples." In another instance, he had alienated some Missouri Democrats when, at a meeting in Kirksville to honor Thomas Jefferson and to promote party unity, he used the occasion to castigate Pendergast and praise his own political record. Senator Truman had followed him as a speaker on the program that evening, and Truman discarded portions of his prepared speech in order to criticize Stark's behavior. Even some of Stark's most ardent admirers admitted that the governor's untimely partisanship annoyed many in the party and unwittingly contributed to Truman's cause.[37]

Stark tried hard to create the impression that he was Roosevelt's favorite candidate, and outward appearances did indicate that he had the president's

Senator Truman with Bess and Margaret during his campaign for reelection, October 1940.

blessings. In the spring of 1940 Governor Stark made numerous visits to the White House on seemingly cordial terms. There were rumors that Roosevelt had called Stark to the capital to offer him the post of secretary of the navy, but by the time of the primary in August it seemed that Stark was receiving only cool and formal treatment from the president.

Meanwhile, the Truman campaign was gaining momentum. If Senator Truman could not win endorsement from Roosevelt, he at least had skewered Stark's attempts to present himself as the president's choice. Toward the end of May, Truman received a bonanza which bolstered his hopes and promised a better chance of victory. His efforts and strong Senate voting record in behalf of labor began to bear fruit. The senator's attacks on Wall Street and financiers had endeared him to labor; he had been successful in preventing wage cuts by the railroad companies in 1938; and unions appreciated his attempts to protect jobs of workers as more automatic machinery came into use on the railroads. The leaders of the railroad brotherhoods, which included over fifty thousand members in the state of Missouri, pledged themselves "to go down the line for Truman." Through their weekly newspaper in Washington entitled *Labor,* the unions printed a special edition showing what a good friend the working classes had in Harry Truman. In July R. H. Wadlow, general chairman of the Brotherhood of Locomotive Engineers, sent a telegram to President Roosevelt announcing a reception in Truman's honor. The telegram disclosed that Senator Alben Barkley and V. C. Gardner, president of the Brotherhood of Railroad Telegraphers, would speak on "what labor thinks of Senator Truman." The telegram asked if the president would send his greetings for the occasion and closed by stating: "Labor needs your support and labor supports you." President Roosevelt declined to send any greetings for the occasion, but in a night letter marked PERSONAL AND CONFIDENTIAL, his secretary, Stephen Early, replied:

> The President asks me to explain to you personally that while Senator Truman is an old and trusted friend the President's invariable practice has been not to take part in primary contests. This is because in contests of this character among members of his own party the President must stand aloof regardless of any personal preference he might have. Of course, after the primary contests have been held the contests then are clear cut between the candidates of opposing parties. The President thought this confidential explanation was due to you in order that you would understand the limitations he is under in sending the message in response to your telegram of July twenty-eight.[38]

Although Truman and Stark never met in actual debate during the primary, on at least one occasion Truman and his opponent Milligan did address the same audience. The Catholic church in Cameron, Missouri, invited all candidates for office to its annual picnic. More than fifty candidates for state and congressional offices accepted the invitation and showed up to drink lemonade, eat fried chicken, pass out campaign literature, tack up posters, and shake innumerable hands. Afterwards, the nearly five thousand voters listened to more than two and a half hours of what one reporter called "old-fashioned 5 minute stemwinding" speeches. Three of the Republican candidates for Senator and Democrats Milligan and Truman were among the stem-winders.[39]

Truman closed his primary campaign on August 4, 1940, in Independence, where several thousand people gathered for a rally on the athletic field of the high school. A sound truck blared a recording of Senator Alben Barkley's address supporting Truman, and the candidate, speaking from a stand on the fifty-yard line, reaffirmed his support of the New Deal.

Although the odds against Truman had seemed insurmountable during most of the primary, factors in his favor had mounted. In addition to Senators Schwellenbach and Barkley, Bennett Clark, who six years earlier had said Truman conducted a "campaign of mendacity and imbecility unparalleled in the history of Missouri," had changed his opinion and worked actively for his junior colleague. Truman did suffer attacks from most of the state's metropolitan newspapers with the exception of the *Kansas City Journal,* but the unfriendly press was offset by the endorsement he received from labor and his strong appeal to black voters. In the spring of 1940 the powerful St. Louis organization led by Robert Hannegan and Bernard Dickmann turned a deaf ear to Truman's pleas for help, but at a critical point in the campaign that summer, the Hannegan-Dickmann forces switched tactics and decided to back him rather than Stark. It seemed that the organization did not want to help the overly ambitious Stark, who had weakened his senatorial chances by striving simultaneously for the vice-presidency. Probably the biggest single factor in Truman's favor arose from the fact that the anti-Pendergast vote would be split between Governor Stark and Maurice Milligan.

Harry Truman admitted that "it looked very dark for the junior senator from Missouri," and on the night of the primary he went to bed believing that he had lost the race. However, when the smoke cleared away and the results were announced, a jubilant Truman discovered that he had won the nomination with a plurality of nearly 8000 votes. The official count was: Truman 268,557; Stark 260,581; Milligan 127, 363.

In the general election Truman was opposed by Manvel Davis, a Kansas City Republican, who ran as much against President Franklin Roosevelt as he did against Harry Truman. Davis charged that Roosevelt was creating a dictatorship and usurping powers not granted by the Constitution. He excoriated the New Deal's "waste of money" and urged a return to private enterprise and local relief administration. He attacked the "Pendergast-Dickmann axis," which he insisted had elected Truman, and he scoffed at the latter for being a "rubber-stamp" for Roosevelt. In the late stages of the general campaign,

Davis stepped up his assaults on Truman and recalled how the senator had been vehemently opposed to reappointment of Milligan as district attorney in 1938. Davis strongly suggested that Truman's turnabout represented part of a bargain whereby Milligan split the opposition in the primary election.[40]

Truman was handicapped during much of the general campaign because of pressing business in the Senate. He made sporadic trips to his home state but could not match the energetic efforts of his Republican rival. Three days after his primary victory, Truman was back in the Senate and stayed there through Friday, September 6. He returned to Missouri to attend a harmony dinner in Columbia on Tuesday, September 10, and to give a speech the next day to Democrats assembled in Jefferson City. By Thursday, September 12, he was back in the Senate. He returned again to Missouri on September 21 to participate in a large rally at Moberly. The speeches at that event in the afternoon featured Truman and the nominee for governor; in the evening, Senator Scott Lucas from Illinois spoke for Truman. Truman's next appearance was as featured speaker at the opening of the Democratic campaign in St. Louis County on September 24.

From September 27 through October 4, Truman resumed his duties in the Senate. Because of the international crisis, the Senate was unwilling to adjourn even though nearly one-third of its members faced reelection contests. In courtesy to those who felt an absence was necessary, the Senate during this campaign period omitted the customary roll call.

Truman returned to Missouri the second week in October and seemed to concentrate his schedule on the smaller cities of the state. On the first day he spoke at Fayette, Fulton, and Mexico. On another day he spoke at Memphis, Kahoka, and Kirksville. On October 18 he delivered an address in Bethany. Following these speeches, he scheduled talks in St. Joseph, Odessa, and Webb City. He closed his campaign much as he had done in August, namely, with a hometown rally on November 1, 1940. At that evening rally, a half-hour band concert began the proceedings, and then Bennett Clark and Harry Truman each spoke, exhorting the voters to go to the polls and do their duty.

Davis and his fellow Republicans were unsuccessful in their campaigns against Roosevelt, and Harry Truman undoubtedly profited from this failure. Truman gained reelection by a vote of 930,775 to Davis's 886,376. The margin had been closer than Democrats had experienced for many years in Missouri, but Truman had kept his Senate seat.

Adding to Truman's elation over his victory in the general election was the knowledge that on the night of the primary in August both the *St. Louis Post Dispatch* and the *Kansas City Star* had put out extras announcing his defeat. He later wrote his version of that win:

> I was nominated by a plurality of 8400 votes [the actual plurality was 7976] in the August primary, after the most bitter mud slinging campaign in

Missouri's history of dirty campaigns. At eleven o'clock on the night of the primary vote I went to bed eleven thousand votes behind and supposedly defeated. The *Kansas City Star* and the *St. Louis Post Dispatch* had extras out telling how happy they were and safe Missouri was from my slimy person as Senator. A lying press cannot fool the people. I came back to the Senate and the doublecrossing ingrate of a Governor was sent back to the nursery.[41]

Second Term Senator (1940-1944)

When he returned to the Senate for his second term, Truman continued his interest in transportation, and until 1941 all his Senate speeches were short and rather inconsequential ones on that subject. The one exception was his short talk on the advisability of purchasing land in Puerto Rico for a military installation. He had requested from his friend Alben Barkley, chairman of the Steering Committee, assignment to the Military Affairs Committee because he said that he was very much interested in the national defense program. If he could not be given a place on Military Affairs, his second choice was the Committee on Agriculture. Truman got his first choice of committee assignment and was also put on Appropriations, Enrolled Bills, Interstate Commerce, Printing, Public Building and Grounds, and a special committee investigating Civil Service.

As the war in Europe widened, American involvement appeared ever more likely. Hitler's string of victories in Europe forced a rapid American armament program, and by the end of 1940 President Roosevelt was proclaiming that the United States would become the great "arsenal of democracy." That year America had taken the first hesitant steps toward the armament program and had passed a universal service law. Both were only small beginnings compared with what would be required later, but they presaged a pattern of increasing tempo and urgency. The problems accompanying armament and mobilization were immense. The country had no camps or even plans for camps to accommodate the huge numbers of recruits inducted under the new conscription law. Those who held elective office were subjected to special pressures from their constituents in regard to where such camps and military bases were to be placed. Because the country was not yet at war, the location of a new camp or defense plant often carried with it a smell of the pork barrel.

Senator Truman tried to volunteer his services as a military officer but was turned down because of his age. The Senate business grew heavier in proportion to the worsening international situation, and in the summer of 1940 while most Americans had watched in worry and horror, France and the Low Countries were felled by Hitler's blitzkrieg. In that summer while the Nazis were making their spectacular advances, Senator Truman, who had become increasingly worried over the national defense effort, made extensive inspection visits to many of the camp constructions and naval installations that were beginning to spring up from Maine to Florida and along both borders north and south.

Although Senator Truman was interested in the defense program in its entirety, he was also very much concerned about the program as it related to the state he represented. He knew his constituents' needs, and many of those constituents clamored for an ever larger share of the programs. Local and state politicians, civic groups, and federal representatives saw the enormous sums being appropriated for defense as a means of combatting unemployment and economic stagnation. Moreover, Truman felt, as did many politicians from the heartland states, that it was bad planning to locate defense plants or military camps near the coastal areas. The Seventh Corps area training center had been planned for land in Iowa purchased by the army, but the camp was shifted to Missouri where it soon became one of the nation's largest training centers, Fort Leonard Wood. Airports, depots, ordnance and ammunition plants, and other military bases were placed in the state. Indeed, Missouri fared so well in getting shares of the burgeoning defense budget that by the middle of 1941 Senator Truman was telling his constituents that he was finding it difficult to recommend further placements in his home state because it already had "55% of all the defense expenditures between the Mississippi River and the Rocky Mountains."[42]

During his campaign for reelection, many of his constituents told him of poor planning and waste that accompanied the construction at some of the Missouri sites. He quickly came to believe that such mistakes might be symptomatic of the whole country. From his Jackson County judgeship he knew that contractors would have to be closely watched if exorbitant profits were to be checked. He made it his business to learn the policies that determined where new plants were to be located, and word soon got around that Senator Harry Truman was the Washington contact who could make the defense agencies listen. Secretary of War Harry Woodring apparently felt that the most reliable source of information on the defense program early in 1941 was the junior senator from Missouri:

> Harry Woodring thought that you could give us more worthwhile information than anyone we might contact, and I share his opinion . . . if there are any shortcuts, please advise.[43]

Senator Truman had a long-time friend and political supporter in Lou E. Holland, who owned a small, prosperous printing firm in Kansas City. Holland and companions from other private businesses found an attentive ear when they complained to their senator that the smaller firms were not getting enough of the defense contracts. Truman, with a Populist's suspicion of large corporations, agreed that there was discrimination against small midwestern contractors when it came to awarding of contracts by Washington bureaus. The army, largest of all defense agencies, argued that it had to place procurement contracts with those firms which appeared most likely to give delivery on a satisfactory date. The small business often could not compete with the mammoth resources in plants, machinery, personnel, production techniques, and financial backing of the large corporation and, as a result, was not trusted by procurement officials. The plight of the small businessman was uppermost in Truman's mind, however, and he rejoined that unless something was done none but the largest companies would survive the defense effort. He told President Roosevelt that it was an unsatisfactory situation when small businesses had to be dependent on ''getting crumbs from the table of the big fellows.''[44]

Truman was not satisfied from his talk with the president that anything at all would be done to help the small businessman, so he planned to take the whole story of defense contracting to the Senate. On February 10, 1941, he presented to the Senate a well-reasoned justification for the creation of an investigative committee. He had done his usual careful job of consulting with party and Senate leaders before expressing his ideas. Three days later, after receiving favorable reactions to his remarks, he submitted a resolution for the establishment of such a committee.

The proposal first went to the Military Affairs Committee on which Truman served. This committee reported favorably on the resolution and raised the membership from five to seven senators. In keeping with Senate custom, the senator moving the resolution was named chairman of the committee. The proposed committee would need money to operate, so it was sent for review to the Committee on Audit and Control, chaired by Senator James F. Byrnes. The latter group accepted the proposal but cut the requested budget from $25,000 to $15,000.

Truman's proposal for an investigative committee was not the only one the Senate had to consider, but his arguments seemed more persuasive than those from other proponents. Moreover, the Roosevelt administration gave tacit if not open approval to his resolution because its scope and wording seemed limited enough to prevent the resultant committee from getting into military and diplomatic aspects of the conduct of the war. Also, the senator from Missouri had been a regular when it came to backing the administration. In March of 1941 when the resolution was reported on the floor of the Senate, only sixteen senators answered the roll call. Little attention was given to the resolution's passage, and probably no one then envisioned the scope of the investigation the newly created committee would ultimately make.

The first appropriation allocated to the Truman Committee did not permit very extensive investigations, and perhaps Byrnes had this restriction in mind when he rejected Truman's request for a larger initial budget. At any rate, Harry Truman never forgot that Byrnes was responsible for the delay in getting his committee created and for the small size of the first appropriation:

James F. Byrnes was Chairman of the Committee on Audit and Control. He is a very cagey politician and he was afraid that the Junior Senator from Missouri wanted a political weapon, although he'd just been returned to the Senate for another six years and could afford to be a statesman for at least four years. Mr. Byrnes finally agreed to give the committee the munificent sum of $15,000 to investigate the expenditure of $25,000,000,000. The Vice President appointed the Committee of seven Senators with Truman as Chairman and we went to work.[45]

The new committee was quickly dubbed the "Truman Committee." The other six members were: Tom Connally of Texas, Carl Hatch of New Mexico, James Mead of New York, Mon Wallgren of Washington, Joseph Ball of Minnesota, and Owen Brewster of Maine. Technically, the members of a Senate Committee are selected by the Senate's presiding officer—the vice-president—but in actual practice the committee chairman has the job of persuading colleagues to serve with him. In this regard, Senator Truman was uncommonly successful in gathering into his committee senators who were established leaders with power in their own rights.

His knowledge of history led Truman into making a parallel between 1941 and Civil War times, when Congress had established a committee on the conduct of the war. He often alluded to mistakes the Civil War committee had made, and he emphasized that his committee would keep aloof from questions of command competency, strategy, and conduct of military campaigns. He left military and naval strategy to the Military and Naval Affairs Committees of Congress and concentrated on the logistical, business side of the war. He believed there was great merit in having a congressional committee investigating the war effort at the time events were taking place rather than waiting until the war was over.

The Truman Committee was extremely active for the next three years. Its members came to see the seamy side of the war effort when they investigated crooked contractors on military installations, manufacturers who made faulty engines or parts, factories that cheated by putting out inferior products, army and navy waste in food and other supplies, and hundreds of similar examples. The committee made some thirty reports in the three-year period of Truman's chairmanship.

As the committee expanded its efforts it gained more credibility within the Senate and with the Roosevelt administration. Consequently, some of the wariness that had characterized the early months of the committee's life began to disappear. In August of 1941, the appropriation was increased to $50,000, and after that date the committee had no trouble in obtaining the money necessary for its operation.

The activities of the committee put its chairman very much in the public eye as newspapers and magazines rendered frequent reports praising the

"Billion-Dollar Watchdog" which Congress had created. This committee's work kept Senator Truman from making a great number of public speeches, but when he did consent to give an address it was a speech prepared and delivered in much the same manner as those given during his first term. He remained primarily responsible for the composition of his messages. Victor Messall, his secretary through the 1940 campaign, reported that Truman wrote all his own speeches in longhand and then dictated them for typing. Although Messall reported that he sometimes "dug up statistics," he did not recall anyone writing speeches for Truman. Truman wrote most of his speeches in the early morning, according to Messall. The senator would arrive at his office and ordinarily write a letter to his mother back in Independence before turning to speech preparation or other comparable work.[46]

In many ways Truman adapted and extended the lessons he had learned in Jackson County politics and during his first term in the Senate so that his committee would have a solid foundation. The committee was his creation; he kept its goals simple and clearly understood. He saw its primary purpose as one of helping to win the war, and to him this meant achieving the maximum and quickest production of war supplies at the least possible cost to the taxpayer. There were always the twin dangers that such a committee might either become overly critical of the administration or subservient to it. Truman made sure that his group trod the difficult path between these two extremes. In criticizing a specific instance or practice, the committee and its chairman were careful not to lay blame at President Roosevelt's door, and thus blanket indictment of the entire war effort was avoided.

There were times when the committee alienated the administration, and certainly there were times when its work angered powerful industrial and business corporations. However, the committee was remarkably successful in establishing a reputation for efficiency and objectivity. It became a force to be reckoned with and soon functioned so effectively that it took on an important role in the shape and management of the defense program. The committee uncovered an extraordinary number of defects, but perhaps more important to the defense program as a whole, the reputation it acquired created a dampening effect and thus prevented more abuses than were actually exposed.

While the degree of influence exerted by Truman on the making of overall defense policy during this period is difficult to measure accurately, it is apparent that as chairman of this increasingly powerful committee he became at least indirectly a participant in policy formulation. In the defense departments, his influence was that of a potentially dangerous investigator who had ready access to the press and public. Furthermore, he ranked high as an objective critic with both these entities. His growing prestige in Congress was reflected in Senator Scott Lucas's remark to the Senate that "as a result of the standing which the Truman Committee has with the American people, whenever the distinguished Senator from Missouri makes a statement we are bound to give it weight.'' One careful student of the Truman Investigating Committee summarized:

> In a very real sense he [Senator Truman] was the Committee; he was responsible for its creation, for its organization, its accomplishments and its influence. He made the Committee what it became through a combination of good sense, hard work, attention to detail and luck, all of which resulted in highly favorable publicity that further increased his effectiveness. By these means, Truman exercised the investigatory power and influenced policy, and in doing so influenced the conduct of the national defense program. Through exercise of the investigatory power, he not only uncovered many things that were wrong but promoted confidence in the program as a whole by creating the assurance that it was being honestly monitored. His influence on policy was considerable.[47]

Aside from talking with the president in early March about his committee's important *Third Annual Report,* Senator Truman had no contact whatever with Roosevelt prior to the Democratic National Convention in late July. However, given the attention and publicity that came to him because of his committee's success, it is no small wonder that Truman's name began to crop up as a possible vice-presidential candidate. Machinery was already in operation which would make that reality occur at the Chicago convention.

6

Building a New Administration

I sit here all day trying to persuade people to do the things
they ought to have sense enough to do without my persuading them. . . . That's all the powers of the President
amount to.

HARRY S. TRUMAN

AMERICAN elections usually are clamorous and dramatic affairs, but in contrast with other years the presidential campaign in 1944 was quite dull. First,
the country was in the middle of a war and both parties showed understandable
restraint. Secondly, other stories vied for the public attention.

It was a time when the Allies were fighting mile by mile through the Nor-
man hedgerows, and in the Pacific an American armada was beginning the
onslaught against Japanese islands. Harry S. Truman was a U.S. senator; Navy
Lieutenant John F. Kennedy was decorated for heroic conduct after his PT boat
was cut in half; Richard Nixon was a navy officer in the South Pacific leap-frog-
ging along a chain of recaptured islands; and George McGovern was behind the
controls of a B-24 bomber flying north from its Italian base. At home, only
after the average citizen's attention veered away from daily war reports did it
turn toward politics and the approaching election.

FDR Chooses His Vice-President

When July of 1944 approached bringing with it the Democratic National
Convention, there was no question that Franklin Roosevelt, then in his twelfth
year of office, would be renominated. Gone was the suspense that had accompanied his decision four years earlier even though he delayed making a public
announcement until shortly before the party delegates were to meet in Chicago. Certainty of Roosevelt's nomination, however, was tempered by concern

over the president's visible aging and declining health. Added to this concern was mounting speculation as to whom he would choose as his running mate.

The leading contenders in addition to Vice-President Henry A. Wallace were Supreme Court Justice William O. Douglas, War Mobilization Director James F. Byrnes, and Senator Alben Barkley of Kentucky. From time to time still more names were thrown into political conversations, but the president himself remained noncommittal.

Vice-President Wallace was admired by the most fervent New Dealers, but he was looked down on by party bosses and lampooned by southern Democrats as a dreamer who wanted "a quart of milk for every Hottentot." Within the Democratic party a powerful group, consisting of National Chairman Robert Hannegan, Postmaster General Frank Walker, millionaire Edwin Pauley, and Mayor Ed Kelly of Chicago, was determined that Henry Wallace should never be in a postion to become president of the United States.

This group of advisers was so strongly opposed to Henry Wallace that all during the first half of 1944 they connived to convince the president that he should choose another running mate. The group's acknowledged leader was Edwin W. Pauley, a California oil tycoon and treasurer of the Democratic National Committee. In the spring the group was joined by Edward J. Flynn, Democratic boss of the Bronx, and Edwin "Pa" Watson, appointment secretary to the president. All were experienced politicians who believed that Wallace would be a serious handicap to the ticket and a potential danger to the country. They had noted the president's decline in physical health and mental vigor, so more than ever they were convinced that choosing a vice-presidential candidate was a critical action.

From their disenchantment with Henry Wallace, the group moved through a long list of possible candidates before deciding on Truman. Pauley, in his capacity as secretary-treasurer of the Democratic National Committee, arranged a series of fund-raising dinners throughout the country, and at most of them he was able to get out the message that Wallace was a dangerous dreamer at a time when the nation needed stability and reality.

On July 11, President Roosevelt held a dinner conference with his top political strategists and announced that he would run for reelection. Thus one answer could be released, but the question of the vice-presidency was as unsettled as ever. That question was pursued by the group of intimate advisers who met privately with Roosevelt in his study after dinner. Pauley gave his version of the meeting with President Roosevelt:

> After dinner, we adjourned to the President's study in the blue oval room on the second floor, where we all went over the various candidates one by one, and, for various reasons eliminated them: Rayburn because of the split in the Texas delegation; Byrnes because of coming from the deep south, too.

Much to my amazement, Roosevelt injected the name of John Winant, at that time Ambassador to Great Britain; and William Douglas. He spent some time extolling Douglas. . . . When President Roosevelt had finished this, there was dead silence on the part of everyone. No one wanted Douglas any more than Wallace. The President sensed this.

The next person discussed was Truman. Roosevelt recalled the occasion when he approved the naming of Truman as head of the War Investigating Committee, and said that Truman had done a good job; that he had not known him too well, but that his work on the Committee had demonstrated his ability and loyalty, and that he had been trained in politics. . . .

The President turned to Bob Hannegan who was sitting next to him on the divan, put his hand on his knee, and said: "Bob, I think you and everyone else want Truman."

. . . On the way back to the Mayflower Hotel, George Allen said to me: "Ed, this is the greatest personal victory you will ever obtain." Allen has always said that he gives me full credit for both the defeat of Wallace and the nomination of Truman. Speaking for myself, I will say only that no one ever worked any harder at it than I did.[1]

The group had leveled its most persuasive salvo and had scored a direct hit. Out of the rival factions and in the privacy of Roosevelt's smoke-filled study a future president was selected. Senator Harry Truman of Missouri was a name that brought no opposition. His voting record had been consistently New Deal; he was from a border state and popular in that exclusive and influential body, the U.S. Senate; and he had won strong newspaper support for his work as chairman of the important Senate War Investigating Committee. Moreover, he was acceptable to the president!

Henry Wallace was not one who gave up easily, however, and had collected a list of 290 delegates pledged to him along with a public opinion poll showing that registered Democrats preferred him over all other potential vice-presidential candidates. At his urging, Roosevelt had agreed to write a letter—dated July 14—stating that if he were a delegate to the convention, he personally would vote for Henry Wallace:

Hyde Park, N.Y.
July 14, 1944

My dear Senator [Samuel D.] Jackson:

In the light of the probability that you will be chosen as permanent chairman of the convention, and because I know that many rumors accompany all conventions, I am wholly willing to give you my own personal thought in regard to the selection of a candidate for Vice President. I do this at this time because I expect to be away from Washington for the next few days.

The easiest way of putting it is this: I have been associated with Henry Wallace during his past four years as Vice President, for eight years earlier while he was Secretary of Agriculture, and well before that. I like him and I respect him and he is my personal friend. For these reasons I personally would vote for his renomination if I were a delegate to the convention.

At the same time I do not wish to appear in any way as dictating to the convention. Obviously the convention must do the deciding. And it should—and I am sure it will—give great consideration to the pros and cons of its choice.

Very sincerely yours,
Franklin D. Roosevelt[2]

Although not a frank endorsement, the note was enough to lead Wallace into thinking that he had presidential support. In fact, it seemed that Roosevelt's strategy was to encourage a potential candidate to think that he was the one on the inside track. As a result, each of several contenders insisted that he was really the president's first choice, and that the latter simply was delaying an open acknowledgment.

James Byrnes, another aspirant, was confident he had captured Roosevelt's approval and even sought help from Harry S. Truman:

In July 1944, as I was about to leave my home in Independence for the opening of the convention in Chicago, the telephone rang. It was Jimmy Byrnes calling from Washington. He told me that President Roosevelt had decided on him as the new nominee for Vice President, and he asked me if I would nominate him at the convention. I told him that I would be glad to do it if the President wanted him for a running mate.[3]

James Byrnes went to the convention assured in his own mind that he had received an unequivocal endorsement from Truman, but the qualification *"if the President wanted him*[Byrnes] *for a running mate"* proved to be significant. It is improbable that Senator Truman was unaware that he himself was being considered for the position. He had been chosen as a delegate-at-large from Missouri and assigned to the National Platform Committee—an assignment similar to ones he had held in 1936 and 1940. Truman could not have been so naive that he went to the 1944 convention with absolutely no expectation that he might be nominated. After the event, he insisted he had tried to forestall it:

When the 1944 election was approaching mention began to be made about Truman for Vice President. Every effort was made by me to shut it off. I liked my job as a Senator and I wanted to stay with it. It takes a long time for a man to establish himself in the Senate. I was a member of three very important standing committees—Appropriations, Interstate Commerce, and Military Affairs and was well up on the list on all of them for seniority, which is very important. My Special Committee was doing good work and I wanted to stay with it. . . . I had tried to make it very plain wherever I went that I was not a candidate for Vice President. . . . There were two dozen men at the Chicago Convention of the Democrats in 1940 who would have gladly taken the honor of the Vice Presidential Nomination and have been exceedingly happy with it. I spent a most miserable week in trying to stave off the nomination.[4]

National Democratic Chairman Robert Hannegan was from St. Louis and an old friend of Harry Truman's dating back to his earliest campaigns for the Senate. Just as the convention in Chicago began to get under way, he visited Truman at the latter's hotel suite to tell him of Roosevelt's decision and was flabbergasted when Truman professed to be backing Byrnes. Here was a fine imbroglio! Hannegan decided that he must talk immediately with the Chief, who was en route by train to the west coast. At Hannegan's urging, Roosevelt consented to stop in Chicago on July 15 for a quick conference. As political ammunition Chairman Hannegan earlier had secured from the chief executive a letter in which Roosevelt had stated, "You have written me about Bill Douglas and Harry Truman. I would, of course, be very glad to run with either of them and believe that either of them would bring real strength to the ticket."[5] Hannegan and other party colleagues were not pleased with the inclusion of Douglas's name, and in the retyping of the letter the two names were reversed. Thus Harry Truman was not yet the unequivocal choice, but it was clear that both Wallace and Byrnes were out as far as Roosevelt was concerned.

The political wheels began churning, and while the presidential train continued toward San Diego, other party leaders started their maneuvers to get Byrnes out of the contest and Truman into it.

Organized labor's opposition to Byrnes had crystallized, and leaders were not shy about stating it. Sidney Hillman, a well-known labor spokesman and then co-chairman of the Office of Production Management, had breakfast with Truman and said flatly that he would not help Byrnes in any way. Truman, seeking support for the man he had agreed to nominate, next met with Phil Murray, head of the CIO, and with A. F. Whitney of the Railroad Train Men. Both expressed positions identical to Hillman's. The following day William Green, head of the powerful AFL, invited the Missouri senator to a breakfast at the Palmer House and revealed that his union did not like either Wallace or Byrnes but would back Truman. To all of these persons and to others, an adamant Truman announced that he was not a candidate, that he preferred to remain in the Senate, and that he was going ahead with his own plans to help James Byrnes.

It is unlikely that coyness prompted such remarks, for Harry Truman had his own assessment of campaign strategies. He was not convinced that he really had received Roosevelt's blessing, and he was too experienced in politics to downgrade its necessity. His reluctance even to nominate Byrnes without encouragement from the president is an indication of the weight he placed on such endorsements. He simply was not going to let himself be thrown into a pot with other common contenders.

With labor showing itself friendly to Truman and knowing the president's inclinations, Chairman Hannegan decided to apply a little more persuasion. He, along with Walker, Kelly, Ed Flynn and Frank Hague, arranged to have Truman visit them at the Blackstone Hotel. "The President wants you to be Vice President," Walker told the skeptical senator. The latter refused to believe it until the phone rang, and it was Roosevelt calling from San Diego. While he sat on one of the twin beds and Hannegan, phone in hand, sat on the other, Harry Truman heard the following exchange:

> Bob, have you got that fellow lined up yet?
> No. He's the contrariest Missouri mule I've ever dealt with.
> Well, you tell him if he wants to break up the Democratic party in the middle of a war, that's his responsibility.[6]

The exact circumstances surrounding the telephone call to Roosevelt are difficult to ascertain. The foregoing is one of Truman's versions, and it differs from those given by others who were apparently privy to the call. Edward J. Flynn states that there was a "committee" meeting in Chicago soon after the convention got underway, and that some members were not yet certain that Truman was acceptable to Roosevelt. They agreed that if they could only get a more definite word from the president then they could all work enthusiastically for Truman's cause:

> We called the President, who was on his private car en route to the Pacific Coast, and I insisted that he again tell these men that he wished Truman for a running mate. In turn he talked to Walker, Hannegan, and Kelly. Mayor Kelly insisted that the President send a note we could use. He agreed, and addressed it to Bob Hannegan, who showed it to various state leaders. Subsequently it was released for publication.[7]

President Truman gave another account of the episode somewhat different from the one that appears in his *Memoirs*. In an autobiographical sketch apparently written while he was president, Truman did not indicate that he was present when the call was made to Roosevelt:

> Hannegan came to see me on Tuesday evening before the Convention met on Thursday and told me that the President wanted me for his running mate. I told Bob I wasn't interested and that the President had never talked with me and would not I was sure. Then Frank Walker told me the same story and got the same answer. Dan Tobin tried to persuade me as did a dozen other influential Democrats. I said no to all of them and said it as positively as I could.

On Thursday night after the Convention had adjourned because of a galery [*sic*] paid demonstration for Wallace, some of the Southern Democrats, Hannegan, Walker and Ed Pauley told me that I was going to be responsible for a split in the Democratic Party which would result in the election of the New York Governor. Maryland's Governor, the Governor of Oklahoma, Harry Byrd, the Junior Senator from Mississippi and Gov. Graves of Alabama along with Tobin and William Green told me that they could all take me and save the party. I caved in then and said all right I'd go. Hannegan and I got Bennett Clark to nominate me with Coffey a great legionnaire and delegate from Ohio to second the nomination.[8]

No matter what the actual details of this incident, Truman seems to have gotten the assurance that he had Roosevelt's support. Consequently, he agreed to run.

The convention itself was without zest or controversy until balloting began on the vice-presidential nomination. Wallace took a strong lead with 429½ votes of the 589 necessary to win. Truman was second with a total of 319½. The delegates had been in session for more than six hours by the time this first ballot was finished, but the convention chairman ordered an immediate second roll call. This time around, Governor O'Connor of Maryland, himself a nominee, threw his support to Truman, and the switching began. One by one the delegations fell into line, and at the end of the call Truman was leading Wallace 447½ to 373. Changes came rapidly when Mayor Kelly of Chicago, giving up on the chances of nominating a favorite son for Illinois, was recognized by the chairman and announced fifty-five more votes for Truman. The stampede began in earnest, and the final vote was Truman 1031, Wallace 105, with a total of only thirty-seven votes going to lesser candidates.

The man who would be only a heartbeat away from the presidency actually had been selected two weeks earlier in a smoke-filled White House study. His selection was confirmed in a Chicago hotel bedroom before actual balloting occurred. It was a time when military campaigns were capturing most of the headlines, but political skirmishes also were taking place. Russian intransigence was not known by the American public; the Cold War had not been christened, and the new vice-presidential candidate was given only the skimpiest of briefings about foreign affairs.

The Roosevelt-Truman Ticket (1944)

Dramatic events occurring throughout the world in the fall of 1944 made it difficult for either major political party in America to arouse public attention over domestic politics. The Republicans faced a particular challenge in trying to defeat Roosevelt because of his tenure and enormous prestige earned as a wartime president. They chose a vigorous young candidate, Governor Thomas E. Dewey of New York, and they attempted to contrast the "new" elements in their party with the aging leaders of the opposition. The forecast was for a light vote in November, and presumably a smaller voter turnout would favor the Republicans.

On his return from a Pacific trip following the Democratic National Convention, Roosevelt made a nationwide broadcast from the Bremerton Navy Yard near Seattle. During the presentation of this speech he wore leg braces for the first time since his return from conferences at Cairo and Teheran. Encumbered by the apparatus, he was forced to hold tightly to his lectern. The result was that he had trouble reading and turning the pages of his manuscript. Gone was the confident, poised delivery that had become one of his major rhetorical strengths. Nor were photographs taken at the time at all flattering, for in them he appeared haggard and querulous. The question of his health remained the one serious issue in the campaign. True, many of the rumors were exaggerated, but there was some visible evidence, too. His leg and hip muscles, frail from disuse, were now almost entirely gone, and he made no public appearances at which he had to stand. Soon public opinion polls were indicating a slump for Roosevelt and an accompanying rise in favor of his opponent.

As the election approached, the possibility of Republican gains stimulated the incumbent president to undertake more active campaigning. At the end of September, in an address before the Teamsters Union, he was at his sardonic best. Rumors and "whispered stories" had accompanied most of his campaigns, but this time the most ridiculous of all the tales got into print. Supposedly, the president's dog, Fala, had been left by mistake on an Aleutian island, and it was alleged that Roosevelt had dispatched a U.S. destroyer just to return the pet. To the delight of the cheering teamsters, chauffeurs, and warehousemen, Roosevelt answered:

> These Republican leaders have not been content with attacks on me, or my wife, or on my sons. No, not content with that, they now include my little dog, Fala. Well, of course, I don't resent attacks, but Fala *does* resent them. You know, Fala is Scotch, and being a Scottie, as soon as he learned that the Republican fiction writers in Congress had concocted a story that I had left him behind on the Aleutian Islands and had sent a destroyer back to find him—at a cost to the taxpayers of two or three, or eight or twenty million dollars—his Scotch soul was furious. He has not been the same dog since. I am accustomed to hearing malicious falsehoods about myself—such as that old, worm-eaten chestnut that I have represented myself as indispensable. But I think I have a right to resent, to object to libelous statements about my dog.[9]

This kind of political derision was hard to answer and it stung the Republicans. The president's sarcasm soon gained wider recognition than the original

story, and delighted Democrats began talking about the campaign as essentially a "race between Roosevelt's dog and Dewey's goat."

After a presidential candidate is nominated he is in demand everywhere.
He immediately surrounds himself with advisers, publicity personnel, writers,
secretaries, and assorted friends. The vice-presidential nominee, by comparison, is almost overlooked. His staff is but a small fraction of that garnered
by the leader, and he often must scrounge if he is to schedule enough suitable
appearances. What help he gets from the Democratic National Committee is
apt to be limited to making certain that he echoes the leader and that he avoids
saying anything that might hurt the ticket.

In 1944, because of momentous changes occurring almost daily in the
course of the war and because of Roosevelt's established prestige, Harry Truman's campaign activities failed to draw much public attention. His entourage
consisted of Hugh Fulton, Matthew Connelly, and three or four newspaper
representatives. Fulton was counsel to the Truman Committee and Connelly,
too, at the time was one of its employees. Other advisers who traveled with Truman or helped with arrangements were George E. Allen, a Washington bon vi-
vant and raconteur, and Edward McKim, one of Truman's chums from his
boyhood in Missouri.

Truman began his campaign with speeches in Detroit on Labor Day. Because of fierce rivalry between the CIO and the AFL he spoke to the former
group in the afternoon and addressed the latter at an evening banquet the same
day. A few days later he went on a tour that started in New Orleans, then
moved to the West Coast, and from there he worked his way through Montana
to Minnesota. In Minneapolis the meeting was chaired by the bright, energetic
state campaign manager for the Roosevelt-Truman slate, Hubert Humphrey.
From the upper Midwest, Truman's campaign proceeded to the Northeast and
into Massachusetts. A ticklish situation developed in connection with his appearance at Madison Square Garden in New York because his earlier rival for
the vice-presidency, Henry Wallace, would also be on the platform. It was
suspected with good reason that friends of Wallace would pack the Garden and
probably dwarf any recognition given Truman. The Truman arrangers,
therefore, contrived to keep their candidate secluded until Wallace arrived.
When Wallace did appear, Truman marched into the huge auditorium
simultaneously with him so that it was not possible to determine who was the
real recipient of the resultant ovation.

The campaign of 1944 opened late and was comparatively brief. The brevity worked in favor of the Democrats because most voters apparently felt it was
no time to swap horses. The incumbent president limited his public appearances to two dinner addresses and three public speeches, all broadcast, and
three special radio talks. Truman was programmed mainly to keep the regulars
in line, and it was hoped that his plain, uninspiring speeches would help ap-
pease some of the disgruntled Democrats.

The early returns on November 7 indicated another Roosevelt sweep, which became greater as more returns were tabulated. The electoral landslide was 432 to 99; the percentages of the popular vote were 53.4 for Roosevelt and 45.9 for his Republican opponent, Thomas Dewey. It is not likely that Truman's name on the ticket helped win many voters. However, he had been no liability, and more important, he now was in line for the presidency.

The Moon, Stars, and Planets Fall on Truman

As the year 1945 began, it was evident to many persons that despite his energetic campaigning in the preceding fall the once robust health of Roosevelt had weakened. His eloquent, moving radio voice had lost its vigor; the famous smile and friendly warmth were displayed infrequently. With his energy gone but optimistic as always, in April he went to Warm Springs, Georgia, for some badly needed recuperation. About 1:15 in the afternoon of April 12, he said simply, "I have a terrific headache." A few hours later a stunned world heard one network radio newsman[10] stumble over the pronunciation of *cerebral* but announce "President Roosevelt has died of a cerebral hemorrhage." It was the end of an epoch.

In America and throughout the world, millions seemed to feel a sense of deep personal loss. For more than thirteen pressure-filled years he had guided his nation's destiny, and from it all had emerged as a true leader and statesman. On the occasion of his death, friends from everywhere offered rich tributes; even old political foes paid him homage.

When the first shock waves of dismay over President Roosevelt's death began to settle, the prevalent feeling in America was one of uncertainty about the man who would succeed him. The obvious contrasts in the personalities of Franklin Roosevelt and Harry S. Truman made speculation inevitable. Could this plain, provincial son of the Midwest fulfil the dramatic role of leader and heroic world figure? No one knew, and many doubted.

Observers don't agree on just which experience is the best preparation for the presidency. Woodrow Wilson spent most of his adult life in universities and had only a short stint as a governor before he entered the presidency. Franklin Roosevelt entered after twelve years of experience in government administration. Dwight Eisenhower came from a lifetime in the military. Lyndon Johnson and John Kennedy emerged from the Senate ranks.

In a technical sense, no man can be prepared for the presidency in the way a dentist or a lawyer can be said to be prepared by several years of experience to extract a tooth or build a legal case. Harry Truman had served in the U.S. Senate; he had been there for ten years before becoming vice-president. His work in the Senate, particularly his chairmanship of the War Investigating Committee, gave him a better grasp of domestic politics and economics than nearly any other public official. He lacked a college degree, but it could not be said that he was uneducated. He had more experience, a better practical acquaintanceship with the workings of government, than Lincoln, Hoover, Eisenhower, Carter, and many other presidents before assuming office. Not a man of brilliant intellectual gifts, Truman nevertheless was smart and had spent his life in serious reading and studying. Insights gained from his self-imposed discipline coupled with his experience in practical politics had created his values and judgments.

Nearly all accounts picture Truman as coming into the presidency entirely untested and unprepared; such interpretations add to the drama of his career but are overly simplified. He himself promoted the impression by saying to reporters and some of his Senate colleagues:

> Boys, if you ever pray, pray for me now. I don't know whether you fellows ever had a load of hay fall on you, but when they told me yesterday what had happened, I felt like the moon, the stars, and all the planets had fallen on me.[11]

It is a mistake, though, to believe that Truman came into the presidency with absolutely no preparation or expectancy of ever achieving that office. As Mark Twain said about the accounts of his death: "Such stories are greatly exaggerated." Certainly Vice-President Truman did not expect to become president less than four months after his inauguration. If he had, he would have schooled himself more fully in such matters as the Teheran agreements, the overall relations with Russia, and particularly the Yalta Conference. Yet no normal man, and certainly not a politician with twenty-three years of practical experience, is immune from the human urge for higher office. For any vice-president, the White House is a magnet, to which that urge, no matter how small or restrained, must be drawn.

For several months preceding Roosevelt's death, there was no lack of rumors about his health; the topic was a lively one at political meetings and social gatherings. In February, while President Roosevelt was en route home from Yalta, a rumor reached the Senate that he had died aboard ship. Later, it was discovered that it was his appointment secretary, Major General Edwin Watson, who had died.

A short time after his return to Washington, President Roosevelt met with his vice-president and discussed the speech he planned to give on his Yalta trip. The president's physical condition did not go unnoticed by Truman, who later recalled:

> I met with the President a week later and was shocked by his appearance. His eyes were sunken. His magnificent smile was missing from his care-worn face. He seemed a spent man. I had a hollow feeling within me, for I saw that the journey to Yalta must have been a terrible ordeal.[12]

President Roosevelt gave his Yalta report to a joint meeting of Congress on March 1, 1945, and many accounts published then noted his weakened condition. A short time later a Washington correspondent for the *Louisville Courier-Journal* described a dinner with Vice-President Truman held before Roosevelt's death and insisted that Truman had acted as if he expected to become president:

> There was Harry S. Truman, seven days before he took the oath as President, sitting with us and, in a shy manner, making it clear to all that he had no doubt he would be in the White House before many months had passed.[13]

Even after his inauguration as vice-president, Harry Truman continued to enjoy the associations and conviviality of the Senate. He presided over that body on April 12, 1945, and when the Senate adjourned for the day he went to Speaker Sam Rayburn's office in the Capitol "to discuss legislative matters and relax a little bit." Responding to an urgent call from Steve Early, Roosevelt's press secretary, Vice-President Truman arrived at the White House at 5:25 P.M. and learned that Roosevelt was dead. An hour and a half later Harry S. Truman was sworn in as the thirty-third president of the United States. An hour later on that same hectic day, he held his first cabinet meeting, announcing that he expected to continue along the path of the earlier administration but that he also intended to be president in his own right.

An incident that revealed his determination to be his own man happened during his second day as president. On that day, Truman called his long-time friend, John W. Snyder of St. Louis, into his office. Truman told Snyder that he was going to appoint him federal loan administrator. Mr. Truman then telephoned Jesse Jones, the administrator for the Reconstruction Finance Corporation, to tell him that "the President" had appointed Snyder as federal loan administrator. "Oh," asked Jones, "did he make that appointment before he died?" "No," was President Truman's grim reply. "He made it just now."[14]

Harry Truman came into the White House having definite ideas about the role of the president in the American system of government; he respected the office of the presidency and always seemed somewhat in awe of it. At the time of his inauguration, some highly placed officials wondered privately and publicly about his ability. One of Roosevelt's closest military advisers, Admiral William D. Leahy, expressed deep concern that a man so "completely inexperienced in international affairs" would have to decide intricate questions dealing with war and peace, and had so much to learn "in the field of international relations."[15]

The new president plunged immediately into his most difficult problems. The day after his inauguration and to the surprise of many experienced

Washingtonians, he was in his office and at work by 7:00 A.M. The secretary of state was first among many high officials who came to give him quick and early briefings. At 11:00 A.M. he met with the government's top military leaders to hear the latest reports on the war. At lunchtime, he decided to visit the leaders of Congress and thus make a gesture expressing his desire for the greatest cooperation between the executive and legislative branches of government. At the luncheon he told the congressional leaders that he wanted to address a joint session of Congress very soon and to assure the world that he intended to carry on certain earlier policies.

A speech to Congress was quickly scheduled for Monday, April 16, and steps were taken immediately for its preparation. Like all modern occupants of the White House, Truman would find himself too busy for personal research and composition. Henceforward, every major speech would have to be filtered through layers of departments and various consultants. The president would be ultimately responsible, but the address itself would represent a group endeavor more than individual effort.

At the outset of his presidency, Truman had no staff of trusted consultants or writers to help him draft messages; yet as president he was faced with three imminent speeches. One was the address to Congress; another was a speech to the armed forces the next day; and on the following Monday, April 23, he was to address a formation session of the United Nations Organization* meeting in San Francisco. He hastily summoned his friend, George E. Allen, and asked him to work with Matthew Connelly in preparing these first three addresses. Allen brought with him an assistant, Ed Reynolds, and together they went into the cabinet room where they started organizing materials for the speeches. Truman only outlined to them in a very general way what he thought might be appropriate for each occasion. They were asked to put the generalizations into reading drafts. The president suggested that the writers ask White House stenographers to type drafts in triple-space in order to allow room for him to make any corrections or interlineations.

The hectic pace of assuming the presidency kept Truman exceedingly busy, and for the next three days he had little opportunity to talk with his two writers:

> It wasn't until after the funeral, on Sunday, that Matt [Connelly] and I had another chance to discuss the speech to Congress with the President. He liked the material we had prepared, made some suggestions, and then proposed that we go over the text with former Supreme Court Justice James Byrnes. After reading our draft, Byrnes outraged my pride of authorship with the remark that he, too, had trouble putting his thoughts on paper.[16]

Organization was later dropped from the official name of this body.

Allen may be inclined to take too much credit for the authorship of this particular address, for it reflected some of the restrained judgment of Samuel Rosenman. Rosenman had offered to resign his office as special counsel to the president but had been pressed into emergency service:

> I had already sent in my resignation . . . in order to give him [President Truman] a chance to get his own staff in. . . . I had difficulty in getting mine [his resignation] accepted, but it was before him on April 14. He said he would like me to help on the Congressional speech, which I did. My difficulty was that this was very different from helping Roosevelt because I found that I was trying to write a speech in the presence of a convention! There must have been fourteen people around the table, all of Truman's old friends: Matt Connelly, John Snyder, James K. Vardaman, and a great many of his friends; and it was very difficult. That was one of the reasons I went in very shortly to press my resignation. It takes five times as long to write a sentence with fourteen people around as it does to be alone with him or one or two others. . . . I did help on this speech. And the next big thing I helped him on was the speech to the United Nations Organization.[17]

The occasion for the speech was a solemn one, and it called for establishing the right mood rather than innovations or exhortations for new endeavors. The first fourth of the address was devoted to an appropriate eulogy of President Roosevelt. The war news, although tragic in its particulars, was encouraging as a whole, and Roosevelt already had persuaded the country to strive for unconditional surrender. Just as expected, in this opening speech the new president assured his listeners that the direction of the war would be "unchanged and unhampered." Then President Truman acknowledged the sacrifices American citizens had made and were making in the service of their country; he shared the hope of all citizens for a durable peace; and he announced that the San Francisco conference to set up the United Nations organization would proceed as scheduled. He praised Americans for being "one of the most powerful forces for good on earth," and then moved quickly into a peroration that centered on his personal role:

> At this moment, I have in my heart a prayer. As I assume my heavy duties, I humbly pray to Almighty God, in the words of Solomon: "Give therefore thy servant an understanding heart to judge thy people, that I may discern between good and bad; for who is able to judge this thy so great a people?" I ask only to be a good and faithful servant of my Lord and my people.[18]

The circumstances of the country's being in the midst of a war, the sudden death of a great leader, uncertainty about the character of a new president—all combined to place this first address within a dramatic setting. Yet in the talk there are no surprises; nor was it overly dramatized. With the exception of its graceful conclusion, the wording was pedestrian and contained many phrases that under different conditions would be considered banal.

Any presidential address, however, creates news and evokes public reaction. President Truman's speech on this occasion was no exception, and it caused a great outpouring of mail which was uniformly laudatory. Most listeners who wrote complimented him for his sincerity, humility, and plainness; many respondents praised him for his references to God and the Bible. Typical of such letters were the following:

> So that I won't remain "just a signature," I'd like to define myself as a typical American young mother of two, who wants to have a word or two with our new President.
>   May God bless you for the spirit behind your wonderful talk to Congress and to us today.[19]

> You charted a wise course toward the haven of justice and peace in your speech to the Houses of Congress yesterday. It was nobly said. I pray that God may bless your courage and humble dependence on Him, both so evident in your speech, and that He may keep you in strength of body, and guide you to the accomplishment of your patriotic purposes is our sincerest wish.[20]

> I am not in the habit of writing letters to people high in our government, but I was deeply moved by your sincerity and humility which I feel were genuine in the speech delivered Monday.[21]

> This noon I heard your address to Congress, and I was deeply moved by the honesty and sincerity of your message, and especially by your closing words from Solomon's prayer.[22]

Approximately 1500 letters in response to the address were received within a week, and all echoed similar praise. A surprising number of letter writers disclosed that they were Republicans or Democrats disenchanted with policies of the New Deal, but they lauded the speech and professed themselves ready to support the new administration.

While it was not to be expected that a single speech could do much to establish trust and credibility in the new president, it certainly in no way lessened respect for him. The address paid tribute to the former president and showed respect but *not* subservience to the past. The speaker seemed confident about the future but not arrogant about the part he himself proposed to play. All in all the speech sounded the right notes of consideration, confidence, and personal humility.

The Close Working Circle

In spite of the obvious success of his address to Congress, President Truman realized that he needed to develop a more permanent team of advisers and speech writers, and do it quickly. Under the presidential system a chief executive picks cabinet members and advisers who will be loyal to him and who more or less share his political philosophy. Because messages are so indicative of character, it is important that he choose writers who are not only sympathetic to his views but who can phrase ideas clearly and in a style that sounds natural and easy for him. The urgency forced on President Truman in April of 1945 did not permit the careful screening and examination that a more normal transfer of administrations would have offered. He inherited Roosevelt's cabinet and most of his advisers, so it was inevitable that occasional bitterness would arise when replacements began to occur. There is no doubt, also, that in his earliest appointments the new president placed more weight on friendship and camaraderie than on specific qualifications for the job to be done. As a result, some persons proved inadequate for the responsibilities given them.

Two days after he moved into his office, President Truman received his first visitor, one of his oldest and closest friends, John W. Snyder. Snyder and Truman had much in common. They were about the same age; they were both from Missouri; each had been a captain in the field artillery during World War I and had kept active in the Missouri National Guard ever since; both were enthusiastic members of various veterans' organizations; they both enjoyed playing poker, which they called their study in probabilities.

The only post that was immediately vacant was that of federal loan administrator, and President Truman quickly appointed his old friend to that position. Actually, the appointment meant much more than that, for Snyder was to serve in many other ways. Three months later, his job was changed, and he became director of the Office of War Mobilization and Reconversion. Then in June of 1946, he was appointed secretary of the treasury. John Snyder's role was even more important during the first months of the Truman administration than his titles suggested, for as a close confidant he was in on nearly all of President Truman's early strategies and decisions.

Eben A. Ayers, who was serving as assistant press secretary to the president when President Roosevelt died, described his first meeting with the new chief executive:

> I got in at 8:30 [Monday morning, April 16] and went to my office where about 9 o'clock I received a call from Rensch [J. Leonard Reinsch, a radio man who hoped to become Press Secretary to the new President] who was in the old office formerly used by Grace Tully [President Roosevelt's private secretary]. . . . Talking briefly with Rensch [*sic*] mention was made of a press conference by the President. Rensch asked me to come in with him and he walked into the President's office. The President was sit-

*Truman's first speech as president to the joint
session of Congress, April 16, 1945.*

ting at his desk and there were two strangers present—strangers to me.
Rensch presented me to the President and I talked briefly with him while
the two other men eyed me coldly. . . .

The two men present, as I eventually learned, were two old friends of
the President, Edwin H. [Edward D.] McKim and John W. Snyder.
McKim is an insurance man in Missouri and Snyder is a former banker who
has been in the government, I believe.[23]

Snyder had more qualifications than mere friendship, however. He had a
good reputation in banking circles, and as a young man had been an officer in
various banks in Arkansas and Missouri. During the worst years of the depression he worked in the Office of the Comptroller of Currency, 1931–1937, and

in the latter year he was appointed manager of the St. Louis Loan Agency—a branch of the Reconstruction Finance Corporation. He returned to Washington in 1940, where he was an assistant to the director of the RFC, and was serving in that job when President Truman called him to the White House.

The appointment of Edward McKim, however, was less rational. Edward D. McKim had been a sergeant serving under Captain Harry Truman in the old Battery D during the war. Afterwards the two had maintained their friendship and had shared many high jinks at veterans' gatherings. When Truman made his tour campaigning for the vice-presidency he had asked his former army buddy and long-time friend McKim to go along with him. Soon after he got into the White House, President Truman appointed McKim to a position called "chief administrative assistant." The appointment was one of several that went sour, and McKim returned to the insurance business.

Eben A. Ayers continued to function as assistant press secretary for the new chief executive, and his diaries describe some of the uncertainty in the White House as President Truman assumed his new responsibilities:

> The situation continues confused. There seem to be all sorts of strange people coming and going. Missourians are most in evidence and there is a feeling of an attempt by the "gang" to move in. . . .
>
> [J. Leonard] Rensch [*sic*] held a press conference this morning in Daniels's office. Daniels introduced him. It was held after the President's press conference. At that time the President announced some of his personal staff—Matthew J. Connelly as his secretary, for one—and said that Rensch will serve as a press and radio "adviser."
>
> . . . Later there were press conferences with Matt Connelly and with Colonel Harry Vaughan, the new aide to the President, at which each gave biographical data about themselves.
>
> Connelly made the best impression.[24]

Reinsch's hopes to become press secretary were never realized, and three days later at a special press conference, President Truman announced that Reinsch had asked to be released so that he could return to his work as a radio station manger in Georgia.

Matthew Connelly, secretary to the president, was an affable young Irishman from Massachusetts, who was tactful and could be close-mouthed when circumstances required. He had been trained both in the Capitol and in federal administrative agencies before Truman selected him as chief of the staff for the Senate War Investigating Committee. During Truman's short term as vice-president, Connelly served as his secretary, and it was not surprising, therefore, that the new president should choose him as his private secretary. It proved to be a fortunate choice. In that position Connelly would not have a lot to do with direct preparation of formal speeches, but he would be privy to many ideas and goals of the president.

Notwithstanding George Allen's contributions to the success of the initial speech, he lacked the rhetorical skills and experience the president needed in a speech writer. President Truman turned, therefore, to Roosevelt's veteran writer, Samuel I. Rosenman.

Samuel Rosenman first met Franklin Roosevelt in 1928 when the latter was running for governor of New York. After he achieved that office, Roosevelt asked Rosenman to become his counsel, and Rosenman acted in that capacity for the next four years. His main job even then consisted of advising Roosevelt on types of messages and in writing manuscripts for speeches. When Roosevelt campaigned successfully for the presidency in 1932, Rosenman organized a "brain trust" of advisers and speech writers. Because Roosevelt earlier had appointed him to the supreme court in the state of New York, Rosenman was not entirely free to act as an official in the federal administration. During the 1936 campaign, President Roosevelt again sought Rosenman's help in communications with the nominating convention and in particular asked him to draft an acceptance speech. Thereafter, Rosenman worked regularly on Roosevelt's major addresses even though he did not have an official post at the White House. Finally, in the fall of 1943, Rosenman was brought into the circle of Roosevelt's official advisers and, largely because of his legal training, given the title, *Special* Counsel to the President. The word *Special* had to be added to his title because Attorney General Francis Biddle argued: "The Attorney General is really the Counsel to the President."

President Roosevelt introduced Rosenman to Truman in 1944 at a White House luncheon where the two candidates had met to discuss the forthcoming campaign. Rosenman did not see Truman again until the latter's inauguration as vice-president in January. The contributions Rosenman made in preparing President Truman's initial address to Congress already have been mentioned, and despite his offer to resign he was persuaded to stay on the job.

Choosing a Press Secretary

Being press secretary to the president of the United States is a demanding job, and the appointment was a critical choice for President Truman. A careless or inept press secretary may send the all-important public image of a president plummeting downhill. The job means always being on call and spending most waking hours at the right hand of the chief executive, ready to offer advice and assistance on any matter that may come up. The press secretary is responsible for explaining to the Washington press corps, and thus to the world, the policies, problems, and actions of any administration. Unofficially, the duties go even further, for to be successful the press secretary must be ready to advise on the most delicate matters and must be privy to some of the president's most guarded secrets and strategies.

President Truman chose his press secretary wisely, although in so doing he again turned to a friend from Missouri. Charles G. Ross had been his classmate when he graduated from Independence High School in 1901; in fact, Ross had stood number one scholastically in that class. As valedictorian Ross was eligible for a small but helpful scholarship offered by the University of Missouri. He entered there in the fall of 1901 and in his next four years gained further academic distinctions. He was elected to Phi Beta Kappa and in his senior year was chosen as one of the ten most outstanding men on the campus. By the time of his graduation he knew he wanted to be a newspaperman. For a short time he worked on the *Columbia Herald;* then in 1906 he landed a job on the *St. Louis Post-Dispatch.* He had a few interruptions to work with other newspapers and served for a short time as a teacher in journalism education at the University of Missouri. While there he decided to write a text for students in news reporting and news editing courses. His book, *The Writing of News,* enjoyed a mildly brisk sale but never made him famous nor brought in much in the way of royalties. Some of his appreciation for the niceties of language can be seen in warnings he offered his students:

Don't think it is necessary to call a child a tot. Don't say a wedding "occurred." Things occur unexpectedly; they don't take place by design.

Don't make the mistake that appeared in this published headline: "Audience of 5,000 see Aeroplane Flight." An audience hears; spectators see.

Don't overwork the word "secure." It is often loosely used where "get," "obtain," "procure," "collect," or some other word would more exactly express the thought.

Don't say "fifty people were present." Use "persons." "People," according to *Webster's Dictionary,* means primarily "the body of persons who compose a community, tribe, nation, or race; an aggregate of individuals forming a whole; a community, a nation"—as "the people of the United States." "Persons" refers to individuals.

Don't call a dog a "canine." "Canine" is an adjective. You wouldn't call a cow a "bovine."

Don't say "an old man 80 years of age." It is sufficient to say that he is "80 years old."

Don't say "completely destroyed." "Destroyed" is sufficient.

Don't call every girl pretty. If a girl is pretty, you are usually justified in telling something more about her.

Don't overwork "very." Through abuse the word has lost much, if not all, of its force. "He's a very good man," as spoken, usually gives the idea that he is only passably good. "He's a good man" is stronger. Be sparing in the use of superlatives.

Don't use dialect to the disparagement of any nationality. Don't use it at all unless you are sure of your ground.

Don't say "one of the most unique." "Unique" expresses an absolute condition; it has no degrees.

Don't use "gentleman" for "man." "Gent" is atrocious.[25]

Newspaper reporting lured Ross away from academia, and in 1916 he resigned his teaching post in favor of another job with the *St. Louis Post-Dispatch*. He served as a Washington correspondent during the Coolidge and Hoover administrations, and then he stayed in Washington through two years of Roosevelt's first term. An extended report on the depression and New Deal measures to combat it won him a Pulitzer prize for distinguished reporting, and in 1934 he returned to St. Louis to become editor of the *Post-Dispatch*.

When Charles Ross heard the news of President Roosevelt's death, his instinctive reactions sent him to his typewriter where he pounded out an essay on "a purely personal impression of Harry S Truman, the Independence, Missouri, boy whom a strange and whimsical fate has made President." In his article, Ross briefly traced Truman's career through Jackson County politics and into the Senate. He recounted the circumstances which led to the vice-presidential nomination, and then offered a short analysis of the Truman character:

> What kind of President will Truman make? The answer is in the lap of the Gods . . . the Republic is in no danger from the accession of Harry Truman to the Presidency. He has shown ability to rise to his responsibilities. He is impeccably honest. He takes advice, but he can be stubborn when he makes up his mind.
>
> He gets along with people. Perhaps he is too amiable; that remains to be seen. But the ability to work out compromises is an invaluable trait in one charged with the day-by-day business of government. Truman has this ability in high degree. . . .
>
> He is a clubbable fellow. He likes to play poker, spin yarns, take an occasional drink. In the Senate, he was popular on both sides of the aisle. He got things done behind the scenes. . . .
>
> Will Truman measure up? A firm answer cannot yet be given. But this can safely be said: Harry Truman has a lot of stuff—more stuff, I think, than he has generally been credited with. He has been called the average American, but he is better than average. He is no nonentity and no Harding. He may not have the makings of a great President, but he certainly has the makings of a good President.[26]

Because of Ross's standing in journalistic circles and also because his article was the most authoritative one yet written about the new president, it was widely reprinted and quoted. The favorable essay may have started President Truman thinking about his old school chum, for he knew, too, that Steve Early, who had been President Roosevelt's press secretary for the past twelve years, had made active plans to leave that job. In the first week of his presidency, Truman invited Ross to Blair House, the president's temporary home, and asked him to become his press secretary. It appears that Ross was not eager to take the proffered assignment, for he asked for time to think it over. He was fifty-nine years old; his salary at the *Post-Dispatch* was $35,000 a year, and despite the higher costs of living in Washington the White House could pay him only $10,000. President Truman persisted, however, because to him Ross was a respected friend with an outstanding professional reputation. That night Ross decided to accept the president's offer and told his wife, "This man needs help."[27]

The following evening Ross returned to Blair House and told the president that he would accept the job. President Truman was delighted, and the two old friends began to reminisce about their school days. In their exuberance they decided to telephone a former teacher back in Independence and tell her that henceforth her two former pupils would be working together in the White House. News of the call spread like wildfire through Independence, and within the hour telephone calls began coming into Washington asking if it were true that Ross had been appointed press secretary. The appointment was not to take effect for another three weeks, and it had been intended to withhold an announcement until that time. The delay would give Ross opportunity to wrap up his work with the newpaper back home. The number of inquiries, however, caused President Truman to call a hasty press conference the next morning and confirm the report which was already out. He and Ross were learning together that anything a president says or does will attract immediate attention.

Not by any means were all of President Truman's personnel problems solved by the appointment of Charles Ross. There would be mistakes, embarrassments, and nagging problems that refused to go away, but the appointment did a geat deal to ensure against a certain clumsiness that many people expected would accompany the new administration. With Ross's knowledge of the nuances of language, President Truman was assured that when he made decisions they would be worded and released to the public in the most favorable ways.

President Truman's Diplomacy Debut

It cannot be stressed too much that in 1945, Americans looked outwardly toward international matters more than inwardly toward domestic politics. Yet foreign policy was the field in which the new president was most untutored and untested. His experience in the Senate had focused on the country's internal war efforts, and his predecessor had not seen fit to acquiant him with the game of international diplomacy as it was being played. It cannot be argued that the transfer of administrations caused an immediate reversal of policy toward the Soviet Union, for there is considerable evidence that President Roosevelt had been edging toward the tougher position some of his advisers advocated. President Truman, because of his inexperience in diplomacy and because he was a person who could accept advice, however, relied at the outset of his administration much more heavily on counselors than did his predecessor. When he was sworn in as president, Truman asked members of Roosevelt's cabinet to stay in office and help him carry on , but within the first week he began making plans for replacements.

On his first full day in office, he met with Secretary of State Edward R. Stettinius and discussed plans for the forthcoming United Nations conference at San Francisco. It is likely that even at this early date President Truman had decided on a change in the position. Most of the newspaper speculation centered around James F. Byrnes. The *New York Times,* on the day it announced Roosevelt's death, carried the headline: "Byrnes May Take Post with Truman."[28] Indeed on that day, President Truman, who found out that Byrnes was at the Shoreham Hotel, had called and asked him to come to the White House. According to President Truman's diaries, Byrnes came to his office on April 13 and April 14, and the two discussed "everything from Teheran to Yalta."[29]

James Byrnes had certain credentials which might lead him to expect a high post in the new administration. He had been an important figure in Washington for several years as Senator, Supreme Court Justice, and more recently as Director of War Mobilization. In this latter position he had been referred to as "Assistant President." He had also attended the crucial Yalta meeting and had kept shorthand notes of what Roosevelt, Churchill, and Stalin had discussed. Additionally, the selection of Harry Truman by the Democratic National Convention in the preceding July had thwarted Byrnes's hopes to become vice-president, and President Truman may have felt a twinge or two of guilt toward the man he had agreed to nominate. Interestingly enough, except for his attendance at Yalta, James Byrnes had little more experience in international diplomacy than did the new chief executive.

Because Byrnes had been a former colleague in the Senate, President Truman knew him far better than he did most other Roosevelt advisers. While President Truman undoubtedly began almost immediately to contemplate new personnel that he would bring in to help in the formulation of foreign policy, he realized, too, that there would be a few Roosevelt intimates on whom he would have to depend heavily, especially in the first few months. One was Admiral William D. Leahy, chief of staff to the president. Leahy had served the former president in a highly confidential role and had participated in most of the wartime conferences held by the Big Three. The crusty admiral quickly won the new president's confidence. President Truman respected him because of his reputation; also, he talked in plain, straightforward language that President Truman understood and appreciated. Leahy was one of the first of Truman's advisers to advocate a tough policy toward the Soviet Union, and he was to grow even more suspicious of Russian intentions before the year 1945 had ended.

No one person did more in 1945 to shape the new president's outlook on the Soviet Union than W. Averell Harriman, scion of a famous and wealthy railroad family. Senator Truman had once castigated the Harrimans along with other railroad magnates who had gained immense fortunes at the expense of the public's welfare, but that unfavorable reference did not prevent him and Averell Harriman from developing a close working relationship in the years ahead.

Harriman had left some of his business enterprises in 1934 in order to become an administrator in an early New Deal program. Later he had served with distinction in several high government posts. He was special envoy for President Roosevelt to Great Britain, and in 1943 he was appointed ambassador to the Soviet Union. A week before President Roosevelt's death, Harriman had requested permission to return to Washington so that he could more fully present his concerns over Russian moves and strategies. Along with that request he cabled his outline of the situation as it appeared to him in Moscow:

> We have recognized for many months that the Soviets have three lines of foreign policy. (1) Overall collaboration with us and the British in a World Security Organization; (2) The creation of a unilateral security ring through domination of their border states; and (3) The penetration of other countries through exploitation of democratic processes on the part of Communist controlled parties with strong Soviet backing to create political atmosphere favorable to Soviet policies.[30]

The news of President Roosevelt's death prompted Joseph Stalin to summon Ambassador Harriman to the Kremlin where the proper condolences were offered. In that meeting, Harriman assured the Russian leader that President Truman would continue to pursue policies and goals agreed upon earlier. Harriman felt privately, however, that differences with Russia were becoming increasingly acute, and was worried lest the Soviets interpret the change in administrations as a retreat from former positions. He left Moscow three days later and returned to Washington to report his fears in person to President Truman.

> I felt that I had to see President Truman as soon as possible in order to give him as accurate a picture as possible of our relations with the Soviet Union. I wanted to be sure that he understood that Stalin was already failing to keep his Yalta commitment. Much to my surprise, when I saw President Truman I found that he had already read all the telegrams between Washington and Moscow and had a clear understanding of the problems we faced. . . . He grasped the importance of the Polish problem and took the opportunity of Molotov's call on him to impress on him bluntly, perhaps too bluntly, the United States' insistence that the Yalta agreement be carried out.[31]

Before his departure from Moscow, Harriman had convinced Marshal Stalin to send his top diplomat, V. M. Molotov, to the San Francisco conference. Molotov would attend the conference, and no doubt the Kremlin saw advantages in having him meet the new American president and make an early evaluation of his character.

The Russian foreign minister arrived in Washington on Sunday, April 22, and the next day President Truman summoned his principal advisers to the White House to discuss Russian relations. At this meeting with the president were: Secretary of State Stettinius, Secretary of War Stimson, Major General John Deane (chief of the U.S. Military Mission in Moscow), Navy Secretary James Forrestal, Admiral Ernest J. King, General George Marshall, Admiral Leahy, and Ambassador Harriman. All, with the exception of Secretary of War Stimson, echoed the call for a hard line in dealing with the Russians. The latter, while favoring firmness, sympathized with the Soviets' desire to establish a ring of friendly, protective states in Eastern Europe. Stimson was doubtful about the wisdom of too "strong" a policy and advised:

> So I . . . told the President that I was very much troubled by it [the Polish problem] . . . I said that in my opinion we ought to be very careful and see whether we couldn't get ironed out on the situation without getting into a head-on collision. . . . I pointed out that I believed in firmness on the minor matters where we have been yielding in the past and have said so frequently, but I said that this [the Polish problem] was too big a question to take chances on.[32]

Harry Truman's nature and training encouraged him to accept simplistic explanations and to plunge ahead. Therefore, he found it easier to side with all those who advocated stern responses to Soviet actions, particularly in the thorny problems in Poland.

This briefing by his advisers provided the backdrop for President Truman's meeting with Russian Foreign Minister Molotov late in the afternoon of April 23. Secretary of State Stettinius, Ambassador Harriman, and Charles Bohlen, who acted as the American interpreter, were the Americans present; Molotov was accompanied by Ambassador Andrei Gromyko, and the Russian interpreter, Pavlov.

President Truman began the conference by using blunt words different from the usual language of diplomacy. He said that failure to agree on the Polish problem might adversely affect postwar collaboration and would be offensive to many Americans. He expressed a determination to carry on the conference in San Francisco despite differences between individual members. When Molotov tried to explain that his government was following what it believed to be correct interpretations of agreements made at Yalta, President Truman cut him off abruptly. He said that the United States wanted cooperation with the Soviet Union but not as a one-way street.[33]

President Truman's statements during this meeting with the Russian diplomats pleased most of his advisers. Admiral Leahy was impressed and declared that henceforth the Russians would know that the United States intended to insist on the right of all people to choose their own form of government. Senator Arthur Vandenberg, to whom Secretary Stettinius narrated the encounter, observed that it was the best news he had heard in months. While from this country President Truman received uniform praise for his statements, there is little doubt that the Kremlin interpreted the episode as marking an end to wartime cooperation and presaging new antagonistic relations.

How would President Roosevelt have met these Russian moves in Eastern Europe if he had lived? No one can answer. The failure of the Russians to carry out the Yalta provision for a genuinely reconstructed Polish government was the most glaring of several Soviet actions which had deeply disturbed Roosevelt and caused him to lose sympathy for the former ally. At any rate, President Truman's briefings and preparation for this first meeting with Russian diplomats came entirely from Roosevelt advisers. The message Truman got from these experienced counselors was unequivocal: the only way to deal with the Russians was to be firm. Inexperienced as he was in the conduct of diplomacy, he had no reason to argue against them. Furthermore, to a man of his blunt, contentious personality the advice reached a sympathetic ear. Actually, his talk to Foreign Minister Molotov did not signify an end to American efforts to reach an accommodation with the Soviets, nor did it announce a radical departure. The policy called "getting tough with the Russians" took time to emerge. In April of 1945, both Americans and Russians shared hopes for the embryonic United Nations as an organization which would help establish collective security. One observer recognized later that before any new policies could be pursued by the new president, persuasion would be needed to change certain fundamental American attitudes:

> "Getting tough with Russia" would also require Americans to depart from certain traditions which had always influenced their diplomacy: non-entanglement in the political affairs of Europe, and fear of a large-scale peacetime military establishment. Under the pressures of the Cold War Americans eventually did give up these assumptions and traditions, but this took time. Even in the unlikely event that in April, 1945, Truman was clear in his own mind on the need to reverse American policy toward the Soviet Union, public opinion would have significantly limited any moves in that direction for some time to come.[34]

7

Persuasion for Change

But at the end, on every point, unanimous agreement was reached. And more important than the agreement of words, I may say we achieved a unity of thought and a way of getting along together.

PRESIDENT FRANKLIN D. ROOSEVELT
Yalta Address, March 1, 1945

You never saw such pig-headed people as are the Russians.

PRESIDENT HARRY S. TRUMAN
Letter from Potsdam to his mother,
July 30, 1945.

THERE can be no question that the policy of cooperation with Russia—a policy nurtured by wartime necessities from 1942 to 1945—was changed under the Truman administration. Lively debates have arisen, however, over questions of why and when President Truman reversed Roosevelt's policy.

Germany's attack on the Soviet Union in 1941 had caught western nations by surprise and had thrust Marshal Joseph Stalin and anti-Bolshevik Winston Churchill into the same camp. In spite of the "Grand Alliance" that came to be forged on the anvil of war, Allied relations often were marred by suspicions rooted in the hostility of former years. In June of 1941, Senator Harry Truman of Missouri seemed to reflect the attitude of numerous Americans when he opined:

> If we see that Germany is winning the war, we ought to help Russia, and if Russia is winning we ought to help Germany and in that way kill as many as possible.[1]

Truman's statement was a common expression which one might expect to be persuasive to the folks back home. He represented a midwestern state where in 1941 isolationism still held great emotional appeal. At the time he had no responsibility except to his constituency, and he could afford to make such an undiplomatic statement. In later years, when he was the nation's leader, the announcement came back to plague him, for it helped Soviet propaganda portray him as an arch betrayer of Roosevelt's programs for peace and international collaboration.

In the early years of the war Russia had borne the brunt of the Nazi onslaught, and the heroic defenses mounted by the Soviets had won the admiration of most Americans. The devastation wrought upon their country led the Soviets to fear that when the war ended, the western Allies would resume their anti-Bolshevik policies. At Yalta, Premier Joseph Stalin expressed this concern and asked for assurances that only friendly governments would be permitted on Russia's immediate borders. Many American and British citizens remained convinced that the Soviet government constituted a menace to world peace and that it was only a question of the war's end before the Kremlin would revert to conquest by encroachment.

Although the Yalta Conference ended with a signed accord covering Poland, the ink was hardly dry before it became clear that Allied understanding was more apparent than real. None of the signatories interpreted the loosely worded agreement in the same way. Churchill began to argue for more western influence; Stalin advocated less. It seems to have been Roosevelt's strategy to operate as a mediator between the British and Russians and to postpone decisions that might disrupt the alliance.

When Truman came into the presidency, he was fond of saying that he had been elected on the Roosevelt platform, and early in his administration he stressed his intention to continue those programs. As time passed, however, he made fewer references to that continuity. There is no record—no graph of the impulses in Roosevelt's mind—to tell us what his assessments of facts and problems in Soviet relations were, but it is clear that Truman, at the outset of his presidency, badly wanted to follow what he thought were ideas and ideals of his predecessor. In response to the deluge of condolences sent to Washington following Roosevelt's death, President Truman assured his countrymen and the nation's allies that there would be no changes in American diplomacy, and he capitalized on universal hopes for peace by giving intensive encouragement to the birth of a new charter in San Francisco for a world of harmony and cooperation.

Like all presidents before him, Truman's attitudes were not entirely self-generated. He had inherited a host of Roosevelt's advisers, and nearly all of them echoed Harriman's call for a harder line when dealing with the Russians. Especially strong persuasion of this sort came from Admiral William D. Leahy, who had a long-standing aversion to the Soviet government. It was the admiral's practice, after summarizing intelligence reports each morning, to report on matters that affected American security. Under this broad umbrella, Leahy became Truman's primary tutor in Russian relations. Leahy by himself, of course, did not persuade Truman to lead the United States through a full 180 degree turn on a course away from Russia, but because of his participation in all of the major wartime conferences and because of Truman's heavy reliance on him, the admiral was in a unique position to influence the new president.

The toughening stance toward Russia was not a change that could be traced to a single event or date. Nor is it likely that the change was part of a carefully planned strategy of the new administration. Rather it was an organic policy that grew on a week-by-week basis as military urgencies lessened and new arrangements had to be made. It is possible, nevertheless, to chronicle certain events that contributed to the rapidly changing diplomatic climate. The advisers, led by Harriman and Leahy, were so persuasive that within a week President Truman was ready to reprimand the Russians. His opportunity to do so came on the occasion of April 23, when he met with Molotov and Gromyko.

It is probable that the first meeting with the Russians was more significant than President Truman realized at the time. Certainly the consequences were important, for there is little doubt that in the aftermath of this stormy session the Kremlin believed that Truman was abandoning the cooperative goals of Roosevelt. The occasion of the interview called for tact and restraint more than threats, but Truman seemed to want the Russians to hear the message he got from his advisers and to hear it phrased in strong language. Given his tendency for forthrightness and occasional overstatement, the tenor of his remarks is understandable. He had been briefed only a few hours before the meeting, and in that briefing he not only had sided with those who called for stern responses but had bared his personal convictions, saying:

> . . . he felt that our agreements with the Soviet Union so far had been a one-way street and that he could not continue; it was now or never. He intended to go on with the plans for San Francisco and if the Russians did not wish to join us they could go to hell.[2]

Another contributing factor to the widening schism between America and Russia was a bureaucratic blunder the inexperienced Truman administration made which resulted in abrupt termination of lend-lease supplies to the Soviets. In America even before the end of the war approached, there had been concern lest the Russians use the huge amounts of food, building materials, and production equipment for political rather than military purposes. President Roosevelt had agreed with congressional leaders who argued for safeguards against such an eventuality. Late in the war Ambassador Harriman in frequent cables urged that Russian requests for aid should be dealt with on the basis of individual requests rather than any long-time commitments, which the Soviets might easily circumvent.

After becoming president, Truman read the Harriman cables carefully and indicated his general agreement with such an intent. Following Germany's surrender on May 9, 1945, the ambassador suggested that it was time to begin curtailing lend-lease shipments to the Russians. Two days later, President Truman enthusiastically accepted Harriman's persuasion and said that it was "right down his alley." Actually, Harriman had placed certain qualifications on his suggestion, specifically, that: 1) lend-lease shipments destined for use against the Japanese be continued as long as Soviet entry into that war was anticipated; 2) supplies be continued if they were needed to finish work already begun on industrial plants; 3) cut off all other lend-lease shipments to the Soviet Union as soon as possible. After listening to the explanations of Undersecretary of State Joseph Grew and Foreign Economic Administrator Leo Crowley, President Truman approved the proposal.

Crowley, who was the administrator charged with implementing the policy, interpreted the directive more literally than either Harriman or Truman had intended. Orders went out that ships containing lend-lease material not specifically intended for use in the Far East should immediately turn around and return to port. Although President Truman soon countermanded this order, he was unable to do so before diplomatic damage was done. Moscow assessed the incident as further evidence of Truman's reversal of earlier American policy.

Adding to the hostility then building between the United States and the Soviet Union were American interpretations of Russian moves in Eastern Europe. The San Francisco conference had hardly opened before Ambassador Harriman flew there to confer with members of the American delegation. He pointed out what he called Russian attempts "to chisel, by bluff, pressure and other unscrupulous methods to get what they wish," and he charged that Moscow was trying to dominate Eastern Europe. This line of talk was reassuring to Senator Arthur Vandenberg, who led the delegation, and to other members who were disturbed over the deteriorating situation in Poland. The delegates were determined to halt what they considered would be further appeasement of the Russians. Such attitudes soon were reflected in public statements, and the Russians were so vigorously denounced that many observers feared the conference was promoting conflict rather than settling difficulties.

Faced with American intransigence on the one hand and continued political resistance within the Slavic nations on the other, Stalin proceeded to turn liberated Europe into a Soviet sphere of influence. The pattern of Soviet policy was clear: using political and ideological identification with local Communist leaders, the Kremlin gradually established a ring of friendly governments in all areas occupied by Soviet troops.

The Potsdam Meetings

Before returning to Moscow, Ambassador Harriman again came to Washington and discussed with Admiral Leahy his latest estimate of Soviet intentions. He volunteered the belief that Stalin would agree to a meeting with Truman and Churchill provided that meeting was not in a territory beyond the control of Soviet troops. Leahy broached the subject of a Big Three meeting to President Truman, and the latter responded enthusiastically. He first sent Harry Hopkins, one of Roosevelt's most trusted envoys and a person who was well received by Russian leaders, to Moscow in order to discuss the questions that seemed to be causing the greatest difficulties and to sound out Marshal Stalin about the proposed meeting. President Truman concurrently dispatched Joseph E. Davies to London to see Churchill and get from him ideas on the same problems. These two missions were the beginning of Truman's preparation for the conference which took place in late July. The Russian-American rift, although frightfully apparent, was still not so wide that all hopes for cooperative agreements could be abandoned.

Hopkins held many long sessions with Stalin between May 26 and June 6, and he reported the substance of these conversations in lengthy cables to the president.[3] Davies returned from his mission to London bringing reports that Churchill, although eager for a Big Three meeting, was increasingly pessimistic about relations with the Soviets. The envoy reported that the British leader was vehement in his criticisms of Russian secret police and other methods being employed by the Soviets in the occupied areas. Churchill told Davies that if American troops were withdrawn from Europe it would be a "terrible thing" and would leave a prostrate Europe at the mercy of the Red Army. At this time Churchill's reputation as a world statesman had been secured, and his arguments were not lost on the new president.

On June 15, President Truman asked Leahy to prepare an agenda which would include a proposed American stand on each question that might arise at Potsdam. Accordingly, Leahy secured agreement from other American military leaders that the highest priority of the United States should be to continue seeking the unconditional surrender of Japan. Consequently, the Joint Chiefs agreed to encourage Russian entry into the Japanese war. Stalin had told Hopkins that he expected Russian forces to attack in that theater by August 8.

The American agenda for the Potsdam meeting was carefully worked out before being approved by President Truman. The outline itself was built around eight major topics: 1) Machinery for peace, 2) Postwar government of Germany, 3) Rhineland industry, 4) Policy toward Italy, 5) Provisional government of Poland, 6) Rumania, Bulgaria, and Hungary, 7) Disposition of captured German ships, and 8) Freedom of navigation in European waters.[4]

The Hopkins visit to Moscow had helped soothe some of the soreness of the Polish problem, and it was expected that postwar Germany would be the biggest single issue facing the conferees. Only three days before his departure, President Truman did as expected and named his friend and former colleague James Byrnes to replace Stettinius as secretary of state. Others among the president's working party accompanying him to the conference were Admiral Leahy, Charles Ross, military and naval aides Brigadier General Harry Vaughan and Captain J. K. Vardaman, Jr., and from the State Department, Benjamin V. Cohen, H. F. Matthews, and Charles E. Bohlen. The White House physician, Captain Alphonse McMahon, also went along.

The party went by train to Newport News, Virginia, where they boarded the cruiser U.S.S. *Augusta* and set off on course to Antwerp. Most Americans at the time knew that a meeting of the Big Three was to take place, but the actual conference site had been kept secret. Even some of President Truman's closest staff were not brought into all of the details of planning, and at least one of them was mildly apprehensive about the possible outcome of such a conference:

> I am not convinced that all of this is a wise thing. It may do no harm, but I cannot help recalling what happened in the case of Woodrow Wilson after World War I. Obviously, the President should go to the conference with Churchill and Stalin—though I hope this will not prove a "babes in the wood" affair. But the President has no experience in these international meetings and discussions, and the other two are tough old hands. Beyond that is the fact that those with the President are almost as inexperienced. His principal adviser will be Secretary of State Byrnes. It is true he was at Yalta with President Roosevelt, but it is doubtful if that experience was sufficient. And he has been in as secretary of state only a few days. They have with them Admiral William D. Leahy, who on the military-naval side is "tops." And there will, of course, be adequate military and naval staffs, so far as any are necessary, as well as others who will join them at the conference. This, however, will undoubtedly be largely a post-war conference, unless there is discussion of Russian participation in the war against Japan.[5]

The meeting at Potsdam did not produce unified strategies of the scope that grew out of earlier conferences in Cairo, Teheran, and Yalta. The Potsdam Conference proved to be significant for Truman and the West in other ways though. First, it marked the end of an era of persuasion that was closely tied to the personalities of the two western leaders. Roosevelt had joined with Churchill and Stalin to create the Big Three, and in this trio he operated as a co-equal. In the West, few persons would deny that the wartime utterances of Roosevelt and Churchill helped tip the psychological scales in favor of the Allies. With Roosevelt's death and Churchill's defeat at the polls while the Potsdam Conference was in session, the tremendous personal persuasions issuing from the respective wartime leaders were ended. Second, Harry Truman at the time had no stature as a world leader except that he represented a nation that was fast becoming accepted as one of the world's two superpowers. Adding to his own lack of experience in diplomacy was the fact that in foreign affairs he was forced to rely almost entirely on holdover advisers from his predecessor or on political friends who were as newly baptized as himself. Third, the strong personal attitudes and convictions Truman carried with him to Potsdam were reinforced by his contacts and exchanges with the Russian representatives. He encountered no discussion nor any person there that would lead him to alter his belief in American supremacy or his concept of Soviet ambitions.

Soviet actions in Eastern Europe led President Truman and the American delegation to believe that the Russians at Potsdam would drive hard bargains—and their expectations proved correct. Stalin insisted that the United States abide by his interpretation of the Yalta agreements and that Truman acknowledge the sphere-of-influence concept, which the Russian leader argued had been accepted earlier by Roosevelt. Under this concept, democratic forms of government in Eastern Europe could be abandoned in favor of the larger cause of Russian-American concord. Though the Allies at Potsdam were unable to settle the dispute over this matter, they did reach agreement on other issues.

In addition to the overriding objective of ending the war against Japan, Truman and his advisers wanted to clear up the remaining problems in Europe so that United States military and economic responsibilities there would be ended as soon as possible. Truman was determined not to repeat the World War I experience on reparations, so he and Byrnes took an unyielding stand against any overall or permanent arrangements. Already the Russians had systematically stripped the German areas they occupied of heavy industry, rolling stock, agricultural implements, and even home furnishings, but they argued that these removals were "war booty" rather than reparations. Byrnes, therefore, proposed that each occupying power take what it wanted from its own zone. The Russian zone included most of the agricultural area of Germany, but the Anglo-American zones contained the bulk of heavy industry. Byrnes agreed to give the Russians a percentage of what could be spared from the Anglo-American zones and to trade certain additional amounts for food shipments from the Soviet zone. Faced with the alternative of getting no reparations at all from the western zones, the Russians reluctantly went along with this bargain.

Russia had long been seeking substantial economic aid, which not only would help rebuild her shattered industry but would carry over into a peacetime economy. American failure to agree to such aid at Potsdam seemed to the Russians to be in line with their interpretation that the western allies were forging a tough new political strategy.

On other issues, Potsdam produced mixed results. In a "package" deal the United States and Britain agreed to set the western border of Poland at the Oder-Neisse line, and the Soviets agreed to accept Italy in the United Nations after a peace treaty could be arranged. The Soviets agreed readily enough to the establishment of a Council of Foreign Ministers which would begin work on peace treaties with the former Axis satellites. Stalin renewed his promise to enter the war against Japan, and a series of smaller matters were referred to the new Council of Foreign Ministers for future consideration.[6]

Themes of Truman's Potsdam Address

Among the legacies that President Truman inherited from his predecessor was the expectation that following a major international conference he would report to the American people. To fulfil this expectation he delivered a radio address on Thursday evening, August 9, 1945.

In the introductory passages of his talk, Truman described the ruined buildings and the bombed cities he had just seen in Germany, and he warned that similar destruction already evident in Japan represented only a fraction of the devastation that would occur in the event of a third world war. Without mentioning them by name, he paid tribute to Roosevelt and Churchill by saying, ''Two of the conferees of Teheran and Yalta were missing by the end of this conference.''[7] Cognizant of adverse reactions already beginning to arise concerning Roosevelt's participation at Yalta, the new president declared that no secret agreement apart from current military arrangements had been concluded at Potsdam. He also stated his recognition that the U.S. Constitution required the Senate to ratify foreign treaties.

When he moved into his main lines of argument, Truman specifically explained that even though many political and economic questions were discussed at Potsdam, there was one paramount military matter, namely, winning the war against Japan. He revealed that the Soviets had agreed to enter the Pacific war before they had been informed of the terrible new weapon, and he predicted:

> The Japs will soon learn other military secrets agreed upon at Berlin. They will learn them first hand—and they will not like them.[8]

Turning from military items to other subjects, President Truman explained that the Big Three had established a Council of Foreign Ministers charged with laying the groundwork for future peace conferences. He reported, too, that there was accord on the admission of Italy to the United Nations.

When he came to the matter of dealing with defeated Germany, Truman explained the agreement that Nazism should be eradicated and that the centralized armament industry, which had made the Nazi war machine possible, would now be broken up. The Allied Control Commission, which was an outgrowth of the conference, was to govern Germany until a more permanent government could be developed.

His explanation of the reparations discussions was likewise specific, and he reported success in moving the Russians away from their earlier insistence on a flat twenty billion dollars. He said that the American and British delegations assented to the provision that Russia get roughly half of the reparations, however, because of the terrible damage suffered by that country.

When he presented his discussion of Poland, Truman said frankly that it had been a difficult issue. He referred to compromises agreed to earlier during the Crimean Conference, but he offered no criticism of those actions. Instead he defended the idea of compromise and the necessity of some of it in every international negotiation. He insisted that the Big Three shared responsibility for helping establish representative government in the liberated nations, and he reported that the three major allies had accepted the idea that establishing fair and representative governments was a joint responsibility.

President Truman next directed his remarks toward the immediate future of Europe by insisting that people there must be fed. In graphic but terse language he asserted that there were hungry people not just in Germany but in countries overrun by the Nazis. European citizens lacked clothes, fuel, tools, shelter, and raw materials. Winter promised them nothing but increased distress, and he warned that victory won at tremendous materiel and human cost would be lost if attention were not paid to this problem.

The final main point in his address dealt with Japan. He said that an earlier warning to surrender had gone unheeded, and he reiterated that now more bombing would occur. He justified use of the atomic bomb because it had been dropped on Hiroshima, "a military target." He asserted that enemy countries had been searching for the atomic secret and had been close to finding it. "We won the race of discovery against the Germans." He said that the bomb had been used against "those who attacked us without warning at Pearl Harbor." He added that he realized the tragic significance of the atomic bomb and insisted that it was too dangerous to "let loose in a lawless world."

In a rather short conclusion, President Truman described the victory in Europe as a victory for democratic government—the type of government that recognized human dignity. He interpreted this dignity not as a vain hope but as a reality and the most creative force present in the world.

Impact of Truman's Potsdam Address

In all theories of communication either modern or ancient, there is the truism that the source of the message is often the most important rhetorical element. In classical rhetoric, which was concerned mainly with speaker-listener relationships, the element was elaborately treated as the *ethos* of the speaker. *Ethos,* loosely translated as the character of the speaker, comes close to embracing all persuasion. Aristotle, the greatest of the rhetoricians in antiquity, summarized the importance of *ethos* by asserting:

> The character [*ethos*] of the speaker is a cause of persuasion when the speech is so uttered as to make him [the speaker] worthy of belief; for as a rule we trust men of probity more, and more quickly, about things in general, while on points outside the realm of exact knowledge, where opinion is divided, we trust them absolutely. . . . It is not true, as some writers on the art maintain, that the probity of the speaker contributes nothing to his persuasiveness; on the contrary, we might almost affirm that his character [*ethos*] is the most potent of all means to persuasion.[9]

Modern rhetorical treatises dealing with forms of communication different from traditional speaker-listener situations continue to recognize the importance of *ethos* but sometimes employ comparable terms such as: *image, source,* or more particularly, *source credibility.*

There were not as many public reactions to President Truman's Potsdam speech as there might have been had his *ethos* been greater at the time. Nor was the address itself in the tradition of Roosevelt or Churchill; no one argued that it was a great speech. There were no hyperboles, alliterative slogans, or striking contexts that might add vividness. It was a report with no attempt to select language to heighten interest. The single simile in the address was a trite one: "Victory in a great war is not something you win once and for all, like victory in a ball game." At times within the speech, however, the speaker's words were very concrete. For example, Truman referred not simply to geographical borders but talked of "the Curzon Line in Poland, east of which there are 3,000,000 Poles who will be returned to Poland."

President Truman as a speaker usually preferred everything short—his speeches, his sentences, and even individual words. In the Potsdam Address, he thought that the several drafts had shortened the message:

> Rewrote it four times and then the Japanese offered to surrender, and it had to be done again. As first written it contained 4500 words and a thousand had to be taken out. It caused me a week of headaches but finally seemed to go over all right over the radio.[10]

As delivered, the address consisted of nearly 5000 words, requiring forty minutes of talking time. The sentences in the address were simple in structure and averaged twenty words in length. This number compares with an estimated average of twenty-six words in most of Churchill's wartime addresses and with an average of twenty-two for the speeches of Franklin Roosevelt, depending on the type of audience.

Throughout the address, Truman's preference for short, common words was clearly evident. The vocabulary of the speech was drawn almost entirely from words of three syllables or less, and those with more than three syllables tended to be well-known terms such as: *eliminated, available, preparation, economic,* and *representative.* When discussing the bomb, Truman likewise phrased his thoughts in short, blunt words, "We shall continue to use it until we completely destroy Japan's power to make war." He reiterated his argument that the bomb would be used "to save American lives."

A careful listener might detect that, throughout his talk, Truman stressed that at Potsdam agreements had been achieved about future hopes rather than on current interpretations and practices. For instance, he said, "There was a fundamental accord and agreement on the *objectives* [italics supplied] ahead of us." Thus Truman tried to meet expectations of an American public that hoped to hear more about friendly cooperation with the Russians. In his report on the Potsdam Conference, President Truman struck out in the same direction of friendly, postwar relations as Roosevelt had expressed in his Yalta address four months earlier. Truman did mention briefly that a difficult problem was developing in Poland, but he repeated his hope that "free and unfettered elections" would be held there as soon as possible.

Although Secretary of State Byrnes as well as Truman himself later stated that they had reason at Potsdam to be pessimistic about future relations with the Soviets, this pessimism was glossed over. For example, Secretary Byrnes later wrote:

> The public at home did not have the clear view of Soviet ambitions that the President and I had got at Potsdam. . . . We had refrained, after Potsdam, from publicly expressing our concern because of our desire to maintain friendly relations with our Russian allies.[11]

There was relatively little public response to the Potsdam address not only because of Truman's lack of persuasive stature at the time, but because the dramatic news of the dropping of the atomic bomb captured most of the headlines. Yet, Truman's talk was a presidential message, and as a result it did not go unnoticed.

The ultimatum to Japan tended to eclipse other ideas. James MacBurney, dean of the School of Speech at Northwestern University and moderator of a nationwide radio discussion program on the subject of "The Potsdam Decisions," gave a clue to the public reaction:

> Last Thursday night President Truman gave his report to the nation on the Potsdam Conference. Before and since that report, we have had momentous news which gives us more insight into this Potsdam Conference. . . . The atomic bomb has been released; Russia has declared war on

Japan; and Japan is now asking for peace. In view of these developments, the military implications of the Conference far overshadow the political and economic decisions affecting the defeated Powers in Europe. The most immediate Potsdam decision, of course, is the ultimatum delivered to Japan to surrender unconditionally or take the consequences.[12]

In Tokyo, the newspapers referred mainly to the speech passages threatening further use of the atomic bomb if Japan did not surrender.[13] In Chicago, Polish-American groups were saddened by the apparent United States acceptance that Poland was not yet to be free.[14] Another newspaper reported a dispatch from Chungking stating that American circles in Asia paid particular attention to the president's statement that the United States would claim permanent overseas military bases, and it was noted that Truman did not bind himself to Pacific bases only or otherwise inhibit American political aims.[15] Truman wrote a memorandum concerning his evaluation of the persuasiveness in his talk:

Well, the speech seems to have made a hit according to all the papers. Shows you never can tell. I thought it was rotten.[16]

If the Potsdam speech is measured not in terms of public response but in terms of how much it revealed of the real international tensions existing at that time, one would have to say that it was not a very accurate expression. Tension was mounting over problems in Poland as well as in Rumania, but Truman's Potsdam speech was consistent with a policy established by his predecessor— the policy of minimizing differences.

It cannot be said that President Truman was unaware of the mounting tension, for in a private memorandum written two months earlier he had charged, "The Russians distribute lies about us."[17] Nevertheless, his Potsdam speech was in keeping with the period of friendly cooperation. His leadership was not so established nor his personal persuasiveness so great as to warrant the bluntness which would become evident the longer he was in office.

Behind Truman's Potsdam Performance

By the time of Potsdam, President Truman had been advised by both Secretary of War Stimson and Secretary of State Byrnes of the development of the atomic bomb. Although the two secretaries differed in tactics, each urged the president to take a tough stance in his bargaining with the Soviets. In Germany, President Truman told Marshal Stalin that America had developed "a new weapon of unusual destructive force," but he made the disclosure in an offhand manner while the participants were standing around waiting for their limousines to arrive. Truman's statement did not evoke much response from Stalin, and explanations of the Russian's failure to react more can only be conjectural. Perhaps he failed to grasp the significance of what he was being told; he may already have received the news from his own sources and he did not want to give any indication that the West might be achieving a military or diplomatic advantage; maybe the translation, done only by the Russian translator because the American interpreter Bohlen did not hear the exchange, was less than accurate. At any rate, Stalin matched Truman's casualness and merely replied that he was glad to hear of it and that he hoped the United States would make good use of it against Japan.

Notwithstanding the fact that discussion of the atomic bomb did not occur in the official sessions at Potsdam, the knowledge that Americans had mastered the engineering difficulties and were about ready to use the new weapon greatly fortified Truman and his advisers. Before he left for Germany, Truman had been told that preparations were well along for the first test explosion. On the eve of his first meeting with the Soviets at Potsdam he confided to some of his associates: "If it explodes as I think it will, I'll certainly have a hammer on those boys."[18]

The day after President Truman and his entourage arrived in Potsdam, the first successful atomic test took place in New Mexico, and the president was informed of the results that evening. The following day, when the plenary session began, he was asked to preside over the conference. That first day the conferees listed the items they wanted placed on the agenda. While this plenary session was taking place, another message detailing more about the test was brought to Truman. As the conference progressed, more messages arrived informing him and the delegation that the test was successful beyond most expectations. Each message seemed to add buoyancy to his confidence, and his demeanor in the sessions reflected that confidence. Stimson observed that the reports provided a "psychological turning point of the conference" and that the president was tremendously "pepped up."[19] Even Churchill was struck by the change in the president's attitude and shared his observation with Stimson:

> [Churchill] told me that he had noticed at the meeting of the Three yesterday that Truman was evidently much fortified by something that had happened and that he stood up to the Russians in a most emphatic and decisive manner, telling them as to certain demands that they absolutely could not have and that the United States was entirely against them. He said, "Now I know what happened to Truman yesterday. I couldn't understand it. When he got to the meeting after having read this report he was a changed man. He told the Russians just where they got on and off and generally bossed the whole meeting." Churchill said he now understood how this pepping up had taken place and that he felt the same way.[20]

Truman and Churchill were tremendously relieved that Stalin did not profess much interest in the bomb nor press them for further details. It should be noted, however, that President Truman did not really tell the Russian leader that an "atomic" or "nuclear" bomb had been developed. Those words were not used; instead Truman offered only the vaguest hint that a "new weapon" had been created. Thus the light of the new weapon, "brighter than a thousand suns," was never fully exposed at Potsdam. Its effects were there, nevertheless; its full impact on diplomacy and power balances had yet to be demonstrated. Knowledge of the successful test did have profound implications, for that information convinced President Truman that he had enough power to talk and act decisively. The knowledge encouraged him to use his characteristics of confidence, bluntness, and assertiveness.

Arguments over the Atomic Bomb Drop

Of all the decisions President Truman made during his nearly eight years in office, none would arouse more debate and continuing reexamination than his approval of the use of atomic bombs against Japan. At the time the bombs were dropped, most Americans were so elated over the end of the war—an end unquestionably hastened by the cataclysmic bombing—that not much public controversy rose to the surface. In the years afterwards, however, vigorous criticisms were mounted over the ethical implications of his decision to employ this terrible new weapon.

At 8:45 on the morning of August 6, 1945, a single American plane carrying one atomic bomb approached the Japanese city of Hiroshima. Within minutes, the project on which American and British scientists had been working so secretly since the beginning of the war exploded over the city of 300,000 people. Only a few minutes later, 80,000 of them were dead and an equal number badly injured. Three days later a second A-bomb was dropped. This time the target was Nagasaki, and the results were similarly devastating. A revolutionary new weapon of destruction had been thrust into modern warfare, and the world could never be complacent again.

The actual destruction wrought by the bomb at Hiroshima was not as extensive as damage done by several earlier fire raids on Tokyo and other cities. Since March of 1945, American bombers had been blasting Tokyo, wreaking very high casualty rates. In the course of these raids nearly sixteen square miles within the Tokyo region were destroyed, and thousands of its citizens were burned to death. Karl T. Compton, president of Massachusetts Institute of Technology and a member of the interim committee that recommended use of the A-bomb, reported that a single fire raid on Tokyo had killed 125,000 people and another raid nearly 100,000.

What made the atomic bomb so different from all other bombings? First, previous campaigns had required thousands of planes, personnel, and a few million tons of bombs. Now a single bomb could achieve what formerly had taken years and had cost many lives and planes. Second, the blast effect of the single bomb surpassed 20,000 tons of the old-fashioned TNT; hence, one of the new bombs (minuscule in comparison with those to be developed in later years) could be expected to completely destroy over ten square miles of a city. Third, radiation effects of the new weapon were at least as frightening and as deadly as the blast itself.

Those government and military leaders who decided to use the bomb considered the goal of ending the war with the least casualties the paramount issue. On the day of the actual event, President Truman was still aboard the *Augusta* en route home, and when first told of the bombing he said to the group of sailors clustered around him in the ship's mess hall, "This is the greatest thing in history." A few minutes later he told the ship's officers that the bomb would bring the war to a speedy end. A formal statement had been prepared by his staff before he had left Washington, and when the Niagara of news bulletins carried ever-enlarging accounts of the drop, Secretary of War Stimson released the statement. It stressed that the new weapon had been developed in order to destroy Japan's power to make war, and it promised more attacks unless Japan accepted the surrender ultimatum issued from Potsdam.

There is considerable evidence that most American leaders were determined to use the bomb *before* the Soviets entered the war in the Far East in order to try to forestall any attempts on the part of the Russians to use a victory over Japan as reason for huge political gains or economic reparations. Accordingly, American and British diplomats at Potsdam sent a message to Generalissimo Chiang Kai-shek asking his concurrence in a warning that could be signed by "all of Japan's principal enemies." Actually, this term included Russia since she was pledged to war with Japan, but technically and legally that country had not yet entered the conflict. When the reply from Chiang came back approving the ultimatum, the warning was duly issued from Potsdam on July 26, and it became known as the Potsdam Declaration. The ultimatum was given out for publication, and a copy of it was sent to V. M. Molotov, the Russian foreign minister. He appeared "disturbed" that the declaration had been released without his knowledge. Secretary of State Byrnes attempted to explain that the declaration had not been presented to him because the Soviet Union was not yet at war with Japan and, therefore, the document might have been embarrassing. Molotov was not satisfied and reiterated that "we should have consulted him."[21]

The discussions and resultant decision to use the bomb have been well chronicled by Secretary Stimson and others. The race had begun nearly a decade earlier in German laboratories where scientists had achieved the original atomic fission. After 1938 the race was joined by American scientists. By 1943, however, economic hardships and manpower requirements forced Germany to concentrate on other aspects of the war, and it became the common objective of Roosevelt and Churchill to be the first to produce an atomic weapon and to use it in war.

President Roosevelt had chosen Secretary of War Stimson to be the president's senior adviser on the military employment of atomic energy, and Stimson continued to serve in that capacity from September of 1941 until June of 1945. Two weeks after President Truman took office, Stimson informed him about the atomic project. At that time an interim committee was appointed to advise the president on questions that would be raised in connection with this new venture. At the beginning of June the interim committee unanimously recommended that the bomb be used without warning against Japan "on a dual target—that is, a military installation or war plant surrounded by or adjacent to houses and other buildings most susceptible to damage."

Secretary Stimson later acknowledged that a separate report from other scientists had been submitted to the panel and had warned against "use of the bomb at all." The authors of this separate memo argued that saving of lives in the Japanese war might be outweighed by the loss of American security in a world where atomic weapons would become accepted means of warfare. The authors of the memo, all knowledgeable and reputable scientists, were nevertheless free of responsibility and had focused their attention on the future. On the other hand, Stimson and his advisers were confronted by the demands of an on-going war and by a war-weary American public. Only he and his close associates had access to all the facts—the plans for invasion of Japan, the estimate of probable casualties, and the number and expected efficiency of American atomic weapons.

Although the war in the Pacific was going well during the summer of 1945, President Truman had been told by General George Marshall, Secretary Stimson, and other close advisers that it might cost a half million American lives to force the enemy's surrender on his home grounds. Consequently, in his public report on the Potsdam Conference President Truman emphasized that the bomb had been used "to shorten the agony of war, in order to save the lives of thousands and thousands of young Americans." At the time, this was an appealing argument to most Americans, especially in view of the Japanese sneak attack on Pearl Harbor and because of their barbaric treatment of prisoners of war. The president also characterized Hiroshima as a military target:

> The world will note that the first atomic bomb was dropped on Hiroshima, a military base. That was because we wished in this first attack to avoid, insofar as possible, the killing of civilians. But that attack is only a warning of things to come. If Japan does not surrender, bombs will have to be dropped on her war industries and, unfortunately, thousands of civilian

lives will be lost. I urge Japanese civilians to leave industrial cities immediately, and save themselves from destruction. I realize the tragic significance of the atomic bomb.[22]

It is true that Hiroshima was the military headquarters for Southern Japan, and it contained several thousand troops at the time of the A-bomb attack. But in reality, the bomb was not aimed only at those troops. To be effective in ending the war, the bomb had to serve as a dramatic demonstration to all Japanese of the hopelessness of continuing their war efforts.

With the special advantage of hindsight, numerous critics later attacked Truman for his role in inaugurating atomic warfare. Although he regretted the need to make such a decision he never agonized over it. He said that the decision to bomb Japan was made at Potsdam during a conference attended by Stimson, Eisenhower, Marshall, Byrnes, Leahy, and "another Naval officer, probably King." President Truman made no attempt to share the responsibility and even assumed more burden for it than the facts may have warranted:

The final decision of where and when to use the atomic bomb was up to me. Let there be no mistake about it. I regarded the bomb as a military weapon and never had any doubt that it should be used. The top military advisers to the President recommended its use, and when I talked to Churchill he unhesitatingly told me that he favored the use of the atomic bomb if it might aid to end the war.[23]

Unquestionably, Truman was sincere in his belief that he alone made the decision to drop the first atomic bomb. Technically, he was correct, and the belief bolstered his self-image of a forthright leader unafraid to do whatever he thought was in the best interests of his country. Many years later he commented that he had "no qualms" about using the atomic bomb and that he had "never lost any sleep over it since."[24]

While there is a large measure of accuracy in the concept that President Truman alone decided to use the bomb, it is also true that he did not have a wide range of alternatives. His senior military advisers concurred in the use of the bomb once it was ready. All of the prestigious government leaders who were privy to plans for development of the bomb expected it to be used if the tests were successful. Moreover, the interim committee and the carefully selected advisory panel on atomic energy told him that they could conceive of no way in which a technical demonstration could be staged to demonstrate the awesome power of the bomb and thus bring an effective end to the war. The test drop in the New Mexico desert could not have remained secret much longer. Had the public learned that a powerful new weapon was in America's arsenal but was being held back by a recalcitrant president, it is doubtful that Truman could have survived the outcry. This is not to argue that President Truman was unduly motivated by political considerations at home; rather it is an assertion that when confronted with consistent and overwhelming advice from all corners, he had little choice to do anything but approve the long planned project. The enterprise started by his predecessor had advanced too far to be halted by a fledgling president just one step short of total success.

Secretary of War Stimson, too, thought there was never any real question that the bomb would be used if the tests indicated probable success. He buttressed the president's arguments by giving a point-by-point rebuttal of the common criticisms that arose over the use of the bomb. He insisted that the entire purpose of the research and engineering efforts had been to produce a military weapon. On no other ground could the wartime expenditure of so much money and time be justified.[25]

Criticism against the decision persisted, however, and Karl T. Compton, a member of the interim committee that unanimously recommended use of the bomb, joined the argument. He wrote an article entitled, "If the Atomic Bomb Had Not Been Used."[26] It was Compton's thesis that the bomb was justified by its result in shortening the war and avoiding larger casualties, both American and Japanese, which would have been caused by prolonged aerial bombardment and invasion of the Japanese homeland. After reading this article, President Truman wrote Compton in December of 1946:

> Your statement in the *Atlantic Monthly* is a fair analysis of the situation except that the final decision had to be made by the President, and was made after a complete survey of the whole situation had been made. The conclusions reached were substantially those set out in your article.
>
> The Japanese were given fair warning, and were offered the terms which they finally accepted, well in advance of the dropping of the bomb. I imagine the bomb caused them to accept the terms.[27]

It required no great persuasion to convince Harry Truman that the atomic bomb should be dropped on Japan. Given Truman's predilection for decisive action, the fact that unquestionably the primary motivation behind the development of the bomb was its wartime application, and Truman's heavy trust in the holdover advisers then close to him, for the president to do other than acquiesce in the action urged on him is almost unthinkable. Moreover, he was absolutely convinced of the truth of his twin arguments that the bomb would save American lives and shorten the war.

In retrospect it is apparent that at least four identifiable currents swept American policy makers during the summer of 1945 toward the use of the atomic bomb. These currents were: 1) to save American lives, 2) to shorten the war, 3) to demonstrate the awesome power of this new weapon, and 4) to forestall Russian expansion in the Far East. The first two reasons were the ones most frequently cited in public discourse, but in the minds of those charged with responsibility the latter two motives were also compelling.

Rising Tensions and Emerging Policy

On his return from Potsdam the new president seemed to view the leaders of the Soviet Union much as Roosevelt had done. They were simply hard, realistic "politicians" with whom "arrangements" could be made through personal diplomacy. When he talked with newspapermen about his meetings with the Russians, Truman spoke of "Old Joe" Stalin with a kind of grudging respect much like that he held for the Pendergast politicians back home in Jackson County. The actions and moves of the Soviets in postwar Europe, however, soon convinced Truman that he was dealing with opponents more aggressive and determined than any he had hitherto encountered. Whenever the Russians moved to expand their control of satellite governments, the Americans and British reacted to try to prevent such consolidation of power.

In the first six months of Truman's presidency, there had been a staggering array of changes on the international scene. The war in Europe ended with Germany's surrender early in May; the former Jackson County judge had gone to Potsdam and acquitted himself well in the company of Churchill and Stalin; the atomic bomb had made its epochal entry; the Japanese war had ended abruptly. In the fall of 1945, President Truman was not accepted as a world spokesman on a par with Roosevelt or Churchill, but he was the leader of one of two superpowers that would dominate the news during forthcoming decades. As far as most Americans knew, he was trying to follow policies and goals developed by the Roosevelt administration, but unmistakably tension was mounting between Russia and the West. Although President Truman had delivered a public report on his conference at Potsdam, he had not yet given what writers and news analysts could call a major foreign policy address. He and his staff had to wait only a short time for a suitable occasion.

As president he received many invitations to speak but declined most of them because he was building his administrative team and was still trying to grasp the limits of his new job. One such invitation had come early in September, asking him to address the powerful National Association of Broadcasters at their annual convention. He asked his secretary to respond "no speech," but he agreed to send a message. Two other invitations, which he found particularly hard to refuse because of his long-standing interest in veterans' affairs, had come in about the same time from the American Legion and from the Veterans of Foreign Wars. He decided that he could not accept both these invitations and that it would indicate partiality if he agreed to only one. Consequently, he turned both down for a while.

One invitation to the president had asked him to speak at Gettysburg, but during his daily staff conference someone pointed out that President Grover Cleveland once had received a similar request. Cleveland refused it "because there had been a speech there before him." Truman laughed and said that would be a good line for him if Cleveland had not already used it.

Navy Day Speech Reveals Hardening Convictions

Out of the many invitations to speak, President Truman and his staff chose Navy Day, October 27, 1945, and New York City for his first comprehensive address on foreign policy. At the time the choice was made, Truman was still relying very much on advice from the "old Missouri gang," and presumably his naval aide, Commodore Jake Vardaman, helped sway him toward Navy Day.

James K. Vardaman, like Harry Truman, had been an artillery officer in World War I. During that war he had attained field rank as an army captain, but later he had switched to the navy and had served in various executive posts with that branch of the service. He had been actively involved in civic and political affairs around St. Louis and called Missouri his home state. During World War II he had risen in the navy to the rank of captain. He was the same age as Harry Truman. The two had become friends while the latter was in the Senate, and Vardaman often had sat at the poker table across from the other Missourian. In May of 1945, President Truman chose him as naval aide and called him Commodore, perhaps in order to help Vardaman compete with that other genial military aide, General Harry Vaughan. Both often accompanied the president on the *Williamsburg* as it cruised the Potomac River. When the three Missourians were aboard, there was assurance of relaxation, usually in the form of cards, a few off-color jokes, and an adequate supply of liquor in case the ship ran aground. President Truman called Vardaman and Vaughan his "chicken gut" boys, referring to the gold braid they wore around their shoulders to identify themselves.

One of the first tasks Vardaman had been given in the Truman administration was to plan details for the travel to Potsdam. He had done his task well although some staff members grumbled that he took the assignment so seriously that the president's most intimate colleagues—those who needed to know his travel plans—were left uninformed. Press Secretary Charles Ross was not told about departure times because Vardaman had stressed the need for absolute secrecy. When newsmen reported details that the president's intimates did not know, there was understandable resentment against Vardaman. The day after Truman and his party left Washington by train for Newport News, Virginia, where they boarded the cruiser U.S.S. *Augusta,* Eben Ayers noted a comment by Connelly:

> Matt Connelly remarked this morning that "censorship" was now off and we, around the offices, might mention the trip. It was a crack at the secrecy maintained by Vardaman.[28]

Vardaman had helped persuade President Truman to chose Navy Day for his foreign policy address, and it was natural, therefore, that the president should ask him to take charge of the physical plans for the event. At the daily staff conference on the morning of Saturday, August 25, Vardaman outlined the physical arrangements that he thought would be most appropriate. The president would travel to New York arriving there early in the morning. He would go first to the navy yard where he would speak for about five minutes; from there he would be driven to Manhattan and north to the Hudson River side where he would go aboard a battleship which would be one of a flotilla anchored in the river. From the ship he would deliver a general address which would be broadcast and carried by loudspeakers to people on the shore. The president seemed ready to give tentative approval to these plans, but he insisted that his main speech should last no longer than twenty minutes.

George Allen, who had helped write the first speech to Congress, was sent as advance man to New York where some of the politicians, particularly Ed Flynn, the Westchester boss, wanted Truman to speak on Columbus Day rather than on Navy Day. The former date offered obvious political advantages, but in a subsequent meeting in the president's office most of his staff opted to stick with October 27. Allen, having in mind President Roosevelt's address from the Bremerton Navy Yard in Washington—an address that was poorly received—expressed opposition to the earlier plan of having the president speak from a ship. Instead Allen argued that Truman should make the address from Central Park, where he said a crowd of 200,000 could be gathered easily. Vardaman questioned that choice but was overruled.

The Navy Day speech was carefully billed as a major policy statement. On the day before the event, Assistant Press Secretary Ayers held a press conference to release details:

> I told them [the reporters] something about the two speeches the President is to deliver tomorrow and I took occasion, purposely, to say of the Central Park speech, the main Navy Day speech, that I think it will be the most important speech the President has made since he came in. That it will deal with the foreign policy of the United States.[29]

The two speeches were not typed in final manuscript form until late in the afternoon of Friday, October 26. The one at the navy yard ran nine minutes, and the one to be given in Central Park was meant to run twenty-five to twenty-eight minutes. Ayers gave advance copies of both speeches to the press at about six o'clock that night. At 10:30 P.M. the presidential party left Washington by train and arrived at Pennsylvania Station in New York at seven o'clock the next morning. They had breakfast with New York political leaders and then left at the head of an automobile caravan through crowd-lined streets across New York and through Brooklyn to the navy yard. There Mrs. Eleanor Roosevelt met them, and they faced several thousand people who had gathered on the flight deck of the carrier. President Truman spoke briefly and named the new ship the U.S.S. *Franklin Roosevelt*. His message was a ceremonial one lauding his predecessor and the naval victories achieved during the recent war. His secretary noted that the president was beginning to show improvement in his speaking:

> At the yard we climbed aboard the new carrier, the Franklin D. Roosevelt, where several thousand people were gathered on the flight deck. Mrs. Roosevelt was there also. The ceremonies of commissioning the ship were followed by the President's brief address which was marked by the best delivery yet of any of his speeches.[30]

After a short lunch at a nearby naval officers' mess, the President led another motorcade to Central Park. There he spoke from a stand erected near the south end of the Sheep Meadow expanse. Estimates of the crowd ranged upwards of five hundred thousand and his address reached millions more because it was carried by all major radio networks.

In short introductory remarks, President Truman acknowledged the reception given him and praised the harbors and ports of New York City. In keeping with the theme of the day, he traced some of the great World War II battles won by the United States fleet: in the European war: North Africa, Sicily, Italy, Normandy, and southern France; in the Japanese theater: Coral Sea, Midway, Guadalcanal, the Solomons, Tarawa, Saipan, Guam, Leyte Gulf, Iwo Jima, and Okinawa. He explained that a process of demobilization had begun but promised that the United States would retain the "greatest naval power on earth." He then listed four reasons why the United States would have to remain militarily strong: 1) to enforce the terms of peace imposed on defeated enemies, 2) to fulfil military obligations accepted under the United Nations organization, 3) to help preserve the territorial integrity and political independence of nations in the Western Hemisphere, and 4) to "provide for the common defense" of the United States in a troubled and uncertain world.

In this address, President Truman stated that the United States sought no territorial expansion and was committed to the eventual return of sovereign rights to all people who had been deprived of them by force. He said that the United States believed that all people who were prepared for self-government should be permitted to choose their own form of government without interference from any foreign source. In his enunciation of twelve points which would be fundamental guides to American diplomacy under his administration, he listed a significant forerunner to what was to be called the Truman Doctrine:

> We shall refuse to recognize any government imposed upon any nation by the force of any foreign power. In some cases it may be impossible to prevent forceful imposition of such a government. But the United States will not recognize any such government.[31]

Further in the speech, the president observed that building a peace would require as much moral stamina as winning the war, and he warned against disillusionment if differences among the victorious nations began to be exaggerated. He insisted that control of the sea approaches and of the skies above them would be absolutely necessary for the protection of America and the peace of the world. As he closed his address, Truman bluntly warned against too much and too rapid demobilization:

> There has been talk about the atomic bomb scrapping all navies, armies, and air forces. For the present, I think that such talk is 100% wrong. Today, control of the seas rests in the fleets of the United States and her allies. . . . The atomic bomb does not alter the basic foreign policy of the United States. . . . The possession in our hands of this new power of destruction we regard as a sacred trust.[32]

Reactions to this speech by Truman were generally more favorable than to any address he had yet given. One reason that he had not delivered a major speech on international problems since his Potsdam report grew from the very pressure of domestic issues. After the war's end in August, the next two months were difficult ones for America's economy. Strikes began to flourish, and old grudges that had been pent up during the war years began to overturn the nation's industrial peace. The administration and Congress had to deal with the strike situation as it arose. President Truman for two months had concentrated on these crucial economic matters and let his secretary of state, James Byrnes, speak on international problems.

The most basic dispute between the United States and Great Britain on the one hand, and Russia on the other, was over the character of the governments in Poland and in the Balkan countries contiguous to the Soviet Union. After the first meeting of the Council of Foreign Ministers in London during September of 1945 Secretary Byrnes reported:

> The chief cause of our difficulties appeared to be our failure to agree on the recognition of Rumania and Bulgaria.[33]

The reception of President Truman's address by the immediate audience assembled in Central Park was very favorable. One observer reported that despite the vastness of the crowd, the speaker held his audience "in rapt attention."[34] The president drew applause when he alluded to the United States as the greatest naval power on earth, when he referred to his earlier proposal for universal military training and to his statement that armed might was necessary to make the freedom of the United States secure. There was prolonged applause again when he pledged freedom for all friendly nations to form governments of their choice without interference. The most enthusiastic and sustained applause came following the enunciation of the sixth point in his speech, namely, the refusal to recognize any government imposed by force.[35]

In the days following the speech, American newspapers reported various reactions, most of which were especially laudatory. The speech seems to have mollified even the *Chicago Tribune,* which usually was highly critical of the Truman administration. On its editorial page the day following the address, the Chicago paper seemed to have been caught by surprise by the message and explained:

> We shall comment in a day or two on the planks of his platform as he stated them. Meanwhile we believe our most useful contribution . . . is to review our diplomacy in the war years.[36]

On Monday, October 29, this same paper interpreted the speech as a notice to the Russian dictator Stalin that "his oppressions in Eastern Europe will not henceforth be condoned by the United States."[37] The *Tribune* continued to report that the speech was widely interpreted as a stiffening of administration attitude toward Russia and was the beginning of a new "tough" foreign stand.

The speech won acclaim from congressional Democrats, including Senator Burton K. Wheeler of Montana, an avowed isolationist who often had criticized the late President Roosevelt's foreign policies. The Republicans seemed to agree that the principles outlined were laudable, but they contended that thus far those principles had not been enforced. Senator Robert A. Taft, Republican of Ohio, said that Truman's statement of principles was "admirable," and he hoped that Truman "could secure the accomplishments of his ideals better in the future than we seem to be able to do in the present."[38] From Albany, New York, Governor Thomas E. Dewey termed it the "greatest speech on foreign policy that had ever been made." Former Secretary of State Cordell Hull called it a "magnificent presentation."

The Navy Day speech also received generally favorable comment in major capitals throughout the world. In London the comment was laudatory, but some editorials were critical of the announcment that the United States would retain the secrets of atomic bomb manufacture. The same principles of cooperation among all the powers, said the *Times of London,* should be applied to the "determination of policy relating to the development of nuclear power."[39] The *London Daily Mail* reported that "American secrecy is likely to lead to mistrust and competition among nations, not trust and collaboration."[40] The speech touched off a British parliamentary debate because of the president's declaration that while the United States was willing to discuss international *control* of the bomb with Britain and Canada, it would not give away any of its manufacturing secrets. Prime Minister Clement Attlee was asked in Parliament to state his government's views on the future of atomic energy and international control in the face of this qualified cooperation.

In Paris it was suggested that the United States might implement its desires to place world riches at the disposal of all by relinquishing sole control of the bomb and of the Panama Canal.[41]

Conflicting reports about the speech came from Moscow indicating its reception there. One report said that Moscow newspapers prominently displayed summaries of the address and that Russians read into it evidence that international relations were entering a less strained period. Another story contained in an Associated Press dispatch from London and printed in the *Chicago Daily Tribune* declared that Moscow Radio had announced, "There can be no lasting peace" if the atomic bomb should influence the foreign policy of the United States. The dispatch continued by stating that this was the first authoritative Soviet comment on President Truman's speech. Cautioning that aggressive nations must be prevented from menacing world peace, radio commentator Anatoli Osipov asserted:

> We hear cynical statements that the atomic bomb should influence the foreign policy of the United States. . . . Obviously you can't have lasting peace with a policy like that.[42]

One American correspondent in Moscow, Brooks Atkinson, wired that the remarks of Truman had come at a good time from the Soviet Union's viewpoint:

> Mr. Truman's reiteration of American principles for the post-war world was most encouraging here. Support for international collaboration has been at its lowest point since the collapse of the Council of Foreign Ministers.[43]

President Truman's Navy Day speech did come closer to revealing the actual tension existing at the time between the United States and Russia than any administration message yet given, but still the denunciation was only implied, and, therefore, not an entirely adequate revelation. Even though a coterie of diplomats may have been aware of the areas of friction between Russia and the United States in October 1945, and even though Russian-American diplomatic relations had been steadily deteriorating, the average American was so elated over the war's end and so concerned with domestic problems that he had little idea as to either the causes or the degree of tension between the two great powers. One sampling of public opinion showed the following response to the question: "Do you think Russia can be trusted to cooperate with us after the war?"[44]

	Yes	No	Undecided
	(%)	(%)	(%)
December 1944	47	35	18
March 1945	55	31	14
June 1945	45	38	17
September 1945	54	30	16

Most American concerns over Soviet policy in other parts of the world had been expressed only in diplomatic councils and conferences not generally known to the public, while leading spokesmen of both major political parties usually had chosen to praise the newly created United Nations Organization rather than dwell on the disquieting relations with Russia. The Navy Day speech, therefore, was a subtle implication rather than an overt revelation of rising tensions.

The wide publicity given the speech by the White House and executive staff both before and after its delivery indicated that the address was considered an important pronouncement. The text was sent to all overseas branches of the Office of War Information, and newsreel cameramen on the spot recorded it for presentation later to millions in motion picture theaters. The event helped usher in a new era of reporting public affairs because it was the first time a presidential address had been televised. Viewers in New York, Philadelphia, and Schenectady were able to see and hear their president.

Those who hailed the speech as an announcement of a strong, new policy of "firmness" were a little premature. Because of its cautious phrasing the talk fell short of revealing the low state of relations with Russia. There was a recognizable change from the tenor of speeches by Roosevelt and even those of Secretary Byrnes, but the change was marked by implication, not outright denunciation. The Navy Day speech brought America a step closer to open ideological warfare, but the time had not yet come for official spokesmen to talk candidly about American-Soviet differences.

8

The Truman Writers

I write the pretty mottoes which you find inside the crackers.

WILLIAM S. GILBERT

GHOSTWRITING of speeches for public figures is not a twentieth-century phenomenon. Isocrates, a doughty Greek of the fourth century B.C. practiced the craft so well that from it he gained a lasting reputation. For more than forty years Isocrates labored preparing messages for those who could afford to pay his heavy fees. He is said to have worked ten years on a particular address—the *Panegyric*, a speech of praise for a Greek state at the time.

From the beginning of the United States, American presidents, too, in varying degrees, have relied on aides, consultants, and writers. A history professor can sometimes add to a graduate candidate's discomfiture by asking the innocent sounding question: "Who wrote Washington's Farewell Address?" At first glance the question sounds like the childish joke: "Who is buried in Grant's tomb?" However, exact authorship of Washington's farewell, particularly the often-quoted passage cautioning the new government to beware of entangling alliances, is far from being clear or undebatable.[1]

The business of being president is too great to permit any one person to have all details readily available in his mind, and the unceasing tasks of office allow no respite when he can retire to his study and go through the labor of preparing a speech—a speech which is liable to have momentous consequences. As a result of these circumstances, modern presidents have turned increasingly to advisers, consultants, and writers who help in the drafting of important messages. But when does speech preparation actually begin? When does a suggestion, which may have been offered orally or in memo form, really become a part of speech preparation? Where is the dividing line between an idea advanced by an aide and the final wording in a public address? The answers to such questions are not always definite and are subject to varying interpretations.

Franklin Roosevelt used ghostwriters extensively and was candid in acknowledging them. Some of his writers, like Robert Sherwood, Archibald MacLeish, Adolph Berle, Jr., Raymond Moley, Tommy Corcoran, Stanley High, Ben Cohen, and Harry Hopkins, helped constitute what he called his Brain Trust. The single writer on whom he depended most for the actual drafting and refining of his public addresses, however, was Samuel Rosenman. Rosenman also served President Truman but did so mainly during the latter's first year in the presidency.

Early Group of Truman Writers

In April of 1945 the new president had to present several important messages almost immediately, and he had no time to assemble his own group of speech writers. As a result, Truman asked Sam Rosenman to help prepare these first speeches but did not put him in charge the same way Roosevelt had done. In the Roosevelt era, there had been two or three main writers for a particular speech; in the early days of the Truman administration there was an extraordinarily large number of friends and political associates—some of whom had few if any writing skills—who swarmed into the White House offering their help.

Among the associates who descended uninvited on the White House was Hugh Fulton, formerly chief counsel on the Truman investigating committee. Truman considered him an excellent lawyer and a first-rate investigator. Fulton arrived at the White House the morning after Truman was sworn in, and he joined George E. Allen and Ed Reynolds, who were already at work on the new president's first speech. Fulton's help apparently was not welcomed:

> Fulton came in and sat in. He announced that he was going to write the speech, so the other boys told me, "We're going to leave."
> I went over to see Truman and I said, "You have a little revolution on your hands."
> He said, "Yes, what's up?"
> I said, "Fulton just announced that he was going to write your speech and the other boys said, "If he's going to write it, we're leaving."
> He said, "Send him in to me. I'll take care of it. Tell the other boys to stay where they are."
> So he brought him into his office and he said, "Hugh, I want you to do something for me. I want you to go back to New York and stay there until I send for you."
> So that was the departure of Hugh Fulton.[2]

Another minor figure who never found a place in the new administration was J. Leonard Reinsch, a radio man who hoped to become Truman's press secretary. Reinsch was from the Cox Broadcasting Company in Georgia and had worked on the technical side of speeches for Roosevelt, dealing with selection of proper microphones, placement, engineering hookups, and similar matters. While Truman was campaigning for the vice-presidency, Matt Connelly made arrangements with Tom Evans, who was a long-time friend of Truman's and who owned a Kansas City radio station, for a studio in which Truman could practice his radio presentations. Evans set aside a studio for that purpose, and Connelly invited Reinsch to sit in on the rehearsals. On several occasions Truman came to the station and recorded the text of his speech; then it was played back, and Connelly and Reinsch made suggestions for improvement.

Three days after President Truman was sworn in, Reinsch called Eben Ayers, assistant press secretary to the president, to say that he wanted to come in and talk about the address the president would deliver to Congress. Early the next morning Reinsch was ensconced in the office formerly used by Grace Tully, Roosevelt's private secretary, and he introduced Ayers to Matt Connelly. Soon after this introduction Reinsch, accompanied by Ayers, walked boldly into the president's office to ask about instructions for the first press conference. When the press conference was held the following day, President Truman announced that Connelly would be his confidential secretary and that Reinsch would "help" with press and radio affairs. That same day Jonathan Daniels, who had been appointed by Roosevelt only three weeks earlier to be secretary in charge of press relations, held his own news conference and introduced Reinsch as President Truman's new "radio adviser." Newspaper reporters asked Daniels if Reinsch would be "Press Secretary," and Daniels replied that although he himself was not appointing the president's secretaries he presumed Reinsch would act in that manner.

Neither Daniels nor Ayers seemed impressed with Reinsch, and Ayers noted:

> Rensch [*sic*] obviously thinks he is to be the press secretary. He impresses me as a light-weight and I am in a state of uncertainty myself. I have no desire to remain here if we are to have a Democratic "Harding administration," as some are hinting. Nor do I wish to be associated with a press secretary who does not know what it is all about.[3]

Reinsch lasted only four days before President Truman held a sudden, special news conference in his office and announced that Georgia Governor Cox, owner of a chain of newspapers and radio stations, had asked to have his former station manager released in order to return and help out with that business. Ayers suspected the reasons for Reinsch's quick departure:

> This bore all the earmarks of Steve Early's [former press secretary to Roosevelt] fine Italian hand. I know Early had formed an opinion of Rensch [*sic*]

and his ability although he had not expressed anything directly to me. However, he stopped me in the lobby recently and asked what he had been hearing about me—evidently something of what I had said as to my doubt about staying. He urged me to "sit tight" and wait.[4]

James F. Byrnes was another friend and associate who wanted to be in on Truman's first speech as president. He did not come to the White House uninvited, but he did come with exaggerated ideas about his role in the new administration. Byrnes only recently had resigned his post as director of war mobilization but had suddenly returned to Washington from his home in Spartanburg, South Carolina. President Truman immediately invited his former Senate colleague to the White House and asked Byrnes to accompany him on the sad journey to Hyde Park. On the train returning to Washington, Byrnes gave the president his observations on the Yalta Conference and his views on upcoming problems in foreign and domestic relations. Most observers at the time expected that Byrnes was in line to become secretary of state, and the expectation proved correct three months later. Byrnes recalled that Truman had said on the trip from Hyde Park that he wanted him to become the secretary as soon as possible, but the two agreed that neither the change nor the announcement should be made until after the San Francisco conference on the United Nations had ended.

There is little doubt that in 1945 James Byrnes felt himself better qualified for the presidency than the man who had defeated him in the vice-presidential struggle. Moreover, Truman's early faith and reliance on Byrnes gave him new encouragement. He tried to make more than a minor contribution to Truman's first address.

> When Truman was sworn in as President, Byrnes came in with a fully prepared speech that Brynes and his boys had written for Truman. I read the thing. Now Byrnes just didn't give this to him as suggestions; he read it to him in his office. After he left, Truman showed me the speech. I said, "Look, we've got ten guys in the Cabinet Room writing your speech, you can't use this. This is Jimmy Byrnes' not Harry Truman's." He threw it in the basket.[5]

A month after Truman's inauguration he was still trying to assemble his own group of speech writers. There was no dearth of persons who wanted a share of this load; the problem was in trying to select trustworthy, capable writers. Even some of his aides grumbled about the confusion in message preparation. On one occasion when he had to make a brief statement on financial matters, Treasury Department officials sent him memoranda containing the gist of the problems and the actions they were prepared to take. He asked that a short speech be drafted on the subject, and those around him in the White House went to work.

Still later someone from the Treasury brought in a draft and while going over this, Daniels [Jonathan Daniels] received a telephone call and left, returning with another draft prepared by someone else. It was not very good and later Daniels commented that the men writing these speeches couldn't make $25.00 a week writing speeches. I said maybe that was the kind of speeches they wanted.[6]

President Truman had asked his secretary, Matt Connelly, to supervise the writing of his initial speech to Congress, and Connelly had called on George Allen and his assistant, Ed Reynolds, to prepare the first draft. They in turn received help from Rosenman; others also volunteered. Considering the hectic pace and disjointed efforts, the end result was very commendable. But that speech was for a ceremonial occasion and did not call for the keen analytical approach nor the shades of meaning so important when the president was to speak on complex matters. More careful judgment would be needed for those addresses. Hence, the veteran Rosenman was the man Truman turned to first as a more permanent writer.

Samuel Irving Rosenman

For more than a dozen years Samuel Rosenman had moved quietly in and out of Washington, never staying long enough for political gossip to get a good start. In 1945, he was a roly-poly, forty-nine-year-old man who stood five foot seven and weighed two hundred pounds. When President Roosevelt died, Rosenman was in London on a special mission, but he had quickly returned and offered his services to President Truman.

Sometimes brusque, Sam Rosenman was known as an aide who "could peg a grammatical solecism or a dubious bit of political policy as unerringly as he could pick a flaw in a law brief." When Rosenman started writing for President Truman, he was bothered by the sheer number of persons who wanted to help. He soon developed a technique for dealing with those who interfered:

We had the same trouble, a lot of people around. It was only until later that I think I convinced the President: "I don't mind these people sitting around making suggestions after the speech is written," I told him, "but spending hours and hours making suggestions about what ought to go in is a prodigal waste of time." I used to try to get rid of some of them in these long sessions who persisted in telling me what ought to go into a speech. I found one very good way of getting rid of them. I'd say, "Now, that sounds fine. I wish you would take this yellow pad and go into the other room and write five paragraphs on it." Well, usually the fellow disappeared; and I wasn't bothered again with him at all. By the time we worked on the Potsdam report speech . . . we were pretty much in the "groove" as Truman would say—Charlie Ross and I. I worked with him alone—and then when they all came around, I didn't pay much attention to what they said. But they'd all come around and make suggestions. As I say, I'd frequently get rid of them then too by asking them to write an insert. It's very easy to make suggestions, but a little more difficult to put it into words.[7]

A meticulous writer himself, Rosenman was not always charitable toward sloppy expression. Charlie Ross, Truman's old friend and press secretary, was one person whose style Rosenman appreciated, but Ross was so hard-pressed in his own job that he seldom had time to help actually draft speeches. He did not serve as a creator, but he always sat in on the review of the final drafts. In those sessions he was a gimlet-eyed editor ready to rule out offending passages or words that might be harmful to the image the administration wanted to establish.

During the first four months in office, the bulk of President Truman's attention had centered on foreign affairs. It was the area in which he had the most to learn, and there had been one crisis after another. He had requested that Rosenman join him at Potsdam, and while they were on the *Augusta* en route home they talked about the need for a message dealing with domestic problems. This shipboard discussion was the genesis of what became known as the "Fair Deal."

Rosenman had served Roosevelt for almost two decades and was thoroughly familiar with the facts and philosophy of the New Deal. He expected that Truman would be more conservative in domestic affairs than his predecessor. There was reason for his expectation because many men who had clustered around the new president did not believe in the New Deal and wanted to get away from it as soon as possible. Fred Vinson, who later became chief justice, Matt Connelly, Jake Vardaman, and other presidential intimates at the time were among those who were only lukewarm toward most New Deal programs. John Snyder, perhaps Truman's closest friend, was convinced that a continuation of Roosevelt's domestic programs would be a disastrous policy for the president as well as for the country. Aboard the *Augusta* Truman discussed with Rosenman some of the social and economic problems that had faced the nation, and he gave his views of the recovery measures enacted by the previous administration. Rosenman was agreeably surprised to learn that far from moving in the direction of "normalcy," Truman wanted a liberal program of action in internal affairs.

As soon as he got back to Washington, Rosenman began preparing a sort of state of the union message on domestic affairs. He consulted with a great many officials and sought from them memoranda summarizing the main problems as they saw them from their respective positions. From this stockpile of response, Rosenman gleaned twenty-one related points and set to work drafting a document. The first draft took considerable time and had many handwritten insertions. When he presented a revised copy to Truman, the president said that he would like to circulate it among the people with whom he worked. Subsequently, there were several meetings in the Cabinet Room where various points of the draft were discussed. John Snyder, Fred Vinson, George Allen, Matt Connelly, and Jake Vardaman, as well as the president and Rosenman, were usually there. Clark Clifford at the time was an assistant naval aide and may have attended some of the meetings. According to Rosenman's recollection, Clifford helped on this message but did not play a major role in its writing nor in the discussions about it. In his *Memoirs* President Truman wrote that most of his aides agreed with the tenets of the proposed document; Rosenman's recall was different:

> "Most of my [Truman's] advisers agreed with the message," is not accurate. I think that the majority disagreed. The statement is accurate when he says that one of those who advised him against it was John Snyder. In fact, that is quite an understatement by the President. Snyder was not only opposed to it, but he became quite emotional about it. I'm sure that at the time the President put an end to the discussion and signed the instrument. John Snyder had tears in his eyes.[8]

The message that resulted from the numerous discussions and revisions was sent to Congress on September 6, 1945. It may seem odd that Truman chose to send such a significant document by messenger rather than present it as a public address. His popularity with the voting public was extremely high, and his quick Friday visit to the Capitol the day after his inauguration had been an overture that many in Congress thought presaged a new equality between the Congress and the Executive.

When he failed to appear in person, some of his former colleagues were miffed enough to remember that Jefferson, too, had felt that as president he ought not go in person to the Congress. One congressman quoted Jefferson and referred to Truman's message as "the speech from the throne." Such criticism was unjustified because the biggest single reason Truman chose not to put the message in the form of a speech was its length. It contained more than 21,000 words, and at his customary speaking rate would have required more than two hours to deliver. The first substantive points in the message concerned dislocations in the national economy caused by the swift end of the war. Cutbacks in war orders already had occurred and most workers had returned to normal work weeks with resultant reductions in pay. Also, many workers were between jobs as industries moved from a military footing toward peacetime production. These dislocations demanded unemployment compensation, an increase in the minimum wage, and extension of selected wartime controls in order to control inflation.

President Truman identified his own goal of full employment with that of

Roosevelt and quoted the former president's "Bill of Economic Rights," which called, among other things, for the right to a remunerative job, a decent home, a good education, and adequate medical care. Truman urged Congress to enact legislation that would provide for the full employment necessary if these rights were to be secured for all citizens. He called for a fair employment practices committee to remove more of the injustices based on race, religion, or color. He challenged Congress to set up new and more effective agencies to deal with labor disputes and to find jobs for veterans. He endorsed the continuation of selective service and announced that he was preparing plans for a comprehensive, long-range, military training program, and for the unification of the armed services.

In closing his message, the president stressed the need to continue shipments abroad in some revised form of the former lend-lease arrangement and in an expansion of the nation's merchant marine. He did not dwell on the nation's earlier unpreparedness for war, but his message ended with the recommendation that Congress enact legislation to acquire and retain supplies of essential raw materials and thereby reduce reliance on foreign sources.

The aggressive tone in this message surprised some persons who thought Truman would be conservative in domestic matters. The communication contained not a single hint that there would be any decrease in presidential power.

The message was not an immediate bombshell because its scope was too broad to be readily grasped. When it did begin to sink in, some New Dealers wondered why so much territory had been covered at once; a few observers and commentators charged it to Truman's inexperience. Predictably, it clearly challenged conservative philosophies, and some diehards scoffed that the message was only Roosevelt's words distilled through the pen of Sam Rosenman. The message was far more than that, however, for it outlined the postwar conversion program and contained a comprehensive statement of the Fair Deal. It reminded the Democratic party, Congress, and the country that there was to be no lapse in the continuity between the new administration and the policies of the old—not only in overseas matters but here at home.

One careful scholar of the period saw the message as heralding a new independence:

> Beyond this, the new President had a very personal stake in his September message: reaffirmation of his own philosophy, his own commitments, his own social outlook; denial of the complacent understandings, the comfortable assertions that now, with "That Man" gone, the White House would be "reasonable," "sound" and "safe." Harry Truman wanted, as he used to say, to separate the "men" from the "boys" among his summertime supporters.[9]

In the preceding April, Truman had become president by chance, but this September message declared that he was going to be an aggressive leader by choice. Undoubtedly, the event marked the end of a honeymoon he had enjoyed with a sympathetic Congress since his inauguration. In the next twelve months he bombarded Congress with special messages, usually detailing the general program sketched in September. There was no order or particular timing; proposals came swiftly in scattershot fashion, but eventually covered the boundaries of social welfare and economic development he had marked out. As a practical politician, he knew he was asking for more than he could hope to get, but he stubbornly insisted that under his administration the nation was not going to return to "normalcy."

As weeks passed into months, some of the irritants in the September message would chafe sections of the public body. The country, like Congress, far from rallying to President Truman's visions of a better future, reacted negatively, and in the elections of 1946 punished his party with its worst congressional defeat in eighteen years. Truman's persuasions were not lost, however, for two years later the September 1945 message formed the core of the successful Democratic party platform.

Sam Rosenman was the primary writer of this September message—a message that became a key document in Truman's presidential career. It was hard for Rosenman, however, to lose the identification he had with Roosevelt. Moreover, Rosenman's meticulous, sometimes discursive, style was better suited to Roosevelt than it was to his successor. Roosevelt enjoyed nuances of language and was ever alert for an appealing word or slogan. He wanted phrases that carried emotional impact; Truman asked only that the speech be as brief as possible and that his statements be accurate. Unlike his predecessor, Truman's part in various revisions of an intended speech was usually slight. When asked which of the two presidents he served gave him the greatest help in preparing speeches, Rosenman replied:

> I think President Roosevelt did. He gave much more help. We knew his style, and the President [Roosevelt] wrote and dictated a great deal more than President Truman.[10]

Loyalty to Roosevelt did not keep Rosenman from praising Truman later when he was asked to compare the two presidents.

> I think there were differences in personality, that were very apparent, between Roosevelt and Truman. . . . President Roosevelt was more equipped towards leadership into new fields than President Truman was. So far as the difference between the way they handled the job, I think they were very similar with one major exception, and that is that President Truman paid much less attention to what his actions were doing towards his chances for re-election than Roosevelt did. President Truman did a great many things that Roosevelt, because he knew the effect it would have, never would have done. For example, seizing the steel works. Seizing the railroads was a different thing, but seizing all the steel plants, which led

... to a fight in the courts, was something that Truman thought was necessary, thought it ought to be done and once he had made up his mind he had no thoughts about the political effect or about his re-election. Roosevelt always was conscious of the fact that it wouldn't be any use for him to be sitting under a tree in Hyde Park if he wanted to continue to do anything about all the pressing problems, that the only place he could do anything about them was in the White House; and he was willing to make many compromises so that he would last to fight another day, as they say. I don't think Truman ever had that in mind.[11]

A good political speech writer must be a selfless person. The passages that may have taken him hours to compose can be ruthlessly discarded in a minute. Someone has said that a ghost writer must be like a Missouri mule and have no pride of ancestry nor hope for posterity. The writer must be willing to let someone else speak his words, and when they are intoned successfully he stands aside to let his chief receive all the plaudits. Usually Rosenman met these requirements well, but he deviated once and commented on his part in the September message:

Personally, I think that the most important thing that I did for President Truman, and perhaps through him for the country itself, was to fight without let-up for that twenty-one point message. Although I believe that it really conformed with the President's general policy, and was wholly consistent with his prior senatorial voting record, it committed him publicly to the philosophy of the Fair Deal or its synonym, the New Deal. Carrying out that message to the extent he did was a great thing for him as well as for the United States.[12]

Rosenman continued as President Truman's chief speech writer until January 1946, when he left Washington to return to New York and enter private law practice. In the approximately six months he served as chief speech writer for Truman, Rosenman had no official assistants. He had begun to call sparingly on the talents of Naval Aide Jake Vardaman's assistant, however. That assistant was Clark Clifford, whom Captain Vardaman had met by sheer accident in San Francisco.

Clark McAdams Clifford

Clark Clifford was a thirty-nine-year-old navy lieutenant in 1945 when Captain Vardaman chose him as an assistant naval aide. When Clifford arrived in Washington to take up his new assignment, he found little outlet for his ambitions and talent. There had never been an assistant naval aide before, and indeed the naval aide himself had little to do. Rosenman soon met Clifford in the course of White House business, and Clifford complained mildly about his inactivity. The overworked Rosenman began giving the personable aide ever larger tasks, and promotions came rapidly for the young officer. Almost immediately he was made a commander, and about six months later he became a captain. In April of 1946, he received a citation for his "superb administrative ability." When Vardaman was appointed to a fourteen-year term on the board of governors of the Federal Reserve System, Clifford succeeded him as naval aide to the president. A few months later in a press conference near the end of June, Truman announced that Clifford henceforth would be Special Counsel to the president; his yearly salary would be $12,000 and he would hold the advisory and speech writing position formerly held by Judge Rosenman.

At this time Clifford was a trim, six-foot-two, gray-eyed, and light-haired officer. Whenever he donned civilian clothes he dressed so well that one newspaper said that he outshone "the clothes conscious President in natty apparel." Many who had known him as a boy and later as a young lawyer were not surprised by his meteoric rise within the president's inner circle. Clark Clifford was born on Christmas Day in 1906 at Fort Scott, Kansas. His mother was a writer and the sister of Clark McAdams, a crusading editor of the *St. Louis Post-Dispatch*. The Clifford family, described by the *New York Sun* as "wealthy and highly regarded," moved to St. Louis, where Clark attended Soldan High School. After receiving his diploma, he went to Washington University, where he joined the Kappa Alpha fraternity and sang with the university glee club. He received his law degree in 1928, and ranked second among 350 applicants to the Missouri Bar.

The young lawyer began his professional career with the firm of Holland, Lashly, and Donnell in St. Louis, and he developed a specialty in corporation and labor cases. By 1938 he was a partner in the firm and also teaching trial psychology part-time at Washington University. Although married and the father of three children, in 1944 Clifford asked for a commission in the naval reserve. He received a rank of lieutenant, junior grade and was assigned to the West Coast in the naval supply offices.

For his services in the navy, Clifford was awarded a commendation ribbon for "outstanding performance of duty as special assistant to the Commander, Western Sea Frontier." More important than the ribbon was a lengthy report he wrote recommending reorganization of the naval supply system. The quality of writing in his report was recognized by Rosenman, who started using Clifford in the drafting of reports which eventually found their way to the president. When Rosenman resigned in January of 1946, he strongly recommended to President Truman that he appoint Clifford as chief writer. This formal action was not taken immediately, however, and for several months while his official title was naval aide to the president, Clifford's chief assignment was to work on speeches and messages. He was chief author of a study of universal military training and helped Rosenman draft the address President Truman gave on that subject to Congress on October 23, 1945. Clifford spearheaded the staff work in preparing for the National Intelligence Authority, which combined the activities of divisions of intelligence in the State, Navy, and War Departments. This authority was the forerunner of the Central Intelligence Agency. Clifford later drafted the bill for unification of the armed forces, which was submitted to Congress in June of 1947.

One event that did much to win Clifford the president's favor came in May of 1946, when the administration was plagued by threatened strikes from both coal miners and railroad workers. At first the railroad unions agreed to postpone the effective date of their strike for two weeks while frantic negotiations led by White House mediators took place. The negotiators were unable to reach agreement, however, and when the two major railroad unions rejected Truman's demands that they call off their intended strike, he signed an executive order for the government to take over the roads.

Angered by the union leaders' refusal to accept the government's directive, President Truman decided to go to Congress in person the next day and ask for the stiffest labor laws in history. He also wanted to take his case to the public, so he scribbled out a speech on tablet paper. The heart of his intended message was a request for authority to draft strikers into the armed services without respect to age or dependency if the strike was judged to be a national emergency. He called a hasty cabinet meeting the next morning to tell cabinet members what he intended to do, and he handed Press Secretary Ross the notes for his radio speech. Ross was so shocked by the vehemence of the intended talk he asked if he and Clifford might redraft it and "tone it down" a little. The president agreed to his request but asked Ross to arrange for a coast-to-coast radio hookup for him that night so that he could explain to the people what was happening.

The original draft that Truman penned for this talk is a rare and remarkable document, for it reveals his basic attitudes and naked passions unadorned by restraints from family or advisers. His intended message praised citizens and soldiers for winning "the greatest war in history," claimed that labor strikes

Truman's draft of a radio talk he gave on the railroad strike in 1945. His writers modified the vehement language in Truman's original draft but left intact the stern intent of the message. From the Papers of Clark M. Clifford, The Harry S. Truman Library.

The President of the United States, under his Constitutional powers has found it necessary to declare a "National Emergency" and to call for Volunteers to support the Constitution of the United States. That Constitution is the greatest document of Government, of, by and for the people ever written.

We have fought the greatest war in the history of the world and that was won by the United States of America. Let no one tell you that any other country won it.

We are a peace loving people and while we like to fight individually, collectively we would much rather have world peace than to have world war. Twice we've shown that when necessary we can win World Wars.

In World War II we furnished the planes, the guns, the ammunition, the ships, the men to bring victory over two of the most despickable nations the world has ever produced — Germany and Japan.

Our young men were drafted for service and they

faced bullets, bombs and disease to win the victory.

At home those of us who had the country's welfare at heart worked day and night. But some people work neither day nor night and some tried to sabotage the war effort entirely! No one knows that better than I. John Lewis called two strikes in <u>War Time</u> to satisfy his ego. Two strikes which were worse than bullets in the back to our soldiers. He held a gun at the head of the government. The Rail Unions did exactly

the same thing. They all
were recieving from four to
forty times what the man
who was ~~being~~ facing the
enemy fire on the front
was recieving. The effete union
leaders reciete from five to
ten times the het salary of
your president.

Now ~~these~~ same union
leaders on V.J. day told your
president that they ~~would~~
cooperate 100% with him to
reconvert to peace time
production. They all lied to
him.

First came the threatened

Automobile strike. Your
President asked for legislation
to cool off and consider the
situation. A yeak kneed Congress didn't have the intestinal
fortitude to pass the bill.

Mr. Murray and his Com-
munist friends, had a con-
niption fit and Congress had
labor jitters. Nothing happened.

Then came the electrical workers
strike, the steel strike the
coal strike and now the rail
tie up. Every single one of
the strikers and their
demigog leaders have been
living in luxury, working

when they pleased and drawing from four to forty times the pay of a fighting soldier.

I am tired of the government's being flouted, vilified and misrepresented. Now I want you men who are my comrades in arms, you men who fought the battles to save the nation just as I did twenty five years ago to come along with me and eliminate the Lewises, the Whitneys the Johnsons, the Communist Bridges and the Russian

Senators and Representatives and really make this a government of by and for the people. I think no more of the Wall Street crowd than I do of Lewis and Whitney.

Let's give the country back to the people. Let's put transportation and production back to work, hang a few traitors and make our own country safe for democracy, tell Russia where to get off and make the United Nations work. Come on boys lets do the job.

were "worse than bullets in the back of our soldiers," condemned strikers "and their demigog [*sic*] leaders," and closed with a rabid appeal:

> Let's give the country back to the people. Let's put transportation and pro-
> duction back to work, hang a few traitors and make our own country safe
> for democracy, tell Russia where to get off and make the United Nations
> work. Come on boys, let's do the job.[13]

It is difficult to imagine what might have occurred had the president of the United States been permitted to give this rabble-rousing speech over national radio. Fortunately for the welfare of the country and for the good of his presidency, Truman's outburst was cooled by his close advisers and a few more hours of consideration on his part. Never in his career was the value of guidance and counsel more dramatically shown. In this case, the administrative system worked.

Immediately after the cabinet adjourned and he had been given Truman's longhand draft, Clifford, with the help of Ross, went to work trying to take the intemperance out of the message. Actually, Clifford rewrote the entire speech, taking out much of the sting and giving it a dignity that had been absent in the original manuscript. Clifford consulted other people, including John Steelman, the president's chief negotiator in this labor impasse, John Snyder, Bill Hassett, and the veteran Rosenman, who came to the White House late that day. The writers worked through the dinner hour trying to get a final draft ready for the president. They succeeded in getting a draft to him about an hour before he was scheduled to go on the air, and while still one of the most emphatic indictments ever uttered by a president, the final version was not the savage attack the president himself had written.

The two speeches President Truman gave on the railroad strike—one over the radio and one to Congress—were successful by nearly every measure. While President Truman was in the middle of his address to Congress, Clifford received a telephone call from John Steelman telling him that the strike was over. Clifford hastily scribbled a note on a scrap of paper: "Mr. President, Agreement signed, strike over." Leslie Biffle, secretary of the Senate, carried the note to President Truman who interrupted his address long enough to say: "Gentlemen, the strike has been settled!" There was a thunderous ovation from the packed chamber, and the remainder of the speech was anticlimactic.

By the time of the 1946 labor crises, a vacuum existed in the Truman administration. Truman's liberalism was still an uncertain quality, and the known liberals around him during that first year were in the minority. With the exception of Fred Vinson, most of the New Deal officialdom departed within the first twelve months: Chester Bowles, Harold Ickes, and Henry Morgenthau. In June the liberal ranks were thinned further when Treasury Secretary Vinson was appointed to head the Supreme Court. Also, Rosenman had left the executive

Truman's special address to Congress on May 24, 1946 urging legislation for industrial peace. Midway through the speech the president received a message—which he immediately read aloud—that the railroad strike had been settled.

branch and with him went the strong liberal orientation he represented. Price regulations, job shortages, smaller pay enevelopes, and ever growing threats of crippling strikes drew the rhetoric of numerous congressmen and worried most of their constituents.

John Steelman, a specialist in labor relations, had become *The Assistant to the President*—a title deliberately awarded to give him a higher status than other assistants. Steelman was put in charge of the delicate labor matters then tormenting the administration. The conservative clique in the White House rotated around him and John Snyder, the old Missouri friend who had been made secretary of the treasury. Steelman's office was in the east wing of the White House and quite distant from the president's working office.

The conservatives were challenged by a more liberal wing of advisers. Clifford's office in the west wing was closer to Truman's Oval Office, and he saw the president more frequently than other assistants. Also because of his unusual persuasiveness, Clifford began to emerge as leader of the liberal group. His allies included Charles S. Murphy (later administrative assistant to the president), Oscar Ewing (director of the Federal Security Agency), Oscar Chapman (undersecretary, later secretary, of the interior), and Leon Keyserling (a member of the Council of Economic Advisers).

Clifford believed in capitalism, but his ideology was hinged on the premise that if free enterprise were to survive, the distribution of the good things in life would have to be more equitable. In contacts with Truman and in his own occasional speeches away from Washington, Clifford hammered away at the disparities: one-third of all American families had incomes of less than $2000 annually; three-fourths earned less than $4000 yearly before taxes; two and one-half million families lacked adequate housing facilities; two million school children were handicapped because of overcrowding and lack of teachers; and one-third of those inducted for military service, between 1940–1945, were disqualified on physical grounds, a total of five million. These alarming statistics gave solid backing to Clifford's repeated assertion that the administration simply could not ''revert to policies which seemed right in McKinley's time.''

Clifford once gave his account of the struggle between the two blocs vying for President Truman's backing in 1946:

> Naturally, we were up against tough competition. Most of the Cabinet and the congressional leaders were urging Mr. Truman to go slow, to veer a little closer to the conservative line. They held the image of Bob Taft before him like a bogeyman . . . it was two forces fighting for the mind of the President. . . . It was completely unpublicized, and I don't think Mr. Truman ever realized it was going on. But it was an unceasing struggle during those two years, and it got to the point where no quarter was asked and none was given.[14]

Clifford's advice and careful writing were tested again during the Henry Wallace fiasco in September of 1946. It happened while Secretary of State Byrnes was in Paris for another meeting of the moribund Council of Foreign Ministers. Relations with Russia had grown steadily worse since the preceding fall. Secretary of Commerce Wallace came to the White House with a speech he planned to deliver in New York City at a rally billed for the purpose of promoting U.S.–Soviet friendship. Wallace told the president about some of the ideas in his speech, and as he talked Truman thumbed through the manuscript. No problems were raised, and the president shifted the conversation to the forthcoming political elections. The president told Wallace that he hoped he would continue trying to garner liberal voting blocs for Democratic candidates on the line in November, and Truman added that he thought

Wallace's speech ought to boost the chances for Herbert Lehman and James Meade, candidates in New York for governor and senator, respectively.

Wallace left the president's office encouraged by what he thought was complete support, and as a result he inserted a new sentence in his speech: "When President Truman read these words, he said that they represented the policy of this administration." The following Saturday night when Wallace spoke in Madison Square Garden, there was considerable clamor and confusion. He was interrupted frequently by applause and occasional booing. The sentences immediately preceding the one in which he stated that he had gained the president's approval read: "In this connection, I want one thing clearly understood. I am neither anti-British nor pro-British—neither anti-Russian nor pro-Russian." At another point in the talk, Wallace asserted that China should remain free from any sphere of influence, and then he ad-libbed: "Mr. Truman read that particular sentence and he approved it." From the references to President Truman within Wallace's address it was not clear whether he was insisting that the president had approved particular sentences or the whole message. Later the secretary contended that in the meeting with Truman the two had gone over the speech page by page.

Taken in its entire context, there is no doubt that Wallace's speech carried severe criticisms of Soviet actions, but it also criticized western powers for failing to recognize Soviet needs and to develop policies suited to Russia's innate suspicions of the capitalist world.

President Truman had fanned the flames further at his press conference two days before the speech was delivered. Most reporters had been given copies of Wallace's planned address, and one of them asked if the line about representing the policy of the administration was accurate. President Truman replied breezily that the statement was correct. The reporter persisted, "My question is, does that apply to that paragraph or to the whole speech?" The president answered, "I approved the whole speech."

The press conference had hardly ended before it was evident that Truman had blundered. The State Department quickly called Ross to ask if such an answer really had been given. The Navy Department was disturbed because it was felt that the statement took the ground out from under Byrnes in his dealings with the Russians in Paris. Indeed, only a few days later the irate secretary of state cabled his chief threatening to resign unless Wallace could be kept from making more criticisms of foreign policy. Senator Arthur Vandenberg, Republican bipartisan leader who had accompanied Byrnes to the Paris meeting, issued an indignant, "I can cooperate with only one Secretary of State at a time."

Two days after the news conference in which President Truman had stated his approval of Wallace's speech, he called newsmen into his office and gave them a written explanation. It had been drafted by Clifford and tried to undo some of the damage:

There has been a natural misunderstanding regarding the answer I made to a question asked at the Press Conference on Thursday. . . . The question was answered extemporaneously and my answer did not convey the thought that I intended it to convey. It was my intention to express the thought that I approved the right of the Secretary of Commerce to deliver the speech. I did not intend to indicate that I approved the speech as constituting a statement of the foreign policy of this country.

There has been no change in the established foreign policy of our Government.[15]

For a week reverberations from the Wallace speech and the president's remarks about it occupied most of Truman's time. Nearly everyone believed that Wallace had marked out a "soft" position opposed to the "tougher" one Byrnes was espousing. Byrnes was not acting unilaterally, however, for in the preceding February he had been mildly chided by Truman when the latter told him "to stiffen up and try for the next three months not to make any compromises."[16]

On September 19, President Truman wrote out a letter in longhand and sent it to Wallace asking for his resignation. The president did this without consulting either Clifford or Ross, who had been set to work drafting a presidential statement on foreign policy, which it was hoped would rectify whatever damage had been wrought. On Friday, September 20, President Truman read the drafted statement on foreign policy to his press and radio conference. It stressed that the government of the United States must stand as a unit with the rest of the world. The statement continued by saying that foreign policy as established by Congress, the president, and the secretary of state was in full force and no changes were contemplated. Truman reiterated his faith in Secretary Byrnes. Then the president read the sentence: "I have today asked Mr. Wallace to resign from the Cabinet." There were audible gasps and a long low whistle from one correspondent. As the conference adjourned, the president turned to Ross and said simply, "Well, the die is cast."

Another major opportunity for Clifford to serve the president came in November 1946 and arose from a strike by the United Mine Workers. In the preceding May, President Truman had signed an executive order seizing the coal mines in order to end a forty-five day work stoppage in the bituminous industry. This action put the mines technically and legally under the control of the secretary of the interior, Julius Krug. The miners were led by the colorful and determined John L. Lewis. Lewis was the son of a miner and had been a miner himself. He had led his union so successfully for thirty years that he had become its undisputed chief. He was a big man of ponderous bearing, overhanging eyebrows, and grave speeches uttered in measured cadences—some of which were said to have been dictated by his wife, who taught literature and Shakespeare. As the date of a threatened coal strike approached, some of Truman's advisers warned him not to risk a showdown with this powerful figure.

In the fall when the crisis deepened, Clifford urged the president to stand up to the labor boss. Late in October, Lewis demanded that contract talks be reopened or else his miners would consider all contracts void—no contract, no work. Lewis's ultimatum was a bold stroke because in effect it challenged the authority of the government. Clifford briefed the legal procedure the administration was to follow. Under his strategy, the first step was for the government to issue an injunction restraining the miners' chief from breaking his union's contract with the government. The injunction affected more than four hundred thousand members of the United Mine Workers. The use of the injunction, which the unions regarded as the most hated maneuver in the antilabor arsenal, so angered the miners that virtually every soft coal mine in the country was immediately shut down. Then began a series of executive moves directed by Clifford. President Truman first instructed the Department of Justice to press contempt action against Lewis for defiance of the antistrike injunction. The contempt action was successfully carried through the U.S. District Court of the District of Columbia, Justice Alan T. Goldsborough presiding, and culminated in a judgment on December 4, 1946, fining the mine workers' boss $10,000 and his union a whopping $3,500,000

Clifford not only had directed the government's case in the courts, but at the same time had prepared nearly all of President Truman's public statements on the matter. The day the judgment against Lewis was announced, Clifford showed David E. Lilienthal, newly named chairman of the Atomic Energy Commission, a paper pad on which he was writing the next speech for the president. The opening line of the address read: "I bring you tonight a report of a major American disaster." The speech was never given, for Lewis called off the strike the day before its scheduled delivery.[17]

The president had won another showdown, and much of the credit had to go to Clifford for his strategy and his adroit handling of details as the matter unfolded. Clifford recalled the circumstances of his advice to the president at the outset of the coal crisis:

> We were split right down the middle on this one. Steelman and some of the others were really afraid that the President would be licked if he locked horns in public with John L. on this issue. The rest of us argued that the President would have to take him on sooner or later, and that the longer it was put off, the worse it would be. Mr. Truman was really in a hell of a quandary at this time. His natural sympathies were on the side of labor, even of the miners, although he had no use for Lewis.[18]

About this time newspapers and magazines began to give increased attention to Clifford. Ayers noted the attention and seemed wounded because his own immediate superior, Press Secretary Ross, was less noticed:

It is interesting to watch how the newspapers and writers trail actual developments, and how little even the reporters who cover the White House from day to day actually know of personalities and of what goes on . Few, for instance, realize the part Ross plays in many things or have any idea of what actually goes on in our office—the press secretary's office. . . . Clifford is, of course, an adviser, and his advice is receiving the President's attention. Perhaps he is the important figure he is being made out to be, but it is interesting to note how long it has taken the newspapermen to discover and to realize how little they still know of what his part is in the day to day events and decisions.[19]

By the time the crisis with coal miners ended, Truman was depending on Clifford for much more than the drafting of speeches and messages. Clifford's judgment was sought on nearly every matter that might have a trace of delicacy or political danger. Department heads and other administrators who came to the Oval Office often departed remembering that the president had told them, "No. I don't need to see it in advance, but it's all right to check it with Clark."

Clifford served as Special Counsel to Truman from 1946 to 1950, and after the coal crisis he was acknowledged as the president's foremost executive adviser. He was in on all of the major decisions and many minor ones taken during these four years. He led the forces within the administration that wanted the president to take a more liberal stand on most of the issues facing the country. He helped steer Truman toward his Taft-Hartley veto, his strong civil rights measures, and other programs in the liberal-progressive tradition. From his influential postion he laid the groundwork for Truman's upset victory at the polls in 1948. He continued to be the chief architect of most of the president's major speeches, although in contrast with his predecessor, Sam Rosenman, Clifford was to become more a planner and organizer of arguments than an actual writer of messages. His administrative talents helped him secure able assistants who could write clearly and who added even more luster to his record.

Clifford came to be so influential that observers of the Truman Presidency were wont to call him the fair-haired Golden Boy. David Lilienthal, who became Clifford's close personal friend, attributed part of his great influence to the fact that he could speak a language Truman understood and appreciated. To Lilienthal, Truman was a man who reacted against the vocabulary of the intellectuals typical of the New Deal—Leon Henderson, Chester Bowles, William O. Douglas. Truman came out of the Midwest at midcentury and represented a twentieth-century version of Populism. He was against big business, Wall Street, and the railroads. He used words and phrases gleaned from Teddy Roosevelt, George Norris, and William Jennings Bryan, and he found it difficult to communicate in the language of the Brain Trusters. Clifford once told Lilienthal that Truman did not like the words "progressive" or "liberal." Truman thought "forward-looking" better expressed his programs and ideas. In this conversation Clifford also recalled that when he first joined Truman's staff they had discussed some earlier liberals.

At that talk the President had said: most of the people Roosevelt had close around him were "crackpots and the lunatic fringe" (Clark emphasized that those were the words Truman used). [Parentheses in the original.] Truman said, "I want to keep my feet on the ground; don't feel comfortable unless I know where I am going. . . . I don't want any experiments; the American people have been through a lot of experiments and they want a rest from experiments.[20]

Late in the fall of 1947 and early into the spring of 1948, President Truman's stock as measured by public opinion polls began to drop. The sag was inevitable because the country was bedeviled by continuing shortages of meat, automobiles, housing, and other needs. The president as usual was the obvious scapegoat. He called a special session of Congress to deal with skyrocketing inflation, and shortly before the session got under way he told his press conference that price controls and rationing were methods used by a "police state." He further said that such methods simply did not fit his concept of a free America. However, when the weak measures advocated by Treasury Secretary Snyder and other conservatives around him failed to improve the worsening economic problems, Truman swallowed his distaste and, with Clifford's constant encouragement, made a fighting speech for both price controls and limited rationing programs.

In attempts to explain the president's sagging popularity more writers began giving their attention to the people around him. A growing number of articles and books began appearing with sharp criticisms of most members of his inner circle. The attacks were whetted, too, by several persons who had been appointed to second echelon positions and were unsuited for their jobs. In part, too, the writers were determined to compare Truman's staff with the brilliant and articulate circle of advisers Roosevelt had assembled. Some critics charged that Truman even drove able and competent men away from him in the early years because he wanted no originality and was insensitive to the ideas of those who served under him. Such charges were not documented, but they found acceptance among those who were not yet convinced that Truman could be a president in his own right. Strangely enough, the more the press criticized most of the staff, the more Clifford seemed to rise in the estimation of the journalists and writers. Perhaps it was his impressive good looks, and most certainly his tact in dealing with the working press helped. He began to be described as the one first-rate adviser surrounded by a group of mediocrities. No one ever charged Clifford with being self-effacing, and unquestionably he had more of the president's confidence than any other single member of the staff.

There is no doubt that Clifford built a staff to do the research and to help him prepare the president's speeches and messages. Clifford had come to the White House with training as a lawyer, and in that field he had learned to be careful with language—the wrong word could lose his case. When it came to writing speeches for the nation's "Number One Voice" he knew that every word would be dissected for overtones and hidden meanings. A word or clause that was too striking or varied too much from the usual formulation might bring verbal rockets from home or abroad. The manuscripts he wrote for Truman were not intended to stir passions; rather, they were planned and drafted in a style that suited a boss who wanted them factual and unadorned. The speeches that Clifford and his staff prepared, therefore, were more in the nature of anticipatory rebuttals for arguments certain to arise. Missing were the eloquent phrases which marked great oratory or the ear-catching slogans which had so often characterized the addresses of Roosevelt: *Nothing to Fear, Rendezvous with Destiny, Arsenal of Democracy, Hand Which Held the Dagger,* or *Quarantine of Aggressor Nations.*

Because of the absence of telling phrases and slogans, Truman's speeches came to be identified only by dates or occasions, not by slogans. Truman's own oral style, which was often distinctive and persuasive, was smothered by tailored speeches overly guarded to make them safe from possible charges of flamboyancy. Journalists had difficulty in coining capsule references, and even an address marking significant changes in policy would have to be referred to simply as the Navy Day Speech, the Greek-Turkish Aid Message, or the Point Four Request.

Perhaps it was the lack of catchy phrases that caused the veteran Rosenman to take a second look at Clifford as a speech writer:

> I think he was a very valuable man in many ways. He was a very hard worker. I think he was a good political adviser; and I think he was a good policy adviser. He did not write well. He was quite a pedestrian writer, and although he was the principal writer after I left, he did not write with facility or with any great inspiration or imagination. However, on the whole he was a great help to President Truman. And I am delighted that I recommended him—for Truman's sake.[21]

Truman was too strong an individual to follow slavishly someone else's suggestions, and he occasionally rejected the counsel Clifford gave. Once during the coal strike Clifford urged a statement which he said might get the president "off the hook," but Truman replied simply that he was "not in favor of doing things simply to get off the hook." Another time when Clifford wanted a blunter statement against Russia, the president turned him down by saying, "I'm not ready to declare war yet." When Truman delivered his speech to Congress on March 12, 1947, asking for aid to Greece and Turkey, the references to Russia were oblique rather than straighforward.

Although he started mainly as a speech writer, Clifford's contributions to President Truman's career went far beyond that. True enough, Clifford was responsible for drafting much of the president's prose on delicate matters, but he also advised the president on what positions he should should take on the most sensitive issues—foreign and domestic. Clifford endorsed and pushed the political strategy that enabled Truman to capture the presidency in 1948. In foreign policy Clifford occasionally might be overshadowed by such towering personalities as George Marshall, Dean Acheson, and James Forrestal, but his insight and analyses were always sought no matter what a prestigious department chief might recommend.

Clifford had Truman's absolute confidence, and he earned this trust by operating as much as possible in strict secrecy within the White House. In mid-1949 he told Truman of his desire to leave government service and return to law practice in order to make more money. In October of that year his salary as Special Counsel was raised from $12,000 to $20,000, but he knew that was a pittance compared with what he could earn in the private sector.

Clifford's departure from the White House staff was mourned by most liberals. After 1950 other issues arose which were beyond the solving of any president or his advisers no matter how talented they might be. The highest points of President Truman's career already had been achieved. In the remaining two years the president would see his public popularity begin to fall toward the low point it reached at the end of his second term. It would be a gross error to imply that President Truman's popularity rose and fell with Clark Clifford, but likewise no explanation of Truman's success in persuasion is complete with acknowledging the role of Clark Clifford.

Clifford spent more time with President Truman than did any other single staff member. He attended nearly every one of the president's daily staff conferences where the day's business was planned and problems parceled out to various persons. Few decisions in the Oval Office between 1947 and 1950 were made without his input. After he left his White House post, Clifford remained on good terms with President Truman, and the latter consulted him often as new crises arose. Democratic presidents who followed Truman, namely, Kennedy, Johnson, and Carter, also saw fit to seek advice from this intimate adviser who served Truman so ably.

Charles S. Murphy

While no other staff member ever attained the influence on Truman that Clifford did, other persons on occasion played important roles in counseling the president and in writing specific speeches. Charles S. Murphy, an exceptionally able administrative assistant who succeeded Clifford as Special Counsel in 1950, was one such person.

Murphy could easily be the forgotten man in the Truman administration. In contrast with the charismatic Clifford, he was a modest, quiet man often overlooked by reporters trying to gather stories about presidential aides. Yet those who worked actively in the Truman administration recognized that Charlie Murphy was the person to see before new ideas or programs were broached to the president.

When Harry Truman was a senator from Missouri, Charles Murphy was working in the office of the legislative counsel in the Senate. The function of that office is to help senators and senate committees with drafts of legislation, with preparation of committee reports, and with various legal questions relating to legislation. Although the two may have met occasionally, it was not until 1938 that Truman first called on Murphy for any assistance. Truman was then chairman of a subcommittee of the Interstate Commerce Committee and asked for aid in drafting a bill dealing with civil aeronautics. A more important service opportunity arose in 1941 when Senator Truman sought Murphy's help in drafting a bill creating the committee to investigate the National Defense Effort.

> The only other piece of legislation I remember particularly, or drafting that I did for him as a Senator was the resolution that created the investigating committee that came to be known as the Truman Committee. I ran into Senator Truman in the lobby just off the Senate floor back of the Vice President's desk one day, and he said, "Murphy, I just made a speech in there on the Senate floor. I want you to get the record tomorrow and read it, then draft a resolution for me of the kind I said I was going to introduce." And that was the resolution that created the Truman Investigating Committee.[22]

In the spring of 1945 not long after Truman became president, his secretary Matt Connelly got in touch with Murphy and talked about a position as administrative assistant to the president. Murphy, having been in the legislative counsel's office for nearly twelve years, was a little restless and eager for a change. He went to the White House early in 1947, and President Truman at first merely told him "to go around and talk to people on the staff." A few days later he got a little handwritten note that read: "Murphy, Take over Rich Keech's files. I want you to look after the Philippines. HST." Actually, there was very little Philippine business to attend to, but Murphy soon found plenty of other matters coming his way. Within a couple of months he was invited to attend the president's daily staff meetings.

Murphy, in cooperation with Clifford, played a leading part in the campaign of 1948. During the early stages of that campaign he remained in Washington, sending material from the capital to writers traveling with Truman. In the decisive final two weeks, he joined the writers and worked directly with others aboard the train.

In February of 1950, Murphy moved from his job as administrative assistant and was sworn in as the president's Special Counsel. The appointment did not create any great stir or indicate that there would be significant changes in the preparation of presidential speeches and messages. As time passed more staff members were added to assist with the construction of messages, and it was not long before Murphy's staff surpassed Clifford's in size. The men Murphy chose to help him had many similarities in their backgrounds. They were usually lawyers or economists rather than professional "writers," and, like Murphy, they were selfless and dedicated to making the administration succeed.

Murphy himself was especially adept at putting on paper the simple words that were Truman's stock in trade; the team jocularly called it "Missouri English." It really meant short, simple sentences, not compound or complex, and the avoidance of long words if shorter ones could be found. In transcript form, the speeches were choppy, sometimes disjointed, but they were typical of Mr. Truman's extempore style. He never learned to read manuscripts well, but they were typed in such a way as to give him many cues and aids. The manuscripts when put in reading form were triple-spaced; pauses were placed at the end of each typed line, not necessarily at the end of sentences, and no page ended in the middle of a sentence or paragraph. These reading devices seemed to help the president somewhat in his pace and intonation patterns.

Murphy never became the close and constant confidential adviser that Clifford did, but after his elevation to the post of Special Counsel the methods used in preparing presidential speeches and messages were greatly modified. Rosenman and Clifford had sought and received assistance, but they approached speechwriting as an individual task, not a departmental project. Murphy assigned and directed writers who worked together in producing a single, finished speech—a true "team" approach that had not developed under either Rosenman or Clifford. Murphy also did more in consulting various department heads during the time a speech was in the drafting stages, and he involved a relatively large number of assistants even after an initial version had been submitted by a designated writer. His staff included George Elsey, David Lloyd, David Bell, Richard Neustadt, and occasional assistance from James Sundquist, Kenneth Hechler, and Stephen Spingarn.

In addition to special messages that had to be prepared as occasions arose, there were three major messages the president was expected to deliver each year. These big three were: the budget message, the state of the union speech, and the economic report. Work on each of these messages began in September when Murphy and his team started seeking recommendations from the Bureau of the Budget, the Council of Economic Advisers, the Department of Commerce, and the Department of Defense. In this connection, Murphy liked to tell a story involving George Marshall about how a final speech might differ from earlier drafts:

> While he [General Marshall] was Secretary of Defense, we were working on some speech of the President's . . . in the field of defense. . . . General Marshall sent a draft . . . over to the White House as a beginning. This

was while Clifford was still at the White House. Well, this draft, as was customary, went through a good many new drafts, finally arrived at the stage where we were sitting down around the Cabinet table with a group which included the President and General Marshall and Clifford. And the discussion proceeded on the basis of this draft that had been revised a good many times in the White House. General Marshall finally reached in his pocket and pulled out a paper, which he referred to from time to time. . . . Finally Clifford said to him, ''General, what is that paper you're reading from over there?''

General Marshall says, ''This is a draft of the message that I sent over here to you last week.''

And I think he was rather hurt that not enough attention had been paid to his draft to recognize it when it was read there.[23]

President Truman's campaign tours in the fall of 1948 were modeled after his successful whistlestop trip through the West earlier that year. His special train—sixteen cars plus the *Ferdinand Magellan,* a lavish suite the railroads had donated to Roosevelt—became a mobile White House containing political headquarters; pressrooms; sleeping accommodations for Truman, his wife, and his daughter; and assorted rooms to take care of twenty staff members and three to four dozen reporters. During most of this campaign, Murphy remained in Washington doing his best to gather materials that could be translated into speeches for the candidate. His most fertile field for material was the research division of the Democratic National Committee, a branch that had been established under Clifford's urging for the express purpose of providing candidates with data and lines of argument to use in the 1948 campaign.

The research division supplied Murphy with information about each city, town, or hamlet at which the train was scheduled to stop. A briefing paper would be prepared detailing civic interests, geography, nature of industries, and any particular matters of local importance. Murphy would winnow through the data and send abbreviated drafts to the working writers aboard the *Magellan.* His job entailed preparing a draft of at least one major speech each day and filling other requests for data that could be used to amplify an earlier speech or remarks.

Most of the time the procedure worked, but the pace was frantic. Sometimes the small White House staff working under Murphy would duplicate the efforts of those aboard the train or being supervised by Clifford and his young assistant, George Elsey. One such occasion came about when two separate groups prepared speeches for Truman to deliver at the National Plowing Contest in Dexter, Iowa. It was one of the most important speeches he made in the entire campaign, and Murphy gave his version of the mix-up:

Well, now, just because it was part of our regular business, we on the White House staff got up and prepared a speech for Dexter, Iowa and unbeknown to us, why, Dave Noyes and Bill Hillman had just come in with a speech for Dexter, Iowa. And so, here's the President with drafts of two speeches and no staff arrangements set up to resolve what to do with them.[24]

On Sunday before he left Washington to start his campaign trip, Truman solved the problem by choosing the draft prepared by Noyes and Hillman—two newer writers he had appointed during the summer to help with the overload that he knew was sure to arise when the campaign got under way.

Murphy's ideas about effective speaking were very similar to the president's. As a writer of presidential speeches he did not want his products to sound too intellectual, and he insisted that it was the president's duty to persuade people, not entertain them. Steelman asserted that Murphy did more actual writing of speeches than did either Clifford or Rosenman. Murphy, like Truman, was careful about grammar and was not impressed by inflated words. He once said that his eighth grade English grammar course was among the most helpful academic courses he ever had.[25]

Murphy continued in his capacity as special counsel until Truman's last day in office, January 20, 1953. Murphy lacked the flair of Clifford, but he expanded the procedure for speech and message preparation. Among the persons he brought into the process of preparing official messages were David Lloyd, David Bell, and Richard Neustadt. He also worked closely with George Elsey, the aggressive assistant to Clark Clifford.

George McKee Elsey

Most observers of the Truman administration refer to George M. Elsey as the *young assistant* to Clark Clifford. That title can be misleading. It is true that Elsey was only twenty-seven years old when Truman came to the presidency, and it is likewise correct that, while Elsey held the titles special assistant to the president (1947–1949) and administrative assistant to the president (1949–1951), he was the principal subordinate on whom Clifford relied. Elsey's role in preparing speeches for President Truman, however, is more significant than the slightly demeaning phrase *young assistant* might suggest.

Thirty-four years junior to Truman, Elsey shared a common interest with Truman—both were students of American history. Once during an informal luncheon aboard the *Williamsburg,* when discussion centered on Civil War operations and generals, Truman told his staff that he would like to have become a history teacher. "Rather teach it than make it?" someone asked. "Yes, I think so," he replied, adding, "It's not nearly so much trouble."[26]

George Elsey was preparing for a career as a college teacher when war broke out. He had graduated from Princeton with a Phi Beta Kappa key in 1939 and was a second-year graduate student in American history at Harvard when the

Japanese attacked Pearl Harbor. Since he held a naval reserve commission, he went on active duty almost immediately. As a junior officer in Naval Intelligence, Elsey was assigned to the White House Map Room and had served there for three years when Truman came into the presidency.

The White House Map Room was an intelligence communications center established the first few days after Pearl Harbor. It was a place where senior officers of the army and navy maintained up-to-the-minute maps and charts of all active theaters of combat. The Map Room was in operation twenty-four hours a day, seven days a week, and was off-limits to all civilian personnel in the White House, except President Roosevelt and Harry Hopkins, his closest friend and adviser. The Map Room was so secret that Vice-President Truman did not first hear of its existence until January 28, 1945. On that date, Roosevelt, who was preparing to leave for Yalta, wrote Truman that any urgent messages should be sent to him through the White House Map Room, but he cautioned his vice-president to make these messages as brief as possible in order not to tie up communications.

The information that the Map Room received from telegrams and dispatches was transcribed onto maps, so that whenever the president or Admiral William D. Leahy, the president's chief of staff, wanted to know what was going on, the data would be instantly available. Officers working in the Map Room also received and decoded messages addressed to the president from outside Washington. As a consequence of their duties the officers became a secretariat for the president's communications with Prime Minister Churchill and Generalissimo Stalin and a few other comparable figures such as Chiang Kai-shek and leaders of the Allied war effort.

In August of 1944, Elsey wrote a lengthy report entitled *Zones of Occupation in Europe*, which was compiled from messages written by Roosevelt, Churchill, the Anglo-American Combined Chiefs of Staff and the United States Joint Chiefs of Staff.[27] Although the plan evolving from these messages angered Roosevelt and he never endorsed it, the plan laid the groundwork for the occupation zones that later came about.

The Map Room staff did more than write policy studies; they occasionally were involved in interpreting executive agreements. Once from Moscow, Ambassador Harriman requested information regarding any promises that might have been made to turn Italian ships over to the Russians. Stalin had told Harriman that at Teheran President Roosevelt allocated one-third of the captured Italian vessels to Russia; hence, Stalin specifically asked for four submarines, eight destroyers, and one cruiser to be delivered no later than February 1944. When Harriman asked Roosevelt about such an agreement, the latter answered vaguely that he thought he might have agreed to give the Russians some ships. The Map Room was astounded because they kept meticulous records of all the Teheran meetings, and they had not heard of such an agreement. Elsey later wrote that the staff was appalled that Roosevelt would agree to give ships to those "untrustworthy Russians," and they hoped that "someone would talk Roosevelt out of the plan." Elsey quoted Leahy as saying, "The Russians are the damnedest double crossers the world had ever seen . . . God, I hate to give destroyers to those dirty crooks."[28]

When Truman came to the presidency, he had no staff familiar with the presidency and with White House procedures, so he found it necessary to assimilate many of the Roosevelt staff members. Then when Clark Clifford came to the White House, first to help Sam Rosenman and later as Special Counsel, he too needed someone intimately familiar with procedures and with White House relations to the Army and Navy Departments and to the State Department. He discovered just such a person in George Elsey.

The first week of the Truman presidency, Admiral Leahy asked Elsey if there were any reports in the Map Room which might be of use to President Truman in learning the background of current diplomatic and military questions. One particular matter that Elsey suggested was in regard to negotiations for the surrender of German forces in Italy—a matter that had upset the Russians, who asserted that the United States and Britain were trying to make a secret agreement with the Germans that would allow the Allies to advance freely into Germany. Elsey wrote a seven-page report for President Truman that summarized British attempts to arrange a meeting with General Karl Wolff, the top German officer in Italy. In his report, Elsey disclosed that although no meeting with the German general had ever materialized and the matter had been closed, the Russians remained very "sensitive and suspicious" of Anglo-American contact with the Germans.

Elsey had a part in helping prepare Truman for the Potsdam Conference. He first combed the White House files for background material on subjects which he expected the president would want to discuss in Germany. Then he wrote more than fourteen short two- or three-page papers summarizing the topics that might arise.

Elsey was among those who went to Potsdam, and there he was kept busy handling the messages that flowed from the military in the Far East and from the civilian staff back at the White House. He also handled the sensitive messages that reported to Truman on the successful atom bomb test at Alamogordo, New Mexico. Stimson's staff had studied cities in Japan and had recommended Hiroshima, Kokura, Niigata, and Nagasaki as possible targets. Elsey remembered that Truman had said that the target "must be a military base," and that he hoped that "no more than one drop would be required."

> It was through us that the President gave the authorization back to the War Department to drop the first bomb, the one on Hiroshima. I recall vividly because he wrote it out in longhand and handed it to me for transmission, that he gave authority for the first bomb to be dropped, at

the discretion of the military commanders on the scene. . . . But in no circumstances did he want the bomb to be dropped until *after* he had left Potsdam. He wanted to be away from the Russians and on his way home before the actual dropping of the first bomb.[29]

In accordance with the president's instructions, the bomb was dropped at the discretion of military commanders a couple of days after Truman and his staff had left Potsdam and were aboard the *Augusta* en route home.

One of the most significant reports Elsey wrote was a one-hundred-thousand-word study entitled, *American Relations with the Soviet Union*. The impetus for this report came from President Truman when he talked with Clifford in July of 1946 and said that the Russians could not be trusted to keep agreements. The president wanted a list of agreements that the Russians had violated, and Clifford in consequence asked Elsey if such a list could be collected. Elsey replied that such a list could be assembled but he thought a list by itself would be too narrow to be helpful. What was needed was a more comprehensive document on the totality of American–Soviet relations. He thought such a document would prove valuable to individuals high in the executive branch of government, and if classified and used judiciously might prevent the kind of trouble the president was having over the public remarks of Commerce Secretary Henry Wallace.

Elsey persuaded Clifford of the importance of his project, and Clifford gave him the go-ahead for it. He spent the last of July, all of August, and the first part of September in writing his report and going over various drafts of it with Clifford. When it was handed to the president in September, Truman felt the document was too explosive to be distributed or even given to members of his cabinet. Accordingly, he asked that all copies be turned in to him, although he permitted Clifford to keep one and he also gave a copy to Leahy.

In later years Elsey stated that he thought the biggest value of his report was that it drew together facts, data, opinions, and materials that hitherto had been available to the president only in piecemeal fashion. The actual writing had begun on July 12, when he made a penciled memorandum summarizing informal remarks President Truman made while talking to Clifford and Ross:

> [Elsey's penciled notes to himself]
>
> Circumstances—
> > CMC [Clifford] in office 4:00
> > Latta [Maurice Latta, Executive Clerk], Matt [Connelly], CGR [Ross]
> > > together with a drink
> > HST began to talk with CMC
> > Latta away, other 2 sat & listened
> > After awhile, CMC began notes, which are attached
> HST—Now is time to take stand on Russia
> > —tired of being pushed around

—here a little, there a little, they are chiseling from us

—Paris conference will bust up—be a failure if Russians want too much because we are not going to back down

—If it is a failure, HST will go on air to entire world—present facts to world

HST just rambled on, talking & "thinking aloud."[30]

From this rough start, the report became an all-consuming eight-week project for Elsey, With Clifford's knowledge and approval, he drafted letters that were sent in the name of the Special Counsel to Leahy, the secretaries of the Departments of Army, Navy, and State, and to certain key ambassadors requesting top secret data on the texts of agreements with the Soviets, commentaries on the manner in which agreements had been carried out, estimates of current Soviet policy with respect to reparations, and recommendations for future policies the United States should follow in regard to reparations. Although the report was prepared under Clifford's general supervision and approval, there is little doubt that Elsey was its primary author. He sometimes chafed that his superior was not paying enough attention to the work in progress:

> I prepared drafts of 6 letters for CMC's consideration.
>
> He told President, in response to President's query, that he *was* doing something on it. (Slight exaggeration) [parentheses in the original.] President then told him to get added dope.
>
> I have kept prodding him this afternoon, & he promised to sit down tomorrow & get into the matter of my drafts.
>
> So far he has done nothing.[31]

When the report was finished and presented to President Truman on September 24, 1946, Clifford's memo of transmittal made no mention of Elsey's role in initiating and drafting the document. It is almost certain that Truman knew of Elsey's involvement, but at the time he may not have realized the extent to which Clifford's assistant had prepared and shaped a product which was to have such profound consequences. The report represented the first attempt to articulate a policy line toward the Soviet Union at a time when the cooperative wartime alliance was falling apart and the United States was searching for a new foreign policy. New York columnist Arthur Krock later asserted that not only did the "Russian Report" supply Truman with the details of American-Soviet relations, but it also charted the course for the future. Krock credited the report for outlining the philosophies that led to such programs as the Truman Doctrine, the Marshall Plan, and the North Atlantic Treaty Organization.[32]

Elsey denied that he or other members of the White House staff had any function in policy formulation or direction, but his denial is less than convincing. He insisted that Clifford, Murphy, Steelman, and all others gave only private advice to the president, who then made his own decisions. While Elsey may have been correct in an abstract sense, it is unrealistic to believe that trusted advisers who select and control the data flow to the president can be overlooked in the course of subsequent events. Moreover, many instances demonstrate that a subordinate's recommendation modified or reversed the chief executive's intended course. For example, after Truman won the election of 1948, he told Clifford to start work on the state of the union message and that it should concentrate on foreign affairs. The inaugural address, coming at nearly the same time, could be devoted to domestic issues. While Truman and many of his staff, including Clifford, went to Key West for a vacation, Elsey remained in Washington starting work on drafts for the two speeches. The more Elsey thought about the occasions, the more convinced he became that the president's order of subjects should be reversed. Elsey phoned Clifford and wrote him long memos arguing that the inaugural was a unique occasion and would be followed by people throughout the world. It would be the one and only time in his life that Harry Truman would be inaugurated as president. That address should be aimed beyond Congress and the American people; it should be tailored toward world problems. Elsey knew that it was never easy to change President Truman's mind once it was made up, but he kept after Clifford and finally the two won out. Truman agreed to the reversal and sent back word through Clifford to write the inaugural so that it, not the state of the union address, would concentrate on world matters.

A more concrete instance of how an adviser can shape eventual policy occurred in December of 1948, when Elsey was approached by Benjamin Hardy, a man who worked in the office of public affairs in the State Department. Hardy came to Elsey to show him a paper he had written on the importance of providing technical assistance to developing countries. Hardy argued that the Marshall Plan was proving successful in Europe but there was nothing comparable to the Marshall Plan that was appropriate to the newly emerging nations of Asia and Africa and to the poorer countries of South America. Elsey, who at the time was groping for a specific program to build into the president's inaugural address, enthusiastically seized Hardy's ideas. Over the objections of some high-ranking members of the State Department who argued that not enough research had yet gone into the proposal, Elsey incorporated the gist of Hardy's paper, and it became known as President Truman's Point Four Program.[33]

As President Truman's programs became successful, several advisers began receiving credit for writing speeches in which he set forth his proposals. Actually, the process of writing speeches for him, particularly before the advent of Murphy as Special Counsel in 1950, was not orderly enough to assign credit to any one individual. There simply was no specific chronology of assignments. Sometimes Elsey would have full responsibility from the very first word of an address; at other times he would not get involved until the second, third, or even fourth draft of a message developed by someone else.

One of the most important speeches President Truman gave during his seven and a half years in office was his address of March 12, 1947, asking for aid to Greece and Turkey. Because it lacked any eloquent phrases or slogans, the address became known as the Truman Doctrine speech although that word "doctrine" was not in the message itself. It is hard to overestimate the significance of this particular address, for it marked the end of American isolationism and set a pattern in the cold war from which retreat would be difficult. The first drafts came from the State Department, but writers there had included so much background data and statistics that Truman commented that the whole thing sounded like an "investment prospectus." He turned that version over to his own writers and asked them to go to work on it. Elsey and Clifford worked together on the message, and the final wording was largely their product. One excellent account of the background and significance of this speech can be found in Joseph M. Jones's, *The Fifteen Weeks*. Elsey, however, was critical of the writing by Jones and his colleagues:

> Now I know Joe [Joseph M.] Jones who then was of the State Department, wrote a book later mostly for which he patted himself on the back for the great speech he had written, and for his fine style that he thought the White House staff had messed up. But look at his beautiful prose. Here's a sentence:
> "It is essential to our security that we assist free peoples to work out their own destiny in their own way and our help must be primarily in the form of that economic and financial aid which is essential to economic stability and orderly political processes."
> Now, I submit, is that the kind of a sentence that President Truman could have delivered effectively, and with force, to the Congress? No, it simply is not his style; it's not a good sentence for anybody, not even a Dean Acheson could have done well with a sentence like that.[34]

The circumlocution Elsey objected to was recast into three separate points that became the heart of the Truman Doctrine speech:

> I believe that it must be the policy of the United States to support free peoples who are resisting attempted subjugation by armed minorities or by outside pressures.
> I believe that we must assist free peoples to work out their own destinies in their own way.
> I believe that our help should be primarily through economic and financial aid which is essential to economic stability and orderly political processes.[35]

The prefatory "I believe" did not appear in any State Department drafts, and Elsey inserted it because he thought it would have more impact and meaning if it introduced in succession the three key sentences. Also, the first person pronoun was consistent with Truman's short, somewhat choppy, oral pattern.

Elsey spent much time and effort on this address as well as on other Truman messages in trying to cut out unnecessary words, in reducing complex sentences to simple ones, and in changing words that were too long, too complicated, or sounded too sophisticated. He found not only that the State Department wrote in swollen phrases and sentences but that material from the military was equally bad because of its jargon. He considered the economists worst of all because they liked to use only technical language. His files soon came to be filled with manuscripts that he had chopped and edited—often to the anguish of the original writer—until he thought they would suit Truman's Missouri habits. He defended his actions and said that most of what he cut out would have sounded false coming from Harry Truman. Elsey insisted that neither he nor others ever tried to polish a speech for President Truman: instead, he said, the efforts were to "depolish" it by removing flowery language that was not in keeping with Truman's everyday oral patterns. He knew, too, that Truman was not one to throw in any Latin, French, or other foreign words. The president always had the final word on what went into a speech or message, and sometimes even in late drafts which he read aloud Truman would catch words he did not like or would decide to say something a little differently.

There is no doubt that under the influence of Elsey and Clifford, President Truman's speeches—although clear and concise—suffered from lack of imagination and subtlety in wording. Inevitably, Truman's own style and what it revealed about him as a person was submerged by the caution exercised by his chief writers. The pattern became increasingly evident as his style receded and was replaced by compositions carefully drafted but ungarnished by his individualistic verbal flavor. There was little that was put into his prepared talks that would attract listeners or readers; Truman and his writers relied on the importance of the subject itself to gain and hold attention. The speeches were devoid of humor or clever phrasing. Although Truman appreciated humor in small informal groups, he was so inept at reading aloud that he could never have read prepared humor in a way that would permit it to sound spontaneous. Anyone reading Truman's addresses will find very little humor in them, but on many occasions, particularly while campaigning, he would get off an unplanned wisecrack or reference that would set his listeners howling.

Once the psychologist and pollster, Hadley Cantril, visited Elsey while the latter was working on a nonsensitive speech. Cantril had been one of Elsey's teachers at Princeton and from time to time had written offering suggestions on how to improve the president's speeches. Elsey invited Cantril to join him and two other writers, and the four of them worked nearly all one night redrafting the talk Truman was to give. Elsey later said that he was disappointed that Cantril's ideas were phrased in psychological jargon and were too esoteric to be of

*Truman delivering his message to Congress calling
for aid to Greece and Turkey, March 12, 1947. The
points in the speech formed the basis for what
became known as the Truman Doctrine.*

much help when it came to the hard realities of drafting a message the president could speak.

On another occasion after Elsey left the White House staff, he was asked what kind of rhetorical proofs, that is, rational or emotional, he used in preparing addresses. In reply he denied having sufficient grasp of such terms to use them consciously in his daily work:

> I think this question implies a greater degree of sophistication than we possessed. I don't believe we, in fact I know darned well, we didn't sit around and discuss the type of proofs to be used nor . . . did we ever discuss the type of reasoning, inductive reasoning or deductive reasoning to be used. I'm not sure that if we had tried to talk about those things we would have known what it was we were talking about, and I'm quite certain that if any one of us had spoken to Mr. Truman and said, "Do you wish to use inductive reasoning or deductive reasoning?" President Truman would have resorted to very simple, very elementary, Missouri farm language in dismissing that kind of question.[36]

Elsey's answer to this question is misleading, however, for any reader so inclined who examines the Truman speeches will find in them numerous examples of inductive and deductive reasoning as well as syllogisms, enthymemes, or any other formal concepts logicians choose for analysis. Like the cook who prepares a fine dinner without knowing the food's actual chemistry, it is not necessary to identify all rhetorical proofs before using them. Whether he realized it or not, Elsey was a practicing rhetorician who used all kinds of "proofs."

Some of the greatest service Elsey gave Truman came in the campaign of 1948. In the early part of that year, the polls showed that the president's popularity had fallen to a dismal 30 percent. Elsey believed that while many newspapers and magazines were opposed to Truman's programs, most voters would support him at the polls if he himself laid his case before them. On June 3, 1948, Truman began a 9500-mile cross-country train tour that was so successful that it formed the basis for the whistlestop pattern that he used in the fall. The technique was to first disassociate himself from the Republican-controlled Congress elected two years earlier, and then to lay the blame for the nation's ills on that group's doorstep. Truman attacked Congress vigorously. He called it an "awful" Congress; then it was a "do-nothing" Congress; next a "good-for-nothing" body, and when he really wound up and linked it all together as that "awful, do-nothing, good-for-nothing, 80th Congress," his listeners responded with encouraging shouts of "Give 'em hell, Harry!"

Elsey did not accompany Truman on the June trip, but he was in constant contact with Clifford, who was aboard the train. The two had prevailed on the Democratic National Committee to organize a research staff of energetic young writers with broad political backgrounds, and later in the fall this group proved invaluable in feeding raw speech materials to the chief Truman writers.

As planning for the fall campaign got under way in earnest, Elsey argued that there could be as many as fifteen whistlestop speeches during the daylight hours and then a major address delivered at a stadium or auditorium that night. The evening address would be broadcast at least regionally, and nationally as often as the meager campaign funds would permit. Clifford took the main responsibility for the evening addresses, and Elsey was to be largely responsible for outlines which Truman could use in each day's extemporaneous talks.

When the fall campaign was launched on September 17, 1948, Elsey already had put in an incredible amount of planning for it. Everything was geared to adapt to changes that were certain to come about. Skeletal outlines of most issues and rebuttals had been prepared, but nothing was so static that it could not be changed as the campaign dictated.

During the fall tour Elsey worked in a little cubicle on the train and wrote outlines for President Truman to use in most of his rear platform talks. Before the campaign was over, Elsey prepared more than three hundred outlines, by far the largest literary contribution of the tour. Each outline consisted of two or three complete sentences which Truman would use as starters for his speech; then these few sentences were followed by a number of simple topics representing separate ideas. Truman could read the sentences consecutively if he were without inspiration or he could improvise on each major thought. The plan provided the president with a reasonably consistent flow of ideas that could support standard themes in a way that intrigued the newsmen covering the episodes.

Unfortunately, the outlines that Elsey prepared for the 1948 tour were not retained because they were considered too primitive to be of lasting value. Whatever item Elsey thought might be of use was simply clipped to a speech outline and passed to the president on the train. In some cases Truman himself scratched out a few lines that he thought should be used, and then an outline was drafted from his sketchy thoughts. Most often, however, the outline was started by Elsey from materials sent him from Washington.

A typical campaign day was September 18, 1948. It began with a speech at Rock Island, Illinois, a strong railroad and labor community. Truman wrote his own outline of an introduction and then a partial text stressing that labor had two chief concerns in the campaign: Taft-Hartley and high prices. The day's main address was at the National Plowing Contest in Dexter, Iowa. The speech there had been carefully written well in advance of delivery and was hard hitting enough to contain some of the strongest language found in any of Truman's manuscripts. He called the Republicans ''gluttons of privilege'' whose

''Congress has already stuck a pitchfork in the farmer's back.'' The itinerary for that single day suggested the pace the rest of the tour would take.[37]

Saturday, September 18, 1948

		MINS.
Rock Island, Ill.	5:45 A.M.	10
Davenport, Iowa	6:09	5
Iowa City, Iowa	7:26	5
Oxford, Iowa	7:50	3
Grinnell, Iowa	8:55	3
Des Moines, Iowa	10:15	15
Dexter, Iowa	12:30 P.M.	(Main Address)
Dexter, Iowa	2:15	Informal remarks
Des Moines, Iowa	4:10	5
Melcher, Iowa	4:52	5
Chariton, Iowa	5:36	5
Trenton, Missouri	7:10	10
Polo, Missouri	8:10	5

With such a schedule it is no small wonder that at the end of a short memo, Elsey added in parentheses, ''(We get a full night's sleep Sunday).'' In fact, the next day was not a complete respite. Truman's voice had shown signs of strain after the thirteen appearances on Saturday, but a night's rest seemed to renew him and the train headed west. He planned no speeches in Kansas, but he conferred on the train with Democratic chieftains who had joined him. At Junction City, Kansas, Truman from the rear of his train told a group that he had made it a rule in his thirty years in politics not to give political speeches on Sunday. He just wanted to meet the folks and compliment them for their community and citizenry. The train also stopped at Lawrence and Topeka where the president offered brief, informal remarks that day which were not recorded.

After the 1948 election, morale at the White House was extremely high. Truman was especially pleased with the work of Elsey, Clifford, and others on his close, personal staff for the team effort which had helped produce victory. Elsey's stock with the president rose higher as a result of the inclusion of Point Four in the inaugural address on January 20, 1949, and later in the summer of that year he was named administrative assistant to the president. Theoretically, in his new position he was not subordinate to Special Counsel Clifford, but in practice little was changed in their day-by-day relationships.

Truman speaking on September 18, 1948, to a crowd in Des Moines during his whistlestop campaign.

Elsey was on duty when the Korean War broke out in June of 1950, and he kept almost an hour by hour account of the president's phone calls, messages, and meetings that went on around the clock during the critical three days of June 24 through June 26. On September 1, 1950, in a broadcast from thē White House, President Truman tried to clarify America's role in Korea. The clarification was necessary because of remarks by General Douglas MacArthur, United Nations commander, which many persons interpreted as a changed policy that would expand the war. Elsey added a point to the president's speech that emphasized the "limited war" aspect of American action and hoped that such a statement by the president would make it clear that he and not MacArthur announced policy for the United States. The September statement by the president, however, was not enough to settle the confusion about United States aims in the Far East, so a conference with MacArthur became necessary.

President Truman flew to Wake Island in October to confer with General MacArthur, and Elsey went along as far as Hawaii. Elsey had joined with Murphy and others on the White House staff at the time in recommending a meeting in Hawaii, but as was learned from later reports, MacArthur did not want to come that far. He did not like to fly at night but would come to Wake Island because it would be only a daytime journey for him. A very small group of advisers, including Averell Harriman and Dean Rusk of the State Department, accompanied Truman on the leg from Hawaii to Wake for the momentous meeting. The conference did not prevent the general from continuing to make public statements which were not consonant with those coming from official Washington, and in consequence President Truman relieved him of his duties in the following April.

During the fall of 1951, Congress worked its way slowly through a foreign aid bill which, among other provisions, established a new post, the director of mutual security under the executive office of the president. Truman immediately named the experienced Averell Harriman to the new position, and in November of 1951, George Elsey was transferred from the White House staff to become assistant to Harriman in his new assignment. Elsey served with Harriman until 1953 and the official close of the Truman administration.

Other Truman Writers

Before the Truman administration ended, numerous other persons were called in at one time or another to help with specific messages. Often a second or third writer was used because of his particular expertise in a subject field, but none of these occasional writers ever approached the prominence or the influence of Rosenman, Clifford, Murphy, or Elsey.

DAVID D. LLOYD. David D. Lloyd, a grandson of David Demarest Lloyd, a noted playwright of the nineteenth century, was a young lawyer whom Clifford recruited for the express purpose of drafting speeches and messages. If any one adviser could be said to have "polished" Truman's speeches that person would have to be David Lloyd. Lloyd was one of the most versatile of the writers surrounding Truman, and even while carrying on full-time professional work he managed to write in other fields. He wrote and published two successful novels, although only one of these—*Son and Stranger,* 1950—came out while Truman was in office.

Lloyd's government career started in 1935 immediately after his graduation from Harvard Law School when he landed a position with one of the New Deal agencies. From 1937 to 1940 he worked as an assistant legal counsel for the subcommittee headed by Senator Robert M. La Follette, Jr., which was investigating the rights of labor. This experience helped him gain an understanding of congressional procedures and outlooks. For a year and a half he worked in the legal division of the Federal Communications Commission examining doubtful applications for radio licenses. Rejected in 1942 from military service because of physical reasons, Lloyd worked for a time in the Office of Price Administration. There, in his job of interpreting rationing regulations for tires, gasoline, automobiles, and licenses, Lloyd supervised fifty-two other lawyers. One young lawyer in the group was Richard M. Nixon, whom Lloyd put in charge of the tire rationing legal section.[38]

When he became a member of the staff helping write for President Truman, Lloyd worked on major matters such as the budget message, the president's economic report, and the annual state of the union message as well as specific legislative programs. One measure of Lloyd's effectiveness on the Truman writing team can be seen in David Bell's assessment that "David Lloyd was far and away the best writer we had." Bell went further in praising Lloyd's work:

> I'm sure he was the most gifted speechwriter of all of us, in the sense of using the English language effectively. All of us admired him greatly, and I suppose that apart from campaign periods when so many people participated, more of the words the President used from his staff would have come from Lloyd than from anybody else.[39]

In 1950 Lloyd came under fire from Senator Joseph McCarthy, who charged that he had "been passed over lightly" by the Loyalty Review Board investigating appointment of government officials. There was no substance to the innuendo and President Truman discounted the senator's claims. Later, Lloyd was somewhat more than an official assistant, for he became a close friend and confidant after Truman left the presidency. He played a key role in the establishment, organization, and financing of the Truman Library in Independence, Missouri. He also continued to help Truman prepare some of the many addresses and messages he was called on to deliver as a former president.

DAVID E. BELL. David Bell was one of several economists from the Bureau of the Budget who joined the White House staff to help draft speeches and messages. Although Bell started as a collaborator during the preparatory stages of the 1947 state of the union address, it was in the latter years of the Truman administration that he made his main contributions as a writer. Early in 1947 when Clifford was short of help he asked the budget director if he could have somebody to help collate financial data pertinent to the intended speech. Bell and Charles Stauffacher, another young economist from the budget bureau, were chosen. In addition to financial data they also gave Clifford their suggestions for what should be the administration's labor policy. Clifford was impressed enough to explore the subject in detail with them, and the result was that when the state of the union speech (1947) was delivered, the section under the heading "Labor and Management" paralleled the first suggestions of Bell and Stauffacher.

In the fall of that year Bell was transferred from the Bureau of the Budget to the White House staff and given the title of special assistant, working under the immediate supervision of Murphy. After 1948 Bell worked on messages dealing with a wide range of issues. A good share of his time was spent with natural resources and conservation problems. He was deeply involved in Truman's trip to the western part of the country in 1950 when the president dedicated the Grand Coulee Dam.

Bell's White House assignments were irregular from 1947 to 1953, and he occasionally went back to full-time duty in the budget bureau. In the winter of 1948–1949 he was on the other side of the table and was put in charge of preparing the budget bureau's draft of a budget message which would then be sent to the White House staff for approval and redrafting. Probably because he knew the treatment his draft would get from White House staffers, he tried to make his first manuscript simple:

> I remember that occasion vividly because we deliberately tried to turn out a brief budget message, and one which was freer than normal of bureaucratese, of gobbledygook. We had some success, I recall, because we got an editorial in the *Washington Post* that complimented the President for the simplicity and readability of that year's budget message—this was in January 1949—and Fred Lawton, who was then the Executive Assistant Director, sent me a little note saying something like, "You have done the impossible; I didn't think it could be done," which I suppose is the incident which makes all this stick in my mind.[40]

In 1952 when Adlai Stevenson was nominated by the Democrats, Bell was asked to join the governor's staff in Illinois. He was given a leave without pay from the budget bureau, and until the end of that campaign he helped in preparing early drafts of Stevenson's speeches. Bell's final responsibility in the Truman administration was to assist in the transition of budget matters to the incoming Eisenhower staff in 1953.

JAMES L. SUNDQUIST. James Sundquist was another occasional speech writer. He, too, worked in the Bureau of the Budget and was borrowed by the White House staff frequently during Truman's tenure. Sundquist had been a newspaperman who left that employment and joined the government in 1941. When Clifford was looking for help in preparing Truman's state of the union message for 1947, he asked Director of the Budget James Webb for a man who could write and who was knowledgeable about complex budgetary data. Clifford and Truman agreed that they needed someone who could translate into English the turgid prose many of the administrative specialists wrote. Sundquist was nominated, and thereafter was used often in speeches on budgets or money matters. He also worked on the president's messages urging consolidation of the War and Navy Departments.

In 1950, after Clifford left his post and was succeeded in it by Murphy, Sundquist was used on speeches outside the budget field. He was asked to write two speeches for Truman's western swing in that year: one on foreign trade and one on foreign policy. Sundquist had never written a speech on foreign policy before, but he was told by David Lloyd, who also was working then under Murphy's direction, to read a couple of Acheson's speeches—maybe that would give him some ideas. Sundquist related:

> I decided I would write my ideas on foreign policy *before* I read Acheson's stuff, just to see how it would work out. I came out with something pretty good, I guess, because hardly a word was changed and it was delivered in Laramie, Wyoming. I was told later that the newspapermen took a poll and voted it the best speech of the trip. On the foreign trade speech, a draft had been done by some expert somewhere, and all I did was give it a literary touch. The one on foreign policy was scarcely even cleared with the State Department; they did contribute a couple of paragraphs at the beginning on a gift of wheat to India, but apart from that, they didn't change anything either.[41]

Early in 1951 Sundquist left the Bureau of the Budget and moved to the Office of Defense Mobilization, where one of his assignments was to prepare for the president a quarterly report on that agency's activities. The substance of these quarterly reports frequently became the basis for a presidential speech or message. Sundquist was pulled back into the White House to work on Truman's message later that year proposing special relief for the Kansas flood areas after the big flood there.

By 1952 the speech-writing team working under Charles Murphy had swollen to include, in addition to Sundquist, occasional service from David Lloyd, Charles Van Devander, Richard Neustadt, and Kenneth Hechler. Hechler specialized in local color, and after Elsey's departure, Neustadt became the writer who concentrated on smaller, whistlestop types of speeches written in outline rather than textual form.

DAVID H. STOWE. Usually the people Clifford, and after him Murphy, summoned to help write messages for President Truman were first "borrowed" from other agencies, most often the Bureau of the Budget. One assistant writer came from the White House bailiwick of John R. Steelman, who from 1946 to 1953 was the "assistant to the president." When Steelman joined the Truman staff he already had held a White House post for more than a year under Roosevelt. Because of his background as a mediator in labor disputes, his expertise was carried over to the Truman presidency. In theory, Steelman was in charge of daily "operations," but it was not always easy to separate operations from policy making. Steelman did not seem to have much direct influence in formulating policies or goals for the Truman administration, however, and there is no evidence that he participated in the drafting of presidential speeches or messages. His first assistant, David H. Stowe, was recruited for that purpose, especially near the close of Truman's administration.

Stowe always remained somewhat within the Steelman orbit even when Murphy called on him for help. Stowe's expertise was used in messages that dealt with civil defense or manpower problems, and because of his long budget bureau background he was involved in a variety of similar questions about post-Korean mobilization.

DAVID K. NILES. Another assistant, but one who had only limited assignments, was David K Niles. Niles had worked in the Roosevelt administration handling problems, contacts, and relationships with minorities, and he continued to do much of the same sort of thing under President Truman. When Niles left the White House staff in 1951, he was succeeded by his long-time assistant, Phileo Nash, who carried on these duties until the end of Truman's tenure.

RICHARD E. NEUSTADT. The final writer of any consequence who helped prepare Truman's messages was Richard E. Neustadt, first assistant to Charles Murphy when the latter was Special Counsel. Neustadt, like Stowe, Bell, and Sundquist, had served in the Bureau of the Budget. In Neustadt's case, he had worked in the legislative reference staff, and had taken a year off to finish his doctorate at Harvard. He had been a personal assistant to James Webb, a highly talented organizer of the budget bureau, and was considered one of the bright young men around the executive office complex. One of the most important pieces of drafting that Neustadt did for President Truman was in connection with the president's farewell message in 1953.

Those who were writing for President Truman at the end of 1952 agreed that they wanted his final address to be their best effort. They wanted the message to express in a sensitive way their personal feelings about the seven years of his administration. Neustadt was assigned to develop the first draft of this delicate message, and he worked almost a month on it, soliciting ideas from other aides, agency heads, and particularly cabinet members who had sat in policy planning sessions with the president. Neustadt's most important single reference came from Truman himself in the form of handwritten notes recounting his career and the major events of his presidency as he saw them. Truman had served in public office as a county judge for two years, a presiding judge for eight years, a United States senator for ten years and fifteen days, a vice-president for two months and twenty-three days, and finally as president for seven years, nine months, and eight days. He wanted his farewell to be brief but indicative of these thirty years. He also wanted to emphasize that in his term as president, the nation had striven to establish a more lasting basis for world peace.

Neustadt led the address through six drafts, reaching the last one on January 14—the day before the president was to deliver it.[42] Truman read the manuscript from his office in the White House, and probably no other address ever did more to reveal his intense sincerity and idealism regarding peace and the country he served.

Summary Statements about Truman's Writers

It should be apparent from the foregoing discussions that no one person, including Truman himself, was the sole author of presidential speeches between 1945 and 1953. The messages were drafted not by men who had established reputations as "writers," but by lawyers, economists, and persons in public administration who had picked up skills as generalists in government. While many of the writers could be considered rhetorical craftsmen, Rosenman, Clifford, Elsey, and Murphy were much more than that. They inevitably became involved in the "timing" of a message. They not only helped the president decide how to say something; they sometimes initiated what should be said about a problem or issue.

By the very nature of the Special Counsel's role, whoever held that position had the overall responsibility for preparation of the president's set speeches, as well as other major public statements, and all presidential messages to Congress. As an extension of these jobs, Truman turned to his Special Counsel for drafting ideas he wanted in the Democratic platform and for serving as captain of the writing and research teams during campaign periods. Because the Special Counsel met with the president daily, his role in policy formulation, although not recognized by statute, became a major force in shaping the administration. True, the president had a final responsibility which he could not delegate, but there is a fine line between wording and substance of an idea. Because of frequent contact and daily advice on all kinds of subjects, the Special Counsel became more than an editor.

When asked which of the major advisers might have had the greatest influence on President Truman, David Bell answered:

> I would say undoubtedly Clifford and Murphy, in succession—that is to say: Clifford in the early years when he was there, and Murphy gradually increasing in stature while he was there with Clifford, and then after Clifford left, Murphy in his position as Special Counsel. It seemed to me that both men had a very strong impact on policy questions, and Mr. Truman it seemed to me had enormous respect for the judgment of both of them.[43]

George Elsey had a far greater role in the Truman speeches than his "assistant" titles would suggest. Elsey's impact was a natural outgrowth of his initiative and huge productive capacity as well as Clifford's tendency to delegate working assignments. No writer in the Truman entourage was more aggressive than Elsey in translating Truman's ideas about the Soviets into a firm, hard cold war policy. During campaign periods, Elsey was a tireless worker who urged other writers to help present a consistent "party line" that would show Truman as a strong, decisive leader. Elsey, more than any other single writer, was responsible for the inclusion of Point Four in the Truman inaugural of 1949. Because others held more exalted positions, Elsey's contributions did not receive the recognition they deserved. Any assessment of Truman's presidential rhetoric, however, would be inadequate if it did not take into account Elsey's writing and related services.

9

Persuading the Congress

We're Democrats, you know, and nobody can boss us.
And we fight like hell.

SAM RAYBURN, *Speaker of the House*

THE American political system works best when an articulate president enunciates public problems and is able to persuade Congress to enact legislation favorable to his goals and strategies. The men who come forward to speak for a vast continental country like the United States can only define policies; they cannot really compel Congress to accept them. A president may suggest what to do about rising prices, unemployment, strikes, the nation's health services, international treaties, and defense plans, but Congress may have different notions.

During the first years of his presidency, Truman sometimes remarked to members of his staff, "You know, I'm not an elected President." He professed that he meant to follow Roosevelt's general course, but his own program was not so clearly charted. He had been chosen for the vice-presidency because of his moderate, middle-of-the-road background, and after he assumed the presidency his policy statements did seem to align him with the more liberal wing of the Democratic party. At the same time, however, he surrounded himself with predominantly conservative cabinet members and advisers who worked against the lingering hopes of New Dealers. Some critics claimed that his heavy reliance on cabinet responsibility resulted in a morass of contradictory policies. Men like Secretary of the Treasury John Snyder and Secretary of Agriculture Clinton Anderson were in open sympathy with the goals of a conservative coalition in Congress. The result was that the early Truman administration drifted toward the right amid considerable uncertainty and confusion.

At the outset of his administration, President Truman also was handicapped because he lacked a loyal and organized congressional team of the sort Roosevelt had energized during the famous first hundred days of New Deal legislation. Truman was so much in awe of the presidency that he seemed to think it enough to announce the good word or suggest a new program without having to follow through with hard political pressures. In the American political system of checks and balances among competing interests, the chief executive can be effective only if he finds a way to lead vigorously. To do this, he must be willing to engage in political give and take. Roosevelt understood such maneuvers and was a recognized master of them; Truman as a new president believed the prestige of his office would be sufficient persuasion.

Truman had been in office for over a year and a half by the time of the November election of 1946. After an initial period of tolerance for the man who had fallen into the nation's top office, opponents and much of the news media became increasingly vehement in their political attacks. Woodrow Wilson had observed: ''In times of crisis, attention is on foreign affairs.'' Now the crisis had passed, and domestic problems commanded the headlines which war and foreign events formerly had monopolized.

By November of 1946, hopes had been discarded that because of his years in the Senate Truman would have at least as much influence with Congress as his predecessor. The biggest single factor causing such hopes to fade arose from the cessation of armed conflict. During Truman's first year in office the country had tired of restrictive measures brought on by war. Added to a feeling that the emergency was over, it became increasingly evident that in dealing with Congress the new president did not have the skills that Roosevelt had developed from his long tenure. Truman was hampered further by a lack of public adulation such as Roosevelt had enjoyed. From the high point of sympathy and popularity he had received when he took office in April of 1945, President Truman had fallen into a trough of unpopularity by the fall of 1946. People gibed: ''To err is Truman.'' Or they roguishly declared, ''If Truman were alive today, the country wouldn't be in this mess.''

To add to the administration's problems, a great many seasoned and capable officials fled their government jobs. Some idealistic New Dealers dropped out when Secretary of the Interior Harold Ickes resigned over the nomination of a wealthy oilman as undersecretary of the navy. Others departed when Truman fired Secretary of Commerce Wallace over the foreign policy imbroglio. When administrators quit or were fired, often their replacements were not equal to the tasks given them. Newcomers frequently were recruited from political and friendship pools rather than for real talent or expertise.

Although it was a boom era, many Americans did not believe the political slogan that told them they had never had it so good. There were too many fears that the bubble would soon burst and that the economy would collapse as it had done after World War I. The expected glut of surplus goods never materialized; instead there were horror stories of shortages—shortages of skilled workers, of housing, of automobiles, and of almost every sort of consumer durable goods. In the process of dismantling the war machinery, new problems of inflation jumped up daily. But if prices were to be checked, wages must be also, and workers were unhappy over the shift from high paying war work to lower paying jobs or from war years overtime pay to a forty-hour work week.

Adding to President Truman's early challenges was the changed attitude in Congress. There he encountered a mood that was entirely different from what it had been during the Roosevelt administrations. Dissatisfaction over Roosevelt's control and his political clout had smoldered under strains first of depression and then war, but with a successor in office the disenchantments began bursting into open controversies. While it is likely that any person following a three-term president would have had difficulty in controlling or even working smoothly with the legislative branch, Truman's lack of experience seemed to enhance Congress's powers and its sense of independence. Former alliances began splitting, and new ones were formed. As a result, Congress proved balky and ineffectual, especially on domestic matters.

When Truman came to the presidency, the war in Europe was rapidly moving toward its conclusion. When it did end in May of 1945, even though the Japanese war was still to be won, political discussions began recapturing the attention of American citizens. In continuation of practices set up by Roosevelt, President Truman invited certain congressional leaders to come to the White House regularly.

Three days after he gave his first address to Congress, President Truman met with Sam Rayburn (Speaker of the House), Senator Kenneth McKellar (president pro tempore of the Senate), Senator Alben Barkley (majority leader in the Senate), and Representative John McCormack (House majority leader). The press soon dubbed these men the "Big Four" in Congress, and Truman asked them to come to his office so that they could receive the latest information about the ongoing war and diplomatic problems. He also wanted to discuss with them certain aspects of the federal budget and what changes in it would be necessary when peace arrived. Although the group's membership would change slightly as a result of elections, President Truman continued to meet regularly with four or five leaders so that he could go over proposed legislation, the status of bills already in the legislative mill, and the new foreign policy that was beginning to evolve. These few key legislators were the ones who would have to maneuver and muscle his programs through Congress. On their shoulders rode his hopes for a successful presidency. It was understandable that Truman, filled with humility and caught without warning in the grip of overwhelming pressures, would turn to established friends in Congress. One man on whom he had to depend most heavily was his friend, the powerful, reigning Speaker of the House, Sam Rayburn, Democrat of Texas.

"Mr. Sam" Rayburn

In the summer of 1944 when Vice-President Henry Wallace proved unacceptable to Democratic stalwarts, some ardent New Dealers were disappointed over the president's proposing Senator Harry Truman or Supreme Court Justice William O. Douglas as suitable vice-presidential timber. John N. Garner had maligned that office by declaring: "The Vice Presidency isn't worth a pitcher of warm spit."[1] Not everyone agreed with his assessment, and several members of Congress hoped that Roosevelt would select Sam Rayburn, a veteran congressman, who was described as "one helluva of a New Dealer."

Samuel Taliaferro Rayburn had won his first term as U.S. representative from Texas in 1913. He arrived in Washington a month early because he wanted to be on hand to watch the inauguration of Woodrow Wilson. During Wilson's two terms, Rayburn voted almost on a straight-line basis for the administration. He was in the jam-packed House chamber the night of April 2, 1917, when Wilson delivered his momentous war message. When America entered that conflict, Rayburn was thirty-five years old and had no military experience. A year later when Rayburn returned to Washington to begin serving his fourth consecutive term, the Democrats were no longer in control of the House, and a Republican, Frederick H. Gillett of Massachusetts, sat in the speaker's chair. Gillett was not as energetic as most speakers, and the editor of the *Boston Transcript,* who knew him well, observed that he never drank coffee in the morning "for fear it would keep him awake the rest of the day."[2]

Rayburn attended his first Democratic National Convention in 1924. Later he would be leader and ranking authority for many such gatherings, but at his first he was observer more than active participant. He and nearly all other attendees were deeply impressed when in 1928 Franklin Roosevelt came out on crutches to make his famous nominating speech for Alfred E. Smith, the "Happy Warrior."

The congressional elections in November of 1930 resulted in a pencil-thin margin for Democrats in the House, and Rayburn's old friend and mentor, John Garner, was elected speaker. With Garner's elevation, Rayburn also advanced and took over the chairmanship of the Commerce Committee.

By 1932 although Rayburn was still a recognized protege of the crusty Garner, he had become an experienced legislator in his own right. As Speaker of the House, Garner had inherited a comfortable separate office, which he dubbed the "Board of Education" room. He was in the habit of relaxing there in the late afternoons with old friends and loyalists. There Rayburn helped down bourbon and branch water in a daily ritual they all termed "striking a blow for liberty." Rayburn served as an intermediary between Roosevelt and Garner in arranging for the latter's name to be placed on the Democratic ticket in 1932, and after his election Roosevelt showed his appreciation for Rayburn's assistance.

Following Roosevelt's reelection in 1936, Rayburn became the House majority leader, but because Speaker William Bankhead was seriously ill Rayburn frequently had to take on many of the speaker's duties. The House then was top-heavy with Democrats—435 of them compared with only 89 Republicans—so Rayburn had an overwhelming majority with which to work. Despite the opposition aroused by Roosevelt's scheme to pack the Supreme Court, Rayburn and his followers continued to dominate all congressional actions.

Speaker Bankhead died in September of 1940, and Sam Rayburn replaced him through a House motion, unusual in that it encountered no discussion or argument. The vote for Rayburn was unanimous, and after twenty-seven and a half years in Congress, he achieved his ambition of becoming Speaker for the legislative body he cherished so much. When he took his oath of office to begin his twelfth consecutive term, he had confessed, ''The House of Representatives has been my life and my love.''[3]

As in earlier years, Roosevelt depended heavily on this congressional stalwart who had become a recognized master of parliamentary maneuvering and strategies. There were countless times that Roosevelt would call the bald, stocky Texan or ask him to stop by to consult about a current problem or forthcoming speech. A typical example of such reliance is seen in the note Roosevelt sent Rayburn on September 6, 1942:

> Can you come to my study in the White House Wednesday morning? Please keep this very confidential as I want Message and Speech contents to be wholly secret until Monday noon.[4]

The authority of the speaker's position when added to his special friendships with key congressmen assured Rayburn a great deal of control over legislation and the entire committee system. He controlled about eight hundred appointments of House members each year that involved membership on special House committees, joint House-Senate committees, various commissions, and international conferences. He had authority over the regular standing committees as well as a host of administrative responsibilities. Among these were general charge of two House office buildings where each representative had a two-room suite, the Capitol bank with millions in assets, the Capitol police force, the stationery store, the page system, press gallery, power plant, and the House chamber itself. His perquisites of office included a chauffeur-driven limousine and two offices, a private dining room, and the ''Board of Education'' after-hours hideaway.

Among the guests who were often invited to the Board of Education retreat was the junior senator from Missouri, Harry Truman. He continued to be quite regular there even after he became vice-president. He was a congenial fellow who liked to talk informally with Rayburn about southern history, farming, and the dangers of Wall Street. The two shared many of the same political beliefs, and by 1944 they had become close friends.

On March 1, 1945, Rayburn and Truman sat side by side on the rostrum in the House while the exhausted Roosevelt delivered his speech on the Yalta conference. The day following Roosevelt's death, President Harry Truman went to the Capitol to see Rayburn and certain former colleagues who met with him in Les Biffle's office. There he arranged for his joint meeting of Congress on April 16. As one of the oldest hands in Congress and because of his long friendship with Truman, Sam Rayburn went to the White House later in the afternoon to call on the new president. Rayburn wanted to assure his friend of wholehearted support and to warn him about some of the problems he would be facing as chief executive. In a separate interview which he gave later to newscaster Martin Agronsky, Rayburn recounted this visit with the new president:

> I wanted to help this fellow. So I went down there and said to him: "You don't have anything in the world that I want. . . . I have come down here to talk about you. I have been watching this White House for many years. I know some of the hazards here and I want to tell you what your biggest hazard is in this White House. You have a lot of people around you here. Some of them are going to be men of outstanding ability and character, and some of them are not going to have too much ability. That is natural when you have a big group around you. And some of them are not going to be able to stand up and battle it out with men of more ability than they've got, and they are going to try to do to you what they have tried to do to every President since I have been here. They are going to try to build a fence around you and in building that fence around you they will be keeping the very people away from seeing you that you should see. That is my first bit of advice.
>
> The next one is the special interest fellow and the sycophant . . . [he] will come like the king of old. He would stand in the snow a week because the king had to see the Pope before he could navigate, and I said that fellow will stay around here for a month and will come in here sliding on his vest and, will say that you are the greatest man that ever lived in order to make time with you; and you know and I know that it just ain't so.[5]

President Truman promptly interrupted to say, "Well, I know I am not." Then as he was leaving the White House, Rayburn asked if he could arrange to see the president without having to walk through a battery of newspaper reporters who would clamor to know what the two were talking about. President Truman replied:

> Just any afternoon after five o'clock, come in the East entrance of the White House, over by the Treasury and walk through there and come up to my study. I'll be in there.[6]

Soon after winning the presidency on his own in 1948, Truman appointed Joseph G. Feeney as legislative assistant to the president. One of Feeney's jobs was to assess congressional opinion before Truman would send over a bill proposed by the administration. Generally, President Truman let it be known that he was thinking of such a proposal, for he wanted no surprises. Feeney observed that in the Senate there was much less "horse trading" than in the House, for in the lower chamber most bills had only to be cleared with Rayburn and his coterie of committee chairmen. Feeney then described the power wielded by Rayburn during most of the time Truman was in the presidency:

> The chairmen in the House were very powerful in their own right, and quite often the President would invite them down for a meeting on a particular piece of legislation. In most cases the President himself carried on a lot of the contact work with the House chairmen. But here again, the House was then being ruled by Sam Rayburn. . . . Sam Rayburn was not only Speaker, but he was director-in-chief of the House. He would decide what bills were going to go through and what were not going to go through. He ran the House with an iron hand. It was a very unusual situation and it will probably never happen again. But most House members were not even able to talk with Sam Rayburn. He only saw the people he wanted to see. And he had a few key people—most of them chairmen—who would be admitted to the throne. So for legislative purposes, Mr. Truman would send for Mr. Rayburn, and they were both very friendly, and they'd go over the bills that were to go through and those that would be sidetracked.[7]

Especially during his first three years as president, Truman tried to preserve his friendly relationship with Sam Rayburn; inevitably the differences between their respective positions would draw them apart, but the personal bond remained close. From time to time, President Truman received valuable help from others in Congress, but no single member would match Speaker Sam Rayburn in terms of power, seniority, and loyalty to the administration.

Senator Tom Connally, Senate Foreign Relations Committee Chairman

Of the myriad problems descending on Truman during the first months of his presidency, none was more serious or more complex than that of grasping leadership in the field of foreign affairs. Because of its seriousness and because it was an area in which he had no experience, foreign relations was the subject that commanded most of his attention during his first year in office. When it came to legislation on foreign affairs, Truman tried especially hard to line up support before any specific proposals went to Congress. He leaned on members of the executive branch and professional diplomats in the State Department, but he also wanted to learn from legislators who were experienced in treaty matters. He understood that he was empowered to sign pacts, but his familiarity with history and the Constitution showed him their uselessness unless they received the "consent" of the United States Senate. The Senate was the arm of Congress he understood best, and in that body he knew that a pivotal position lay in the leadership of the powerful Senate Foreign Relations Committee. Its chairman was another Texan, Democrat Tom Connally.

Connally was an old-fashioned senator who embodied the popular image of a traditional southern politician. The portly, silver-haired, homespun Texan liked to wear boiled white shirts, gold studs, a black string tie, and a slouch hat of the same color. He had first come to Congress in 1917 as a member of the House of Representatives where he quickly won a seat on the Foreign Affairs Committee. There one of his first votes was in favor of a motion "advising" President Woodrow Wilson to declare war on Germany.

Connally wore his southern allegiance plainly and was every ready to help filibuster against any proposals that section disliked. He enjoyed his reputation as an orator of the old school, whose remarks might be a whiplash or soothing syrup as occasion demanded. He could be a genial and amusing companion but a dangerous antagonist in debate. His seniority encouraged a natural sarcasm, which frequently was personal and demeaning. He once advised an opponent:

> Now, if the Senator would only approach these matters with an open mind, instead of an open mouth.[8]

In the House and throughout his career in the Senate, Connally was a party regular until the time of the New Deal. Then he split with Roosevelt on many issues of domestic reform; however, he was a convinced internationalist and backed Roosevelt's foreign policy to the fullest before and during the war. When Truman came into office, Connally immediately aligned himself with the latter's attitudes toward international relations. In his role as chairman of the Committee on Foreign Relations, it was Connally's task to explain foreign treaties to the Senate, and as the ranking Democrat on the committee he was expected to push those treaties through to ratification.

United States foreign policy had been moving the nation toward confrontation with the Soviet Union since at least the beginning of 1945, but the critical cold war did not start until about a year and a half later. The next several years were marked by one crisis after another as tensions between East and West mounted alarmingly.

In 1946 when American diplomats strove to find a basis for a peace treaty, their efforts were stalled by Soviet intransigence. That year, Connally accompanied Secretary of State Byrnes to the meetings of foreign ministers first in London and then in Paris where he was the eyes and ears of the United States Senate. The meeting in Paris was a disappointment, and the various ministers went home to report a lack of progress. The breakdown came over disagreements concerning the future of the port of Trieste in the Adriatic, Italian reparations, Italian colonies, and the French-Italian border.

By the beginning of 1947, the Truman administration was attempting a major restatement of its position toward the Soviet Union. The change of position, which became known as the Truman Doctrine, thrust the United States into the role of dominant power in the Mediterranean and committed the nation to using its strength to stop communism everywhere. Despite charges to the contrary, the Truman Doctrine was not an abrupt change in direction but represented instead the culmination of trends that had begun early in 1945.

In the Mediterranean, Great Britain had been the traditional guarantor of western interests, but at the close of the war the British economy collapsed, and the country's military weakness became apparent. Russia had long held designs on Turkey and the Dardanelles, the crucial passage between the Black Sea and the Mediterranean. In nearby Greece, that country's economy had been shattered by the harsh Nazi regime, and new forces were struggling for power. By late 1946, the tottering Greek government, which had relied heavily on British military and economic aid, found itself unable to deal effectively with guerrilla forces which received increasing support from their Balkan neighbors—Yugoslavia, Bulgaria, and Albania.[9]

The expected British withdrawal from Greece and Turkey materialized on February 21, 1947. By this time President Truman was convinced that any success of the Greek rebels would mean automatic extension of Soviet power, so he moved quickly to mobilize his forces in Congress. He invited congressional leaders to the White House for a meeting on February 27, where he brought out his biggest persuaders hoping to win support for a decision he already had made. In addition to Connally, others present at this important meeting were: Arthur Vandenberg, Styles Bridges (chairman of the Senate Appropriations Committee), Joseph Martin (Speaker of the House), Sam Rayburn (minority leader in the House at the time), Charles Eaton (chairman of the House Foreign Affairs Committee), and Sol Bloom (ranking Democrat on the House Foreign Affairs Committee).

Secretary of State George Marshall opened the meeting by announcing Britain's withdrawal and by describing the implications that action would have on American interests. Believing that Marshall had "flubbed his opening statement," Undersecretary of State Dean Acheson then asked for the floor. Acheson outlined the situation in more bold and threatening terms than Marshall. He asserted that failure of the United States to act decisively in the crisis would open three continents to Soviet penetration. The meeting had been arranged not to discuss alternatives but to allow President Truman to tell the congressmen that he already had decided to provide quick military and economic aid to the two beleaguered nations. He was so sure that his decision in this emergency was correct that when it came time to prepare his address to Congress, he rejected drafts which were uninspiring or coldly statistical. On one draft, he scratched out the word "should" and penciled in "must." Looking back on his message, he explained:

I wanted no hedging in this speech. This was America's answer to the surge
of expansion of Communist tyranny. It had to be clear and free of hesita-
tion or double talk.[10]

When the Foreign Relations Committee held open hearings on Truman's
proposal, Senator Connally as chairman closely questioned Acheson and other
administration spokesmen. Subsequently, Connally did a great deal to help
dispel the arguments that charged the United States with moving unilaterally
and ignoring the United Nations. He insisted that the new international
organization was not yet equipped to handle the situation of Greece and
Turkey, but that later the United States would waive its veto power if it found
that action by the United Nations would make American assistance unnecessary
or undesirable.

In a related area, Connally helped line up Senate support for the administration's proposed peace treaties with Italy, Hungary, Rumania, and Bulgaria
long before they were presented for ratification. Another instance of Connally's
support for Truman occurred in October of 1947. It was then that Truman
called Congress into special session and asserted that immediate congressional
action was necessary to control inflation and to provide $642 million in stopgap
aid for Europe. During this special session, the Senate acted on an additional
foreign policy measure which was closely tied in with the new containment
policy. An inter-American treaty recently had established the Organization of
American States and provided for collective action among nations in the Western Hemisphere against any aggressor. President Truman carefully had included Connally and Vandenberg among the United States' negotiators for the
treaty, and in so doing had assured bipartisan support in advance.

In 1949, Truman gave Connally the main responsibility for obtaining Senate approval of the North Atlantic Treaty—the first peacetime alliance for the
United States. When Britain, France, Belgium, the Netherlands, and Luxem-
bourg concluded a fifty-year agreement for economic cooperation and defense,
Secretary Marshall told British Foreign Secretary Ernest Bevin that the United
States was entirely sympathetic to the arrangement. Moreover, Congress appeared willing to consider a regional defense pact with European nations based
on Article 51 of the United Nations Charter. Connally helped his Republican
colleague Arthur Vandenberg draft a resolution expressing the Senate's support
for such an alliance and then engineered the statement through his Foreign
Relations Committee, where it received unanimous endorsement. Vandenberg
presented the resolution to the full Senate, and after only one day's debate that
body approved the measure. The resolution called for the United States to arm
signatory nations against any possible attack by Russia, and Senator Connally
refuted arguments from those who objected to such rearmament commitments.
Three weeks after the Senate adopted its resolution, State Department
negotiators began discussions with European representatives, and these discus-

sions led to establishment of the North Atlantic Treaty Organization in August of 1949. In this as well as in other instances dealing with foreign problems, Connally worked closely with Arthur Vandenberg. The election of 1948 made Connally rather than Vandenberg chairman of the Foreign Relations Committee, but together they symbolized the bipartisan leadership without which most of the Truman foreign policy programs would not have survived in Congress.

In June of 1950, Senator Connally was instrumental in getting Truman's Point Four program through the Senate despite stiff opposition, especially from Senators Robert Taft of Ohio and Eugene Milliken of Colorado. Congress already had authorized a fractional part of the whole $3.2 billion foreign aid bill, but Point Four had been set at a tentative and compromise figure of only $35 million. The debate centered on whether this "bold new program" would steer too much private capital into underdeveloped areas of the world without giving American investors any hint that their investments would be protected. Taft argued that Connally, as chairman of the Foreign Relations Committee, had introduced an entirely new bill rather than a compromise version coming from a conference with House committee members. Taft was joined by Milliken in charging that in this new version for granting technical assistance, the government offered no insurance to investors against losses overseas. They also objected to the bill as presented by Connally because they said there was no time limit to it.

Connally had his party members in line, however, and he rebutted the allegations by insisting that the language of the bill assured investors "that they will not be deprived of their property without prompt, adequate and effective compensation."[11] He ridiculed the language and actions of his opponents and scoffed that they were showing statesmanship "with a little 's'." When the vote was taken, it was a personal triumph because the Senate voted 47 to 27 for the proposal as he had presented it.

It would be difficult to explain the Truman record without recognizing the services of Senator Tom Connally. Most of the successes Truman won from Congress were in the field of foreign policy, and these achievements were made possible only because he was able to get a bipartisan coalition going, particularly in the Senate. Connally was a faithful Democrat who, notwithstanding his monumental ego, contributed immeasurably to that bipartisanship. At times, notably near the close of Truman's administration, bipartisanship broke down, and some observers believed the breakdown occurred largely because of Connally's resentment toward Senator Vandenberg. Connally felt that all too often he, as chairman of the Foreign Relations Committee, was not awarded newspaper attention and recognition equal to that given his Republican colleague from Michigan. Actually, President Truman placed great trust in both veteran legislators, and he once acknowledged their value to him:

I frequently talked to Senators Connally and Vandenberg, who were the ranking members of the Senate Foreign Relations Committee. I wanted these two key figures to have direct access to me at all times, and I wanted the benefit of their counsel and experience.[12]

Arthur H. Vandenberg, Republican Senator from Michigan

It is ironic that so much of the reputation fervent Democrat Harry Truman achieved in foreign policy matters can be traced to backing he received from an equally fervent Republican. Arthur Hendrick Vandenberg of Michigan and Robert A. Taft of Ohio generally are considered the two outstanding leaders in the United States Senate during the time President Truman was in office.

Arthur Vandenberg was the same age as Harry Truman and similarly had known hard work and meager income during his teens. He had begun hauling freight in a pushcart, and he continued to work at different odd jobs throughout his high school career. He attended a prelaw course at the University of Michigan for one year, but had to drop out when he could not meet school expenses and earn his living at the same time. He went into newspaper work for the *Grand Rapids Herald* when he was twenty-two, and when he became editor of that paper he rapidly made a name for himself in Michigan political circles. He wrote three books extolling the virtues of Alexander Hamilton as the "Great American," and consistently proclaimed his own faith in the nationalist point of view.

In 1928, Vandenberg was appointed to the Senate to fill the unexpired term of a senator who had died. Six months later he was elected to the Senate in his own right. When he survived the New Deal landslide and won reelection in 1934, his position in the tiny Republican hierarchy was assured. On the floor of the Senate, he spoke often in his booming voice and was inclined toward purple prose and cliches. For nearly a decade after 1934, he opposed New Deal programs and was a leading spokesman for isolationism.

With American involvement in the war, Vandenberg began to reconsider his position. The rain of robot bombs that Germany showered on England convinced him that their range could be vastly extended, and on January 10, 1945, he arose in the Senate to deliver a speech on which he had worked long and painstakingly, writing and rewriting it while bent over his typewriter and puffing away on his ever-present cigar.

In a passage that seemed to echo what Roosevelt had been arguing even before Pearl Harbor, the Michigan Republican declared that the United States must appeal to its allies to choose between alternatives of living in a postwar world on the basis of individual action, in which each nation would look out for itself, or on the basis of joint action, in which "we undertake to look out for each other."[13]

The speech was an immediate sensation and brought Vandenberg a surge of popular support. The *Washington Star* said that he spoke for "those millions of Americans who want to cooperate fully with our Allies both in winning the war and writing the peace." Political columnist David Lawrence wrote that the senator had "swept away completely any idea that the Republican party . . . is to obstruct in any way the movement for the establishment of an international organization to assure peace." President Roosevelt, who was to leave for the Yalta Conference only a few days afterwards, hastily requested fifty copies of the senator's remarks. Many observers complimented Vandenberg for his forthright admission of a change in his basic beliefs. Walter Lippmann, noted journalist and authority on world affairs, later was asked just how he thought historians would view the overall contributions made by Senator Vandenberg. He answered in part:

> We do not any of us like to change our minds, particularly in public. And when we have taken a public stand we tend to be stuck in it. Once an issue has been fought over a long time, most of us are too proud and too timid to be moved out of our entrenchments by reason and evidence alone. Nothing then is likely to change quickly, and in time before it is too late, the minds of a whole people, except a collision with the brutal facts and being run over by them—as in Pearl Harbor.
>
> But when a sudden and tremendous change of outlook has become imperative in a crisis, it makes all the difference in the world to most of us to see a man whom we have known and trusted, and who has thought and has felt as we did, going through the experience of changing his mind, doing it with style and dash, and in a mood to shame the devils of his own weakness. I would argue at the bar of history, if ever I got the chance, that his (Vandenberg's) spiritual experience, which great masses of our people entered into vicariously, was the creative element which made his other political powers so enormously effective.[14]

Franklin Roosevelt appointed Vandenberg as a delegate to the San Francisco conference where the United Nations took form, and subsequently the Michigan senator collected Republican votes for its approval. President Truman next sent him to the United Nations General Assembly meeting in London where Vandenberg saw firsthand the obstructive tactics of the Soviets. As a result, he came out quickly in favor of the emerging policy of firmness and bluntness when dealing with the Russians. Most Republicans in the Senate followed his lead in foreign affairs, and this voting pattern gave him a firm veto over any and all treaties espoused by the Truman administration. Democrats might outnumber Republicans in the Senate, but to obtain ratification of any pact it was necessary for a sizable number of Republicans to vote with them. Vandenberg aided Truman in another way: usually he was able to tell the president, most often through Secretary of State Byrnes, what bills his Republican colleagues would or would not support.

Vandenberg's participation in most of the foreign aid and defense programs enacted during Truman's administration was invaluable. The senator often started by leading the opposition but ended by supporting those proposals which he felt were in the national interest. His method was to go through an initial period of public doubt and skepticism; then in due course he would suggest a few minor changes before giving his stamp of approval and handing the proposal to his colleagues.

Vandenberg was instrumental in getting the Truman Doctrine endorsed by Congress and in presenting it primarily as a measure to combat the Soviets. At the meeting on February 27, 1947, when President Truman told his select group of congressional leaders of the action he contemplated in the Greek-Turkish crisis, Vandenberg insisted on a dramatic step. After Secretary of State George Marshall, Undersecretary Dean Acheson, and finally Truman himself had presented their case for immediate economic and military aid to the two threatened countries, a long silence ensued. Then Senator Vandenberg responded:

> Mr. President, if you will say that to the Congress and the country, I will support you and I believe that most of its members will do the same.[15]

Vandenberg believed that the only way to persuade legislators to enact such a far-reaching change in foreign policy was for the president to go before Congress and "scare hell" out of the country. And that is precisely what President Truman did on March 12, 1947, with his blunt warning that Communist actions were gravely and directly threatening American security.

After President Truman delivered his Greek-Turkish aid speech, the press and various organized groups alleged that the administration had bypassed the United Nations. Vandenberg joined Senator Connally in rebutting these attacks, and he introduced an amendment which provided for withdrawal of military and economic aid if and when the United States found that any intergovernmental body, including the United Nations or any of its branches, could offer similar assistance. The amendment was nothing but window dressing, but it was sufficient to take the steam out of charges that the United Nations was being ignored, and it permitted the bipartisan congressional bloc to feel that it had a larger part in shaping the new policy.

The Truman Doctrine speech before Congress on March 12, 1947. In the background is Senator Arthur H. Vandenberg.

Three months later when the Marshall Plan was first proposed, Senator Vandenberg started by viewing it with alarm; he was afraid of where such largesse might eventually lead. However, he held great respect for General Marshall and soon became convinced of the soundness of the entire concept. Vandenberg believed that national unity was of paramount importance, and again, economic aid seemed imperative if the war-wracked nations of Western Europe were going to be able to join American efforts in halting the spread of communism. In June of 1948, Vandenberg presented a successful resolution which informed the president that it was the sense of the Senate that the United States should enter into such regional and collective arrangements as "are based on continuous and effective self-help and mutual aid, and as affect its national security."[16]

In his inaugural address the following January, President Truman incorporated the Vandenberg resolution into his speech and made it his third point. The president asserted that such agreements would "provide unmistakable proof of the joint determination of the free nations to resist armed attacks from any quarter." The Vandenberg resolution made the North Atlantic Treaty possible, for it was an idea around which both supporters and opponents rallied; they felt that it fulfilled the Senate's responsibility to give the president "advice and consent" regarding treaties.

Over the course of his presidency, Truman's personal standing rocketed up and down like a roller coaster, but his peaks of popularity were reached during his dramatic diplomatic moves. Senator Vandenberg's cooperation was vital in such matters, for he controlled the reluctant opposition. President Truman and his aides initiated the moves, but they became possible only when he was able to persuade Vandenberg of their correctness. Not until then would Vandenberg use his tremendous influence and rally the congressional backing that was needed. The senator's score in such rallies was uniform and remarkably high.

Alben W. Barkley

When Harry Truman entered the White House, Alben Barkley already had served in Congress for thirty-two years. Barkley was elected to the House of Representatives in 1913—the same year as Sam Rayburn—and he served fourteen years in the House and later twenty-one years in the Senate. He was one of the best known, best liked, and most experienced legislators on whom President Truman would have to rely.

Barkley was introduced to politics during the years William Jennings Bryan was national standard bearer for the Democratic party, and because of Barkley's infatuation with oratory it was only natural that he came to share the Great Commoner's political beliefs. When Barkley went to Congress he got to meet his idol, Bryan, and more than one observer has noted that Barkley liked to compare his own career with that of the free silver advocate.

The young Barkley was abetted in his Democratic leanings because nearly all members of his immediate family were staunch Democrats. A renowned storyteller throughout his adult years, Barkley liked to recite an anecdote he first had heard from his college mentor. The story concerned a young fellow who sent a letter to the editor of an "advice to the lovelorn" column. The fellow wrote:

> I am in love with a beautiful girl of fine character and want to marry her. She knows about my sister who is a prostitute, my brother in the penitentiary and my uncle in the insane asylum, but she doesn't know I have two cousins who are Republicans. Shall I tell her?[17]

Barkley was elected to Congress in 1913, and was sworn in as a freshman congressman on March 4 of that year—the same day President Woodrow Wilson was inaugurated for his first term. Barkley admired Wilson and called him "the greatest statesman and greatest President under whom I ever served."[18]

Barkley was in Congress during the twelve Republican years of 1920–1932. While Franklin Roosevelt campaigned for the presidency in 1932, Barkley was campaigning for his own second term in the Senate, having won a seat in that body six years earlier. Barkley worked hard for Roosevelt's nomination that year and served as temporary chairman and keynote speaker of the convention which selected Roosevelt. Some observers thought that Barkley's speech on the occasion was too long. For example, in his syndicated column Will Rogers commented on the keynoter's speech:

> Now comes Senator Barkley with the "keynote." What do you mean, "note?" This is no note. This was in three volumes. Barkley leaves from here to go to the Olympic Games to run in the marathon. He will win it, too, for that race only lasts three or four hours.[19]

Barkley met and liked Harry Truman almost immediately upon the latter's arrival in Washington. In fact, when it was time for the Senate to vote on a successor to Majority Leader Robinson, the race was a close one between Barkley and Pat Harrison of Mississippi. Senator Truman sought out Barkley and promised him his vote. However, soon so many pressures were put on Truman that he felt compelled to switch his vote to Harrison. It was characteristic of Truman that he then went to Barkley and asked to be relieved of his earlier commitment. Barkley won the contest for majority leader by one scant vote and later wrote that he admired Truman very much for having had the courage to come in person and admit his intention to change his vote.

When Truman was installed as vice-president in January of 1945, Barkley established the same sort of close working relationship he had held with Vice-President John Garner. For the three years in which Truman served out the unexpired term of Roosevelt, Barkley was the administration's leader in the Senate. He was always loyal, but because of the new administration's ineptitude, he sometimes was caught flat-footed by proposals of which he had no previous notice. Despite briefings given him in the White House and his regular attendance there at the so-called Big Four conferences, it seemed that too often such conferences were informal get-togethers, not revealing enough to tell attendees what was coming up. The metaphor-prone Barkley complained mildly that it was like playing catcher in a night baseball game, in which the administration not only failed to give adequate signals but often turned out the lights just when the ball was thrown!

In the summer of 1946, President Truman tried to crack the whip and line up congressional support for his proposal to draft strikers into the army. The gusts of labor's anger over this shocker were soon whipped into a hurricane. Loyal Majority Leader Barkley tried to avert the storm by moving to send the bill back to a committee for further study, but his move was soundly beaten, 70 to 13. Then he offered a series of amendments that weakened the bill in almost every section, and he fought against other amendments that tried to put teeth back into it. After midnight on the fourth day of snarling debate over the issue, the Senate under Barkley's adroit handling finally voted approval of the battered emergency antistrike bill, 61 to 20. It was a much weakened measure which called only for more labor responsibility, but it did give the president authority to negotiate wages and working conditions in plants seized during a national emergency. The president's prestige had been rescued again by his faithful majority leader but not before being cudgeled and nearly destroyed.

It was an open secret that Alben Barkley was not President Truman's first choice for the vice-presidential nomination in 1948. His preference was Supreme Court Justice William O. Douglas, but the justice was unwilling to leave the Supreme Court to run in what appeared to be a most unpromising campaign. When the Democratic National Convention opened on Monday, July 12, 1948, in Philadelphia, President Truman's personal popularity, according to most polls, had fallen to a depressing low. The nearly sixteen hundred delegates assembled in an atmosphere heavy with gloom. Several days before the convention got under way, one newspaper reported that the "Democrats act as though they have accepted an invitation to a funeral."[20]

The dispirited delegates responded to every speaker with only polite applause until Senator Barkley appeared to give the keynote address. He had served as keynoter at the conventions of 1932 and 1936 when the party's hopes were justifiably high. Now, at seventy years of age, he was a speaker whose vigorous voice and rhetorical flourishes soon brought the apathetic audience to its feet. He spoke for more than an hour, praising the New Deal and condemning the other party. The delegates cheered to the rafters his charge that Republicans were responsible for high prices and that the Eightieth Congress would be the supreme issue of 1948. He derided opponents for their attacks on the administration and exhorted his listeners to stand by their party in time of need. It was old-fashioned, hackneyed oratory, but the crowd loved it. Barkley had intended to shorten his manuscript, but the audience response was so enthusiastic that it spurred him toward ever more interpolations and sallies. His sharp, biting phrases caught the fancy of the partisan listeners, and they guffawed when he said that Republican promises to houseclean in Washington reminded him of 1932, when even the spiders in the federal cobwebs were weak from starvation. The delighted Democrats went wild when the Kentucky senator drawled out his analysis of Republican campaigning:

> Whatever their [the Republicans'] platform may or may not promise, whatever their candidate may or may not stand for, we have in all this confusion and vague atmosphere of promise and threats, one clear true clarion call. They are going to eliminate all the *bureaucrats* from Washington.
>
> What is a *bureaucrat?* Congress creates a bureau in some department and the President appoints the head of that bureau. And then he becomes a *bureaucrat* in the minds of those who do not like him or cannot get from him all the things they want.
>
> What is a *bureaucrat?* A *bureaucrat* is a *Democrat* who holds an office some Republican wants.[21]

When Barkley finished his talk, a twenty-eight minute demonstration broke out on the floor. The band played "My Old Kentucky Home" and the audience joined in the tune. Meanwhile, a long line of dignitaries paraded across the stage to shake the orator's hand and pose with him for photographs. The reaction to Barkley's address removed all questions about who would be the nominee for vice-president. National Chairman Howard McGrath phoned Truman and told him that Barkley was going to be the convention's preference. By this time, Truman had given up on hopes of persuading Douglas to run with him, and he had no other strong choice. So he replied, "If the convention wants Alben, of course, he is acceptable."

It was raining hard in Philadelphia at 12:42 A.M. on Thusday, July 15, when Truman was finally nominated, and a little more than an hour later Barkley accompanied the president as he made his entrance into the hall. Truman arrived with a carefully prepared speech which had not been written in manuscript form but was eighteen pages of outline, full of short, punchy sentences. At the outset of his speech, he energized his audience by telling them:

Senator Barkley and I will win this election and make the Republicans like it—don't you forget it. We will do that because they are wrong and we are right.[22]

It was a fighting address throughout, and its biggest punch was the sentence which called for a special session of Congress.

A few weeks after the convention when President Truman was departing Washington for the start of his formal campaign, Barkley saw him off. As the two shook hands, Barkley wished the president good luck and said, "Mow 'em down, Mr. President." The exuberant Truman responded, "I'm going to fight hard, and I'm going to give 'em hell." While President Truman whistle-stopped his way across the country, Barkley as vice-presidential candidate did the same elsewhere. He visited thirty-six of the forty-eight states in six weeks, traveled 150,000 miles, and delivered more than two hundred and fifty speeches.

At noon on January 20, 1949, Barkley stood on the steps of the Capitol along with President Truman and took his oath as vice-president. From his own experience, President Truman knew how little opportunity could be afforded vice-presidents, so he tried, whenever feasible, to send more responsibility and assignments to the cooperative Barkley. When he began his elective term, President Truman had Vice-President Barkley attend cabinet meetings, and he encouraged Congress to pass an act making the vice-president a member of the National Security Council. As vice-president, Barkley presided over the Senate but could no longer engage in the active debate he had enjoyed for so many years. He joked about the vice-presidential character in a popular musical who had nothing to do but sit in the park and feed the pigeons. In his boredom the stage vice-president thought he would join a library, but he discovered he "had to have two references," so he gave up and did not get in.[23]

Relations between Barkley and Truman were exceptionally cordial even if the vice-president was not always privy to some of Truman's secret aspirations and biggest political gambits. Barkley admired the spunky Missourian and thought that the president was often far too kind and loyal to certain old friends who took advantage of him. Near the close of their terms in office, Barkley summarized his impressions of the Truman record:

President Truman, however, did not "pop off" on the big issues. His big decisions were invariably taken only after serious consideration, in which he invited the opinions of his Cabinet and advisers. Among the big issues which, in my opinion, Truman met wisely and courageously were the decision to employ the atomic bomb in Japan and thus end the war; the decision to act in Korea, which, although it has since been subjected to base and ignoble criticism by political partisans, was applauded at the time as a brave and necessary act; the Berlin airlift, which probably saved Europe for us; the Truman Doctrine in Greece and Turkey and the Marshall Plan, which also held off the advances of world communism, and the decision to recall General Douglas MacArthur.[24]

On his part, President Truman recognized that his genial vice-president had an unmatched record both for partisan loyalty and bipartisan popularity. During his seven and a half years in the White House, Truman had no other figure around him who commanded so much good will as did the beloved Barkley. There were instances when Barkley's unfailing good humor and conviviality buoyed the president's spirits and rescued him from the inevitable loneliness of his office.

Senator Scott W. Lucas

Scott Lucas, Democratic Senator from Illinois, was another person who was often among the important legislators who met regularly with President Truman. As a congressional adviser, Lucas not only helped the president on questions of policy, but more importantly, he aided in planning and blocking strategies for getting Congress to act favorably. During most of the Truman presidency, Lucas held several vital liaison posts. Besides the position of majority leader after 1948, he played key roles as party caucus chairman, steering committee chairman, and policy committee chairman. No matter what legislative proposals Truman initiated or backed, Lucas was the man to shepherd them through the Senate.

Lucas was known as a studious lawmaker whose vote invariably went to the New Deal. By 1945, he had made his mark as a friend of the farmer and a down-the-line party man, the only exception being the time he had jumped the fence to attack Roosevelt's "court-packing scheme." He was not considered a creative politician; he dug no new channels. In his fourteen years as congressman or senator, Lucas sponsored little major legislation; rather, he toiled loyally on Capitol Hill for whatever administration he served, and he stuck staunchly by Harry Truman in the dark days before Philadelphia.

After the Republican congressional landslide of 1946, Lucas moved into the position of minority whip. Then in 1949 when Barkley left the floor to become vice-president and preside over the Senate, loyalist Lucas was unanimous choice for majority leader. A Senate majority leader, unlike the speaker of the House, does not enjoy the authority by which he can cut down dissidents and reward the faithful. In the Senate the majority leader must wheedle and persuade; he cannot twist and force the way his counterpart in the House does. He cannot even control from one hour to the next the order of business on the Senate floor. Nor can he get action on anything on the floor before it has gone through a committee, and a committee chairman in the Senate is almost unchallengeably powerful in his own right.

In Senate debate, Lucas was considered the voice of the White House. His job was to back the president's view on such issues as labor, taxation, housing, civil rights, and inflation controls. It was also his duty to keep Truman advised of the entire Senate situation, telling him what realistically could not be accomplished. As majority leader he was supposed to be ready to speak at a moment's notice on any subject of current importance. When attacks were made on the president, he was to rebuff them or see that they were answered at once. His predecessor, Barkley, had done this well because of his personal popularity and gift of humor. Lucas was effective enough as a speaker but more given to solemn forcefulness.

Though Truman had won the election of 1948, he did not win control of the Senate—if by that one meant an effective majority in carrying out presidential programs. Theoretically, as majority leader in the Eighty-first Congress which opened in January of 1949, Lucas led fifty-four Democrats, but actually day in and day out he could not count on more than forty stalwart supporters. Arrayed against him were usually the forty-two Republicans plus whatever roaming bands of southern Democrats might elect to go along with them on individual issues.

On foreign affairs, Lucas usually left the spotlight to Foreign Relations Committee Chairman Tom Connally. Lucas, however, was a genuine supporter of antiisolationist policies even though he came from a state where there was always considerable danger in espousing such views. When the isolationists arose, Lucas was ready to do battle and argue against their attempts to limit foreign aid. The Marshall Plan, the North Atlantic Pact, the Military Assistance Program, and the liberalized Displaced Persons bill were Truman victories in which he aided immeasurably.

President Truman twice went against advice from his majority leader— once when the latter wanted to hold back the civil rights filibuster fight until the Senate accomplished other legislation on which southern Democrats could be expected to go along, and once again when Lucas wanted the president to put a flat limitation on what the public could really expect from the Eighty-first Congress. Truman was never publicly willing to forgo a single major item he sent to Congress.

In the civil rights battle Lucas realized, perhaps before Truman did, that the armistice among Democrats following the 1948 election was apt to be brief. He expected that southerners would organize on the issue, and they would then join Republicans to create a formidable bloc of opposition. He himself was caught by Democratic colleagues from the South who claimed he was destroying their state sovereignty; he was lashed simultaneously by ''liberal'' associates who thought he was not driving hard enough. In one conference with his legislative leaders, President Truman pressed for more action by his majority leader to break up Senate filibusters over civil rights. Lucas, he felt, ''was not a fighter but was inclined to take things too easy.'' According to his assistant press secretary, the president said:

Lucas would rather recess the Senate and go out and play golf and then come in the next day than to get down to hard work and keep the sessions going at night, which he [President Truman] said was the only way to break a filibuster if one starts.[25]

That same day Lucas told newspaper reporters that the president had ordered a fight to the finish against any compromise that would encourage the filibuster techniques of southern Democrats, supported by some Republicans, who wanted a change in the rules so that they could talk the civil rights legislation to death. Thus Lucas was irrevocably committed to the Truman program, and once the decision was made to go ahead he saw his first function as being one to persuade Congress. If persuasion failed, he hoped to have enough solid party votes to blast the administration's measures through the Senate.

The fears were justified when throughout January of 1949 a Dixiecrat-Republican coalition threatened to torpedo Truman's civil rights measures. Lucas did not win the battle to restrict filibusters on the matter and had to be taken to the hospital in utter exhaustion. Just when the entire program seemed ready to go down in defeat, he came back to the Senate floor and threw himself into a pressure-packed schedule of sixteen-hour arguments and conferences. Although Truman lost the congressional battles both over his civil rights programs and repeal of the Taft-Hartley Act, the efforts of Lucas helped turn the record of the Eighty-first Congress in a general direction of credit to the Truman administration.

In 1950 Lucas faced the biggest election fight of his career when he was challenged by former Congressman Everett Dirksen. The campaign was an intense one, and Lucas stumped the state of Illinois piping prosperity and defending Truman's leadership. He met head-on the criticisms of actions in Korea, and he insisted that American moves there may well have headed off a third world war.

Two years earlier when Truman had campaigned through the grain states of the Midwest, the president had reproached the Eightieth Congress for failing to provide storage bins for the bountiful harvest that year. Such appeals had helped put Illinois in the Democratic victory column. In 1950 Lucas used the bin issue as a reminder of what his constituents had received from a Democratic administration in which he himself was heavily involved.

Lucas faced in Everett Dirksen, his Republican opponent, an effective campaigner backed by an isolationist bloc led by the powerful *Chicago Tribune*. Also working to the disadvantage of Lucas was a sensational uncovering of crime linked with underworld figures in the Chicago area. When the final votes were counted in the fall of that year, they showed that President Truman had lost one of his steadfast lieutenants in the Senate.

Other Congressional Contacts

After he entered the White House, Truman found it was no longer possible to keep the same relationships with friends he had made while serving in the Senate. Then he had allied himself with Democratic moderates such as Joseph O'Mahoney of Wyoming, Sherman Minton of Indiana, and Millard Tydings of Maryland.

President Truman knew who were the established leaders in government, and he usually courted them assiduously. However, leadership in Congress seldom follows a straight-line pattern—there are major figures whose support must always be pursued, and there are others who hold positions of power on specific issues. Certain leaders were responsible for Truman's successes with the various Congresses; other individual legislators played parts in his several defeats.

John W. McCormack, Boston Democrat and majority leader of the House when his party was in power, was a person whose vote Truman knew was assured. Unusually talkative and ingratiating on occasion, McCormack was Speaker Rayburn's principal lieutenant on the floor when it came to executing the administration's strategy.

McCormack was an intense New Dealer who had risen near to the top of the Democratic hierarchy because of his unwavering allegiance. He faced trouble in the second year of Truman's first administration because of divisions within the party. To southern congressmen, McCormack was too New Dealish and liberal to win constant support. In 1946, conservative southerners emerging from fourteen years of storm cellar existence under the New Deal had great cause for hope. Their aim was to seize control of the party reins in the lower branch of Congress. In the elections of the preceding November, Republicans had gained the majority edge (246 to 189), but within the Democratic party itself southerners commanded a solid bloc of 109 members from twelve southern states; they outnumbered their northern colleagues by about eleven to eight. Southern Democrats were so opposed to McCormack that they promised to revolt at the opening of 1946 if this Boston liberal were to assume the minority leadership. When added to pressure from the White House, their threat persuaded Rayburn to take the post himself and thus for a time quell the growing intraparty conflict.

McCormack often served the president by echoing assertions that came first from the White House. For instance, in 1947 several high-ranking Democrats told Truman that he could gain political advantages by sending a regular series of antiinflationary measures to Congress. The president assented and told his aides that he wanted "a baby to lay on the doorstep of Congress every week."[26] In line with such strategy, McCormack wrote his colleague Helen Gahagan Douglas of California encouraging her to organize a group of Democrats who would speak out against inflation and place the blame on Republicans in Congress. McCormack told the congresswoman that he thought such an organized campaign would be "constructive and important political-ly." At every opportunity, he repeated the administration's line that blame for the nation's economic woes lay only with the opposition party. Such efforts demonstrated his chief contributions to the Truman legislative record. First, the accusations demonstrated unswerving allegiance to his party chieftain; sec-ond, by demanding inflation-control legislation that the president was not like-ly to get, the charge helped Truman link the Republican-controlled Congress with the high cost of living.

Senator Millard Tydings, a tall, gray-haired patrician with an impeccable record of respect for law and decorum in the Senate, served on the all-important Foreign Relations Committee. During both Truman administra-tions, he was a strong supporter, particularly throughout the tortuous back-ground of the Internal Security Act of 1950.

Questions about what the government could do to protect itself against subversion began bursting onto front pages as early as 1947. For more than a decade, charges and countercharges flew like shrapnel in the halls of Congress and in living rooms across the land. The demagoguery that came to be known as McCarthyism did not attain full growth until after Truman left office, but it started and grew at an alarming rate while he was in the presidency.

As Russia rose to become a superpower, Communist penetration into es-tablished governments throughout the world likewise increased. In the years following World War II, the Communist threat to free governments was ever present. In part the threat was real and in part shadow, and the line between the two was seldom clear. President Truman began receiving reports of es-pionage operations within the government almost as soon as he entered office, and throughout his administrations there was to be no let-up in his battle with Congress over who was to manage the nation's internal security—the executive branch or the legislative branch.

When the Republicans in 1946 captured control of Congress for the first time in eleven years, one of their campaign pledges was to "clean the Com-munists and fellow travelers out of government." As a result of such oppostion, Truman set up a Commission on Employee Loyalty. He did it reluctantly because even though he predicted that such a commission would lead to legalized witch-hunting, he thought the risk was better than letting the whole issue go by default to the growing body of fanatics.

The event that did the most to start a torrent of congressional investiga-tions occurred in 1950 when a hitherto obscure senator, Joseph McCarthy of Wisconsin, told a Wheeling, West Virginia, audience that the State Depart-ment was riddled with Communist spies:

> And ladies and gentlemen, while I cannot take the time to name all of the
> men in the State Department who have been named as active members of
> the Communist Party and members of a spy ring, I have here in my hand a
> list of 205—a list of names that were made known to the Secretary of State

as being members of the Communist Party and who nevertheless are still working and shaping policy in the State Department.[27]

The Wisconsin senator knew when he made the charge that it was not true, but it became an immediate sensation. A Senate Foreign Relations Subcommittee was quickly empowered to look into McCarthy's allegations. The blue-ribbon Senate investigating group was headed by Truman's friend, Millard Tydings, and included the equally distinguished Francis Greene of Rhode Island and Brian McMahon of Connecticut. Chairman Tydings tried hard to keep the public hearings from becoming a circus, but he was up against a wily, headline-seeking opponent. In one instance—the Owen Lattimore case—McCarthy said that he was ready to let his case "stand or fall" on the committee's findings. When those findings exonerated Lattimore and were expressed publicly by Tydings, McCarthy then told reporters: "Either Tydings hasn't seen the file, or he is lying. There is no other alternative."

McCarthy stepped up his attacks against individuals and alleged that the entire Truman administration was lax in permitting Communists to work in sensitive government posts. Eventually, even most Republicans recoiled against McCarthy's twisted logic and seamy tactics. Respected Republicans said that Truman's administration had provided them with enough campaign issues without resorting to political smears and demagoguery. When the Tydings committee finally closed its investigations and made its report, the record showed that the committee had taken almost three-million words of testimony from twenty-five witnesses and had endured four months of acrimony and insult. Although the report castigated McCarthy for his behavior, the furor he created did not subside until well into the administrations of Truman's presidential successor.

In addition to Joseph McCarthy, President Truman had other detractors in Congress. The so-called China lobby proved to be an effective if not willing ally of the Wisconsin demagogue. The China issue served as a rallying point for such constant Truman critics as Senator William Knowland, Republican of California, Senator Styles Bridges, Republican of New Hampshire, Senator Pat McCarran, Democrat of Nevada, and Representative Walter H. Judd, Republican of Minnesota. This group was joined by others who clamored for greater American assistance to the Nationalist Party led by Chiang Kai-shek and condemned the priority given to Europe in the global policy of the Truman administrations. When the Nationalist rule in China began crumbling in spite of years of gigantic American assistance, critics tried to pressure the administration and relieve their own embittered feelings by agitating for more investigations of the State Department.

President Truman's position was to let the ongoing Chinese civil war take its inevitable course, and in the spring of 1949 the State Department became convinced that further aid to prop up the tottering Chiang regime would be wasted. Nevertheless, Senator Pat McCarran introduced a bill to extend $1.5 billion in further economic and military aid to the Nationalists. Secretary of State Acheson, speaking for the administration, opposed the bill and wrote that there was no evidence "that the furnishing of additional military aid would alter the pattern of current developments in China." He argued that on the contrary, effective assistance would require the use of an unpredictably large American armed force in actual combat and would be inimical to the long-range interests of the United States.

The dispute over Far Eastern policy had many ramifications, some of which included the matter of Hong Kong, a British colony which all Chinese considered rightfully a part of China. Hong Kong might be one of the first attack points if the Chinese Communists should be victorious and try to extend their conquests beyond China's recognized national frontiers. Yet an attack on Hong Kong would involve American as well as British interests, both as a violation of the United Nations Charter and as a simple matter of Anglo-American solidarity. There was also the question of protection for the large island of Formosa (Taiwan), wrested from China by Japan in 1895 but returned to China at the end of World War II. Formosa presented a particularly complex problem because of its uncertain legal status pending the conclusion of a peace treaty with Japan.

As a rule, Truman did not hold grudges very long, but in the case of McCarran he made an exception. In addition to McCarran's identification with the China lobby, other instances helped spark Truman's ire. One instance was a bill to liberalize the Displaced Persons Act of 1948 by increasing the number of European displaced persons to be admitted outside the regular immigration quota from 205,000 to 339,000. The 1948 act had been shown to be restrictive because of its low ceiling and its discriminatory pattern of preferences regarding the country of origin. A new bill to eliminate these features was passed by the House in 1949, but the parallel bill bogged down in a subcommittee chaired by Senator McCarran. A declared foe of the administration-backed revision, McCarran devised ingenious obstacles including a self-imposed "survey" trip to European displaced persons camps. The trip took him away from Washington but filibusters by his cohorts Harry P. Cain, Republican of Washington, and James O. Eastland, Democrat of Mississippi, were sufficient to get the bill sent back to committee. Such delay tactics infuriated Truman, who had hoped to obtain favorable action on the bill before Congress adjourned for the fall elections.

Truman was equally incensed over McCarran's attempt to attach an amendment to an extension of the European Recovery Program (Marshall Plan) which called for setting aside $50 million in loans to Franco of Spain. At one of his morning conferences, Truman told his staff that McCarran had been trying for some time to get recognition for the Spanish dictator and had threatened Secretary of State Acheson unless an ambassador to Spain was appointed.

"I think," said the President, "McCarran has been reached." He [President Truman] said that Acheson had told him that in 1945 McCarran came to Acheson, then Assistant Secretary of State, and demanded that McCarran and his wife be sent to the U.N. organization meeting in San Francisco, and threatened them that if they weren't, the Department's appropriations would suffer. The President said that he told Acheson to tell McCarran to "go to hell." However, the Department decided to pay the shot and he went. President Truman said blackmail worked then and McCarran was trying it again now. Clifford said that a certain Senator had said that McCarran was the only U.S. Senator of whom he had positive proof [that he] was a crook.[28]

During Truman's elective term which began in January of 1949, his contacts with former Senate colleagues tended to become sketchier and more formal. The diminution of his relationships with old friends progressed as he came to rely ever more on those people around him, especially Clifford, Marshall, and Acheson. Often he was able for the first time to see that people in the Senate, many of whom he had thought earlier were so great, were highly partisan and really had a limited view of national problems.

When it came to domestic legislation, President Truman got few of the things he asked for. His domestic requests formed a package labeled the Fair Deal and included his attempt to get the Taft-Hartley Act repealed, to establish the Fair Employment Practices Commission, a national health program, the Brannan Plan for relief of agriculture, and federal aid to education. Some observers felt that he exaggerated his demands on the theory of asking for the moon and being satisfied with even a glimpse of the heavens. One veteran reporter, Jack L. Bell, head of the Associated Press staff covering the Senate from 1940 until 1969, believed that Truman had no real expectations of getting his domestic recommendations accepted by Congress. Bell insisted that throughout 1947 and most of 1948, Truman was intent on getting himself reelected; his demands were a "grandstand operation" preparing the way for the presidential race in the fall of 1948.[29]

Certainly, President Truman did use the "Do-Nothing Eightieth Congress" as a whipping boy in his subsequent campaign. In retrospect, the Eightieth Congress which he targeted gave him most of what he asked for in the field of foreign policy, although it rebuffed him on nearly every front when it came to legislation concerning national affairs. There was considerable truth to a statement made by Charles Halleck, Republican majority leader in the House during the Eightieth Congress, when he later complained:

It always galls me to think that Harry Truman won in 1948 by attacking the Congress which gave him his place in history.[30]

10

Persuading the People

Neither candidate made a speech on the stump that will
survive in the schoolbooks, but those of Truman at least
had some human warmth in them.

HENRY LOUIS MENCKEN *(on the 1948 Campaign)*

IN a passage that is often quoted, the English historian Thomas Macaulay once declared grandly: "Parliamentary Government is Government by speaking." And indeed there were periods in both British and American history when an outstanding party leader was that eloquent parliamentary spokesman who could sweep colleagues along on the flood of his legislative debating. But the golden age of American oratory—an age that produced such giants as Webster, Hayne, and Clay—had passed long before Harry Truman was born. By the time Senator Harry Truman arrived in Washington, the party leaders were not necessarily those who could persuade their colleagues but were instead those popular politicians who could bid successfully for the confidence of the voters. Congress was not so apt to assert its independent will as it was to elicit, register, and reflect that shapeless entity known as public opinion.

The beginning of the second quarter of the twentieth century saw an ever-accelerating growth in public reliance on what has come to be called mass communication. Mass communication has several characteristics that distinguish it from person-to-person communication and from traditional speaker-audience relationships. Among these characteristics is the ability of the various media—newspapers, magazines, movies, radio, and television—to reach vast, widespread, and unseen audiences. For example, a large metropolitan newspaper may be read by literally thousands of persons, and a single voice via radio or television can be heard by millions.

A second characteristic is that for the most part modern mass communication is a one-way process. Usually there is scant opportunity for reader, viewer, or listener to seek additional clarification, challenge assertions, or offer more information. There may be letters to the editors, or in the case of presidential remarks, there may be subsequent correspondence sent to the White House. But no matter how carefully tabulated, these subsequent messages represent only a tiny fractional response.

Third, the amount of information available to newsgatherers and awaited by an eager public is obviously far greater than the scanty information often used to persuade in an earlier day. Ideas disseminated by the mass media are the result of much selection; it simply is not possible to print everything or to broadcast complete accounts of most events. The medium is forced to choose material particularly selected for the audience it wishes to reach. In the case of presidential remarks, many circumstances, facial expressions, gestures, and related matters are omitted necessarily.

While Franklin Roosevelt had little experience as a legislative speaker, his extraordinary popularity would be hard to explain if one were to ignore the matchless radio appeals that captured the minds and emotions of millions of ordinary citizens. Harry Truman knew that he could not match the oratory of his predecessor when it came to making radio appeals to the citizenry. He did believe, however, that if he himself fully understood the facts, phrased those facts plainly, and repeated them often enough to the public, his arguments would prevail. The major test of his belief would come with the general election of 1948.

Press Conferences

Truman had been an active politician for more than twenty-five years before he came into the White House. He realized that even as president his remarks would have only minimal effect until they were converted into newspaper paragraphs and radio reports. Actually, his relationship with the working press had been extremely good during his years in the Senate, and as president he moved quickly to maintain these healthy contacts. Newsman James E. Pollard quoted *Editor & Publisher* as stating that Truman began his presidency with "a larger acquaintance among newspaper men than Hoover or Coolidge ever enjoyed or than Roosevelt had in 1933."[1]

President Truman held his first press and radio conference five days after he took the oath of office. He held his last one just five days before leaving the White House in January of 1953. In the intervening period of nearly eight years, he met the reporters in a total of 324 press conferences at fairly regular weekly intervals. Knowing the impact these conferences would have on the voting public, Truman prepared for them very carefully. While most of the conferences were general ones open to authorized press representatives, approximately a dozen were held for such restricted groups as the executive committee of the Negro Newspaper Publishers Association or the editors of monthly magazines for the Standard Railroad Labor Organization.

It was Truman's practice to hold a briefing session with his staff about one week prior to a scheduled press conference. At these preparatory meetings, Ross and Clifford, or in the later years Joseph Short, Roger Tubby, or Irving Perlmeter, would submit notes of probable questions and points likely to be raised. As well as their questions, the various press secretaries would have information which they had collected from agency heads or from other officials. This information then was shared with the president in order to give him pertinent data and probable answers. On the day of the press conference and approximately a half hour before it began, President Truman would hold a second meeting with his press staff for a quick review of possible questions and suggested responses. These two separate briefing sessions were planned to enable him to respond succinctly and accurately to any issue that could be foreseen. While it was impossible to anticipate every question, most of those who participated felt that there was great merit in the practice sessions and that their batting average was quite high.[2]

There were exceptions, but usually Truman's manner in conducting his press conferences was relaxed and confident, seldom stiff or formal. Most of the time he was patient with journalists, although he could be sharp if he thought they were trying to pressure him or if he felt they were trying to take control of the conference. He took to these meetings a bluntness bred in the army and nurtured in the rough and tumble world of big city politics. His comments and conduct soon put reporters at ease, but also demanded respect. He demanded that respect not so much for himself as for the office he held.

One observer, in analyzing the press conferences of three presidents, found that Franklin Roosevelt held an average of 6.9 conferences per month; Truman's average was 3.5, and Eisenhower's was 2.0. The same researcher concluded that President Truman "found his press conference the most effective channel through which to reach the American people and the rest of the world."[3]

Douglass Cater once characterized Truman at press conferences as "the backwoods Baptist laying down a personal testament of God and Mammon to the congregated reporters."[4] Truman was ever quick to defend himself if he felt his authority was being questioned. His tartness with reporters who he felt were pushing him too hard can be seen in an exchange that occurred in 1948 during a discussion of a severe drop in commodity prices:

> QUESTION: To recapitulate, you do not think, then, sir, that the drop in commodity prices has lessened the—
> PRESIDENT: Now, you needn't put what I think into the question, because I can't answer it.
> QUESTION: I was trying to clear up my own mind—
> PRESIDENT: All right, then ask it, and see if I can answer it or not.[5]

Another example typical of Truman's determination to speak for himself is seen in his sharp retorts during a press conference discussion of atomic energy:

> QUESTION: Are you intending to say that you didn't think public discussion does any good?
> PRESIDENT: No, I am not. You needn't put words of that kind into my mouth. I will answer your questions—
> QUESTION: I thought I was asking one—
> PRESIDENT: All right, proceed. You don't put words in *my* mouth [emphasis Mr. Truman's].
> QUESTION: Do you think that public discussion will answer the situation?
> PRESIDENT: Public discussion helps every situation.[6]

Occasionally, Truman was evasive in his answers to journalists, but reporters who attended his conferences also noted that in contrast with his predecessor, who liked to wander over all sorts of terrain and give discursive responses, President Truman tried to stick closely to the material at hand. Certain reporters represented special challenges, and Elizabeth May Craig was one who gave him frequent trouble. Craig was a Washington correspondent for several Maine newspapers, and her column, *Inside Washington,* was a regular feature in the Gannet chain. On several occasions she was involved in sharp exchanges with presidents. Once when Franklin Roosevelt, in a rare moment of petulance, had complained about newspaper unfairness, Craig defended the press corps and reminded him that he had a columnist in his own family (Eleanor Roosevelt, writer of the newspaper column, *My Day*). At a time when President Truman was making plans for adding a balcony to the south front of the White House, Craig told him at a press conference that it was not his privilege to alter the exterior appearance of a historic mansion. She added that anyway Republicans regarded him as a temporary tenant of the mansion. Although he considered Craig often impertinent, President Truman did invite her to go along on several overseas trips as one of the privileged press representatives. One of her colleagues noted Craig's disturbing effect on the President:

> In the case of Mr. Truman, he had one bete noire who drove him crazy, and it was May Craig. He could not stand that woman and I've seen him clasp his hands and shake them as though he had them around her throat. And I think had he had them around her throat we would have had murder in the White House because he was not very fond of her.[7]

Frequently the reading public was misled into believing that President Truman's press conference remarks were spontaneous and ill considered. As a result of this impression, some people came to think that he was overly quick and careless in making other judgments. In actuality, he realized that much of his public image depended on whatever prominence and interpretations writers would give his press conference statements and demeanor. His positions and indeed his remarks, therefore, were usually the result of planning and rehearsal even when they appeared to be impromptu and casual.

In public meetings Truman was inclined to repeat phrases used by questioners, and this tendency got him into trouble several times. One instance occurred in the furor over the dismissal of Henry Wallace. At a conference on September 12, 1946, Truman was asked if his approval of Secretary of Commerce Wallace's remarks applied to a particular paragraph or to the whole speech. Mr. Truman picked up the reporter's phrase and replied, ''I approved the whole speech.'' Two days later he called reporters into his office to clarify what he then termed ''a natural misunderstanding.''

Another occasion occurred during a discussion of possible action the United States and the United Nations might take against Communist China. A questioner asked the president if there were any consideration of using atomic bombs in retaliation, and Truman inadvertently replied, ''The military commander in the field will have charge of the use of the weapons, as he always has.''[8] This comment was interpreted by the press to mean that President Truman had said the commander in the field had the choice of using atomic bombs. The interpretation brought British and French ministers scurrying to Washington seeking a quick clarification.

The single incident stemming from press conference remarks that gave Truman his greatest and most continuing embarrassment concerned his alleged ''softness'' toward Communist infiltration in the government. The original exchange centered around the phrase ''red herring'':

> QUESTION: Mr. President, do you think that the Capitol Hill spy scare is a ''red herring'' to divert public attention from inflation?
> PRESIDENT: Yes, I do, and I will read you another statement on that, since you brought it up.[9]

At that point, the president read a statement in which he quoted his instructions to federal agencies telling them they could permit congressional committees access to certain unclassified forms relating to their employees, but nothing ''relating to the employee's loyalty.'' President Truman stressed that ''no information has been revealed by these committee investigations that has not long since been presented to a federal grand jury . . . that has not long been known to the FBI.'' He added that the hearings served no useful purpose and instead were doing irreparable harm to certain people. Ending his prepared statement, the president then said that the hearings were simply a ''red herring'' to keep the committees from doing what they ought to do. After further elaborating the point that the information had been presented previously to a grand jury, President Truman was asked:

QUESTION: Mr. President, could we use a part of the quote there, that last: they are simply a "red herring"?

PRESIDENT: Using this as a "red herring" to keep from doing what they ought to do.

QUESTION: Are we going to get copies of that?

PRESIDENT: Yes.[10]

President Truman maintained unusually good relations with the news media most of the time, but he was not above making sarcastic references to what he called "Monday morning quarterbacking by the press." His reactions to editorials of certain publications varied from enjoyment to disgust. The editorial which seemed to bother him more than any other that was published during his two terms in office was one which appeared in the February 13, 1951, issue of his newspaper archenemy, the *Chicago Tribune*. The editorial writer charged that Truman had brought the presidency to its lowest point in history through his protection of grafters, corrupters, and the Pendergast spoils system. The editorialist concluded by saying, "Truman is crooked as well as incompetent. That is sufficient ground for the impeachment of any official." The president was understandably indignant and sent a fast memo to his attorney general in which he intimated serious consideration of libel proceedings against the *Tribune*. Despite the fact that he sought legal grounds for ascertaining the libelous nature of these attacks, the evidence is clear that after a while he simmered down and adopted an attitude of philosophical forbearance. He later wrote Clifford:

> I am wondering if all the libelous statements, particularly this one and several others that we are familiar with, could not be kept until sometime in the future when we could make use of them not for gain but for historical purposes.
>
> There have been only two or three Presidents who have been as roundly abused and misrepresented in certain sections of the press as I have.[11]

Truman's favorite newsman was Arthur Krock, Washington bureau head for the *New York Times*, and in 1949 Truman wrote Krock:

> I enjoy immensely reading the editorials of the *New York Times*, the *Baltimore Sun*, the *Washington Star*, the *Washington Post* and others. The McCormick and Hearst editorials are not fit even for publication, let alone for reading matter.[12]

Krock had met Truman on a couple of social occasions and had been impressed by his conversations. He suggested to the president that his opinions about news reporting and editorializing would make a good newspaper story. Truman invited Krock to come to see him, so an appointment was made for Monday, February 13, 1950. Krock's visit was off the record, but he and the president talked for some time. Later Krock talked with Press Secretary Ross and told him he had offered to submit what he wrote to the president who could then have it checked for accuracy. Truman had replied that he need not do that, but Ross did go over the article and made some minor corrections—removed a few quotation marks—and then went over it with the president. The story was displayed on the first page of the *Times* with a three-column head, first line reading, "An Interview with Truman."

At his next press conference the first question to come up dealt with quotations that had appeared in Krock's article. Truman snapped back at the questioner asking him if he had even read the story in the paper. When the answer was affirmative, the president told him to read it again and he would have his question answered. After another short question, President Truman spoke testily:

> May I say to you gentlemen right now—you seem to be in a kind of disgruntled mood this morning—that the President is his own free agent. He will see whom he pleases, when he pleases and say what he pleases to anybody that he pleases. And he is not censored by you or anybody else. I have tried my best to be as courteous to you gentlemen as I possibly can be, and I expect to continue that, but I don't like your attitude this morning, so just cool off.[13]

A few of the correspondents appeared sulky and disturbed, so after another question President Truman assured them that his remarks were not meant to be a reflection on every bureau chief and reporter in the White House. Eben Ayers, the president's assistant press secretary, recorded his version of the continuing dialogue:

> Doris Fleeson, woman columnist, who called Ross yesterday and almost weeping, protested, entered the controversy, asking if the giving of interviews went by favor "and there is no longer a rule." She said they were under the impression there was a rule or custom which had the binding force of a rule.
> "It is a custom," the President replied. "It will continue," but he said, "I will do as I please with regard to breaking it."
> Fleeson said that was the information she wanted, and President Truman added, "That is the answer. You have the information, and I am not disgruntled in the slightest."
> Fleeson, "Why should you be?"
> President Truman returned to restraint, and turning away from her, said, "I am in as good a humor as I can possibly be, but I would like to answer some questions that have a bearing on the present situation."[14]

Like other presidents before him, Truman smarted under newspaper or radio criticisms. He once complained to a friend, "Of course, there isn't a newspaper editor in the United States who doesn't know how to run the

Government better than the President does." On another occasion he said forthrightly that there were only two classes of newspaper columnists—the "ivory tower" ones and the "guttersnipe" variety. He went on to make his simple distinction, "One writes from an ivory tower and the other writes from the gutter, and not one of them tells the truth except by accident."

In one of his amusing flights of whimsy on the subject of columnists, Truman wrote the following memo:

> I have just made some additions to my Kitchen Cabinet, which I will pass on to my successor in case the Cow should fall when she goes over the moon.
>
> I have appointed a Secretary for Columnists. His duties are to listen to all radio commentators, read all columnists in the newspapers from ivory tower to lowest gossip, coordinate them and give me the result so I can run the United States and the World as it should be. I have several able men in reserve besides the present holder of the job because I think in a week or two the present Secretary for Columnists will need the services of a psychiatrist and will in all probability end up in St. Elizabeth's.[15]

Despite his occasional blasts at the press, the majority of working reporters gave Mr. Truman high marks for his conduct of press conferences. The marks were a tribute to the efforts of several close advisers—notably Clifford and Ross—who had grown wise in public relations and who often cautioned restraint in presidential utterances. The briefing and practice sessions were invaluable in helping present Mr. Truman as a knowledgeable, competent leader who knew the facts before he made his decisions. By the beginning of 1948 many reporters had come to appreciate Truman's candor, and many of them secretly admired his feistiness. Republican gains in the congressional elections of 1946 led most journalists to think that Truman had little chance of recapturing the presidency in 1948, but press and public would soon learn more about his effectiveness as a political campaigner.

Planning a Strategy

Nearly every observer of the American presidency regards Truman's upset of the pollsters in 1948 as one of the most remarkable episodes in his entire career. Indeed the victory was so dramatic that it tends to obscure other substantive achievements of his administrations. Contrary to popular explanations, the win was not just another example of the Truman "luck"; nor did it happen because Thomas Dewey was a weak opponent. The victory was more than an example of a determined man fighting against discouraging odds. Such explanations are misleading in their simplicity, and they ignore the shrewd analyses and meticulous staff work that lay behind the Truman campaign.

Clark Clifford is often credited with being chiefly responsible for Truman's successful strategy, and certainly Clifford's influence was so great that it cannot be overlooked. As Special Counsel to the president, he was the funnel through which all major proposals and suggestions had to flow. The record shows, however, that Clifford functioned more as synthesizer of various strategies than as their originator. Some suggestions he rejected outright; others he endorsed, and in case of doubt he passed them on to the president for his consideration.

There is no hard evidence that President Truman needed encouragement to run for a full term, but an initial show of support for doing so came from a small unofficial group that began meeting early in 1947. The so-called liberal wing of advisers formed the group's nucleus, and it included Oscar Ewing, Matt Connelly, Leon Keyserling, and Robert Hannegan, who then was chairman of the Democratic National Committee. Clifford frequently joined the informal gathering which met regularly to eat dinner and to discuss long-range economic and political goals. On another level, memoranda came steadily through administrative channels informing the president of the constantly changing political situation and recommending certain courses or attitudes for him to take.

Throughout the twentieth century, presidents usually have been able to control their party conventions, and for that reason Truman himself was confident that he could not be denied the nomination if he desired it. Others were not so sure. His popularity had soared soon after he succeeded Roosevelt but had dipped alarmingly during the congressional elections of 1946. The following year his stock as measured by public opinion polls had risen due in large part to such measures as the Marshall Plan, his advocacy of government action to curb high prices, and his resolution in meeting the challenges of the labor titan, John L. Lewis. Most of the Truman advisers thought the election would be won or lost on domestic rather than on foreign policy issues.

James Rowe, a Washington lawyer who had worked in the White House during the Roosevelt years, began planning a 1948 strategy. Under the general direction of Clark Clifford, Rowe developed a thirty-three-page, single-spaced memorandum entitled "The Politics of 1948."[16] The analysis was done at the specific suggestion of Director of the Budget James Webb, and Rowe was unequivocal in his assessment of political realities. He was equally blunt in advising the president of what he should do if he wanted to win in the following year. Rowe's lengthy memorandum of strategy was funneled through Clifford who refined it very little but added a section mostly on civil rights. When the memorandum finally reached President Truman it was forty-three pages of double-spacing, dated November, 1947, and bore the familiar initials "CMC" above the typed name, Clark M. Clifford.

It is understandable that because of Clifford's highly visible position and because of his administrative talents this key document began to be attributed to him rather than to its primary author. Only a few insiders at the time realized that much of the original analysis came from Rowe. George Elsey, when asked if he had assisted Clifford in the preparation of the memorandum, recalled:

> I did not. I did not write it; I did not assist him in it. I did see some drafts of it. I read portions of it from time to time, but . . . I was more of a casual observer of the process at work than a participant in it. I would say that the thoughts that Clifford was expressing there, were as I understood it then, and have no reason to change my opinion since, were pretty much the outcome of those discussions that he was having on a fairly regular basis with the Oscar Ewing group. . . . The group of people who would meet from time to time in Oscar Ewing's apartment at the Sheraton Park and talk over political matters. *Also, Mr. Clifford had the benefit of memoranda that other keen observers on the political scene around town had written and had sent to him* [italics supplied]. He took all of this material and considered it, and studied it, material both written and oral, and consolidated it in a fashion that he thought would be meaningful and helpful to President Truman.[17]

When asked if there were any particular ''observer'' to whom he referred, Elsey answered:

> Well, I do recall that James Rowe had sent one memorandum to Mr. Clifford which he found particularly impressive.[18]

Rowe's sizable contributions to this key document can be inferred from entries made on the daily calendar of Budget Director Webb. Early in the summer of 1947 Rowe started meeting regularly with Webb, and almost invariably after each meeting, Webb then met with President Truman and Clifford in the White House. Democratic National Chairman Hannegan also attended these latter meetings.

Moreover, Rowe's primary input for the blueprint of strategy Truman adopted is substantiated by an item on Webb's calendar for Monday, December 1, 1947:

> Brother Webb,
> Do you have any objections if I give to Senator-Chairman McGrath [McGrath succeeded Hannegan as Democratic National Chairman] (who has asked me for suggestions) my copy of a memo I wrote last September on several interesting matters?
> I will not reveal who got the memo in the first place—unless you have no objection.
> Will you have Mrs. A. phone me yes or no?
>
> JHR[19]

When queried about the extent of his authorship of the significant memorandum, Rowe offered a modest reply:

> So far as I know the Truman memorandum you refer to is essentially mine. It was done for Truman in 1947 at the suggestion of Jim Webb, then the Director of the Budget.
>
> It was sent to Clark Clifford at the White House. I know he added something, I think mostly on Civil Rights, and sent it on to the President. Clark tells me he is not sure what he added because his papers are at the Truman Library. . . .
>
> In the past, some scholars have told me that my memorandum is single-spaced and the Clifford revision is double-spaced.
>
> So far as I know, the above is an accurate account of the memorandum you are interested in.[20]

A premise underlying most of Rowe's and Clifford's arguments was that the Democratic party was an "unhappy alliance of Southern conservatives, Western progressives, and Big City labor." In an earlier age, John Hay had called the party "a fortuitous concurrence of unrelated prejudices." As election year 1948 approached, the party was indeed a conglomerate that drew elements not only from the South, West, and big cities, but was a magnet for the doctrinaire liberals and radicals, Jews, and blacks then newly recognized as a voting bloc. The great majority in these disparate factions had voted Democratic regularly in the past four elections, but no one could be sure whether they had done so because of party or had swung into line due to Franklin Roosevelt's commanding leadership.

The strategy described in the Rowe-Clifford memorandum—which was sent to the president over Clifford's signature in November of 1947, almost a full year before the election took place—set forth seven major assumptions:

1. Governor Thomas Dewey of New York would be the nominee of the Republican party.
2. President Truman would be elected if the Administration would concentrate on the Democratic alliance between the South and West.
3. Henry Wallace would become the candidate of a third party.
4. The independent voter in 1948 would hold the balance of power and would not actively support President Truman unless a great effort were made.
5. The foreign policy issues of the campaign would center on relations with the USSR and the Administration's handling of foreign reconstruction and relief.
6. The domestic issues of the campaign would be high prices and housing.
7. Tensions and conflict between the President and the Legislative Branch of Government would increase during the Congressional Sessions of 1948.[21]

The document then moved into a discussion of how President Truman could best take advantage of the seven probabilities. The analysts asserted that entrenched political leadership was senile and dying; the party needed rebuilding from the ground up. It was necessary to revitalize the administration's working contacts with progressive labor leaders, and the cultivation of these leaders could be done only by President Truman himself. To counter the third-party threat posed by Henry Wallace, the strategists urged the administration to persuade known liberals and progressives to move into the fray; they *"and no one else"* should point out that the core of Wallace's backing was made up of Communists and fellow travelers.

A section of the document dealt with practices that might improve President Truman's public image. Members of the cabinet and the administrative staff should do more to point out his qualities as they observed him in his working habits. There were assertions that the American people had tremendous interest in their chief executive and were invariably hungry for news about him. With that hunger in mind, the memorandum suggested that the president have an occasional lunch with such prominent scientists or business men as Albert Einstein and Henry Ford II.

Rowe and Clifford stressed that President Truman should be identified more clearly as leader and shaper of American foreign policy. Secretary Marshall was a fine man, but the plan which bore his name gave away too much credit in an election year. In the American republic it is the president who is responsible for foreign policy. Military affairs would continue to capture the attention of most voters, who, if nothing else, would feel the matter through their pocketbooks—seventy-four cents of every budget dollar would go for defense. Therefore, announcements on military matters ought to come not from the Department of Defense but from the White House. The American voter must not be allowed to forget that the president is the commander-in-chief.

It should be remembered that this document of political strategy originated in the summer of 1947, and it urged the president to recognize even then the advantages in persuasion accruing to him through his powers of office. The presidency is vastly more flexible than Congress, and this flexibility meant that the president could act much faster and more often in persuasion than any group of senators or congressmen. President Truman was encouraged to seize the "great opportunity of presenting his program to the American people" in his message on the state of the union, scheduled for delivery the following January. The writers candidly explained:

> He [the president in his State of the Union Message] can present his recommendations simply and clearly to the Congress so that the people will know what the President is asking the Congress to do. There is little possibility that he will get much cooperation from the Congress but we want the President to be in position to receive the credit for whatever they

do accomplish while also being in position to criticize the Congress for being obstructionists in failing to comply with other recommendations. This
will be a fertile field for the development of campaign issues.[22]

The writers predicted that high prices, housing, the Marshall Plan, tax revision, conservation of natural resources in the West, and civil rights would
become the main points of conflict between the two major parties. Prices at the
time were considered high but were expected to spiral toward even higher
points during the following year. The issue probably would crest in the summer
of 1948, and that would be a "propitious" time for the president and the
Democratic administration.

Housing was an issue that could be presented in a light favorable to the
Democratic party. Truman earlier had approved a rent control bill but in doing
so had criticized the rent control lobby that had worked against any governmental action on housing. The strategists took a cue from Machiavelli and
declared:

> It is the essence of politics to wage an attack against a personal devil; the
> Real Estate Lobby should be built into the dramatic equivalent of the
> Public Utility Lobby of 1935. Purely on the merits, the performance of the
> real estate interests in their post-war gouging fully deserves everything they
> get in the way of retaliation. There can be no possible compunction in us-
> ing such tactics against them.[23]

It was expected that Congress would go along with President Truman's
recommendation for the Marshall Plan, but there was likely to be intense controversy over the type of organization set up to administer the program. The
memo acknowledged that Congress might turn down Truman's recommendation that the European Relief Progam be administered by the secretary of state,
and such a turn-down would allow political benefits to be reaped. If a separate
agency were created and the job poorly performed, then the president could
argue that Congress had refused to follow his recommendation and the confusion, inefficiency, and waste—inevitable elements in any large undertaking—
were the result.

In earlier pages the memorandum had stressed that the South was safely
Democratic and that the administration should concentrate on winning electoral votes from the West. In that section of the country, conservation of
natural resources, reclamation projects, better roads, and more public power
plants would be especially persuasive themes.

Rowe and Clifford approached the matter of civil rights more gingerly
than any other issue. They recognized that the Democratic party was
"vulnerable' insofar as the Negro* vote was concerned. The writers acknowl-

---

*Throughout most of Mr. Truman's active life, *Negro* was an acceptable term. The term *black*
did not come into popular usage until later. Truman would have felt that *black* was pejorative.

edged that Republicans were making great efforts to garner black votes through a fair employment practices commission, an anti-poll tax bill, and an anti-lynching bill. The memorandum departed from its pattern of specificity elsewhere and on civil rights only cautioned:

> The Administration would make a grave error if we permitted the Republicans to get away with this. It would appear to be sound strategy to have the President go as far as he feels he possibly could go in recommending measures to protect the rights of minority groups. This course of action would obviously cause difficulty with our Southern friends but that is the lesser of two evils.[24]

The Rowe-Clifford report concluded by recommending that a small working committee be set up and given the assignment of coordinating all political activities in and out of the administration. The committee members must be "Truman men," who would be ever alert in discovering how the president could seize political advantage from programs, agencies, and daily events. The committee would give the president a monthly estimate of political trends, including the rise and fall of popularity of leading Republican candidates and any liabilities or particular troubles the Democrats might face. There should be intensive research on each of the major candidates likely to be involved in the next presidential campaign. To lead these research efforts, there should be created a "Dewey expert," a "Taft expert," and in order to be safe even a "Truman expert," who could play the role of devil's advocate.

No one can examine the presidential campaign of 1948 and fail to be impressed with the part played in it by this Rowe-Clifford memorandum. Right or wrong, the authors believed that preservation of what was good in American life depended on a Truman victory. This end was so overriding in importance that almost any means were justifiable. The operational guide charted the exact course the campaign would follow. Moreover, it was a coldly pragmatic document that assessed the needs of the president and devised a pattern of tactics that closely fitted his personality and temperament.

The memorandum was cynical but accurate in predicting that labor would vote its pocketbook. There was a strong demagogic flavor in advising that the Taft-Hartley Act ought to be played up as a "slave-labor act" even though President Truman himself had benefited from its provisions several times earlier. There was further demagoguery in trying to garner all the credit for victories in foreign affairs—victories which had come about through congressional bipartisanship—and then assuming that such cooperation would vanish if Republicans were elected. Perhaps the most Machiavellian aspects of the strategy lay in proposing that President Truman submit legislative programs to Congress even when he knew they would be defeated.

Overstatement and hyperbole are handmaidens for political campaigning in America. Timothy Dwight, clergyman and president of Yale University at the opening of the nineteenth century, had said that if Thomas Jefferson were elected his victory would make "our wives and daughters the victims of legalized prostitution." In similar exaggeration, Republican Robert Ingersoll in 1888 had charged the Democrats as being "the friend of an early frost and believers in the Colorado beetle and the weevil." The pattern in 1948 was not entirely dissimilar when President Truman hammered away at the derelictions of the Eightieth Congress.

Traditional debate strategy calls for the incumbent to defend his administration and most of the status quo, but the Rowe-Clifford memorandum reversed such tactics. President Truman was the "in" candidate, but in 1948 he became the attacker. He was an incumbent who seized the offensive and succeeded in putting his challengers on the defensive.

Truman's 1948 Campaign: Phase I

The nature of his office brings political shadings into nearly every presidential remark. Sometimes the shadings are so light as to be hardly discernible; at other times they are garishly apparent. In the case of major addresses, the political ramifications may be staggering. There are three messages of consequence the president is expected to submit each year: the state of the union address, the budget message, and the economic report. Each of these demands months of preparation and represents efforts from many advisers and administrators within the executive branch.

The state of the union address traditionally is given early in January, and by that month of 1948 President Truman and his confidants already were determined that the speech would be the opening salvo in their battle for the presidency. George Elsey, perhaps the most sanguine of all the Truman writers, viewed the speech as a political maneuver. He believed it should be "controversial as hell" and should draw the line between Republicans and Democrats. Clifford concurred, and President Truman accepted their advice. The earliest drafts of the message were even more partisan than its final wording. Because of the sharpness of its attack on the Eightieth Congress, there was little doubt of the strategy Truman Democrats were going to follow.

The Rowe-Clifford memorandum had pointed out the unique setting for the state of the union address. All senators and representatives attend such sessions as well as members of the cabinet. Most ranking foreign diplomats are invited to the event, and the press reports it in great detail, usually giving it the best position on page one. In Truman's time television had not come into accepted use, but such addresses were broadcast live over all major radio networks. Thus on January 7, 1948, when he appeared in the House chamber to make his speech, President Truman had assurance that his remarks would be heard or eventually read by millions of American voters.

The manuscript that President Truman read made no direct mention of the forthcoming election, but it did not require much imagination to look beyond the overt wording to find an underlying belief that progress was identified with Democrats and that failures would inevitably result if Republicans were elected. A subject on the minds of many voters at the time was adequate housing, and the president denounced the absence of any long-range housing program. He declared that before the severe shortage of homes could be overcome, rent controls would have to be extended and strengthened. Among other ambitious proposals incorporated in his message were: increases in unemployment compensation, improvements in old age and survivors' benefits, more federal aid to education, and a nationwide system of medical insurance. He called for increased efforts toward the conservation of natural resources and asked for more multipurpose dams and more developments in the nature of the Tennessee Valley Authority. Turning to agriculture, he advocated continuing price supports, establishment of more farmer cooperative associations, and extension of rural electrification. He then appealed to wage earners by asking that the minimum wage be nearly doubled, raising it from forty cents to seventy-five cents an hour.

Most presidents find it advantageous in their state of the union addresses to praise the goal of world peace, and Truman was no exception. He did not dwell long on foreign affairs, however. He asked for full support of the United Nations and urged Congress to appropriate 6.8 billion dollars for the first fifteen months of the Marshall Plan. There was also a passage that appealed to many Americans with strong loyalties to other lands and countries. He requested new legislation to permit thousands of displaced persons—persons then living in refugee camps overseas—to enter the United States.

Two months earlier Truman had given Congress a ten-point plan to combat the rising costs of living. In his state of the union speech, he did not repeat these ten points, but he stressed the need to grapple with the threat of inflation, which he called the "one major problem which affects all our goals." He surprised the legislators by suggesting a specific tax reduction plan that would allow each taxpayer to deduct forty dollars for himself and for each dependent from his final tax bill.

There was little favorable reaction to President Truman's speech. His immediate audience was attentive but seemed to sit on its hands until at least the midpoint of the message. There was a ripple of applause from Republican ranks when he pledged to enforce the Taft-Hartley Act even though he disagreed with it. However, Truman's tax reduction scheme almost caused apoplexy among some Republicans, and the next day Senator Robert A. Taft of Ohio delivered a half hour "reply" to the president over the American Broadcasting

Company's radio network. Taft estimated that Truman's tax device would cost an extra five billion dollars a year, and he charged that Truman was presenting the federal government as "Santa Claus himself."[25] Other Republicans were equally indignant. Harold Knutson, chairman of the House Ways and Means Committee, exclaimed:

> My God, I didn't know that inflation had gone that far! Tom Pendergast paid two dollars a vote and now Truman proposes to pay forty dollars.[26]

Other Republicans rose to the bait Truman offered them. Charles Halleck, majority leader in the House, responded to the forty-dollar tax cut by harkening back to the Reconstruction slogan of "forty acres and a mule." The Hoosier senator snorted derisively, "What, no mule!"

But criticism came not only from political opponents. During presentation of the address and in the weeks immediately following it, there was conspicuous silence from Democratic partisans. One press survey indicated that only seventeen Democrats would admit to being generally in favor of President Truman's proposals. A few Democrats who were usually recognized as "liberal" legislators approved his domestic themes, but it could not be said that he had won in any way his party's endorsement.

Moreover, press comments were less than enthusiastic. Arthur Krock of the *New York Times* described the address as promising "everything including the kitchen stove." That newspaper seemed to like some parts of the speech but criticized the tax credit as demagogic gimmickry which could only add to the nation's problems with galloping inflation.[27]

Harry Truman had been in the Senate long enough to realize that there was little chance of getting his programs enacted quickly by Congress. That group might accede to certain requests in the areas of military preparedness and foreign aid, but those were not the areas Truman intended to use in political campaigning. He understood full well the prestige of his office and knew that it would generate publicity for any messages sent from the White House to Capitol Hill. He agreed with his close advisers, therefore, that it was simply prudent politics to bombard Congress with presidential messages. During the first months of 1948, he showered Congress with an unceasing barrage of requests, suggestions, and counsel. Most observers understood his maneuvers. Jack L. Bell, chief political writer for the Associated Press and the journalist then covering the Senate, was one of many who saw Truman's actions as a political gambit:

> Truman always exaggerated his demands. His theory was to ask for the moon . . . and hope to get 10% of what he asked for. Truman knew the score. He had been in the Senate; he knew how it worked, and he knew

how the operation went. He knew exactly what would happen to his recommendations. But he was intent on getting himself elected to the Presidency and his was a grandstand operation.[28]

Though Truman's state of the union address failed to win much immediate support from his party, there is no doubt that his message was planned as a framework for the Democratic platform to be written at the Philadelphia convention in July. A presage of that hectic convention arose in February when the president sent to Congress his special message on civil rights. His message adhered closely to strategy devised earlier, and as foreseen in the Rowe-Clifford memorandum, the action caused more than a little "difficulty with our southern friends." His thunderclap on civil rights went far beyond what any predecessor had offered, and in doing so it opened a fissure that grew until it led ultimately to the Dixie revolt. There were political gains though, because Truman's forthright requests ensured that the important black vote would be solidified behind the party he led.

The origin of Truman's civil rights program went back to an executive order he had issued in December of 1946. That order had created the Committee on Civil Rights, a prestigious group led by Charles E. Wilson, then president of General Electric. The committee had prepared a lengthy, widely publicized report—To Secure These Rights—which among other things called on the federal government to take the initiative in trying to end discriminatory employment practices, in protecting the right to vote by establishing an anti-poll tax law, in seeking enactment of antilynching laws, and in setting up a permanent commission on civil rights.

If judged by today's standards, President Truman's call for action on civil rights in 1948 seems rather innocuous, but it was an audacious document at the time it was issued. The message brought southern tempers to an immediate white heat, and Dixie Democrats lost neither time nor opportunity in denouncing the man responsible for it. A conference of Southern governors had been long planned, and when that group held its scheduled meeting in Florida the president's message preempted all other matters. One proposal there asked that the assembled governors notify national party leaders that "we no longer will tolerate the repeated campaigns" for civil rights legislation. The governors voted instead for a forty-day cooling-off period during which time a committee from their group would interrogate the Democratic national chairman about the administration's program on civil rights. A short time later, four thousand southern Democrats gathered in Jackson, Mississippi, and endorsed Governor Fielding L. Wright's call for a new grouping of "all true white Jeffersonian Democrats" to act against the Truman leadership.

On February 19, traditional Jefferson-Jackson Day dinners were held in cities throughout the country. The purposes of such meetings were to bring the faithful together, to enrich the party's coffers, and to stimulate enthusiasm for the forthcoming campaign. That year, discord and bitterness worked against such goals. In Little Rock, Arkansas, when Truman's voice began coming in over the radio to the Democrats assembled for the Jefferson-Jackson Day dinner, nearly half the 850 guests arose and walked out. In Washington, the meetings were held in two separate hotels—the Statler and the Mayflower. President Truman addressed both throngs, but an unpleasant public rebuke was effected at the Mayflower. Senator Olin D. Johnston of South Carolina had purchased a block of seats at a table conspicuously near the speaker's dais, but the senator and his guests had connived to avoid the meeting. When reporters asked about the empty table, the senator's wife blithely told them that she and her guests had decided not to attend "because I might be seated next to a Negro."

When an angry delegation of southern governors subsequently called on Senator J. Howard McGrath, chairman of the Democratic National Committee, to see if the president might modify his proposals, they were told that Truman would not budge from the course he had charted. A veteran White House correspondent for the *Washington Post,* Edward T. Folliard, was one of many who credited Truman for political courage on the issue of civil rights:

> A lot of people seemed to think that the civil rights movement began with Roosevelt, and I just don't believe that. He did do something about Federal employment. I've forgotten what it was, but I'd like to remind you that Roosevelt never lost a Southern state in an election. But we did have this revolt against Mr. Truman in the South because, well, he had appointed a commission to look into the matter of civil rights. He also had started integrating the troops in the armed services. At any rate, the South thought, as they would put it, that he was a "nigger-lover" and they couldn't understand why he was doing it, because they knew that his grandparents had fought in the Confederacy. I remember that some Governor in the South called him a "dead Missouri mule."[29]

Despite the movement begun in the South to wrest the party away from Truman's leadership, the response of most Democrats serving in Congress was restrained. In the House, the powerful Rayburn, although a Texan, declared: "I am not going to vote against the Democratic ticket just because I don't agree with President Truman on these matters." Rayburn's sentiments were echoed by other southern leaders in Congress, who thought Truman's message was a "foolish piece of politics" not serious enough to risk a rupture in the national party.

In 1948 as spring became early summer, there was little doubt that President Truman had won support from most Americans for his militant stand against the Soviet Union. On the domestic front, his achievements were more controversial. He had not pushed vigorously for his civil rights program since its unveiling in February. Nevertheless, his popularity as measured by public opinion polls kept dropping steadily. In his own party, there were burgeoning efforts to drop him. Moreover, third-party threats from the camp led by Henry Wallace as well as the Democratic coalition in the South grew more ominous each day.

The November memorandum of strategy had stressed that if the campaign were to be successful, numerous particular interest groups would have to be aroused. The authors of the memo had considered one interest group, the South, to be "safely Democratic," but the West was "Number One Priority." Accordingly, Truman's advisers and writers suggested to him that he "find occasion to visit the West on business." His trip could be ostensibly nonpolitical, but on it the president would be free to "explain" why the Republican-controlled Congress was not carrying through on his proposals.

An opportunity came when the University of California invited the president to speak at its commencement exercises on June 12. The invitation was accepted and quickly expanded into a fourteen-day excursion across the country. The trip was seen by Truman staffers as a rehearsal for a scenario that would show the voters a fighting president. He was not an insignificant, inarticulate farm boy. He understood the presidency and knew how to win it. Arrangements were quickly made for him to deliver numerous short talks intended to establish just such an image.

The itinerary called for five major speeches—Chicago, Omaha, Portland, the University of California at Berkeley, and Los Angeles. The special train left Washington about midnight on June 3. President Truman was accompanied by twenty members of his personal staff and about one hundred reporters and photographers. For the next two weeks the train doglegged its course across the states giving Truman a chance to hammer away at his political opposition. He was at his best with the small gatherings around the train's rear platform. He delivered more than sixty of these rear platform talks in the course of his June trip, and his folksy, sometimes corny manner seemed particularly appropriate for his immediate listeners.

If judged as a set of speeches aimed toward opening a debate, Truman's talks on this western trip—both his prepared texts and his informal remarks—clearly showed a three-pronged strategy: 1) Get to know your president. They say a lot of things about me that are not true. Here I am. Look me over and decide for yourself. 2) The present Congress, dominated by Republicans, is not working for the greatest good for the greatest number of citizens. Next November you should elect a Congress which will be devoted to the public interest. 3) You in the audience are to blame for having an unsatisfactory Congress. Two-thirds of you stayed home in 1946 and let the other one-third of the voters give you a Congress which is responsible for all these things that are not good for the country.

President Truman did not flinch from the charge that his trip was a political one. At Santa Barbara, California, he told his listeners:

Informal snapshot of speech writer George Elsey waiting to board President Truman's campaign train during a whistlestop at Danville, Illinois, in October 1948.

> If you are on my side, it's [the trip] nonpolitical; if you are not, it's a low-down political trip, to come out and tell the people what they ought to hear.[30]

Senator Robert Taft again answered for the Republican opposition and gave two separate speeches on June 11: one before the Union League in Philadelphia and a condensed version over a national radio hookup. At Philadelphia the Ohioan used a term which offered the doughty Truman too good an opportunity to overlook. Taft referred to what he called Truman's "blackguarding Congress at every whistle station[*sic*] in the West."[31] Jack Redding, director of public relations for the Democratic National Committee, immediately seized on the senator's blundering language. In telegrams to thirty-five mayors of towns where President Truman spoke, Redding asked if civic leaders agreed with Taft's description of their town as a whistlestop. As might be expected, most of the replies were sarcastic and anything but complimentary. Only a small seven percent of the total group of cities answered that it had not occurred to them that Senator Taft's statement could be interpreted as applying to their town. Twenty percent took no position and asked for more details about the original statement. The bulk of the answers made Taft look ridiculous, and some typical responses to his gaffe were:

> (From Seattle) Seattle is not a whistle stop, but everyone who sees her stops and whistles, including Presidents and Senators.

> (From Grand Island, Nebraska) Grand Island was never a whistle stop. Third largest city in Nebraska with 25,000 of the finest people in the Midwest; first sugar factory in the United States here; largest livestock auction market in the world.

> (From Gary, Indiana) Senator Taft in very poor taste to refer to Gary as quote whistle stop unquote. 135,000 citizens of America's greatest steel city resent this slur.

> (From Los Angeles) The term hardly applies to the Los Angeles metropolitan area in which presently live one-thirty-fifth of all the people in the United States, considerably more than half of the population of Ohio. The number of new permanent residents within the city limits of Los Angeles since 1940 approximates the total population of Taft's home city, Cincinnati. I feel quite confident that anyone who could have been in Los Angeles last Monday, a perfect day in June with Southern California sunshine and blue skies, and witnessed nearly one million good American citizens lining the streets to welcome their President, would have both whistled and stopped. (From Fletcher Bowron, Republican Mayor of Los Angeles.]

> (From Crestline, Ohio) Senator Taft's description of our town as a whistle stop is rather misleading in view of the fact that Crestline, Ohio, a town of 5,000 population, is served by two of the world's greatest transportation systems, Pennsylvania Railroad Company and the New York Central. Forty-two passenger trains make regular scheduled stops here daily. Suggest Senator Taft consult time tables of the above referred to transportation systems for a proper classification, proper description of a "whistle stop."[32]

While he was on this preliminary campaign trip, President Truman lambasted Congress for its record on every significant domestic issue except civil rights. He apparently agreed with most of his advisers, who preferred criticism for neglecting that issue to risking further negative reaction from the southern wing of the party. He likewise stayed away from foreign policy as a debating issue because he knew that Congress, although Republican controlled, had marched in step with nearly all of his requests in that area.

His debate technique became evident in his big city speech themes and in his talks before smaller, informal groups. In Chicago, he chose lines of argument that would appeal to listeners representing many nationalities and who had maintained close ties with relatives in Europe. Accordingly, the text he read in Soldiers' Field stressed the need to overcome communism by further improving the American standard of living and by broadening the social security program. He emphasized, too, the desirability of admitting a substantial number of displaced persons, for they, like American pioneers of an earlier age, would help build a better nation. At Los Angeles, he listed eight major pieces of legislation on which Congress had refused to act, or if it had done so, had acted primarily for the benefit of what he called "special interests," including price controls, housing, labor, social security, health insurance, aid to education, reclamation, and the "rich man's tax law."

In small towns President Truman's sallies and optimism were especially effective, for listeners caught his mood and bounced it back to him. He was one of them, speaking their language—the language of the local service club, the small businessman, the farmer, the veterans' organization, and the town's church groups. He capitalized on careful briefings his staff gave him about regional products or projects of civic pride. At Wenatchee, Washington, well known for its abundant apples, he said, "I am familiar with your apple situation, and I am trying to get it worked out." At Idaho Falls, he tried a joke indirectly complimenting the citizens for their handling of the surplus potato problem:

> I understand you grow a lot of potatoes here. . . . You also have a very loyal citizenship. During the war I was up in Presque Island [*sic*], Maine, making an investigation of an air field up there, and I heard that there was an Idaho boy in the guardhouse. I inquired as to why he was in the guardhouse. I was told he had been on kitchen police and refused to peel Maine potatoes.[33]

The trip was not all pluses, for there were mistakes due to careless planning and irresponsible staff work. At the outset, several of the president's old friends failed to make proper arrangements for his appearances. One of the most egregious incidents happened at Omaha, where Truman spoke in the huge Ak-Sar-Ben auditorium. The auditorium had a seating capacity of 12,000, but because of poor ticket distribution only about 1000 people showed up. National news magazines promptly ran stories and unflattering pictures suggesting that the poor attendance was an index of Truman's popularity. At

Carey, Idaho, his briefing was erroneous, and he made several inaccurate statements before discovering that the airport he was dedicating had been named for a young girl who had died in a private plane crash, not named for "the brave boy fighting for his country." In Eugene, Oregon, his offhand comments about Stalin became hot national copy for several days. There he recalled some of his experiences at the Potsdam Conference and lapsed into a folksy evaluation of the Russian leader:

> I got very well acquainted with Joe Stalin, and I like old Joe. He is a decent fellow. But Joe is a prisoner of the Politburo. He can't do what he wants to. He makes agreements, and if he could he would keep them. But the people who run the government are very specific in saying that he can't keep them.[34]

Truman's carelessness on this occasion dramatized the potential importance of any statement made by an American president. It simply was too good a news story to pass up, and one enterprising newsman, Robert J. Donovan, was the first to capitalize on it:

> Apparently, Donovan was about the only writer aboard the train to get his immediate story filed about Truman's remark at Eugene, Oregon, "I like old Joe." The train left, and writers had to climb aboard. When it stopped next at a junction in the Cascades, there was only the telegraph operator, and Donovan reached him with a $5.00 bill and asked for an open dictation line to the *New York Herald Tribune,* his paper at that time. Later he became editor of the *Los Angeles Times.*[35]

The description by President Truman was contrary to views then being put out by Soviet experts in the State Department. They pictured Stalin as an undisputed dictator who controlled the lives and fates of millions in Russia and its satellite nations. Robert A. Lovett, undersecretary of state, immediately telephoned Clifford about Truman's indiscretion. Charles E. Bohlen, a Kremlinologist who later became ambassador to the Soviet Union, also contacted Clifford aboard the train and said that he was mystified about the president's remarks. Advisers convinced Truman that he ought not repeat his statements, and on this matter he followed their advice.

President Truman's western tour gained momentum as the end of the second week drew near. Crowds were larger, and they seemed to relish his attacks on the Eightieth Congress. His debate case had taken definite shape. In Washington during his absence, Congress was driving toward adjournment. Preparations for the party conventions were also well underway. When the president got back to the White House, he expressed confidence that voters would rally to his support in November if he could continue to reach them as he had done for the past two weeks. Few persons, including his closest staff members, were so avowedly optimistic.

Campaign, Phase II: Acceptance Speech

The Republican convention met in Philadelphia on Monday, June 21, only two days after Congress adjourned. For three months preceding that convention, Republicans had been engaged in narrowing their field of candidates. The primary elections had presented a confusing picture because of ballot restrictions and because there were few states where all candidates were entered. One brief contender was General Douglas MacArthur, but he was eliminated early when an expected groundswell for him failed to develop. Next to fall was Harold Stassen of Minnesota, who in May led all other Republican candidates according to the popularity polls. Stassen's fall followed his radio debate with another leading contender, Thomas E. Dewey of New York.

Stassen and Dewey were entered in the Oregon primary where they agreed to a radio debate before a small, select live audience. Their debate was the first one with a nationwide listening audience, so it generated a great deal of public interest. At the time the debate occurred, the question of outlawing the Communist party had emerged as the primary issue for the two debaters. Their confrontation lasted for an hour, and after it was over, the consensus seemed to be in Dewey's favor because of his eloquent portrayal of dangers involved in trying to "outlaw" ideas or associations per se. From that time onward, the Republican contest lay between Dewey and Senator Robert Taft of Ohio.

After Republican successes in congressional elections of 1946, Robert A. Taft was regarded as an almost inevitable presidential candidate. He had grown up in politics, for his father had served the country as its twenty-seventh president. Moreover, Robert Taft had strong credentials in his own right. He had won election to the United States Senate in 1940 and was well into his second term. He was respected as a knowledgeable legislator with a keen mind and one who had attained undisputed leadership of the conservative bloc in Congress. Party stalwarts had chosen him on several occasions to rebut the criticisms President Truman had leveled at Congress. Taft's name was familiar to most voters, for he had derived considerable prestige from his co-authorship of the Taft-Hartley Act. His political liabilities included the fact that he lacked public charisma and that he was regarded as an unfeeling conservative. While a good many persons seemed to agree with him in private, they doubted that he could win a national election.

Taft's obvious rival for the nomination was Thomas Dewey, who had lost to Franklin Roosevelt four years earlier. In 1948 Dewey and his followers believed that his time had arrived. Four additional years as governor of New York had enhanced his credentials. After a rather lethargic start, the Oregon contest made him realize that he would have to bestir himself if he were to win the nomination. As a consequence, he decided on an all-out effort in that state; he invaded nearly every major town, most hamlets, some crossroads, and even hamburger stands. One journalist commented that the New York governor was the greatest explorer of Oregon since Lewis and Clark.

As soon as the Republican National Convention began, it was evident that Dewey had more delegates committed to him than any other candidate. He did have to reckon, however, with strong party tradition against naming a one-time loser, on the principle best expressed by Alice Roosevelt Longworth: "You can't make a souffle rise twice." However, the Dewey forces were extremely well organized, and they simply outmaneuvered those of his opponent. The usual conferences and secret bargains took place, and the first ballot showed Dewey with 434 votes compared to Taft's 224. A second roll call brought the New Yorker to within 33 votes of the 548 required to win. While voting for the third time was under way, dissenters jumped on the bandwagon, and the Dewey choice became unanimous. The next day the convention picked Earl Warren of California as his running mate. With formidable candidates from the two states with the greatest number of electoral votes, Republican hopes soared.

Three weeks after Republicans chose the team of Dewey and Warren, Democrats gathered in Philadelphia for their national convention. By this time it was clear to most observers that the president had enough committed delegates to assure him the nomination. His opposition from within the party certainly had not vanished, but by the sheer political strength of the presidency sufficient votes had been garnered so that he and his forces knew he would head the ticket. But perhaps winning the nomination would not be enough. Truman aides were acutely aware that Democratic disunity might prevent a November victory. George Elsey was one of those worried about the internal strife:

> The Democrats have splintered in all directions and at the moment I see little prospect of any early or happy family reunion.[36]

The Democratic convention opened with less than the usual confidence; in fact, there was an air of gloomy resignation. The caustic columnist, Henry Louis Mencken, suggested that there was fear among traditional New Dealers:

> The convention hall is being repainted for the Democrats, but in the same baby blue that greeted the Republicans. The only portraits so far hung are one for Roosevelt 2d and one of President Truman. The latter shows His Excellency smiling affably, but Roosevelt looks grim and even somewhat alarmed.[37]

The real heat of the convention grew out of the civil rights issue. President Truman had soft-pedaled that matter since his explosive request in February, but southern conservatives were not appeased and threatened to boycott any ticket with Truman on it. Hubert Humphrey, the energetic young mayor of Minneapolis and then a candidate for senator from Minnesota, was one of the leading advocates of a solid civil rights plank in the party's platform. Among those who rallied to his side were James Roosevelt, Franklin D. Roosevelt, Jr., and G. Mennen Williams, destined to become a five-term governor of Michigan. Opposing them were Strom Thurmond of South Carolina and his phalanx of followers from the deepest parts of Dixie.

Many delegates thought a civil rights fight could be avoided by simply repeating the ambiguous language of the 1944 party platform, but the Humphrey-led forces would not allow it. They held out for a flat endorsement of the program President Truman had sent to Congress the preceding February. Arguments finally got beyond the control of the platform committee and came before the full convention for a final vote. On this vote, the Truman proposals as championed by Humphrey won decisively, but the victory did not come cheaply. When the results of the vote were announced, thirty-five delegates, mainly from Mississippi and Alabama, rose from their seats and conspicuously strode from the hall. Actually, the walkout was smaller than feared, and the bulk of southern delegates remained and accepted the more moderate position that the issue should be settled within the party.

Truman's nomination was threatened not only by southern conservatives but by Democrats who did not believe he was adhering closely enough to New Deal philosophy. Indeed, most of the early liberals had not survived the transition from Franklin Roosevelt to Harry Truman. By convention time in 1948, only two acknowledged liberals—Oscar Chapman, secretary of interior, and Governor Ernest Gruening of Alaska—had been retained in the official top administration echelon.

To offset some of the criticisms coming from liberals within the party, Truman was urged to persuade Supreme Court Justice William Douglas to become his running mate. Douglas turned down the offer, however, and Alben Barkley, largely on the merit of his compelling convention oratory, was nominated for the vice-presidency.

The heat in Philadelphia during the convention was almost unbearable, and the humidity was higher than the temperature. The sweltering weather was a topic that arose in nearly every conversation and was forgotten only during the intensity of the civil rights bitterness and during Alben Barkley's keynote address. The enthusiastic reception given that performance was recounted earlier, and many delegates expected that President Truman's acceptance speech would be anticlimactic.

There had been much discussion within the circle of Truman advisers about his reputed weakness as a public speaker. Those who attended the Wednesday suppers in Oscar Ewing's apartment worried about Truman's ineffectiveness on the platform—a place where his opponent, Tom Dewey, was expected to excel. There was no doubt that President Truman could not read a speech well, but some of his supporters had begun to notice that he could extemporize quite impressively. The first realization that Truman had talents in this pattern had surfaced in April during his talk to the American Society of Newspaper Editors. That speech had gone through the usual drafts and corrections. The prepared address dealt with the subject of inflation, and he gave the manuscript his customary wooden interpretation. There was more to the occasion though, for he also had written, on nineteen pages of White House stationery, his version of Russian activities since he had come into office. These nineteen handwritten, five-by-eight-inch pages became the basis of a two-and-a-half-page typed outline, double- and triple-spaced between major points. The outline was to be used as a reminder for extemporaneous remarks offered after his manuscript speech was completed. *Mirabile dictu!* It was his extempore speech that captivated his listeners and won great applause. The outline approach had proved successful for him, and it became the basis for his whistlestop technique used later in June. After Truman began to demonstrate his effectiveness in extempore speaking, several persons were ready to assume credit for recommending the changed mode of delivery. William L. Batt, director of the research division of the Democratic National Committee, was one of those who believed that Truman had added a new weapon to his rhetorical arsenal:

> The President was not an effective public speaker before the campaign began. He was searching for a style which would be most comfortable for him. He didn't read a script well. . . . So I recall he was always experimenting with something different and at some point in the proceedings Clifford, and/or Murphy developed this idea of a speech written in the form of an outline where every topic sentence was a complete sentence and it was also a jumping-off point for extemporaneous remarks. . . . He used this technique down at the Departmental Auditorium . . . . For the first time he tried this technique of prepared sentences and extempore remarks intermixed, and it went over great. I remember all of us concluding, "This is it. He's found it!" This was the technique that was used mainly from then on. He could, if he wanted to, stick to everything that was prepared, that he'd worked on, or he could take off from it, and he just fit in that like a hand in a glove.[38]

On his western trip and in the weeks immediately following it, Truman turned to extempore delivery more and more. When he went to Philadelphia to accept his party's nomination, he went armed with twenty-one pages of carefully screened ideas that had been typed in a combined outline-essay form. The outline was triple-spaced and each page, with the exception of the conclusion, contained only one main point.

Preparation of the speech had started early, and several persons had submitted ideas or even drafts to the writer-in-chief, Clark Clifford. Samuel Rosenman, who was not so active a Truman writer as he had been before the ascendancy of Clifford, urged a "fiery" approach that would center on foreign policy, but that subject was not acceptable to Truman. He had discovered that voters were more interested in hearing him castigate Congress for its failures to act on domestic matters as he saw them. One draft for the acceptance speech was dated July 9, and was prepared by William Batt. This draft was sent to Clifford but was not directly used. Batt discovered, however, that all his input was not in vain:

> I listened carefully because I was curious to see if any of my language stayed in; only one idea I had in my draft stayed. . . . When I paced up and down our little apartment the night when Clark [Clifford] had given me this assignment, I was asking my wife. . . . "We've got to give some reason. What reason can the President give for wanting to be re-elected?"
>
> She said, with that gorgeous, deceptive simplicity that women are capable of, "It's all very easy, because we're right and they're wrong."
>
> So, I put that in. "We're going to win because we're right and they're wrong." And out of the entire draft which ran for over fifty minutes, that one sentence is the only thing that stayed.[39]

On Tuesday, July 13, two days before the address was to be given, Sam Rosenman joined the writers Truman mainly depended on at that time—Clifford, Murphy, and Elsey—and the four of them holed up in the cabinet room to develop a bona fide draft. This version in turn went through three other drafts before one was acceptable to President Truman. He already had decided to use a modified outline form, so he asked his writers to cast the message in just such a mold. The result was the twenty-one-page outline-essay he carried with him to Philadelphia.

President Truman left Washington by train early in the evening of Wednesday, July 14. The convention hall in Philadelphia was packed hours before the night session began and was insufferably hot and humid. Outside was a crowd estimated at twenty-five to thirty thousand, milling around, hoping to slip inside if a chance arose. It would not have been proper for the prospective nominee to appear in the hall before his nomination was confirmed, so Truman chose to wait in a small bare room beneath the stage that held the dignitaries. His room had a tiny balcony and doorway which led to a service alley. That doorway was the only ventilation he had because the only air-conditioned office had been scheduled for meetings of various attendees. There is no evidence that the small room was deliberately chosen as an affront as some opponents and scribes were to assert later—it was simply the nearest space that offered the president any measure of privacy. Most of the time he sat on a wooden straight-backed chair waiting out the long evening session. As hours dragged on, it became obvious that the roll call of states would not be reached until after midnight. Truman was asked if he wanted the convention to recess for the night in order that his address might be given the next day. He declined the offer because he and his advisers believed there would be great dramatic effect in an acceptance speech delivered as a climax to the evening's momentum.

The convention had its other moments of drama: Dixiecrats had walked out; Wallace-ites had condemned the meeting; a former mess sergeant with a booming brass voice led a continuous demonstration outside the hall to nominate General Eisenhower; and before the president greeted the delegates the pigeons were turned loose.

Emma Guffey Miller, an experienced and dedicated committeewoman from Pennsylvania, conceived the idea of releasing "doves of peace" over the crowd inside convention hall. The "doves" were supposed to symbolize the president's concept of peace. Pigeons were easier to come by in Philadelphia than doves, so several crates of the birds were secretly brought to the hall. When Truman was nominated, someone opened the crates, and the birds fluttered out. Leonard Reinsch, one of Truman's advisers on the scene, described the happening:

> The first time we heard about this was when the *Life* photographer, perspiring as all of us were, came in and said, "They won't let me photograph those dying pigeons." This shook us up, but there were enough things shaking us up at that time so we didn't get particularly concerned about the remark. The next thing we knew, apparently crates of pigeons that were pretty well beaten down by the heat were opened somewhere in the hall. Some tired, hot pigeons staggered out of the crates. They spotted the fans in the ceiling and when they got enough energy several of them headed for the ceiling fans. The spectators immediately below the fans lost all interest in what was happening on the platform and kept their eyes on the pigeons flowing around the ventilating fans.
>
> Some other pigeons had a little more energy and a couple of squadrons of them spotted Sam Rayburn's perspiring bald pate, which made quite a target near the rostrum area. They zoomed in on this shiny target, and the first time Rayburn knew what was happening, pigeons were coming at him from all directions. He waved his arms around and got them scared off for awhile; then they regrouped. This target looked pretty good, so they zoomed in again—and by this time it was a little bit too hot in the auditorium anyway and all of us were tired—and the Speaker started moving his arms around; the pigeons started going in all directions, and he finally leaned over, and the radio audience from coast to coast heard the Speaker utter in despair and disgust, "Get those goddamned pigeons out of here."[40]

Oblivious to the shenanigans taking place on the convention floor, Truman kept going over the remarks he planned to make. In later years when compiling his *Memoirs,* he wrote that he also fell into a reverie and reviewed the lives of former presidents. About 2:00 in the morning of Thursday, July 15, the signal came that the delegates were ready to hear him. He was escorted down the aisles and onto the speaker's platform in a manner befitting the president of the United States and a nominee just selected. Before Truman spoke, Alben Barkley, who had accompanied him to the rostrum, made a short speech accepting the vice-presidential nomination.

Always a dapper dresser, Truman had chosen for the occasion an almost white Palm Beach suit, and he presented a cool contrast to most of the tired, sweaty delegates and functionaries. As soon as he was formally presented, Truman walked to the lectern and placed on it the familiar black notebook that now contained his twenty-one pages of outline. Smiling broadly, he then stepped back, bowed, and waved repeatedly while waiting for the tumult to die down. When that began to happen, he approached the lectern again. As he prepared to speak, there were shouts from the crowd for the bustling photographers to get out of the way and for Truman to lower the battery of microphones hiding him from his listeners. He responded with an offhand comment that tickled many partisans because of its double meaning:

> I can't. I have to have them [the microphones] up where I can see. I am sorry that the microphones are in the way, but they have to be where they are because I've got to be able to see what I am doing. As I always am able to see what I am doing.[41]

After this sally, the president began his extemporaneous talk. Listeners today probably would be very surprised if they were to hear the speech as he delivered it. Modern listeners first would notice his short, staccato rate, in sharp contrast with the practice encouraged by voice coaches for contemporary presidents. Also, listeners would learn that his voice, always somewhat nasal, lacked the resonance that marks most successful political speakers in an age dominated by television. Moreover, his enunciation was sometimes so blurred that "foreign policy" came out almost like "farm policy," and final consonants often were missing from the words "accept" and "worst." But these were only minor problems, if Truman's talk is to be judged by the way in which the crowd responded. The first burst of real enthusiasm generated by what he said, rather than by his mere appearance as the party's choice, came early in the introduction. On the first page of his outline, this introduction was suggested by only ten words:

1. Introduction
   (a) Thanks for nomination
   (b) Acceptance
   (c) Reference to Vice Presidential candidate.

President Truman's interpolations can be best appreciated if one examines what he actually said as he started his speech.

> I can't tell you how very much I appreciate the honor which you have just conferred upon me. I shall continue to strive to deserve it. I accept the nomination. [Applause] And I want to thank this convention for its unanimous nomination of my good friend and colleague, Senator Barkley

of Kentucky. [Applause] He is a great man and a great public servant. Senator Barkley and I will win this election and make these Republicans like it. Don't you forget that! (Outburst of sporadic yells and sustained cheering.) We will do that because they're wrong and we are right, and I will prove it to you in just a few moments.[42]

As he moved through his speech, Truman continued to make insertions worded in the type of language that had proved so successful during his previous tour of the West. Indeed, it was his on-the-spot interpolations, not the outlined remarks prepared by his writers, which rallied the weary delegates and brought them to their feet cheering the man they had chosen to lead them. For instance, Truman did not mute the obligations of the American farmer as he saw them. That blast came out while he was extolling the record of the Democratic party, and the record includes the statement: "Farm income has increased from less than two and one-half billion dollars in 1937 to more than eighteen billion dollars in 1947." Then he barked out his own assertion:

> Never in the history of any republic or any kingdom or any other country were farmers as prosperous as farmers of the United States, and if they don't do their duty by the Democratic Party they are the most ungrateful people in the world.[43]

The audience howled in agreement. When he began reciting improvements gained by labor, he ad-libbed an equally blunt declaration:

> Labor's had but one friend in politics, and that was the Democratic Party and Franklin D. Roosevelt.[44]

After these thrusts, President Truman insisted that increased income should benefit all the people. He then added his unwritten observation that this "last, worst 80th Congress proved just the opposite for the Republicans." His accusation brought forth more loud applause and one voice shouting above all others: "Pour it on, Harry." He answered in American vernacular: "It is the business of the Democratic Party to see that all the people get a fair shake."

When he began citing his party's record in foreign policy, Truman departed from his text long enough to insert a reference to Woodrow Wilson and the League of Nations, which he declared had been "sabotaged" by Republicans. Next his outline showed the following points:

(b) Now the United States accepts its full responsibility for leadership in
   international affairs.
   i—United Nations.
   ii—Foreign aid.
   iii—Removal of trade barriers.

Truman's remarks as given, however, did not follow the exact order in his outline, for he first mentioned the United Nations and apparently overlooked the next item. He discussed "removal of trade barriers," and then without any noticeable gap in communication, he returned to the skipped item, namely, the subject of "foreign aid." On this point, he ad-libbed his contention that "Politics should stop at the water's edge, and I shall continue to preach that throughout this campaign."

From the Democratic party's record, Truman moved into a series of accusations against the Republican party. Here he was on equally familiar ground, and he marched through the subjects of high prices, housing, labor, federal aid to education, social security, health, basic human rights, and taxes. When discussing taxes, Truman declared that the Republicans had passed a tax bill that was so "rotten" they could not stand it themselves. When they finally passed a slightly improved version, the new law was one that "helped the rich and sticks the knife in the back of the poor." No such intemperate language had appeared in his prepared outline.

The more Truman referred to Republicans, the more strident became his utterances. He belittled the Republican record in each of the areas he had marked out. For example, he said that when the Republican Congress finally got around to submitting a housing bill, it "isn't worth the paper it is written on." Referring to the Republican platform section dealing with slum clearance, he said, "I wonder if they think they can fool the people of the United States with such poppycock as that!"

On the labor issue, he reminded his listeners that while the Democratic party platform called for repeal of the odious Taft-Hartley Act, Republicans, although professing to be friendly toward labor, had cut labor appropriations so much that only one bureau was left. Then, in a grammatical lapse that was untypical of him, he added, "And it *can't hardly* function." It is unlikely that any in the crowd noticed his grammatical error, however, as he approached the climax of his speech.

Rhetoricians agree that a well-built speech, like a poem, should have a structural climax, that is, a high point of interest toward which the speech moves. A person could search the annals of American public address and not find a better example of a rhetorical climax than the one Truman used on this occasion. The undeniable high point of interest came when he revealed his intention to recall Congress:

> On the 26th of July—which out in Missouri they call Turnip Day—I am going to call that Congress back and I am going to ask them to pass laws halting rising prices and to meet the housing crisis which they say they are for in their platform.[45]

A necessary feature of an effective rhetorical climax is that it occur near the end of the address, and when the tumult over Truman's surprising decision began to subside, he moved into a brief conclusion. In this section, his writers had forsaken the outline format and had returned to essay form. For the first time in his address, President Truman began carefully reading his manuscript. He closed with a paraphrase of words from Franklin Roosevelt, but no peroration could really add to the drama and excitement he had aroused a few moments earlier.

President Truman had decided early to deliver this talk extemporaneously. Nearly one week before he gave it, he told his staff that he intended to speak off-the-cuff and hoped he could "keep the swear words out."[46] Of course, the speech was in no way impromptu, for it went through several carefully drawn drafts before being put in outline form. One draft written two days before the actual address did not mention the special session. This omission has caused some historians to conclude that the decision to call Congress back was not made until a few hours before the speech was given.

The idea of recalling Congress was suggested to President Truman by several persons. William L. Batt from the Democratic National Committee offered one explanation:

> It was between the Republican and the Democratic convention, and it was also at the time I was working, at Clifford's request, on a draft for the President's acceptance speech that the idea came to us [i.e., the group working in the Research Division of the National Committee] for calling Congress into a special session. So we went up that Wednesday night and I made the best case I felt I could make advocating the callback of the Congress to this little "Kitchen Cabinet" [the group meeting since early January, 1948, drawing plans for Truman's re-election and consisting of: Ewing, Brannan, Murphy, Clifford, Elsey, Bell, and Keyserling]. I was voted down. . . . The group didn't accept the idea. . . . I came back the next morning rather sheepishly and reported to my team that I'd made the best case I could, that there was some support for it, but on balance it had been voted down . . . conceivably by Jack Ewing. . . . I asked Clifford for an appointment to talk further about it. . . . Then I talked to him on the phone, and he said, *"Put it in a memorandum"* [emphasis added]. I'm not sure whether or not I did put it in a memo . . . but I went down and talked to him, and he was far more receptive to the idea that next day than the group had been the night before. Clifford, undoubtedly, was the guy who persuaded the President to adopt the idea of calling the Congress back.[47]

In files of other advisers to Truman at the time, there are references to an unsigned memorandum dated June 1948, entitled, "Should the President Call Congress Back?" This mysterious memo advocated a recall because:

> 1) The reactionary record of the 80th Congress would be spotlighted, 2) it might force Dewey and Warren to defend the actions of Congress, 3) it could keep the glare of publicity on such "Neanderthal men" as Martin,

Halleck, Wolcott, and Allen, 4) it might split the Republicans on such issues as housing, inflation, social security, and 5) it could give the President an excellent chance to follow through on his fighting western trip and also show him *in action on Capitol Hill* fighting for the people [emphasis in original].[48]

When shown this unsigned memorandum recommending a special session, Batt surmised that it came from his group because the ideas were so familiar. Undoubtedly, persuasions from Clifford and Sam Rosenman also helped bring about Truman's decision, but because the suggestion for a special session came from so many persons it is difficult, if not impossible, to pin down the first source of this advice.

The acceptance speech was a bold and typical Truman action. His promise to recall Congress helped accomplish his immediate purpose of buoying the hopes of dispirited delegates. He conceded later that he knew the session of Congress would be fruitless as far as any legislation was concerned. He had to have something to run against, and his speech focused national attention precisely on the target he and his advisers had marked out earlier—that "awful, do-nothing 80th Congress." He had begun his case well, and in the next three and a half months he would drive it home.

Campaign 1948, Phase III: Talking to Voters

Almost as soon as the convention ended, President Truman set his writers to work preparing a message for him to deliver to the special session of Congress. He saw the occasion as another opportunity to reach the voters. Again, he received memoranda from many quarters advising him of topics and approaches that could be used in this delicate situation. The situation was bound to be delicate because his congressional listeners could hardly be sympathetic toward a speaker who had been so relentless in his criticisms of them during the past six months. Senator Carl Hayden of Arizona, an old friend from Senate days, sent him a six-page memorandum that included eleven points that the senator thought should be emphasized. This list was turned over to writer George Elsey, who was given the task of preparing the first draft.

Elsey also had materials from the president's Council of Economic Advisers. From these two sources he put together a first draft and discussed it with Clifford. The latter agreed with most of the script but recommended eliminating any kind of endorsement of specific bills in the field of civil rights. The election was going to be too close to risk further alienations on that score. Clifford ranked the topics in an order of importance: 1) inflation, 2) housing, 3) education, 4) minimum wage, 5) social security, 6) health—omit, 7) civil rights—omit, 8) federal pay, 9) displaced persons, 10) United Nations—undecided, and 11) wheat.

Within one week, this proposed speech went through six major drafts. On July 21, Clifford showed the latest version to Truman, who gave it tentative approval. Truman also called in numerous Democratic leaders and checked with them. He invited their suggestions, for he realized that he must infuse a fighting spirit into a badly splintered party. Press Secretary Charles Ross began feeding to reporters details from the forthcoming speech piece by piece, thus ensuring that more attention would be drawn to the event.

Meanwhile, more suggestions were coming in from organized labor. Phil Murray, the CIO president, gave Truman a list of twelve items his union wanted stressed; only four of these were not accepted or were noted "not at this session." The four were: 1) repeal of Taft-Hartley, 2) national health program, 3) adjustment of veterans' benefits, and 4) a farm program, including price supports and soil conservation.

Inflation was given highest priority in the speech. When discussing the final draft with his staff of writers, President Truman remarked that they should all keep in mind that Congress was not made up only of rich men. If most congressmen doubted the impact of rising inflation, they ought to ask their wives about the cost of feeding a family in 1948 as compared with those costs a year ago. He said that he would remember to say something like that. His final manuscript showed this passage:

> Since last November, prices have gone even higher. As every housewife knows, food prices rose rapidly throughout 1947. They are climbing even faster now. Month after month the cost of clothing, fuel, and rent keeps on going up.[49]

When he read these lines to Congress, Truman recalled the former discussion and ad-libbed:

> The cost of living is now higher than ever before in our history; there are not very many rich men in the Congress of the United States. Most of you have to live on your salaries. All you need do is just go home and ask your wife how living costs are now as compared with what they were January 1, 1947.[50]

President Truman gave this speech to Congress on July 27, and Republicans greeted him with open hostility. Some members did not even rise from their seats as he entered and left the chamber. There was scattered, perfunctory applause only six times during his thirty-minute address, but in reality he was talking to a much wider audience. He appreciated the coverage his address would get in the nation's press and radio. The whole event was planned publicity that came through just as expected.

Truman's strategy left the Republicans in a quandary. Should they do nothing as he had predicted and adjourn immediately? Or should they attempt to rebut his criticisms by taking their not insignificant record, especially in foreign policy matters, to the people? Should they select a few of the less controversial measures and try for early enactment? They looked to their own nominee for directions, but strong leadership was not forthcoming.

By the time of Truman's nomination, his Republican opponent, Governor Thomas E. Dewey of New York, already had determined the broad outlines of the battle he meant to wage. He intended to run a "dignified" campaign and avoid any real confrontations with the president. After all, public opinion polls gave Dewey overwhelming assurance. At that time the Gallup poll gave him 48 percent of the vote and Truman only 37 percent; Wallace got 5 percent, and the remaining 10 percent of the respondents were undecided.[51] The Roper poll taken slightly later was even more encouraging, for it showed Dewey with 46.3 percent, while Truman's vote dropped to 31.5 percent; Wallace received 3 percent, and the remaining 19.2 percent expressed, "no opinion."[52] Strongly influenced by these findings and guided by unanimous opinions from his advisers, Dewey believed that his lead was too great for Truman to overcome.

Moreover, it was evident that President Truman intended to continue his pattern of unrestrained attacks. It was argued that if Dewey were to respond in kind, there might be a groundswell of sympathy for the embattled president. Dewey's analysis was reinforced by memories of the 1944 campaign in which he had been extremely aggressive in his attacks on Roosevelt. Reviewing that defeat four years later, the New York governor and his advisers concluded that such assaults had hindered, not helped, his case for the presidency.*

President Truman's western tour in June had buoyed his own spirits although few on his immediate staff shared his optimism. He began his official campaign the first week in September with outings that would last nearly two months, cover eighteen states, and give him opportunity to deliver numerous short, extemporaneous talks in addition to formal manuscript addresses.

He and his staff had learned much from the June experience, and this time planning for his appearances was carefully assigned and meticulously carried out. His two major advance men were Oscar Chapman, undersecretary of the Interior, and Donald Dawson, an administrative aide normally in charge of personnel assignments. Their job was to visit each major city and check on local arrangements before the president's train arrived. State and civic dignitaries were selected to board the train when it arrived, meet the president, and then

---

*While it is impossible to examine a political campaign from one side only, the focus of this work is on the persuasive practices of Harry Truman; hence Dewey's campaigning will not be recounted in detail. Other books cover the 1948 election from a variety of different angles, including analyses of Dewey's campaign strategy. Among such books are: Jules Abels, *Out of the Jaws of Victory;* Robert J. Donovan, *Conflict and Crisis;* Susan M. Hartmann, *Truman and the 80th Congress;* Irwin Ross, *The Loneliest Campaign;* Joseph C. Goulden, *Mencken's Last Campaign.*

travel a few miles with him through their home territories before being bounced off in favor of a similar group from the next region.

When the campaign train left Washington on Sunday, September 5, it consisted of sixteen cars. Aboard were more than eighty reporters and photographers, agents from the Secret Service, technicians from the Signal Corps, and more than a dozen Truman aides and secretaries. The last car of the train was a Pullman especially equipped and adapted for the president and his family. The car was dubbed the *Ferdinand Magellan* and contained its own galley and dining area, two bedrooms, a combined living area and office, and an oversized rear platform covered with a protective striped canopy. Thousands of American voters would always remember the image of a smiling, waving President Truman standing alone beneath that canopy on the rear platform as his train pulled slowly away and faded from sight.

The first manuscript address was scheduled for Detroit on Labor Day, September 6, but on that day Truman also gave numerous shorter talks at stops en route to his major destination. He spoke first at Grand Rapids, Michigan. Shortly before 7:00 A.M., several hundred persons came to the station to greet his train when it arrived. Then he climbed into one of the several open automobiles, and escorted by local candidates he led a parade to the downtown square. There 25,000 persons jammed into the area to listen to his remarks.

Within an hour and a half Truman was back on his train rolling away from Grand Rapids and toward his next stop, Lansing, Michigan, where he made another extemporaneous talk. His talk there was based on one of the more than three hundred outlines writer George Elsey prepared for him during the final two months of campaigning. In the Lansing talk, there were ten points, each worded in a short sentence and triple spaced in the outline:

(1) an introduction [in which he ad-libbed]
    (a.) this a fine crowd
    (b.) recall labor's contribution in winning the war
    (c.) nowhere are contributions greater than in industrial cities of Michigan
(2) mean to give several speeches in honor of Labor Day, five in Michigan today
(3) Republican philosophy ignores labor
(4) stress that Republicans have not changed
(5) Republican failures during special congressional session I have called
(6) tax bill was enacted because Republicans thought it would be good politics
(7) bad effect of tax bill on average worker
(8) effect of tax bill on rich is in sharp contrast

(9) Republican Congress should have passed anti-inflation program that would help everybody, including farmers

(10) a conclusion: this is election year, choice between a Republican government and a Democratic government. ''Republicans will take you back to policies that led to disaster in the 1920's.''

This ten-point speech set a little drama that would be reenacted more than two hundred and fifty times in the next two months.[53]

Truman spoke briefly at Hamtramck, Michigan, before proceeding to Cadillac Square in Detroit. There he was given a boisterous welcome by more than 250,000 persons. His speech in Detroit was not simply another Labor Day address; it was aimed at all great labor centers—New York, Pittsburgh, Dallas, Chicago—wherever there were tightly reined labor groups capable of turning out a large vote. He knew very well that by condemning Republicans for passing the Taft-Hartley Act over his veto, he would be drilling on labor's most sensitive nerve. Furthermore, he warned in Detroit—one of the greatest labor centers of the world—that if a Republican president were elected, labor should expect treatment even worse than Taft-Hartley. He excoriated the ''do-nothing 80th Republican Congress'' and declared that Republican leaders were men ''with a calculating machine where the heart ought to be.'' In its verbal exaggeration the Detroit speech seemed to be just what laboring men and women wanted to hear. The crowd was with him all the way, for his denunciations frequently brought forth the chorus: ''Pour it on'' and ''Give 'em hell, Harry!''

Encouraged by his Detroit reception, President Truman returned to Washington for a few days before embarking again on his arduous schedule. By this time his entire strategy was well set; everything would be planned to give his speeches an air of honest spontaneity. One reporter at the time noticed the president's confidence:

> Coming back from Detroit, Roscoe Drummond, who I believe, was still with the *Christian Science Monitor,* then, he and I got Clark Clifford into the compartment and said, ''Now look, Clark, the President talks about winning. He is very optimistic; he's very, very sanguine. Does he really believe he's got a chance to win this election?''
> And Clark laughed and he said, ''We don't know. It's a wonderful thing for the staff. We all feel we are on our own goal line and we've either got to punt or pass or do something desperate, but the boss doesn't seem worried, and it's very morale-building for us.''[54]

The Rowe-Clifford memorandum entitled ''The Politics of 1948'' had assured Truman that he would be elected if the administration would capitalize on the traditional alliance between the South and West. The two writers agreed that the South could be considered safely Democratic—a judgment that failed to foresee that area's dissensions over the civil rights stand. Truman was urged to concentrate on winning the West. If Democrats could capture the West, they also would pick up enough votes from doubtful midwestern states to assure victory even if states with big electoral votes—New York, Pennsylvania, Illinois, New Jersey, Ohio, and Massachusetts—were lost. The farm vote lay mainly in the Midwest and was judged as identical with winning the West. Both were given "the Number One Priority." This line of reasoning led Truman to follow his exhortations to labor with a tour of midwestern states where he centered his fire on the critical farm vote.

President Truman decided to deliver his major farm policy address in the heart of Iowa, a state proud of its agricultural heritage. This significant address was given on September 18, a day during which Truman also delivered twelve other extemporaneous talks. That Saturday was a day filled with commitments but was representative of his endeavors and schedule in the period between September and the election in November. He and his advisers chose the occasion of the finals of the National Plowing Contest, which were held on the farm of Mrs. T. R. Agg. Her model farm was near Dexter, Iowa, a small town of 635 inhabitants, only thirty-five miles from the state's capital.

An enormous crowd, variously estimated at sixty-five to eighty thousand persons, had gathered on the farm by the time President Truman arrived. How many had come for the plowing contest and how many out of a desire to hear the president could not be determined.

Truman began his address by recounting hardships farmers had endured during the Great Depression and before their subsequent rescue by the New Deal. It was the Democrats, he asserted, who passed legislation which lowered interest rates, reduced farm mortgage indebtedness, and permitted many American farmers to begin tasting some of the fruits of prosperity that were standard fare for "the Wall Street reactionaries" and "these gluttons of privilege."

The year 1948 was a good one for grain production in the United States: the corn crop of 3.7 million bushels was the greatest in history up to that time—55 percent greater than in 1947. The wheat crop of 1.3 million bushels was the second greatest in history. In part because of this huge production, grain prices had declined drastically. Corn, which was $2.46 per bushel in January of 1948, fell to $1.78 by September. In the same nine months, wheat had dropped from $2.81 per bushel to $1.97. It was Secretary of Agriculture Charles Brannan who brought forth a related issue that, when added to farmers' natural concern over tumbling prices, was to play an important part in Truman's pursuit of the farm vote. That issue was the availability of storage bins.

The shortage of storage bins was closely linked with the system of government price supports for various farm products. The system might seen complicated to city folks, but it was all too familiar to those on farms or working in businesses related to agriculture. Under this support system, the federal government guaranteed farmers that they would not have to risk selling their products below a certain price level. When the market price was above the established support level, a farmer could sell his crop through the usual commercial market. When the market price fell below the support level established by the government, the farmer was entitled to a farm loan at the support price, pledging his crop as collateral. If prices later rose, he sold his crop, repaid the loan, and pocketed the difference. If prices fell below the support level, he forfeited his collateral but could keep the money.

In that year of 1948, because of the enormous grain production, farmers had to store their grain if they were to get an available loan. To qualify for such a loan, the grain had to be stored in approved bins or granaries, but few farmers at that time were able to provide their own storage facilities. In normal years the grain could have been accommodated in commercial storehouses, and any slight excesses could be put in additional bins provided by the Commercial Credit Corporation. However, that agency's charter had come up for renewal in June, and through a legislative quirk the revised charter had specified that the CCC "shall have no power to acquire or lease any such plant or facility or acquire or lease real property except office space." This dilemma left many grain farmers in a plight not of their own making.

President Truman had found another cudgel which he could use against his opponents, and he quickly blamed the shortage of storage bins on the Republican Congress that he alleged was manipulated by wealthy grain speculators. One of Truman's chief strategists in the campaign was Oscar (Jack) Ewing, administrator of the Federal Security Agency, and he offered his evaluation of the storage bin issue:

> There was an enormous crowd of farmers present because it had been advertised that the President would be making a farm speech. It was in that speech that he picked up and made an issue of a matter that had been brought to his attention by Secretary Brannan. The 80th Congress, which of course, was President Truman's chief political opponent at that time, had appropriated nothing with which to build storage bins in which farmers' grains might be stored. . . . The President made the most of the failure of the 80th Congress to provide the necessary storage space. I remember his classic expression was that the 80th Congress had put a pitchfork in the farmer's back. I know the President repeated this all through the campaign.[55]

The pitchfork analogy was a homely exaggeration deliberately chosen to appeal to Truman's agrarian-minded listeners. Years later after President Truman left office, writer Clark Clifford said that he still cringed at the memory of that "pitchfork in the back" expression although he approved the wording at the time.[56]

The storage bin issue was one that Truman could tie in with his denunciations of the Eightieth Congress. Also, it was an issue with strong echoes of the Populist credo of the little fellow in the Midwest pitted against the big financial interests in the East. The issue allowed Truman to identify himself with the farmer or with the man and woman living in a small town. Wherever he went through the farm areas, he hit it hard and with devastating effect.

By this time his short train stops followed a definite pattern. The stopovers were usually ten minutes long, and his appearance took up about half that time. His extempore remarks always began with references to local scenery, industry, agriculture, or history, and his detailed knowledge of small towns and regions seldom failed to surprise and delight listeners. By such adaptations to local audiences, Truman created the impression that he knew a great deal about nearly every community west of the Mississippi. If he himself had never visited the community before, it was likely that Mrs. Truman or one of their relatives, no matter how far removed, had done so. The president made extensive use of his maternal grandfather, Solomon Young, who had accompanied several wagon trains through the West. The frequency of these references to his grandfather led one reporter aboard the Truman train to observe dryly:

> According to a Pennsylvania Railroad representative on the Truman train, this campaign trip is just about the most elaborate tour ever made of this country. I suspect that he is referring only to railroad trips and has conveniently overlooked, for the sake of rail propaganda, those wagon-train trips made by Grandfather Young.[57]

After concluding his four- to five-minute talk, President Truman then would ask the crowd: "How would you like to meet my family?" He knew that indeed many in the crowd were there for that express purpose, so he would say something like: "First, Mizz Truman." Right on cue, Mrs. Truman would come through the door and stand on the right side of her husband beneath the striped canopy. President Truman usually would identify her as "the boss" and wink familiarly at the men in the audience. After Mrs. Truman had exchanged a few greetings with the well-wishers, the proud father would announce: "And now I'd like to have you meet my daughter, Margaret." Some observers noticed that when he was in border or southern states, the president referred to his daughter as "Miss Margaret."

In general, the whistlestop speeches did not define policy for the first time. They simply were reiterations in local terms of policies the president had enunciated previously. The information about specific localities that showed up in Truman's introductory remarks appeared to be firsthand knowledge but in actuality was the result of careful staff work. Truman advisers working with representatives from the Democratic National Committee prepared a list of twelve questions, and this list was sent to leading citizens in each town to be visited. The list was as follows:

QUESTIONS ON TOWNS TO BE VISITED BY THE PRESIDENT

1. What are the particular complaints the people have about high prices in your town? Give us the details and any local incidents on prices.
2. What is the principal problem facing your town and its citizens right now?
3. How did your town vote in the 1944 and 1946 elections? Is it traditionally Democratic or Republican? Who are the candidates for the Senate and the House? Do they have strong popular support? What are their chances of election?
4. What is your town proudest of?
5. Who are the half-dozen most notable citizens of your town? Do you have any Olympic stars? Any war heroes? Any citizens who have won the affection of your citizens, such as ministers, priests, rabbis, or well-loved people in other fields besides religion?
6. What is the size of your town? This means population, physical characteristics (hilly, spread out, etc.), main industries, etc.
7. Give us a brief, colorful history of your town, stressing the events likely to be remembered by most citizens.
8. Does your town have a slogan, such as "the biggest little city in America" or something along such lines?
9. What are some of the local phrases, sayings, familiar jokes about your town?
10. What are the nicknames for political leaders and others?
11. What is the housing situation in your town? Are there any slums? Any public housing projects? How many housing units were built in the town last year? This year? How many units are needed?
12. How many veterans do you have?[58]

The answers to these questions were added to other available information, and a summary sheet, usually one page and never more than a page and a half, was prepared. The summary would show the town's population relative to other cities in the state, major industries, significant dates and events in the town's history, election statistics, and the number of registered Democrats and Republicans. The data was then fed to Truman writers who put it into outlines for the whistlestop talks. Matt Connelly, secretary to the president, described the process:

We'd get material from the National Committee on what was to be identified with this town. Did they have a paper mill or something they were kind of proud of, and that research would be done by the National Committee and passed along to Clifford and his crew. And we'd go into like Haverstraw, Iowa, and there'd be something about they had the state pig production or something of local interest that we worked in at the beginning of the draft. Usually they were just outlines because they used to run twelve or eighteen a day, so you couldn't have a prepared speech at every stop . . . the whistlestop speeches were largely outline speeches or off-the-cuff completely.[59]

After his farm policy speech in Iowa, Truman swung back down into his home state of Missouri, where he spoke briefly at Trenton and Independence. The next day was Sunday, so he attended church in Independence. Later that day he borrowed a car and visited friends and relatives in the vicinity. That night he boarded his train again and left for the West. His next manuscript speech was given in Denver on Monday evening, September 20. He invaded Utah the following day and spoke at Price, Helper, American Fork, and Ogden. Often a town would have some kind of planned camaraderie, and a typical example occurred at Ogden. There he was appointed an honorary captain in the Weber County sheriff's posse, and Miss Utah put a boutonniere in his lapel.

From Utah, the Truman train went into Nevada, and the president spoke at Reno and Imlay. From Nevada, Truman entered California, and among the first places he spoke were Truckee, Roseville, Oakland, and Sacramento. Reflecting the hectic work pace, the speech outlines began to show frequent deletions and corrections, usually made in pencil. A note in Elsey's handwriting appeared on the outline used for the Sacramento speech:

> This was done in about 2 hrs. It was to be a speech on 160 Acre farm limitation—then was completely altered to be about Public Power![60]

On that Wednesday, September 22, Truman gave an important speech in the evening to an audience in San Francisco. By that time writing pressure aboard the train was intense, and Elsey scribbled a note to Clifford:

> Outside Sacramento less than three hrs before speech with no one having seen it! Is there any possibility of detaching you to look at San Francisco outline?
>
> GME
>
> I'm standing outside in corridor. R.S.V.P.

Clifford's response:

> "Hold it. Will get to it later."
>
> CMC[61]

On Thursday, there were brief stops at Bakersfield and Burbank, where James Roosevelt, who earlier in the spring had led the abortive attempt to keep Truman from getting the nomination, boarded the train for the short ride into Los Angeles. The president had spoken in that major California city only two and a half months earlier and had been delighted with his reception. During September, however, neither Truman nor his rival Dewey drew capacity crowds when they appeared in the Los Angeles area. The night Truman spoke, the glamorous Hollywood Bowl was not available; Dewey forces had rented it in order to "rehearse" certain lighting effects to be used when their man appeared the following evening. Truman had to be satisfied with a larger hall, Gilmore Stadium, which made the numerous empty seats even more conspicuous.

The Los Angeles speech was one of the few occasions during the campaign when the president referred publicly to threats from a third party. After delivering his standard attack on Republicans, he changed direction and took a verbal swipe at the party led by Henry Wallace. First, he complimented those people with "true liberal convictions" who were worried over the state of world affairs and were being tempted to vote for the Progressive party candidate. Then he insisted that such action would be throwing a vote away:

> A vote for the third party plays into the hands of the Republican forces of reaction, whose aims are directly opposed to the aims of American liberalism.
>
> A vote for the third party will not promote the cause of American liberalism; it will injure it.
>
> I say to those disturbed liberals who have been sitting uncertainly on the outskirts of the third party: Think again. Don't waste your vote.[62]

As the campaign intensified, it became clear that Truman was aiming his appeals at four distinct groups: farmers, labor organizations, blacks, and consumers. Sometimes the groups would overlap, but usually in the large cities Truman could be counted on to hit hard on the labor arguments. His appearances in cities on the West Coast brought out such tremendous demonstrations by labor groups working in his behalf that when Dewey arrived there and saw all the banners flowing from these organized groups, he lamented, "I wondered whether I was running against labor or the Democratic Party."[63] The more Truman poured it on about Taft-Hartley, the more organized labor responded.

The Democratic National Committee followed Truman's tour carefully to see how his speaking was being received. Sometimes suggestions from the central campaign headquarters in Washington were ridiculed by those advisers caught up in the hurly-burly of the hustings. For instance, one memorandum from Batt to Clifford noted that during a manuscript address the "rattling" of paper was audible to radio listeners. Batt asked, "Would it be possible to use either linen or parchment paper?" His suggestion elicited a one-word rejoinder in Elsey's handwriting, "Nonsense." In the same memorandum, Batt criticized sentences for being too long and involved, with too many dependent clauses. The penciled response was "He can't talk kindergarten all the time."[64]

Truman barnstormed the West Coast from September 17 to October 2; in the period he covered a total of 8600 miles and gave 135 talks, ranging from prepared addresses to informal remarks. Whenever he talked about conservation, he reached sympathetic ears. That subject was considered vital by voters in the vast Rocky Mountain and Pacific Coast areas, for to them conservation meant the reclamation of formerly arid land by turning water on it so it could be opened up for farming and homesteading. Great quantities of cheap power were necessary to pump this water in and out of the huge reservoirs and distribute it where it was needed to provide electricity and energy for new industries.

As the Truman train wound its way through the western areas, pressure to write material for the next stop mounted. Sometimes routes were changed, and a talk prepared for an intended stop had to be discarded. For example, one speech had been prepared for Denison, Texas, but the president spoke instead without preparation from a platform at Sherman, Texas. Elsey noted, "No preparation for this —our route was changed!"[65]

No town was too small, and press associations were quick to capitalize on any quirk or oddity in a local community. At Temple, Texas, Truman referred to an article in the *Washington Star* under the caption, "Truman's Stop in Texas Required by Town Ordinance." The accompanying story explained that once a town marshal in Temple had halted a presidential train:

> It's a good thing President Truman scheduled a campaign stop here. The town marshal halted one presidential train that was scheduled to pass through without stopping.
> It's a law.
> The city ordinance goes back to 1904, when Temple residents heard that President Theodore Roosevelt intended to go straight through town without a pause. The City Council . . . passed an ordinance requiring all presidential trains to stop at least five minutes. The city marshal and county sheriff halted Mr. Roosevelt's train, climbed aboard and served papers on the engineer. Mr. Roosevelt made a speech, complimenting the city on its nerve. The ordinance never has been repealed, but it never has been needed since.[66]

Truman laughed about the ordinance and told the crowd that it really was not needed; he was going to stop anyway because "your Congressman says I promised him to come here."

President Truman and his advisers on the campaign train kept getting messages from Washington that his speeches should include more statements about the threat of communism. Memoranda from the Democratic National Committee insisted that the American people were being "saturated" with propaganda in the press and radio to the effect that the Truman administration had done a poor job in dealing with communism. Moreover, those persons in Washington who were helping plan Democratic strategy believed that Dewey intended to make communism one of the major issues in the campaign.

The whistlestop campaign—President Truman with his running mate Alben Barkley and his daughter Margaret.

It was important to choose the right time and location for a major speech dealing with communism. Batt wrote Charles Murphy recommending against making such an address in California, and Murphy concurred. Another occasional writer for Truman, Stephen J. Spingarn, advised Clifford:

> My opinion is that this speech should be made as far East as possible and, in any event, not West of the Central Time Zone. I say this because I think it is the type of speech that should have the widest possible radio audience. I believe it will be the kind of fighting speech that will have more impact on the air than in print. Because of the three hour time difference, relatively few people in the East would hear the speech if it were given in California. At the same sime, I think the speech should be made as early in the campaign as reasonably possible. I think Mr. Batt is right when he says that the middle West is the place where the cries of Communism are doing the most damage. . . . In all the circumstances, I think that Oklahoma City would be an appropriate place for the speech.[67]

Oklahoma City was selected as the place to strike hardest at communism. Because of the emotionalism in that issue, the writers aboard the train weighed each word in this manuscript speech very carefully. From Washington, Murphy wired a suggested change in one sentence reading: "I charge that the Republicans have impeded and made more difficult our efforts to *apprehend* communism in this country." Murphy suggested that the word, "apprehend," be changed to "cope with." The change was made accordingly.[68]

Life aboard the campaign train began to take on more and more the marks of a fast-moving road carnival, and reporters eagerly seized on any happenings that would help them draw such a picture. Every community wanted to honor the president but also to offer him a glimpse of civic character. At Lordsburg, New Mexico, a company of the national guard in full uniform was present, and Truman accepted Indian purses for his wife and daughter, Margaret. He was given a letter opener in the form of a totem pole from the Bataan Veterans Association. At Deming, forty miles east, the mayor presented him a specially made silver belt with the inscription, "To Harry S. Truman from Deming, N.M." Leather-bound albums engraved with forty-six views of southwestern New Mexico ranches and industries were presented to Mrs. Truman and Margaret. The Deming Lions Club distributed small bags of Mimbres Valley pinto beans to everybody on the train, and three hundred Mescalero Indians, given the opportunity to vote in the presidential race for the first time, entered the train and talked with the president prior to his address.

In Texas, Cactus Jack Garner met the train at 6:50 A.M., and the former vice-president escorted the Truman party to his home at Uvalde. There a huge breakfast was served that included orange juice, bacon, ham, chicken, dove, scrambled eggs, three kinds of preserves, and coffee. Truman also received a Mexican sombrero from the president of the local chamber of commerce. As a special fillip, a member of Truman's old Battery D Battalion, Henry L. Warren from Corpus Christi, had been brought to the festivity.

In Texas, the civil rights issue presented Truman with a particularly delicate problem. His aides had convinced him that he would have to aim his persuasion at blacks as one of the main voting blocs if he were to win the presidency. Oscar Ewing, federal security administrator and one of the key aides behind Truman's campaign, announced in a speech to the National Urban League in Richmond that any black who voted against Truman would be "betraying his race." Then Ewing echoed one of Truman's themes, namely, that victory for the GOP would "wipe out every vestige of social and economic progress which the American negro has made during the past decade and a half." Such expressions from the Truman election team raised doubts in the minds of many Texans, and as a consequence while the president campaigned in that state he avoided making any direct references to civil rights.

The intensity of the feelings over civil rights could be heard, however, in the mild boos that greeted him for merely shaking hands with a black woman at Waco, Texas. There Truman did declare that every child was entitled to an education regardless of color. This statement, which seems so innocuous viewed from the hindsight of history, was a bold statement for a politician to make in a public meeting in Texas during the year 1948. No segregation was imposed at the Texas meetings Truman attended, but custom had not died and blacks and whites segregated themselves voluntarily. In Dallas, he made a graceful gesture toward an American idol, who happened to be black. Truman was introduced by Attorney General Tom Clark, and the latter made an awkward misstatement in presenting him as the "man who stopped *Joe Louis* [heavyweight boxing champion]." Truman replied, "No, that was John L. [Lewis], I don't have enough muscle to have stopped Joe."

After his tour of the West, Truman made a quick three-day swing through the states of New York and New Jersey. The following week he was back in the critical area of the Midwest. At Crawfordsville, Indiana, his writers had given him an opening line which read: "I am happy to be here in Crawfordsville—" Truman penciled in his own addition drawn from his long-standing interest in history and reading:

> in the home-town of General Lew Wallace. A couple of hours ago, I was in Greenfield, James Whitcomb Riley's home. I read Riley's poems and Lew Wallace's books when I was a young man and I've always been interested in this part of the Hoosier state.[69]

Truman's excursion into the Midwest was followed by a two-day trip to Miami, Florida and Raleigh, North Carolina. On October 21, he was back in Washington for a day in his office. The next two days were spent in Pennsylvania, and it was in Pittsburgh that he first used his imaginary dialogue:

> Now, let's imagine that we, the American people, are going to see this doctor. It's just our usual routine checkup which we have every four years.
>
> Now, we go into this doctor's office.
>
> And, "Doctor," we say, "we're feeling fine."
>
> "Is that so?" says the doctor. "You been bothered much by issues lately?"
>
> "Not bothered, exactly," we say. "Of course, we've had a few. We've had the issues of high prices, and housing, and education, and social security, and a few others."
>
> "That's too bad," says the doctor. "You shouldn't have so many issues."
>
> "Is that right?" we say. "We thought that issues were a sign of political health."
>
> "Not at all," says the doctor. "You shouldn't think about issues. What you need is my brand of soothing syrup—I call it 'unity.' "

Then the doctor edges up a little closer.

And he says, "Say, you don't look so good."

We say to him, "Well, that seems strange to me, Doc. I never felt stronger, never had more money, and never had a brighter future. What is wrong with me?"

Well, the doctor looks blank and he says, "I never discuss issues with a patient. But what you need is a major operation."

"Will it be serious, Doc?" we say.

"Not so very serious," he says. "It will just mean taking out the complete works and putting in a Republican administration."

Now, that's the kind of campaign you have been getting from the Republicans. They won't talk about the issues, but they insist that a major operation is necessary.[70]

Wherever Truman spoke, his aides would circulate among the crowd, if time permitted, and then report various audience reactions. For the manuscript speeches the system was a little more organized. George Elsey usually kept a written record of reactions. For example, after an address was given in Philadelphia he wrote in on the president's reading copy observations of crowd responses:

36 applause
5 laughter only
2 no's
1 Boo (at a Taft-Hartley passage][71]

At Cleveland, Truman talked for the first time about the public opinion polls which were showing him at such a disadvantage compared with his rival, Dewey. Truman termed them "sleeping polls," and said that most people would not be fooled because "They know sleeping polls are bad for the system . . . an overdose could be fatal."

The president seldom referred to his opponent by name, but as election day drew nearer, Truman's implications became plainer. At Boston, he said:

The Republicans tell us they stand for unity. In the old days Al Smith would have said that's baloney. Today, the Happy Warrior would say that's a lot of hooey, and if that rhymes with anything that's not my fault.[72]

While Truman was campaigning, his opponent, Governor Dewey, of course was doing the same. Dewey and his entourage of advisers, well-wishers, and favorite reporters and journalists had toured the country since mid-September. A greater number of newspaper and radio people accompanied Dewey aboard his *Victory Special* than went on the Truman train. Many observers commented on the efficiency of the Dewey organization and predicted that there would be a carryover of that effectiveness after the election. Dewey's speeches were ready and given to the press usually twelve to twenty-four hours before delivery. Occasionally, speeches were printed in local newspapers before they were made. The ultraefficiency of the Dewey train was such that when some tomatoes were thrown at the train, Jim Hagerty, Dewey's press chief, rushed to the press car to report how many were thrown. In contrast, correspondents on Truman's train often missed deadlines because his speeches so frequently were extempore or were in final script only a few minutes before delivery. Thomas Stokes, a correspondent who traveled on both trains, wrote that to transfer from Truman's train to Dewey's was "like leaving a casual free and easy theatre stock company on tour to join up with a sleek New York musical." Another reporter who wrote from both camps, Richard Rovere, gave an even more graphic comparison:

> As far as the arts and techniques, as distinct from the political content, of the campaigns are concerned, the difference between the Democratic and Republican operation is, I calculate, thirty or forty years. It is the difference between horsehair and foam rubber, between the coal-stove griddle and the pop-up toaster. Dewey is the pop-up toaster.[73]

During most of the campaign, Governor Dewey lifted his rhetoric into the clouds. In contrast to Dewey's abstract pronouncements, Truman's gibes were specific. As is customary, both candidates ended their campaigns with predictions of victory. Opinion polls reported that Truman through his arduous campaign had narrowed the gap somewhat, but his rival still had what seemed an insurmountable lead. On the eve of election, Gallup predicted that Dewey would get 49.5 percent of the vote, and Truman would receive 44.5 percent. The Crossley Poll credited Dewey with 49.9 percent, and Truman with 44.8 percent.[74] Moreover, nearly all of the nation's leading magazines and newspapers lined up with the pollsters and flatly predicted a Dewey victory.

As the campaign moved toward its end, Truman worked back in his home state. On October 30, he appeared before an enthusiastic audience in St. Louis's Kiel Auditorium for a final rally. In the period between Labor Day, September 6, and Election Day, November 2, he made seven campaign trips extending over 19,928 miles. He spoke in twenty-nine states and gave major addresses in the following cities:[75]

Detroit, Michigan	Oklahoma City, Oklahoma
Dexter, Iowa	Louisville, Kentucky
Denver, Colorado	Charleston, West Virginia
Salt Lake City, Utah	Akron, Ohio
Oakland, California	Springfield, Illinois
Los Angeles, California	St. Paul, Minnesota
Bonham, Texas	Milwaukee, Wisconsin

Philadelphia, Pennsylvania	Cleveland, Ohio
Buffalo, New York	Boston, Massachusetts
Miami, Florida	New York City
Raleigh, North Carolina	New York City (Brooklyn)
Pittsburgh, Pennsylvania	St. Louis, Missouri[75]
Chicago, Illinois	

With the exception of speeches given in Detroit, Dexter, Denver, Oklahoma City, Miami, and Raleigh, the major addresses were delivered at night in order to take advantage of extensive radio coverage. In addition to these twenty-six major addresses, Truman gave approximately 244 extempore talks of the whistlestop variety. Generally, these were delivered from the rear platform of his private car, although in some of the larger towns he left his train and went on a motorcade through the main part of town to a spot where a larger crowd could be accommodated. These speeches were repetitive and tended to be more "corny" than the prepared addresses. In his whistlestop talks, Truman seldom tried to define any major policy; instead he simply reiterated in local parlance the goals or policies he previously had discussed.

Truman was at his home in Independence on election day, and he and his family voted about midmorning at the town's Memorial Hall. At lunchtime, he attended a party in his honor given by the mayor of Independence and some selected friends. Later that afternoon he drove with two Secret Service men to the Elms Hotel in Excelsior Springs, some thirty miles from Kansas City, and settled down to await the results.

Those results are well-known history. To the astonishment and chagrin of pundits and pollsters, Truman won despite the loss of four of the largest industrial states—New York (47 electoral votes), Pennsylvania (35), Michigan (19), and New Jersey (16). Truman captured 24,105,000 popular and 303 electoral votes while Dewey collected 21,969,000 popular and 189 electoral votes. The relatively small number of remaining ballots was divided between Thurmond and Wallace.

For years to come, analysts would attempt to explain Truman's surprising upset. One distinguished pollster, Elmo Roper, candidly admitted: "I could not have been more wrong."[76] The political strategy planned and adopted by Truman a year in advance proved eminently productive. Throughout the campaign tours, it seemed that the platitudes of Dewey could not stand against the common sense utterances of Truman. In the last analysis, the slim margin of victory might have been provided by the personalities of the two men. Truman seemed a more human and attractive person than did the detached and lofty Dewey. No one could gainsay the adroitly planned and orchestrated campaign conducted by the president and his aides, but the bottom line of the campaign report showed that Truman outhustled his opponent. Harry Truman did just what he had done in nine earlier political campaigns—talk more often, talk plainer, and work harder than the person running against him.

THE ONE MAN ARMY.

DES MOINES REGISTER AND TRIBUNE

J. N. "Ding" Darling's cartoon commenting on
Truman's victory in 1948.

11

Truman the Debater

The give and take of debating, the testing of ideas, is essential to democracy.

PRESIDENT JOHN F. KENNEDY

CONTROVERSY is inherent in democratic government, and those who aspire to leadership must be willing to engage in public discourse. Their discourses inevitably consist of arguments, and these arguments in turn touch off responses from other leaders. Thus public debate is born, usually not from any prearranged schedule or agreement, but because in democratic government the decisions of leaders are examined and evaluated by the citizenry.

Some persons might think it odd to call Harry Truman a debater, for the term debate conjures up different images for different individuals. To a few people debate is a depreciatory word suggesting a speaker who prefers victory even at the expense of truth. Others argue that an authentic debater is an effective persuader forever in search of that elusive entity called truth. Still other persons when thinking of debate immediately envision a declamation contest or an orator like Daniel Webster with his magnificent voice rolling through the Senate chambers. Debate need not have such narrow definitions, however, for it takes many forms and occurs under a multitude of circumstances. If debate is thought of as being wider than school exercises or legislative actions and is construed as the advancement of arguments which audiences must weigh and consider, then Harry Truman necessarily was a debater.

Truman's debate was not one that took place on a single occasion, nor was it limited to a few opponents specified beforehand. Instead his debate was a running argument that lasted for seven and three-quarters years. It continued, with slight modifications, even after he left the White House. All of the necessary elements of traditional debate were involved: investigation to find the best lines of argument, discovering which issues would be relevant at a given time, collection of evidence to support the case, and, whenever necessary, development of patterns of refutation to answer attacks made on the administration's case.

The basis for productive debate depends on a proposition, which is the central judgment that a debater asks listener or reader to accept. One does not argue phrases or words but argues instead for an overall judgment embodied in an underlying proposition. This proposition is a declarative sentence, either implied or stated, and may be phrased formally or informally. The single proposition President Truman argued during his tenure in office can be reduced to: *The United States is best served by my administration.* Neither he nor his colleagues put the core of their arguments in such bald terms, but this basic proposition lay beneath Truman's case as it was presented to the public.*

Building the Truman Case

In examining the Truman case there is no attempt to maintain that it was a coordinated effort that developed according to a set plan adopted at the outset of his administration. On the contrary, his case can only be seen in retrospect, for it grew out of his efforts and supporting ones from key members of his administration to meet exigencies as they arose. The nature of the presidency made it impossible to schedule long in advance just when major parts of the total case would be presented. There were general positions staked out, of course, such as those he announced in the Truman Doctrine and the Fair Deal, but the nearest document that might be construed as a plan for the overall case is Truman's message, drafted largely by Rosenman, sent to Congress on September 6, 1945.

In traditional debate a case is an outline of issues and supporting materials that are chosen in order to argue for or against a proposition. The affirmative case—the one advanced by those in favor of the proposition being argued—must include a need for that proposition, must explain the workings of what is being supported, and finally must convince listener or reader that this side of the proposition brings greater benefits than would accrue if the other side were accepted.

Truman's case would have failed miserably had he been unwilling to back up his public persuasions. Rather than being reticent, he often seized opportunities to advance his case or to refute attacks made on it. In addition to his formal platform addresses, hundreds of statements, informal remarks, and campaign speeches were made from trains or other casual settings during his run for the presidency in 1948. His real success as a debater lay in the credibility

---

*A good perspective on President Truman's "case" can be gained by examining the sequence of some of his important public persuasions. See the Chronology.

of his messages, and this credibility was enhanced because he was willing to take resolute action. When he did so, the move generally added to his overall credibility. Without the resolution to make accompanying military and economic commitments, the world would have judged his arguments mere bombast.

Berlin Airlift

Throughout most of 1947 the Truman Doctrine, with its goal of halting the spread of communism, gathered momentum. The military phase of the doctrine was first evident in aid to Greece and Turkey, and a few months later the Marshall Plan took form as its economic counterpart.

One of the first actual confrontations immediately pertinent to Truman's argument that the Soviets wanted to take over Europe arose early in 1948 and grew out of problems in the occupied zones of defeated Germany. While there was disagreement at Potsdam in 1945 over the formula for fixing the amount of reparations from Germany, it was agreed that each of the Allies—the United States, Britain, Russia, and France—would be granted various zones of occupation. Each of these four nations was entitled to reparations from the zone assigned to it. In addition to the matter of reparations, the conferees at Potsdam had agreed to a loosely defined Allied Control Council. Among the responsibilities given the Control Council was the administration of greater Berlin.

The Potsdam agreements did not settle all questions, however. The Soviets maintained that because their country had suffered most from the war's devastation, they were entitled to an extra share of reparations. But most of the raw materials and industrial equipment that the Russians claimed was necessary to rebuild their national economy lay in the Ruhr—an area in Germany that was assigned to the British.

On the last day of March in 1948 the Soviet military administration issued an order forbidding Allied trains from crossing the occupation border and entering the city of Berlin unless those trains, both passenger and baggage, were checked by Russian personnel. The following day Soviet representatives decreed that no freight could leave Berlin by rail unless permission had been granted by Russian authorities. These moves by the Soviets, if unanswered, would put them in full control of Berlin. General Lucius Clay, the military governor in the American zone, cabled the War Department:

> We have lost Czechoslovakia. Norway is threatened. We retreat in Berlin. When Berlin falls, western Germany will be next. If we mean . . . to hold Europe against Communism, we must not budge. We can take humiliation and pressure short of war in Berlin without losing face. If we

withdraw, our position in Europe is threatened. If America does not understand this now, does not know that the issue is cast, then it never will and communism will run rampant. I believe the future of democracy requires us to stay.[1]

Numerous earlier events clearly indicate that President Truman was predisposed to accept this line of reasoning. The other Allies, led by the United States, responded with charges that the Russian directives were inconsistent with the free and unrestricted right of access in Berlin that had been agreed to earlier. The Russians denied that any such agreement had been made and claimed that they had full right to control all traffic in their zone.

President Truman saw the Soviet moves in Berlin not as a contest over legal rights but as a struggle over Germany and, in a larger sense, all of Europe. Many Americans seemed to share his conviction that through quick action the Communist encroachments had been halted in Greece and Turkey. The European Recovery Program was proving very successful. Truman believed, therefore, that the blockage of Berlin was communism's counterattack.

Accordingly, General Clay and other commanders were ordered to make emergency arrangements to have essential supplies such as food, medicine, and clothing flown into the city that had been effectively blockaded by land and water. The airlift soon was averaging 2400 to 2500 tons of supplies a day. This was enough to sustain the beleaguered Berliners during the spring and summer months, but additional tonnage would be required during the winter.

In July General Clay was called to the White House to give a complete report on the situation in Germany, and he reiterated more firmly his advice that the United States should maintain right of access to Berlin no matter what the risk. It was a precarious dilemma. Clay was asked what risks would be involved if the United States attempted to send armed convoys into the city. His answer in effect was that there might be Russian interference with such obvious land challenges, but the United States still had air access and could increase the level of supplies through that route. The Air Force chief of staff was not so sure and argued that the concentration of aircraft necessary to provide Berlin would mean reducing air strength elsewhere. Truman, however, gave a different analysis:

> I did not agree with the Air Force Chief of Staff. I asked him if he would prefer to have us attempt to supply Berlin by ground convoy. Then, if the Russians resisted that effort and plunged the world into war, would not the Air Force have to contribute its share to the defense of the nation? I answered my own question: The airlift involved less risk than armed road convoys. Therefore, I directed the Air Force to furnished the fullest support possible to the problem of supplying Berlin.[2]

There is no doubt that Truman was adamant in his determination to defend American access to Berlin, but he preferred to treat the matter as one falling squarely within the province of the State Department. As a result, he insisted that Secretary George Marshall, and later Secretary Dean Acheson, were the proper spokesmen on the issue. Truman himself had no speeches or messages prepared on the subject, and he rebuffed attempts of newspersons to draw him into public discussions about it.

On June 30, 1948, Secretary of State Marshall released a statement to the press which read:

> We are in Berlin as a result of agreements between the Governments on the areas of occupation in Germany, and we intend to stay. The Soviet attempt to blockade the German civilian population of Berlin raises basic questions of serious import with which we expect to deal promptly. Meanwhile, maximum use of air transport will be made to supply the civilian population. It has been found, after study, that the tonnage of foodstuffs and supplies which can be lifted by air is greater than had at first been assumed.[3]

This statement embodied the official policy of the United States government toward the Berlin crisis—a crisis that lasted nearly a year. At his news conference the same day that Marshall gave his statement to the press, Truman was asked: "Mr. President, what is your attitude toward the Soviet blockade?" He replied succinctly:

> I have no comment. General Marshall expressed the attitude of the Government after a conference with me.[4]

Three weeks later at another presidential press conference the opening question was: "Mr. President, what do you make of this situation in Berlin?" This time the reply was even terser: "No comment." Then reporters asked if General Clay and General Marshall were coming in for an appointment at 12:30. President Truman confirmed that they were. Next, referring to a speech that was being prepared for him to deliver to the special session of Congress, reporters asked Truman if he would discuss the Berlin situation in his forthcoming address. He replied: "I will not. I will not."[5]

At another news conference a week later, one reporter referred to British Foreign Secretary Ernest Bevin's statement regarding an approach to the Berlin impasse and again attempted to get President Truman to discuss the crisis. The reporter asked:

> Mr. President, Mr. Bevin made a statement today regarding the next approach to Moscow regarding the Berlin situation. Held out, too, his hope for settlement of the whole European problem. I wonder if you could give us any American view—[6]

President Truman broke in and said:

> I haven't seen Mr. Bevin's statement, and I have no comment to make on it, or on the European situation.[7]

Later in that same news conference, another reporter said that there seemed to have been some disappointment in Congress that the president did not send them a report on Berlin. The reporter asked if the president planned to prepare such a message; Truman's reply was typically terse: ''I do not.''[8]

On September 9, Secretary Marshall held a press conference during which he denounced attacks by Communist-led mobs on the city government of Berlin. He said that Communist efforts to disrupt conferences on the future status of Berlin must be firmly resisted and that he hoped the forthcoming talks at the Council of Foreign Ministers could proceed in a quiet and orderly atmosphere. At the president's news conference the following day, reporters again tried to entice Truman into a discussion of Berlin. They asked him if the secretary's trip to Paris could be tied in with the blockade crisis. President Truman answered first by referring to Marshall's own press conference. The persistent reporters then asked specifically, ''Mr. President, can you give us anything new on the Berlin situation?'' Truman's reply was:

> No, I cannot, I have no comment on the Berlin situation. I think Secretary Marshall covered that yesterday as well as it can be covered at the present time.[9]

In an attempt to get further clarification of Secretary Marshall's statement the president was asked if the Soviet blockade efforts would be resisted. His answer was:

> Yes. We are still standing up for our rights in Berlin. There are still some more arguments to be had on the subject. We are doing everything we possibly can, through negotiation, to straighten the thing out.[10]

Then the questioning took a turn toward the meaning of ''negotiation'':

> QUESTION: That is still all confusion to me, to say we are negotiating, because I had understood that we would not negotiate as long as the blockade was on.
> PRESIDENT: No, that is not—no such statement as that. We have been trying to negotiate all our difficulties. We have been negotiating ever since the war ended, and we are going to continue negotiating, hoping to get a settlement. You can't settle it any other way.

QUESTION: I didn't understand it. The statement said that we would not negotiate under duress. I think that was the phrase.

PRESIDENT: No, we are not negotiating under duress. We have not been negotiating under duress.

QUESTION: The blockade is not under duress?

PRESIDENT: It is attempted duress, but we are not negotiating under duress. We have been negotiating right along ever since the war ended. We will continue to negotiate, always hoping, we will get a peace.

QUESTION: Well, sir, is the action of certain civilians, and Russian policemen and Berlin policemen—is that part of the negotiation, or is that outside?

PRESIDENT: That is outside. I think Secretary Marshall commented on that very fully yesterday.[11]

President Truman issued a public statement on October 9, 1948, following Secretary Marshall's return from a meeting of the Council of Foreign Ministers in Paris. In his statement President Truman briefly explained that he had contemplated sending Supreme Court Justice Vinson to Moscow and that he had discussed such a possibility with Secretary Marshall. His discussion with the secretary convinced him that such a step would be unwise, and he decided against it.

On November 13, 1948, Trygve Lie, secretary general of the United Nations, and Herbert V. Evatt, president of the United Nations General Assembly, sent a communique to the heads of government of Great Britain, France, the United States, and the Soviet Union, appealing for four-power conversations to end the Berlin dispute. On November 17, Secretary Marshall answered the letter that had been sent to the president. Marshall's answer stated that the United States was willing to engage in conversations as soon as the Soviet Union lifted the Berlin blockade so that the negotiations could take place under conditions free from duress. He added that the United States government was ready to take part in all efforts of the Security Council to solve the Berlin problem. In his news conference on November 16, President Truman was asked about the joint communique. He answered:

> I received a message like that, but I have no comment on it at the present time. General Marshall and—[inaudible]—prepared an answer which I have approved.[12]

The Berlin crisis hung on until the spring of 1949 when the Soviet authorities indicated they were prepared to remove the blockade. In a press conference on April 13, Secretary of State Dean Acheson, who had replaced General Marshall at the latter's request to be relieved from further government duty, announced that official avenues of communication were still open if Russia wanted to discuss lifting the blockade and undertake four-power talks on Germany. Acheson reiterated the official position that the blockade must be removed in advance of general discussion about Germany. In a presidential press conference the day after Acheson's announcement, Truman was asked if there were any new approaches by the Soviet government toward settlement of the Berlin crisis, and he replied:

> I think Mr. Acheson answered that adequately yesterday at his press conference. He sent me a copy of what he said, and that covered the situation.[13]

During the first week in May of 1949 the Russians removed their blockade of Berlin, and the crisis passed. General Clay asked to be relieved of his duties as military governor in Germany, and President Truman used the occasion to express satisfaction that the blockade was being lifted. He added that he was "happy that there is a chance to take up where we left off, over ten months ago."[14]

Thus ended one of the serious international crises during his presidency. Throughout the entire controversy Truman had kept from being drawn into public debate over what to do in Berlin. He felt his case on this particular issue was so strong that no defense by the president was needed. Nevertheless, his steadfastness in refusing to be cowed and his resolution in pushing emergency plans for the airlift had given his overall arguments weight and credibility. The Truman Doctrine had withstood the challenge. Through persistence and persuasion open warfare between the world's superpowers had been postponed.

Debate over Korea

The Truman Doctrine was slightly more than three years old when another international crisis arose. It was a crisis that was to test severely Truman's resolution and the philosophy around which his basic arguments in foreign policy had been structured. The event was the Korean War, and the philosophy was containment—a policy of continued United States resistance to the spread of communism.

As chief executive, it fell to Truman to present the case for containment to America and the world. His Greek-Turkish aid message in March of 1947 was his first major expression of containment. That address unveiled military aspects of the policy; later economic aspects were added by such programs as the Marshall Plan and Point Four. Generally favorable responses to his containment pronouncements convinced him that there had been a significant change of attitude in American public opinion since the years of wartime collaboration with Russia. President Truman had further reason to believe his case had won popular support, for the out-and-out opposition that had come from liberals led by Wallace and from isolationists had been largely erased by his election victory in 1948.

On several occasions after he left the White House, Truman said that he regarded the decision to act in Korea as the most important decision of his presidency. In his *Memoirs*, he recalled other instances when aggressor nations were encouraged because democratic governments had failed to act. He was sure that events in Korea represented but a part of the Soviet plan for world conquest:

> I felt certain that if South Korea was allowed to fall Communist leaders would be emboldened to override nations closer to our own shores. If the Communists were permitted to force their way into the Republic of Korea without opposition from the free world, no small nation would have the courage to resist threats and aggression by stronger Communist neighbors. If this was allowed to go unchallenged it would mean a third world war, just as similar incidents had brought on the second world war.[15]

The Korean War was rooted in agreements made at the end of the Second World War. With the consent of the Allies in 1945 Japanese forces north of the thirty-eighth parallel in Korea surrendered to the Soviet army; those forces south of that parallel surrendered to American troops. By happenstance the thirty-eighth parallel just about split the country into geographic halves, and a dividing line of sorts was thus established. This line became a factor a year and a half later when, at the request of the United States, the United Nations assumed responsibility for efforts to unify Korea. In 1948 elections were held in South Korea, and as a result of these elections the section south of the parallel proclaimed itself the Republic of Korea and installed Syngman Rhee as its president. Within a month the northern part of the country took a similar step and proclaimed itself the Democratic People's Republic of Korea.

The next two years saw no real peace between the two sections of Korea. John J. Muccio, United States ambassador to the Republic of Korea in 1950, reported that prior to the actual outbreak of war there were probably as many incursions from the South into the North as there were from the North into the South.[16] The fragile peace was shattered in June of 1950 when North Korean troops en masse crossed the parallel into the southern zone. Until that date American response to Communist pressures anywhere in the world had been in rhetoric, money, supplies, aid, and advice—not in the use of military power. The import of the incursion by the North into South Korea was that it represented a direct military challenge to Truman's policy of containment. His persuasions had seemed logical and effective to most Americans and indeed to most non-Communist countries throughout the world, but how strong was his case really? Would he and the country under his leadership be willing to use force if that was needed to repel force? Korea provided the answers.

This is not the place for a detailed discussion of the background, the conduct, or the outcome of the Korean War. There are general histories as well as many excellent articles and books that deal with special aspects of that event.[17] Our purpose is to look at the arguments President Truman presented in justifying his decisions and American actions during that crisis.

Periodically in American history there seems to arise a series of public controversies that get to be labeled as "great debate." There were the Webster-Hayne speeches in the Senate in 1830, the Lincoln-Douglas debates of 1858, the Senate debates over the League of Nations following World War I, debates over isolationism during the decade of the thirties, and the so-called "Great Debate" over Korea in 1950. The last-named exchange could not match its forerunners in eloquence perhaps, but the issues were global and grave in their implications.

It cannot be said that Truman and members of his administration were persuasive enough to make the war in Korea a popular one. On the contrary, it was the subject of acrimonious, often partisan debate. The public debate ostensibly was over a faraway war, but the controversy had overtones from the clash of domestic politics. There were two tangential factors that bore on the public arguments: 1) the initial serious military reverses in Korea, and 2) the marked Republican gain in the midyear election.

One point of view in the debate over Korea was advanced by such men as former Ambassador to Great Britain Joseph P. Kennedy, former President Herbert Hoover, and Senator Robert A. Taft. Their thesis was that the policy of containment had failed and a major revision of foreign policy was necessary. Though differing on some points, these men and those who sided with them believed essentially that Korea had proved that America could not defend successfully the great Eurasian land mass because of the vast superiority of military manpower which the Communist world could put into the field. The best policy for the United States, they argued, would be to conserve its resources rather than to spend them by pouring large quantities of troops and material into countries around the world.

Against this view was arrayed the official policy of the United States as argued by President Truman and supported by Secretary of State Dean Acheson. A few Republican leaders lined up behind Truman on the Korean issue, and among those who agreed with him was his rival in 1948, Governor Thomas E. Dewey of New York. General Dwight Eisenhower, who was not yet identified publicly with either major political party, also endorsed the administration's basic position. Truman and his supporters insisted that the policies advocated by the Kennedy-Hoover-Taft school would be a "retreat" which could only ensure eventual world victory for the Communists.

Joseph Kennedy opened the debate with an address at the law school forum at the University of Virginia in Charlottesville. In his speech Kennedy declared that, in contrast to the weakness of the West, the Soviet bloc had manpower and military strength of a type the world had never seen, and he warned:

> To engage these vast armies on the European or the Asian continent is fool-
> hardy, but that is the direction towards which our policy has been
> tending. That policy is suicidal. It has made us no foul weather friends.[18]

Joseph Kennedy had been a strong Democrat during the Roosevelt era, and for that reason the American press gave unusual attention to this speech. Some writers declared that it heralded a widening rift within the current administration. When former President Herbert Hoover and Senator Robert Taft delivered separate public addresses that echoed Kennedy's line of argument, the press at home and abroad began to speculate whether there had been an orchestrated attack on Truman's foreign policy. Kennedy denied that charge and said that he had given the speech merely at the invitation of the university forum through his son Robert, who then was a law student and president of the student senate:

> I was invited by the committee of the Law School whose duty it was to get
> speakers to talk on topical questions. I spent about three weeks working on
> the speech. I did no consultation because it covered subjects that followed
> my line of thinking for the last fifteen years.[19]

Other journalists joined the fray, and some declared that Kennedy's remarks meant a return to isolationism; others interpreted them as expressing the "disillusionment" among the nations of Europe which had believed that the United States could successfully defend them against aggression. Kennedy gave a private assessment of his talk:

> I think my evaluation of the public response is not of any particular value. I
> feel very happy that it instigated the speeches of ex-President Hoover and
> Senator Taft along my general line. I also feel that I spoke for a great mass
> of public opinion that felt the way I did but up to that time had not had
> their feelings expressed for them.
>   The speech was coupled with Mr. Hoover's by the *New York Times* on
> numerous occasions as the basis of the Great Debate in the United States
> Senate. I think the speech speaks for itself.[20]

Kennedy's speech was given on December 12, 1950, and two days later Thomas Dewey, governor of New York and titular head of the Republican party, gave a rejoinder supporting the policy of containment. Then on December 15, President Truman delivered a radio address dealing with the "grave national emergency." Thus it happened that the president spoke at the end of a week in which the sense of urgency in the nation's capital seemed to rise rapidly.

Truman was keenly aware of the need to present his strongest arguments if he were to rebut criticisms that were being leveled at containment as a policy.

This awareness can be seen in his official activities in the days preceding the address. Two weeks before the speech, he had conferred almost daily with British Prime Minister Clement Attlee on the Korean War and the larger world crisis.* Likewise, during the week immediately before his speech, Truman had been in prolonged daily sessions with members of Congress and his administration leaders, charting the course he was to disclose in his speech.

President Truman began this radio and television address to the American people by putting the blame for the Korean War and the world crisis squarely on Soviet Russia. In the third sentence of his speech, he charged: ''This danger has been created by the rulers of the Soviet Union.'' Then he listed four lines of policy his administration meant to follow:

> First, we will continue to uphold, if necessary to defend with arms, the principles of the United Nations—the principles of freedom and justice.
>
> Second, we will continue to work with the other free nations to strengthen our combined defenses.
>
> Third, we will build up our own Army, Navy and Air Force and make more weapons for ourselves and our allies.
>
> Fourth, we will expand our economy and keep it on an even keel.[21]

Truman then amplified in turn the ways in which each of these four policies would be followed. He declared that United States' representatives in the United Nations would continue their efforts to find ''peaceful means'' of settling the dispute in Korea but promised that his administration would not engage in ''appeasement.'' He said that we would continue to build military defenses against aggression in Korea as well as strengthening our participation in the North Atlantic Treaty Organization for the possibility of an outbreak of hostilities in Europe. He next insisted that adjustments in industrial production would be necessary in order to make more weapons and military equipment. Then he discussed citizen responsibility in helping construct a stronger internal economy. In connection with this point, Truman referred to a current labor strike in a railway union, declaring that since the strike constituted a danger to the nation's security, he was asking the striking union members to return to their jobs at once.

The American people were not entirely unprepared for this speech by the president, and the bulk of reaction was favorable to it. One major newspaper in New York, after a survey taken by its regional correspondents, concluded that

---

*Prime Minister Attlee's visit seemed to point up another example of the psychological importance of statements by an American president. Speaking in an offhand manner before the press on November 30, 1950, President Truman had intimated that the field commander in Korea could use the atomic bomb there against the Communists any time he so desired. A ''clarification'' of this intimation did not come out in time to prevent world wide repercussions, for almost immediately the British prime minister had boarded a plane and had come to America to find out what was in the president's mind. (See earlier mention on p. 241.)

the citizens generally not only were ready to make the adjustments demanded by Truman's mobilization arguments, but in some cases the people seemed ready to meet even greater demands than he had laid down.[22]

In New England, the people expressed themselves as willing to accept the controls, the sacrifices, and the greater drafting of manpower proposed by the president because they thought such measures were essential in meeting the emergency.[23] In the South, a Nashville, Tennessee, newspaper was quoted as saying that Truman would find the people of that region "ready to go along with him" in his plans for mobilizing the nation. From Atlanta, Georgia, came the report that the "vast majority of people" was willing to make whatever sacrifices were necessary for a speedy buildup of defenses.[24] In the West, the *Salt Lake Tribune* said: "The call for a sharp step-up in the national mobilization was long overdue." And from Los Angeles came the report that there was a "unanimous sentiment against appeasement," yet a strong desire to extricate the United States from its disadvantageous situation in Korea.[25]

President Truman's speech, as expected, did not prevent response from the other side in the debate. Former President Hoover gave an address a week later that was interpreted as a rejoinder, and five days after Hoover spoke, Senator Taft, in a widely heralded Senate speech, also challenged the president's case. Taft accused Truman of acting beyond his presidential authority in committing American troops to Korea. In direct rebuttal to Truman's contention that a buildup of arms and support for NATO was vital, Taft maintained the first consideration should be to defend America, "the citadel of the free world." The Ohio senator admitted that "an army of reasonable size" has a place in the defense of the American continent, but he insisted that it need not be such a large force as might be necessary for a land war on the continents of Europe or Asia. He went on to argue:

> It seems obvious that the immediate problem of defending this country depends upon control of the sea and control of the air. . . . We have a powerful air force, but it seems to me vitally necessary that that air force be increased until we have control of the air over this country and over the oceans which surround our continent.[26]

Taft addressed the relationships between mobilization and the domestic economy, but he disputed the economic issues as analyzed and presented by Truman. Taft then concluded his speech by warning that only a carefully planned and retrenched military policy could prevent economic collapse or inflation in America.

President Truman's major address on Korea and the subsequent supporting arguments he gave in press conferences and on lesser occasions did not keep the issue from being debated throughout his last full year in the presidency. Korea remained an unsettled issue, but there can be little doubt that Truman was able to rally public support for his decision to act in that crisis. As wars go, Korea was a clean-cut victory for the United States and the United Nations. The fact that the United States was willing to intervene showed that containment was more than a hollow phrase; as a policy it may have stopped a major Communist lunge southward which, if successful, might even have engulfed Japan.

Nor was Truman's case hurt by the dismissal of General Douglas MacArthur in April of 1951.[27] When the initial oratory aroused by that dramatic event had spent itself, Truman's position seemed even stronger. On the issue of dismissal, the president felt his position was so strong that once the step had been taken he could remain aloof from the public outcry. Truman even defended the general's right as a private citizen to plead his case before Congress. General MacArthur conceded Truman's right to relieve him, so as months passed it became apparent that the core of the controversy was whether the president's or the field commander's strategy should prevail. Time proved to be on Truman's side, and the results of the MacArthur episode did no real damage to Truman as far as containment and particularly Korea were concerned. His stature as a persuader was reinforced; although battered and challenged, his case remained intact enough to be supported by Congress and the American public.

Truman's Debate Profile

Formal debates in colleges are judged according to ballots which may range from simple to complex. The simplest ones, like the outcome of a political election, merely ask for the winner's name. The more common debate ballot asks judges to rate the debater in such categories as analysis, reasoning, evidence, organization, refutation, and delivery. Three of them—evidence, organization, and delivery—are inherent in all persuasion and for that reason are treated in detail in the next chapter. The remaining three categories—analysis, reasoning, and refutation—are more closely linked with debating, and it is interesting to note briefly Truman's habits in these regards.

It may seem unusual to attempt a cursory evaluation of argument that stretched over more than seven years, but in doing so one can get a better picture of Harry Truman as a political and practical debater.

Analysis. In chemistry, analysis refers to discovering the number and qualities of elements present in a compound; in argument, analysis is the process of discovering the issues. Issues are those points that must be proved if the debater is to win his case.

In debate there is also a responsibility called burden of proof. The phrase roughly means that a speaker who advances a case is expected to change listeners' minds. When Truman came into office in 1945 the prevalent feeling, undergirded by fervent hope, in the minds of most citizens was that America and Russia would cooperate in peace as they had in war. It soon became clear, however, that under Truman's leadership America was moving away from a position of cooperation with Russia at all costs—a position Roosevelt had marked out during the war and had enunciated in his Yalta address. The causes for the widening gap were hotly disputed, but it was up to Truman to change public attitudes before the program of containment could be accepted by the American public.

Foreign policy became Truman's strongest issue in his general argument that the nation's welfare could be entrusted to him and his administration. Though his earlier years had been spent entirely in domestic affairs, the schism between the Western democracies and the Soviet bloc provided the most persistent theme marking the Truman presidency.

Truman entered the White House with two predispositions: a belief in America's invincibility and a conviction that Communist Russia meant to conquer the world. These convictions were made even stronger by the success of the atomic bomb and the establishment by the Soviets of satellite governments immediately after World War II.

Especially in 1946 and 1947 when the doctrine of containment first began to take shape, Truman encountered stiff opposition. Henry Wallace, former vice-president and secretary of commerce, led a sizable and vocal opposition which charged that the "get-tough-with-Russia policy," as it then was called, would lead inevitably to war. Wallace and others maintained that America was in no danger from Russia and that Truman was trying to frighten the country in order to get his requests approved by Congress. He was charged, too, with deliberately ignoring the infant United Nations. The burden of proof fell on Truman to rebut such attacks and to reestablish his argument that his foreign policy programs were necessary for world peace.

Of course, it was not through Truman's persuasions alone that public opinion was changed. Undeniably, the plight of satellite governments, the Berlin blockade, and other actions by the Soviets gave urgency to Truman's case. Nevertheless, the fact that American public opinion did reverse itself so far in five years as to support a military war in Korea is tangible and indisputable evidence of Truman's success in winning approval for basic foreign policy issues as he analyzed and presented them.

While he was eminently successful in winning legislative approval for his foreign policies, Truman was less so when it came to domestic matters. Although his election campaign was waged mainly on national issues, he won in 1948 not because of demonstrated successes or positive programs but because he capitalized on mistakes of the opposition. Truman's analysis of domestic issues was in essence a divisive one; it aimed at convincing four groups of voters—labor, farmer, black, and consumer—that "the Republican Party is the party of big business and that the Democratic Party is for you." At times it seemed almost as if Populists had returned from their graves, for Truman railed against corporations, financial institutions, and the establishment wherever he found it. The Congresses gave him little that he asked for in national programs, and as a result a public image was created of a debater who spoke for the ordinary citizen. It was an image that, coupled with commanding scores in foreign policy issues, was enough to win election.

Reasoning. In formal logic the two large classes of reasoning are called induction and deduction. In the former, one moves from considering specific instances to acceptance of a general conclusion, and in the latter a person starts his argument with a general proposition and reasons toward a specific conclusion. Every person employs both these types of reasoning. In actual thought and argument the two types are used so regularly and are interchanged in the mind so quickly that it is often impossible to separate them.

The pattern of reasoning most visible in Truman's public communications, however, is basically deductive. He usually started with certain general beliefs or convictions. These ideas formed general premises from which a specific decision could be drawn. For example, one can trace his thinking through such steps as the following:

1. Whatever the Soviets do is a part of their plan for world conquest.
2. The danger to Greece and Turkey is a Soviet action.
3. Therefore, the danger to Greece and Turkey is part of their plan for world conquest.

The basic premise in this thought pattern provided many other specific conclusions which lay behind actions initiated by Truman. Russian military buildups and displays, deteriorating economic conditions in Europe, creation of the iron curtain, internal espionage, invasion of South Korea—all could be minor premises which, when applied to a major belief, would justify a specific course of action.

The deductive thinking pattern was likewise evident in Truman's approach to domestic matters:

1. If Congress failed to heed his recommendations, then the blame for the country's troubles must fall on Congress.
2. Congress failed to heed his recommendations.
3. Therefore, the blame for the country's troubles must fall on Congress.

The deductive pattern of thought makes for clarity but is dependent on listeners or readers agreeing with each of the basic premises. Truman's preference for deductive arrangements made his rhetoric understandable even though opponents could and frequently did disagree with the premises from which his conclusions were drawn.

Refutation. Argument against an opponent's case is known as refutation. The word itself comes from Latin and originally meant to repel. In modern argument refutation has come to mean answering attacks and presenting evidence or reasoning designed to weaken an opponent's case.

George B. Shaw once observed: "The way to get at the merits of a case is not to listen to the fool who imagines himself impartial, but to get it argued with reckless bias for or against." Argument is the meat of a politician's life, and Harry Truman was a practicing politician throughout most of his adult years.

It is a truism that effective refutation must keep the opponent on the defensive. In this regard, Truman was especially adept, for both by nature and by planning he wanted to challenge the opposition, to ask detailed questions, to demand more evidence, and in general keep the burden of proof on the other side. His speeches, notably those given during campaigns, were models of a technique advised by that wily propagandist Sam Adams in the days of the American Revolution: "Put your adversary in the wrong and keep him there."[28]

Truman as a debater needed little encouragement in refutation, and sometimes his vehemence needed to be restrained. His eagerness came from a paradox that marked his peculiar talents as a persuader—he was both humble and arrogant. In the first place, he never pretended to be something he was not. In his character were threads of modesty that became a great political asset. Whatever eloquence he was able to develop came from his exemplification of the common man. Moreover, his genuine humility enabled him to develop a penetrating responsiveness to the ego needs of other persons. On a personal level, his sincerity and humility were unquestionable. On other levels, there was a basic arrogance that sprang from his overriding confidence in himself and in the rightness of his decisions. This confidence gave him encouragement when others thought the debate was going against him.

The essence of good refutation is aggressiveness, and Truman's aggressiveness can be seen in such acts as his calling Congress into special session, his subsequent success in placing the plight of the country squarely on the shoulders of the Republican majority in Congress, and in his skillful use of the Taft-Hartley issue.

The final Taft-Hartley bill had modified harsher provisions that originally had been submitted in the House by Representative Fred A. Hartley, Jr., Republican of New Jersey. The modified version was passed by both houses and sent to Truman June 9, 1947.

Among the provisions of the bill was a prohibition against the closed shop—a shop in which membership in a particular union was a prerequisite for being hired. Labor regarded this as the most odious section of the bill because the section also permitted states to pass their own "right-to-work" laws—laws which if enacted by state legislatures could forbid even the requirements that workers in a given industry must belong to a union. Other restrictions included one that in the event of a national emergency the president, through his attorney general, could seek a court injunction to prevent strikes or lockouts.

While the Taft-Hartley bill was being debated in Congress, Truman remained out of the public controversy, but as the legislation gained steam a mass of lobbyists and pressure communications came to his office. The overwhelming portion of these efforts urged a veto. Most of his advisers agreed with him that the problem the bill presented was primarily a political one. If he signed the bill after his intemperate stand against railroad strikers a year and a half earlier—a time when he had proposed drafting strikers—the traditional labor support for his party might evaporate. On the other hand, if he vetoed the bill his standing with organized labor would improve. By a veto he might also refute some of the arguments against him that Wallace and other liberals were leveling. He owed many of his political triumphs to labor anyway, so it was no great strain for him to decide on a veto. Oscar Ewing, the unofficial leader among his more liberal advisers, described the candid strategy that lay behind the veto decision:

> In organizing the group it was my idea that we should try to develop a pattern of things for the President to do that would convince the various groups of voters that President Truman was pitching on their team . . . one of the early subjects we considered was whether or not President Truman should veto the Taft-Hartley bill. He was under great pressure from the leaders in Congress and I think from all of his Cabinet, except the Secretary of Labor, to go along with that bill and approve it. Our group, after discussing it, felt very strongly that it was unwise for him to approve the bill. We argued that labor was very much opposed to it, that the chances were the bill would be passed over his veto anyhow and thus become law so that he would lose nothing by the veto. Our view finally prevailed and the President vetoed the bill. Congress promptly overrode the veto, but Truman had greatly increased his popularity with labor thereby.[29]

A good debater must select arguments for refutation which fit in with an overall strategy. Taft-Hartley was not the "slave-labor" Truman called it, but it represented an opportunity for him to refute his opponents' case without seriously endangering his own. There can be little doubt that Truman chose to attack the Taft-Hartley Law because it fitted in with his main contention that labor troubles and economic ills were products of his political opposition. This is not to say that Truman was dishonest or believed that Taft-Hartley was good legislation; on the contrary, he had a long-standing record against some of its provisions. He simply joined with others in overstating the "terrors" of the act.

Truman was criticized for using the Taft-Hartley Act after he had inveighed so often against it. He invoked the powers granted him under the act six times before his presidential campaign officially opened in 1948: three times in maritime strikes, twice in coal mine disputes, and once before an impending strike at the Oak Ridge, Tennessee, atomic plant.[30]

There are several explanations for what at first blush may appear to be an inconsistency arising from the fact that Truman tried to prevent Taft-Hartley from becoming law and then used the very provisions he had argued against. First, in assessing Truman's record as chief executive one can never overlook his tremendous awe and respect for the office of the presidency. He took his oath and responsibilities seriously and was not about to ignore his duty to use presidential power whenever he felt the welfare of the country was threatened. If this meant calling on laws to which he personally was opposed, so be it. Second, he was too shrewd a politician to underestimate the harm that could come to him and his party if prolonged strikes and resultant economic disruptions were allowed to spread across the country. He had more to lose from continued labor unrest than from the use of a weapon designed for the enemy's arsenal. He chose, therefore, the lesser of two evils and opted to employ legislation that had been handed him.

Truman's political strategy in vetoing Taft-Hartley was vindicated soon after Congress passed the bill over his veto, because labor groups quickly swung in behind him. As predicted, he also won applause from a great many liberals who had wavered because of what they charged was his militancy in foreign policy.

When President Truman appeared before Congress in January of 1948, he used his state of the union address in part to refute his Republican opposition. In arguments that were clearly anticipatory refutation, Truman outlined what he felt the country needed. He was fully aware that Congress would vote down ninety percent of his requests, but he was determined to show the country an aggressive debater. It was an honest image that would be of immeasurable value in the campaign that lay ahead.

12

Truman at the Rostrum

If truth were self-evident, persuasion would be unnecessary.

CICERO

AN assumption underlying the preceding pages is that an understanding of a person's speech patterns provides a special kind of index to understanding his character and accomplishments. If that assumption is at all valid, it is time to take final stock of Truman as a persuader measured by some of the usual standards of speech criticism.

What Is Good Speaking?

There has been a great deal of private and public comment over the question: "Was Harry Truman a good speaker?" To answer that question we first need a set of standards by which to judge. Just what constitutes good speaking? Through the centuries men and women have given the question a lot of thought but have not reached total agreement. It is possible, however, to compress their thought into four closely related criteria.

There has been a great deal of private and public comment over the question: "Was Harry Truman a good speaker?" To answer that question we first need a set of standards by which to judge. Just what constitutes good speaking? Through the centuries men and women have given the question a lot of thought but have not reached total agreement. It is possible, however, to compress their thought into four closely related criteria.

First, one school of thinking says that good speech should be measured by its nearness to truth. If a person speaks the truth, his speech is good; if what he says is false, his speech is bad. There can be no real argument over the importance of truth in any lasting persuasion, but that does not mean that truth alone is an adequate standard for judging a person's speech. There have been instances when a learned teacher or scholar could not communicate ideas effectively. Moreover, "truth" often is not ascertainable. For example, did the failure of the United States to join the League of Nations cause that international body to die after World War I? The absolute truth cannot be determined.

Another standard sometimes used in speech evaluation examines the speaker's motives and intentions. This standard is called the ethical theory, the word *ethical* being derived from Greek *ethos*, meaning the sum total of all attributes that made a person believable. Obviously, good character and attitudes are huge assets in persuasion; indeed, no persuasion can survive long without them. Journalists and advertisers often depend on the ethical theory by using terms like *source credibility* or *public image.* The weakness of depending too much on the ethical theory in judging a person's speech, however, is that all too often we do not know the speaker's motives or we disagree with them. And all of us are familiar with instances when good intentions did not prevent wrong action or inept performance.

A third approach to judging speeches is called the results theory. Speech is considered good if it gets the desired results and poor if those expected results do not follow. Did the salesman sell the product? Did the candidate win election? At first glance, this theory seems sensible, but again the results theory by itself is not enough. It does not explain those instances when remarkable speakers failed to win support for the cause they espoused. For instance, Woodrow Wilson's speaking did not persuade America to join the League of Nations—a cause he pursued intensely and eloquently. Likewise, few people would want to deny that Winston Churchill was one of the great orators of the twentieth century, yet he failed to convince his countrymen of the seriousness of the gathering storm in the years prior to World War II. Also, in 1945 when his prestige was at its highest, Churchill's speaking did not win him reelection to the post of prime minister. Obviously, the results theory cannot serve as the single measure by which speech is judged.

The final theory holds that good speech can be judged best on the basis of methods used by the speaker. The methods have evolved through centuries during which men and women observed speaking and speakers. Through these observations and evaluations has come a system or set of principles known as rhetorical theory. Rhetoric as a field of study had its genesis in the Greek democracy, but rhetorical principles are being adapted constantly to meet changing situations and new practices. Moreover, modern communication technologies have made rhetoric more pervasive and more vital than ever before.

The classical approach to rhetoric was a very broad one, encompassing the source and validity of the speaker's beliefs, the organization of his ideas, his language, his education and experiences, and finally his voice and physical actions while speaking. Aristotle, the most lucid of all the ancient Greek rhetoricians, defined rhetoric as "the faculty of discovering in the particular case what are the available means of persuasion"[1] This extensive declaration permits examination of all methods and techniques an individual might employ to influence the belief or actions of others. Let us see how these established principles can be applied to the speech practices of Harry Truman.

Ideas and Beliefs in Truman's Speech

It is indisputable that American presidents have relied on ghost writers and speech advisers; what is not certain is the extent of such reliance. In hectic, busy days demanding almost continual communication, ghost writers can save time for their hard-pressed chief executive, and they can develop felicitous phrases that are not so likely to cause trouble. The rapid rise in use of mass media and instantaneous communication by presidents makes writers and speech assistants more important than ever before. Harry Truman did not establish as large a coterie of writers, public relations experts, and assorted advisers as did presidents who succeeded him. Nevertheless, he used writers enough that one might reasonably ask: "How can we be sure that Truman was speaking his own thoughts and not merely those concocted by a skillful writer?"

One clue to whether a particular speech was really Truman's or the product of someone else's thinking is its consistency with Truman's known philosophies, opinions, and previous utterances. On this scale, Truman scores high, for there is remarkable consistency among the major ideas he expressed during his years in the presidency. Any differences, when they appeared, were differences in detail or in political strategy, not in basic convictions.

Another strong indication that Truman's speeches were primarily his own can be found in comparing his manuscript addresses with his extempore talks. In extemporaneous presentations, Truman had to rely on his beliefs and his grasp of information at the time he was talking. He often was briefed and had assistance in planning lines of argument or possible answers, but the decision of what to say and how to say it had to come from his own inventiveness at the moment.

Patterns of Thought in Truman's Rhetoric

Truman's basic outlook and attitudes, like those of every other human being, were formed by circumstances of his training and experience. One set of circumstances consisted of personal associations, and these associations helped crystallize most of his beliefs long before he got to the White House. The first and most lasting of the associations was the unusually strong influence of his mother. It was she more than any other person who implanted in him a simplistic orientation; and throughout her life, the dutiful elder son tried hard to please the strong-willed mother. Like his mother's concept of good or evil with no middle ground, for Harry Truman everything was black or white with seldom any gray. Usually there were only two paths, and he had to choose one. No matter whether it was a question of paving or not paving a road in Jackson County or halting or continuing lend-lease shipments to Russia, there had to be a decision. The decision would be either right or wrong, and once made there would be no agonizing over it. This pattern of thinking was both Truman's strength and his weakness, for it made him decisive but dogmatic.

Another predilection that was evident throughout Truman's speech career was his faith in established institutions. He was no iconoclast smashing away at cherished images. On the contrary, his decisions often reflected recognition of civic and political establishments, his sense of loyalty to family and friends, his faith in the supremacy of his country, and his reverence for the Constitution. Congress might be a convenient target for him to attack during campaign periods, but he recognized its role in helping to govern the country. This recognition and his knowledge of history helped him deal effectively with executive-congressional relations even though he was always extremely sensitive to whatever might be considered an attack on the prestige of the office of the presidency. He once shared with Averell Harriman his idea of the importance of protecting presidential authority:

> When I [Harriman] was Mutual Security Director, President Truman had a very definite concept of his authority and power in Mutual Security. I went to Truman and asked that we accept the Congressional recommendation to set up a watch dog committee to guard expenditures of the Executive for the Mutual Security. President Truman said, "Averell, you don't understand that the greatest responsibility I have as President is to protect the power of the Executive from the zeal of Congressional action."[2]

Truman had reason to be proud of his military service in World War I. That short but intense experience left an indelible imprint on his outlook and approach to problems. The experience reinforced his preference for discipline, orderliness, and for following established lines of authority. The experience also nourished his belief in the innate superiority of his government and his countrymen. As a United States senator, his assessment of world problems was myopic, but it was compatible with isolationist sentiment that prevailed throughout the Midwest for a score of years after World War I. During the Red-baiting years in the twenties and early thirties, Truman was in local politics in

Missouri, and he made no public statements of consequence about the Soviet Union. His general attitude toward that county and European "squabbles" was typical of the isolationist mood that flourished in America's heartland prior to World War II.

Truman's army experiences as a young man helped etch his image of military commanders in heroic proportions. Throughout his life he recalled his disappointment over being disqualified for attendance at West Point because of poor eyesight. Notwithstanding the brouhaha over the dismissal of General Douglas MacArthur—a case sensational in itself without the popular fabrications found in many semifictional books, films, and television shows[3]—Truman admired most military men. Witness his veneration of General John F. Pershing, commander of the American Expedition Forces in World War I—a man Truman could have known only from afar and by reputation. In the presidency, Truman chose to rely heavily for guidance in diplomatic matters on such military figures as Admiral William Leahy, General Omar Bradley, and General George C. Marshall. On numerous occasions he referred to Marshall as "the greatest living American." He likewise praised General Dwight Eisenhower right up to the time the latter began to show interest in becoming a political candidate. In 1951, Truman sent one of his aides into the state of New York in order to assess political opinion regarding likely Republican candidates. The aide returned and reported that party professionals there had little enthusiasm for either Taft or Dewey. Some mentioned MacArthur, but most thought it would be Eisenhower in 1950. This report led Truman to comment about Eisenhower:

> The President expressed a very high regard and liking for Eisenhower as a man and as a soldier, who he said had made one of the greatest records in history. The President pointed out that education of an individual for a military career does not equip him for the Presidency. The officer accomplishes things by giving orders; a President, Mr. Truman said, has to accomplish things by persuasion—though, he added, he can perhaps give some orders—but what he accomplishes is largely by persuading others. The president referred to the case of General Grant and his experience as president.[4]

There is little doubt that the person in American history whom Truman admired most was General Andrew Jackson. Truman was instrumental in getting a stature of his hero placed in front of the Jackson County courthouse in Kansas City, and it is significant that in Independence at the courthouse where Truman and his fellow county judges presided, there is a statue of Jackson at the east entrance and a statue of Truman at the west. The county in which Truman lived and won his first political offices was named in honor of the hero from Tennessee. Whenever an opportunity presented itself, Truman liked to quote or refer to Jackson. Truman's extensive reading and his emphasis on biographies made him well acquainted with Jackson's military and political careers. He praised Jackson's decisive actions in both war and peace, and he seemed to interpret Old Hickory as the single great American figure able to make a successful transition from military achievements to government leadership.

It requires no great imagination to find parallels between Andrew Jackson and Harry Truman. One hundred and seventeen years separated their presidencies, but both were nominal Democrats. Both were criticized for rudeness and irascibility, and both bore reputations of being intemperate, arbitrary, and decisive. Each was identified as a people's president—a choice of the common man. Both were willing to battle against great odds including assaults on financial aristocracies. Each shared the burden that when he first entered office, most people predicted that nothing much of consequence should be expected from his administration. Truman did not find such comparisons at all unflattering and no doubt pictured himself as a kind of modernized Andrew Jackson.

Harry Truman was considerably more intelligent and capable than most people at the time realized. His reliance on generals and admirals has been criticized by revisionist historians, who link such reliance to his decision to drop the atomic bomb and to the origins of the cold war. Problems of controlling atomic warfare and dealing with the Soviet Union posed obvious dangers and created enormous frustrations for him. He came to the presidency woefully uninformed and untutored by the dying Roosevelt in these two most critical areas. Foreign policy dominated his administration—he began with the close of World War II and ended with the Korean War. His approach to foreign policy matters were those that might be expected from a typical self-made, middle-class, midwestern, sixty-year-old man with strong ties to veterans' groups.

Emotion has always been considered to play a vital role in persuasion. What is not always clear, however, is the precise way in which emotion is brought to bear in a particular speech. Also, most of us tend to be somewhat suspicious of "emotions" used in persuasion even though few observers would deny that emotional appeals exert great influence. Emotion is not necessarily contrary to good thinking, and we should not be misled into thinking that because a speech contains an emotional appeal it is illogical. Indeed, because emotions are human traits and because persuasion aims toward human responses, it is impossible to find persuasion that is devoid of all feeling. Rhetoricians do not agree on the number of specific wants and needs that often energize our responses; nor is there agreement on what names should be given to these forces. Names that at one time or another have been used include: instincts, human drives, impelling motives, motivational appeals, or reaction tendencies. One drive that is included in every such listing is the drive that is variously called fear, security, or safety. This deep human want was a drive underlying many of Truman's public speeches.

*Truman addressing a crowd of over 250,000 people
in Detroit on Labor Day, 1948.*

Perhaps the clearest example of a Truman speech that appealed to fear is found in his address of March 12, 1947, calling for military and economic aid to Greece and Turkey. The gravity of the situation then should not be forgotten, and there is no attempt to present the address as being emotion without substance. The speech, one of the most consequential of any made by an American president during the twentieth century, announced what came to be known as the Truman Doctrine. The address was consequential because it marked official departure from traditional noninvolvement in the political and economic affairs of Europe. Senator Vandenberg, it will be remembered, insisted that it would be necessary to "scare hell" out of the country. Truman did just that by declaring that the "United States must take world leadership and quickly to avert world disaster." He did not mention the Soviet Union by name, but by equating the new threats with previous actions by Germany and Japan, he aroused the fears of millions of Americans that the two superpowers were teetering on the brink of another world conflict.

Fear was also a recurring theme in Truman's political campaigning. He relentlessly tried to convince his targeted voting groups that if Republicans were elected, another depression would be inevitable. Nowhere was the appeal to fear better demonstrated than in his pursuit of votes from organized labor. He repeatedly preached that the "odious" Taft-Hartley Act was only a foretaste of what could be expected if more Republicans were voted into office. At the official opening of his campaign, he warned a huge Labor Day audience in Detroit:

> If you let the Republican administration reactionaries get complete control of this government, the position of labor will be so greatly weakened that I would fear not only for wages and living standards of the American working man but even for our democratic institutions of free labor and free enterprise.[5]

The appeal was a potent dose carefully prescribed for labor's latent fears; reactions to the medicine were immediate and favorable. From the AFL and its Labor League for Political Education came the message that at least seven million of eight million workers in the AFL would be for him. Phil Murray, head of the CIO, visited Truman and told him that out of the 6.5 million members in that group, no more than one million could possibly be against him. The appeal helped labor return to Truman and his party.

Another appeal found often in Truman's rhetoric involved what has been called the motivation for fighting or aggression. Much has been spoken and written in an effort to explain why human creatures fight one another— why they engage in acts of aggression. There seems to be an almost innate desire for competition, fighting, or even admiration for a fighter. Truman used the drive well and depicted himself as fighting against the establishment represented by the Eightieth Congress, corporate newspapers, or conservative opponents within his own party. He was an unlikely champion from the Midwest determined to win against the forces of evil wherever he found them. The election of 1948 showed that many citizens supported him out of sheer admiration for his spunk in battling against what seemed insurmountable odds. Respect for a fighter also helps explain the growing number of people who have become interested in the career of the peppery thirty-third president.

Patterns of Organization in Truman's Speeches

Modern rhetoricians divide a public address into three essential parts: an introduction, a body, and a conclusion. Some speakers strive hard to find an introduction that will capture immediate attention, arouse interest, and clarify the main discussion which is to follow. Truman paid scant attention to the introduction as an integral part of his talk, no matter whether he was preparing it himself or going over it with advisers. Indeed, it often seemed that he approached an address as if it had only two parts—a beginning and an end—and he wanted the two as close together as possible. When talking about Freemasonry or his interpretation of the Constitution, he was not apt to be so constrained, but in contrast with the stereotypes of long-winded politicians, throughout his life Truman's speeches were noted for their terseness. Circumstances frequently would dictate opening references to the meeting or group, but Truman used this technique more than most presidential speakers. It was his favorite way of identifying himself quickly with his listeners.

Truman was not shy about using the personal pronoun "I," and his openings often contained references to members of his family. Three examples of his introductions will show the pattern he preferred.

(Outside the railroad station at Ft. Worth, Texas, September 27, 1948.)

Governor Jester, Mr. Mayor, Mr. Carter, distinguished guests on this platform, and fellow Democrats of Ft. Worth, Texas:

I am exceedingly and highly pleased at the turnout here in this great city at this time of day (2:30 P.M.). I can't tell you how very much I appreciate it. I want to say to you that ever since the minute I hit El Paso, Texas, I have been most agreeably surprised every time we've stopped— and at a great many places at which we didn't stop. The station platform has always been full, and the station platform here in Ft. Worth is full. It looks to me like about 15 acres of people. It is much better to measure by the acre than to measure them individually. You don't miss any when you count them by the acre.

I have always been told that Ft. Worth is where the West begins. When I was a very young man, 17 or 18 years old, I paid my first visit to Ft. Worth. I have paid regular visits to Ft. Worth ever since that time for one reason or another.

I was down here in Ft. Worth during the World War. I was down here before the Second World War and during the Second World War. I made some inspections here of bomber plants on several different occasions as Chairman of the Special Committee to Investigate the Defense Program—and much to your credit, I found things were in excellent shape, and I found that we were turning out the machines which we needed to win that war.

When I was a kid, my father used to take a daily telegram to Kansas City. It always quoted prices from the five markets, and Ft. Worth was then, and still is, one of the five great cattle markets of the world. Ft. Worth depends upon the cattle business and the farming and the oil business of Texas for its being one of the greatest cities in this great State of Texas. Therefore, you are vitally interested in the policy of the Federal Government as it affects these various industries.[6]

(Short speech at a supper for Democratic senators and representatives, held at the Shoreham Hotel in Washington, D.C., on January 12, 1950.)

Mr. Chairman, Mr. Vice President, Mr. Speaker, and fellow Democrats:

It is a very great pleasure for me to be here again on this occasion. I was here last year and discussed with you certain experiences of mine as a Member of the Senate of the United States, and the difficulties I had in being elected at various times—in 1934, 1940, 1944, and I think I said something about the election of 1948.

But you have heard excellent advice from the Speaker of the House, and from the Vice President, and I hope that all of us will remember that the Democratic Party is the party of the people of the United States, and has been ever since Thomas Jefferson.[7]

(Labor Day address in Milwaukee, Wisconsin, September 1, 1952.)

I am very glad to come to Milwaukee and speak to you tonight. Milwaukee is a great city in a great State—a State that has a long, proud record of progressive government. A lot of progressive measures that the State of Wisconsin adopted many years ago became part of the New Deal—and were spread over all the country from here. Wisconsin has a great liberal tradition which was made famous by the two Bob La Follettes. I served with young Bob in the Senate, and he is one of the finest men I have ever known. I am sure that this year Wisconsin will return to that tradition and elect a United States Senator you can be proud of.

I am especially glad to be here on Labor Day. This is our day to honor the working men and women of America. It is also a day that marks the official opening of an election campaign—at least on the Democratic side. The Republicans don't seem to attach much importance to Labor Day.

I am going to get a great deal of satisfaction out of the presidential campaign this year. In the first place, we have a splendid candidate for the job, and in the second place, I won't have to do much of the work myself, this time.[8]

In this Milwaukee speech, Truman then proceeded to praise Adlai Stevenson, the Democratic nominee, for his record of concern for labor during his terms as governor of Illinois.

In his extemporaneous whistlestop talks, Truman tried hard to identify himself or some member of his family, no matter how remotely, with the community or local history. Regardless of which approach he used to introduce his speech, Truman seldom allotted the introduction much time before getting into the main part of his message.

When it came to the body of the speech—the part that carried the gist of his message—Truman invariably used simple and direct organization. He had no inclination toward presenting facts first and letting those facts help listeners form their own conclusions. Instead his preference was to use what rhetoricians term the *didactic* method of arrangement. This method means that he first would state the idea he wanted his listeners to accept, and then he would present concrete materials or proof supporting that contention. There is no evidence that he or his writers knew the meaning of the term *didactic* or consciously followed it as a guide, but it was the consistent pattern that appeared throughout his speech career. A few examples will demonstrate his customary pattern of assertion first, then support.

The arrangement pattern is evident in a radio address explaining his reasons for vetoing the Taft-Hartley bill. The speech was broadcast from the White House at 10:00 P.M., EST, on June 20, 1947, and he began his talk with blunt assertions:

> My fellow countrymen:
> At noon today I sent to Congress a message vetoing the Taft-Hartley bill. I vetoed this bill because I am convinced it is a bad bill. It is bad for labor, bad for management, and bad for the country.[9]

The president then presented reasonings that underlay his contention that the bill was faulty. He closed his fifteen-minute speech by explaining his hope that the bill would never become law. (In spite of Truman's hopes and persuasions, Congress on June 23, 1947, passed the bill over his veto.)

Truman's preferred organizational pattern was evident also in his state of the union address at the opening of 1947. On January 6 of that year, he appeared before Congress to give an address which centered on industrial tensions then tormenting the nation. After introductory statements, Truman came to his first major contention:

> Certain labor-management problems need attention at once. . . . We should enact legislation to correct certain abuses and to provide additional governmental assistance in bargaining. . . . I propose to you . . . the following four-point program to reduce industrial strife:
> Point number one is the early enactment of legislation to prevent certain unjustifiable practices. [Truman next explained in sequence the practices of jurisdictional strikes, interunion disagreements over which union is entitled to perform a certain task, secondary boycotts, and the unjustified

use of economic force by either labor or management in deciding issues.]. . . .

    Point number two is the extension of facilities within the Department
of Labor for assisting collective bargaining. . . .

    Point number three is the broadening of our program of social legisla-
tion to alleviate the causes of workers' insecurity. . . .

    Point number four is the appointment of a Temporary Joint Commis-
sion to inquire into the entire field of labor-management relations.[10]

After enumerating each of the points mentioned in the above example,
Truman gave his supporting evidence and reasoning.

    Another instance demonstrating Truman's pattern of contention followed
by rhetorical proofs occurred when he appeared before a special session of Congress later in 1947 to plead for immediate economic assistance to certain European countries. He delivered this speech on November 17, 1947, and after formal recognition and salutation to the members of Congress, he laid down the
thesis he had come to argue:

> The Congress has been convened to consider two problems of major con-
> cern to the citizens of the United States and to the peoples of the world.
> The fate of the free nations of Europe hangs in the balance. The future of
> our own economy is in jeopardy. The action which you take will be written
> large in the history of this Nation and the world.
>
>   The Secretary of State and other representatives of the executive
> branch have appeared before the committees of Congress during the past
> week to present the facts regarding the necessity for immediate assistance
> by the United States to certain European countries. Austria, France, and
> Italy have nearly exhausted their financial resources. They must be helped
> if their peoples are to survive the coming winter, and if their political and
> economic systems are not to disintegrate.[11]

    A fourth example illustrating Truman's typical order in presenting ideas
stands out in his radio report to the American people on Korea and on United
States policy in the Far East. This address was broadcast from the White House
on April 11, 1951, at 10:30 P.M., EST—the day Truman had issued his statement and order relieving General Douglas MacArthur of his commands. At the
outset of his address, Truman stated clearly what he saw as America's purpose
in Korea: "In the simplest terms, what we are doing in Korea is this: we are trying to prevent a third world war."[12]

    Next Truman insisted that the action taken by the United States the previ-
ous June was "right," and it was "still right" in April of 1951. He then traced
aggressions by North Korea which he said had threatened world peace and were
just like the aggressions that had menaced Greece and Turkey in 1947 but had
been forestalled by effective American military and economic aid.

    Then Truman launched another major contention:

> The aggression against Korea is the boldest and most dangerous move the Communists have yet made. The attack on Korea was part of a greater plan for conquering all of Asia.[13]

He followed this assertion with his supporting evidence, which included two secret intelligence reports that he said showed the invasion by North Korea was but one step in a plan to dominate the Asian continent.

After setting forth the reasons for American involvement in Korea, President Truman approached the end of this radio address and thus came to the crisis that had prompted the occasion:

> I believe that we must try to limit the war to Korea for these vital reasons: to make sure that precious lives of our fighting men are not wasted; to see that the security of our country and the free world is not needlessly jeopardized; and to prevent a third world war.
>
> A number of events have made it evident that General MacArthur [this was the first time Truman mentioned MacArthur's name in this particular address] did not agree with that policy. I have therefore considered it essential to relieve General MacArthur so that there would be no doubt or confusion as to the real purpose and aim of our policy.[14]

That was his simple, direct explanation, and Truman followed it by announcing the name of the new commander. He closed his speech by laying down the terms under which a peace settlement in Korea could be reached if the enemy were willing:

> One: the fighting must stop.
> Two: Concrete steps must be taken to insist that the fighting will not break out again.
> Three: there must be an end to the aggression.[15]

Many more instances could be found where Truman would first state his basic contention and then present his supporting reasoning. After one or more central contentions buttressed by supporting evidence, Truman would move quickly and sometimes abruptly into a conclusion. His speeches lacked rhetorical climaxes of the type found in the orations of Cicero, Webster, Lincoln, Wilson, or Franklin Roosevelt. In fact, Truman did not do well in marching his speech toward an ever-rising pitch of audience fervor. To be sure, there might be excitement and emotion generated during his address, but when that happened it was because of some dramatic announcement, not because of any rhetorical arrangement. A case in point could be his acceptance speech in July of 1948. When he announced in that address that he was going to call Congress back into session, the feelings of his listeners exploded into wild enthusiasm. From that point on, his address began to grow anticlimactic, and his final passage, paraphrasing words from Roosevelt, sagged below the high point reached by his dramatic call for a special session.

The arrangement of ideas within a Truman speech was predictable. Surprises, if they came, had to result from either the substance of what he said or from the words and expressions he used.

Harry Truman's Language

The seventeenth-century English playwright, Ben Jonson, wrote, "Language most shows a man; speak, that I may see thee!" While language may not be an infallible index to character, particularly in modern times when advisers and writers are used ever more in the preparation of presidential messages, it is still true that vocabulary and language patterns offer us insights into a person's character and abilities.

Beliefs about Truman's language are beginning to take on legendary proportions, and like most legends, those beliefs are seldom rooted in fact. The most common belief is that because he did not possess a college degree, his vocabulary was narrow and laced with vulgarity. More careful examination will show that this belief is unwarranted.

Anecdotes usually grow up around most persons who become famous, and often it is impossible to dislodge those stories from the public mind. One anecdote about Truman that has made the rounds for years begins by recounting a conversation Mrs. Truman is supposed to have held with ladies attending her bridge party. One guest, after complimenting Mrs. Truman for the job her husband is doing in the White House, then adds: "However, I do wish, Bess, that you could do something about Harry's awful language. He's always talking about unpleasant subjects and choosing the word 'manure.' Can't you get him to stop saying that?" Whereupon Bess is supposed to have replied, "But, my dear, for years I've been trying to get him to use the word 'manure.'" That story comes up in nearly every casual conversation about Truman, and yet there has never been a shred of documentation indicating that such a conversation ever took place. When it is pointed out that there is no evidence for such a story, people are apt to say, "But that is what we might expect from Harry Truman." The anecdote is as fictional as stories of George Washington chopping down his father's cherry tree, or of Abraham Lincoln's alleged romance with Ann Rutledge. Nevertheless, as Harry Truman's life and career becomes more obscured by time, it is likely that pertinent facts about his language will be forgotten and such anecdotes remembered.

Truman actually possessed a broad vocabulary because of his extensive reading, but this fact usually went unnoticed because of his fondness for terseness. His goal in choosing words was accuracy, not ornateness. Short speeches, short sentences, and short words were characteristics of his language even when he had no battery of assistants. In his presidential years, he often told his writers that what he wanted was a direct statement of facts without trimming or oratory. As a result, the Truman language, whether entirely from his own mind or modified by opinions of persons working closely with him, became noted for its simplicity and clarity. Clifford called it a style well suited to the "Missouri Mind" and admonished assistants to phrase presidential messages accordingly.

The fact that President Truman used speech writers should in no way suggest that he was incapable of writing his own speeches. On the contrary, his best persuasions came when he had no prepared text. Even if a manuscript went through several drafts, the final product always bore an unmistakable Truman imprint. A journalist once questioned Clifford about such speech preparation:

> I went in to talk with him [Clifford] one day about writing speeches for the President, and I must say that Clifford, although not ordinarily a modest man, was modest this day. He said, "Well, really, it's his [Truman's] speech when I finish with it. I'll write a speech and then he [meaning the President] will write in between the lines, write changes out in the margins, then I'll do it the second time. Sometimes I have had to write a speech seven times before he's satisfied. In the end, it's really his.[16]

In rewriting drafts submitted to him, Truman invariably tried to reduce the length of sentences. In a speech for the American Association for the Advancement of Science on September 13, 1948, one can see his mind at work as he pared unnecessary phrases. One draft proposed an opening statement which read: "As President of the United States, I welcome you to Washington as you open your centennial meeting." Truman penciled out the last clause, and the sentence became: "As President of the United States, I welcome you to Washington." Later in a fifth draft of the same speech, he shortened a long sentence which first appeared as: "In the one hundred years since this Association was organized, science has helped transform this Nation from a relatively undeveloped wilderness into the most powerful Nation in the world today." His shortened version became simply: "In the one hundred years since this Association was organized, science has helped transform the United States into the most productive nation in the world."[17]

Another example of Truman's preference for short sentences can be seen in the way he improved a long sentence given him by his writers for a radio address on the Railroad Strike Emergency on May 24, 1946. One sentence in that message originally read: "After consideration, this compromise was accepted by the operators and by eighteen of the unions, who were cooperative, and who placed the interests of the country first." Truman made this somewhat involved sentence into three shorter ones:

After consideration, this compromise was accepted by the operators and by eighteen of the unions. The eighteen unions were cooperative. They placed the interests of their country first.[18]

In a speech for the Jefferson-Jackson Day dinner, March 23, 1946, Truman looked at a proposed sentence: "The problem of changing over to the ways of peace involves much more than a physical shift in producing civilian goods rather than war goods." He then eliminated the last phrase, "rather than war goods," and changed the rest to read simply: "The problem of reconversion involves much more than a physical change over to the production of civilian goods." Likewise later in the draft for this same speech, he took the sentence: "That is the reason for the plan of premium payments, which would be used to break bottlenecks and to remove the burden of price increases from those least able to afford them." He shortened the sentence to a simple explanation: "That is the reason for premium payments, which would be used to break bottlenecks."[19]

Truman not only wanted his sentences direct and simple; he chose short words whenever possible. In drafts submitted to him, he frequently struck out a word like "individuals" and substituted "people." He would replace the word "formula" with his preferred word, "plan." In one early speech during his presidency, he scratched out "subsequently" and replaced it with "later." A few paragraphs further on in the same speech, he deleted "periodically" and wrote above it "in every age." In a speech dealing with the Railroad Emergency in May of 1946, Truman was given a sentence which read: "Returning veterans will be held at ports and demobilization centers." He chose shorter words and simplified it to: "Returning veterans will not be able to get home." In other instances, he changed the word "indivisible" into "cannot be divided," and "individual initiative" was replaced with "individual efforts." On the occasion of a speech for the Jefferson-Jackson Day dinner on February 19, 1948, he was given a sentence that included the word *engulfed*: "Jefferson liberalism thus gave birth to and was engulfed by Jacksonian democracy." Truman rubbed out the *engulfed* and wrote in its place "carried on."[20]

On at least on one occasion, President Truman enjoyed a little banter about overblown words. It happened at his news conference on August 9, 1946. He began that conference by stating that he had no particular announcements to make but was ready to try to answer any questions. The first question and his response took the following form:

QUESTION: Mr. President, the Republican national campaign director [Representative Clarence J. Brown of Ohio] today accuses you of *inganna-tion* [emphasis added] in connection with your budget.

PRESIDENT: Well, I guess that's just to add to the obfuscation of all the rest of his statement. [Laughter] That's about in line with what he's trying to say.[21]

Actually, Brown's use of the word, *ingannation,* had sent Truman and his aides to dictionaries. They were unable to find the word there, but one of them did locate the word in a thesaurus where it was likened to synonyms deceit, deception, and fraudulence.

After the president's initial response, there was a series of questions on other matters until a little later in the conference when a second reporter returned to the word *ingannation:*

QUESTION: Mr. President, getting back to the ingannation—
PRESIDENT: The obfuscation. [Laughter]
QUESTION: Get him to spell that, will you?
PRESIDENT: Well, I will spell it for you. I had it looked up in the dictionary. It means deceit or deception, and it is spelled i-n-g-a-n-n-a-t-i-o-n. I don't use $40 words like that in my language.
QUESTION: Is that a double n, Mr. President?
PRESIDENT: It says so here. I never saw the word until I heard or saw it in the paper, and then I had to get a dictionary and look it up.[22]

Another questioner then asked the president if he had secured any opinions from his aides about the word, and he answered:

PRESIDENT: Yes, I discussed it with Dr. Hassett [William D. Hassett, then secretary to the president]. Dr. Hassett's opinion was the same as mine, that it was a good Republican word, and that the Democrats wouldn't use it.[23]

On a rare occasion, Truman himself might indulge in a pretentious word. The indulgence was most likely to occur when he was talking about his favorite subjects of history or Freemasonry. Once while he was a senator he gave a speech, which he wrote out beforehand, praising the Masons for their contributions in building America. He said repeatedly that Masons as an organization followed principles of public "benignancy." Although most everyone was familiar with this word in its adjectival form, it is an uncommon speaker or writer who uses it as a noun.

As a result of his preference for short words and sentences, President Truman's communications usually were unmistakably clear even if they were not always graceful. In his writing, he was a careful speller, and he had an excellent command of grammar in both written and oral expression. One veteran correspondent complimented him on that score:

I'd like to call your attention to something else. I told somebody this, I think they were interviewing me in connection with an oral history on Eisenhower. If you went back and looked at transcripts of press conferences or speeches, off-the-cuff speeches, you'd be very much impressed by Mr. Truman's syntax, his rhetoric in general—it marched. He didn't clutter up his speeches with adjectives or adverbs. He was a man who liked nouns and verbs. It would be hard to find a grammatical error in any of his remarks, either in press conferences or off-the-cuff speeches.[24]

Even in his schooldays, Harry Truman had been a good student of language. He was more traditionalist than innovator with words, but as he rose to higher political office he never lost his appreciation for accuracy of expression. His early appointment of Charles Ross as presidential press secretary was an assurance that language coming from the White House would be carefully screened for grammatical correctness. One Truman writer, David Bell, recalled Ross's role as an editor:

He [Ross] also, incidentally, had high standards of English style. To this day, I feel strongly about certain matters of English usage that date from some of the matters that Charlie Ross used to snort about when he went over drafts of material that we had prepared for the President. For example, Ross was highly scornful of the word "presently" to mean "now." As far as Charlie Ross was concerned, the word "presently" meant "in the future." I have not forgotten that, and I have the same bias today.[25]

Truman's vocabulary, like that of every person's, reflected his interests and culture. He had grown up in Missouri at the turn of the century, had served in the army, had been a farmer, and had been in politics most of his adult life. It was only natural that his language would contain echoes from his varied past. He had some old-fashioned phrases that he used from time to time—phrases that were descriptive of persons or events. Many of these terms were homely, farm vernacular and would pop out often during his informal discussions. For example, during a conference with his board of economic advisers in March of 1949, he commented that someone there must be as "crazy as a pet coon." In another staff conference when the name of Senator Harry Byrd came up, Truman used an old rural colloquialism in saying: "He doesn't know straight up from crossways."[26]

One of Truman's favorite expressions, which he often uttered in an amused, half-curious way, was "Oh, pshaw!" In press conferences, he referred to newsmen as "men," not "fellows" as Roosevelt had done, and he frequently showed his border state upbringing by saying, "You all." He was at his best when he could lapse into the axioms and colloquialisms that had guided him throughout his life. During the campaign of 1948, after he had delivered his major farm policy speech in Dexter, Iowa, he stayed around to inspect some plowing and tractor exhibits. Then he chatted with visitors about his early days on a farm. He delighted his listeners with his knowledge about horses and mules, and it seemed only natural for him to tell them, "I'm going down to Berkeley to get me a degree." It was not an expression contrived to make him seem more folksy; it came out that way because it was easy for him to be familiar with people when they gathered before him in small crowds. He could identify with them on such occasions, and his ad-libbed comments were sprinkled with remarks like: "I certainly appreciate," "It certainly is a pleasure," or "I certainly will."

At Sanderson, Texas, he told the people who had come to the railroad station to greet him, "This is a mighty fine whistlestop, out here where it is a long way between stops." Then at Bells, Texas, during the same tour, he said:

> I'm going over to Bonham with Sam [Rayburn]. I don't feel like it would be fair to Sam, fair to Bonham, for me to stand here and make the speech I am going to make at Bonham in Bells so I am going to make a deal with you. It's only twelve miles—why don't you just get in the car and come over to Bonham, and I will give the Republicans the gun over there? I think you will like it.[27]

Whether it was to "make a deal" or to "give the Republicans the gun," Truman liked to use metaphors. They enriched his language in a way that made reporters take notice. Readers in turn remembered his unusual and sometimes mildly irreverent comparisons. A case in point was Truman's comparison of his own efforts with an inscription on a grave in Tombstone, Arizona: "Here lies Jack Williams; he done his damnedest." Truman insisted that was all he was trying to do in the presidency.

Truman once used a comparison that never came to public attention. The incident occurred in early September of 1950, when he decided that he would have to ask Louis Johnson to resign as secretary of defense. He called Johnson to the White House for an off-the-record meeting, and almost at the outset told him that he would have to ask for the resignation. Johnson had bounced in full of pep and ideas, but with this unexpected blow he wilted and left terribly depressed. The next day, President Truman confided to Ross:

> This is the toughest job I have ever had to do. I feel as if I had just whipped my daughter, Margaret.[28]

Even in his written communications, Truman liked to use vernacular expressions, and frequently his words were common but pungent. Once when criticizing the Scripps-Howard chain of newspapers, he wrote to the editor of the *Washington Daily News* about that paper's publication of an editorial entitled, "The Korean Stalemate."

> The attached editorial . . . contains a double-barreled, barefaced lie which I've marked with a red line. . . . Of course, truth means not one thing to Roy Howard or your snotty little *News*—but these are the facts.[29]

On another occasion, when recalling his relations with the *Kansas City Star*, Truman made it clear that he never had been given any real trouble by the management of that newspaper. He said that it was only on their editorial page that they "attempted to skin me." [30]

So much has been written about Truman's use of profanity that he often is pictured as an uncouth and frequently vulgar person. The picture could hardly be more distorted. There is no doubt that once in a while he did use language ordinarily considered obscene, and because that language was uttered by the president of the United States it offended some persons. The words were not unfamiliar, but many citizens had come to believe that every American president was cast in a mold of more than human proportions, and therefore would never fall to common expressions.

Considering his life experiences, Truman's occasional bursts of profanity should not be surprising. It would have been truly unusual if he never used profanity. What was surprising was that he, unlike most presidents, made no attempt to conceal his language habits. On the contrary, he seemed to take a puckish delight in criticisms about his vocabulary. If the truth were known, Truman was probably far less profane than most of his predecessors, and certainly less so than several of the presidents who have succeeded him. If judged on a scale of profanity frequency, Truman would rank well below most recent presidents. Eisenhower could and did swear like the army trooper he had been. John F. Kennedy's private conversations were interlarded with vulgarities that were filtered out by careful White House public relations experts. Lyndon Johnson swore often and at times seemed almost obsessed with scatological terms. In his debates with Kennedy in 1960, Richard Nixon vowed that if he got into the White House the schoolchildren of America would never hear him use the kind of language Truman had employed. Nixon was right on that score—at least partially—for it was not until the expletive-deleted Watergate tapes were played that his penchant for vulgarities was exposed. The main difference between Truman and other American presidents was that Harry Truman in public was very much like Harry Truman in private.

The profanities that Truman uttered had carried over from his years on the farm or his army career. Most of them were pretty mild if measured by today's permissive standards. The word *damn*, for instance, could be considered a strong word when it was spoken by President Truman. Language, of course, is always a reflection of time, place, and circumstance. One circumstance arose in September of 1947, when King Carol of Rumania was presented to Truman. Carol asked the president if he spoke French, and Truman, who did not care for Carol mainly because of his reputation as a woman-chaser, answered abruptly, "No, and damn little English!" [31]

Truman used the word *hell*, but not as often as writers, movies, and television shows have depicted. He gave the word more popular acceptance with his remark that he merely told the "truth" about Republicans, and they in turn thought it was "hell." The remark was picked out to become the title of a highly successful stage play based on selected episodes in his life, "Give 'Em Hell, Harry!"

An expression that was a Truman favorite was "son-of-a-bitch." He used it carelessly; sometimes it was pure name-calling, and at other times it was in a friendly manner much like Owen Wister's Virginian—"When you call me that, smile!" An example of Truman's use of the term in a friendly vein occurred in 1950 when his long-time Assistant Press Secretary Eben Ayers asked him to autograph a book. Ayers apologized for asking because he said that he realized the president had to sign his name so often during the course of a normal day's business. Truman laughed it off:

> I have to sign my name for so many sons-of-bitches that it's a pleasure to sign it for someone I like.[32]

It had taken Ayers, who was serving as Roosevelt's assistant press secretary when Truman came into office, several weeks to adjust to Truman's casual use of "son-of-a-bitch." At least the phrase seemed to surprise Ayers enough that he entered a note in his diary one day during Truman's first month in office that the president had just told him he had written a nice letter to a "son-of-a-bitch."[33]

A strange use of this phrase came up in connection with the appointment of Paul Stark, a fellow Missourian. Paul Stark was a recognized horticulturist who was recommended for a job with the U.S. Department of Agriculture soon after Truman assumed the presidency. Paul Stark was a brother of Lloyd Stark, a former governor of Missouri. Truman had done several favors for the Democratic governor, but despite such assistance Stark had chosen to run against Truman for the United States Senate in 1940. When asked if he would endorse Paul Stark for the position in the Department of Agriculture, President Truman said, "Paul Stark is a brother of the Governor, who is a son-of-a-bitch." Then perhaps realizing the possible overtones, Truman added hastily, "I meant no reflection upon their common mother—the Governor is a self-made son-of-a-bitch."[34] Mr. Truman never attempted to explain this genetic oddity!

In other instances Truman used this phrase more from habit than from any real name-calling. For example, when the publisher of the *Tulsa Oklahoma World* wanted an office appointment, Truman told his secretary that the publisher was just another "son-of-a-bitch." The term seemed to pop out easily whenever he was talking about newspaper publishers. Once when someone advised him that it would be good political strategy to court the news media and in particular to try to heal wounds with publishers Meigs and Hearst, he replied, "I'm not sending for any of those sons-of-bitches."[35]

During his campaign for the presidency in 1948, Truman spoke in Fresno,

California, where he excoriated the Republican legislator representing that district and said that he was the worst congressman in the House of Representatives. Edward Folliard, a newsman covering the Truman campaign, related an incident that stemmed from the president's public remarks:

> Later that day, I was in the press room in Los Angeles writing my story, and I felt somebody behind me. I looked around, and it was the President. I said, "Oh, Mr. President, I was just writing what you said about Congressman So-and-so." He said, "Well, probably I've re-elected the son-of-a-bitch." Well, it turned out that the man he had excoriated was defeated. . . . It's too long ago for me to remember names, but I remember the incident very well.[36]

There were times when Truman's use of the term was more malicious and closer to pure name-calling. For instance, once when he was talking with his aides about General Charles DeGaulle, he told them, "I don't like the son-of-a-bitch."[37] Perhaps the most widely noted instance of his use of this term occurred in February of 1949, when he went to a dinner given at the Army-Navy Country Club in honor of Major General Harry Vaughan. Vaughan was a former army buddy of Truman's and had been elevated to a position as the president's military aide. Jack Romagna, the presidential stenographer, had been told to attend the dinner in order to record any remarks the president might make. In his speech, Truman defended Vaughan against attacks by Drew Pearson and other columnists because Vaughan was awarded a medal by the Argentine government. Truman said:

> I want you distinctly to understand that any son-of-a-bitch who thinks he can cause any of those people to be discharged by me, by some smart alec statement over the air or in the paper, has got another think coming.[38]

Reporters rushed to their telephones and were after Romagna for a transcript of the actual words. Romagna telephoned the White House staff asking what to do about it. Secretary Ayers in turn telephoned President Truman, who said that indeed he had seen some of the reporters at the dinner and, therefore, had decided to say what he thought. He agreed, however, that it might be better to leave the phrase and even the initials out of the official transcript. Thus began the habit of substituting "x x x" or "– – –" for Truman's actual words in newspaper accounts.

Truman occasionally used other profane phrases. The other phrases were rare and more apt to be shared only with his closest staff. On one occasion he called Nelson Rockefeller of New York "a little piss ant."[39] At another time he referred to the industrialist Henry Kaiser as a real "pisscutter."[40] In exasperation over Eisenhower's flirtation with politics in 1948, Truman called the general, then at the height of his popularity, a "s – – – a – –."[41]

In Truman's later years as president, he asked Eben Ayers to check the historical accuracy of data being compiled about Truman's early career. Ayers took to the president certain articles written by William Bradford Huie that had been published in the *American Mercury*. The articles had appeared in the May and August issues of 1951, and were critical to the point of being scurrilous. Ayers reported another instance of Truman's profanity:

> The President said he had not seen it [the article] and I told him I was not bringing it to him. I explained what was in it in a general way and told him that I thought some of the boys around the White House were a little excited about it. I said that I felt, and I thought he agreed, that no attempt should be made to answer these articles. . . . The President agreed and quoted advice attributed to Calvin Coolidge—"never enter into a pissing contest with a skunk."[42]

Yet Truman could turn his vulgarisms against himself, too. Once after being shown a picture in which he was included, he harkened back to his days on the farm and said that it looked just like "sheep s – – – on a shingle."[43] At different times he jokingly told his aides that if he had not gone into politics, he probably would have become "a piano player in a whorehouse."[44]

Truman nearly always avoided profanity if there were any women present. Early in life he had put them on a pedestal, and there they remained. He believed it was a gentleman's duty to shelter them from the seamier sides of life, including coarseness of language or conversation. His sensitivity on this score can be seen in an incident involving Beth Short, his corresponding secretary. Following one press conference during which he had used the word *damn*, he followed Mrs. Short into the elevator and offered her an apology:

> Beth, I didn't know you were present. If I had known you were there, I wouldn't have used that word.[45]

In many ways, Truman was an old-fashioned man even for his day. In social gatherings he showed impeccable manners and sensitivity to the feelings of others. He seemed so genuine that most persons found it impossible not to like him. Robert K. Walsh, a reporter for the *Washington Star*, described an incident that helps portray Truman's common touch. It emerged at a reception given for Charles Ross when the latter became the president's press secretary:

> Well, anyway, we had this—there were free drinks—great big turnout for Charlie. He was very well respected and very well liked. I suppose the Press Club committee knew it, but Truman showed up unannounced, walked in and stood as we all lined up to shake hands with him. This was late in the afternoon, about five or five thirty. They had a bar at one end, everybody had a drink in his hand, and there again, the line moved much more quickly than I thought. I had a drink in my hand, left hand, I guess, bour-

bon and water or something. I got right up to the President, and I tried to find a place to put this doggone drink, going up to the President of the United States with this—that was very new then. I couldn't put it on the floor, and there was no table there. I got up to him and he sort of grinned, so I said, "Congratulations, Mr. President, glad to see you," and all that. I said, "I must apologize for having this thing in my hand."

And as I remember he replied: "What the hell do you think I have in my hand?" In back of him there was a little table he had pulled around, and he had a glass in his hand.[46]

Truman seldom held grudges very long, and eventually forgave nearly all his enemies. He made up with nearly everyone with whom he had quarrelled: John L. Lewis, Dwight Eisenhower, Harold Ickes, even in part with Richard Nixon. Truman was especially angered with Eisenhower in 1953 when the latter, who was then president, went to Kansas City to make a speech before the Young Farmers. At that time Truman had an office in Kansas City, and he, not his secretary, called the presidential suite at the Muehlebach Hotel where Eisenhower was staying and said he would like to come around and pay his respects to the president. He was told that the president's calendar was filled and that he could not make an appointment. No one ever ascertained who actually gave Truman this response, but even if it was a mix-up, Eisenhower never apologized nor tried to make amends. George Allen, a crony of President Eisenhower's, said later that an investigation had been ordered, but there was no real follow-up. Even Richard Nixon, when told by one reporter about the incident, said, "Oh, that was wrong. The president should have called up Mr. Truman and told him he was sorry, and that would have ended the whole thing."

The acrimony of this incident faded with time, however, and on the day of the funeral for John F. Kennedy, Eisenhower and Truman together with their wives were driven in the same limousine to Blair House where Truman was staying at the invitation of President Lyndon Johnson. As the limousine stopped, Truman said, "Ike, how about coming in for a drink?" Ike and Mamie agreed. Later when the little gathering was about to break up, Mamie thanked Truman for something he had done just before Eisenhower's inauguration in 1953, namely, inviting their son, John Eisenhower, to be in attendance at the inauguration ceremony. At that time, John Eisenhower was serving in Korea, so Mamie thanked Truman for his considerate action and then kissed him. That was the end of the feud, and as far as Truman was concerned, they were the friends they had been for many years.[47]

Although Truman usually forgave his former enemies, there were two persons toward whom he remained embittered. They were Clare Boothe Luce and Adam Clayton Powell, both of whom had hit Truman in his tenderest spot, his love and respect for the women in his family. Clare Boothe Luce once made a sneering remark about Mrs. Truman having worked in Senator Truman's office. The remark was true, for Bess was on his senatorial payroll. What Mrs. Luce did not explain, however, was that Truman had gone bankrupt and had vowed to pay back every cent he owed. As a senator, he was still paying off those debts, and that was one big reason for Mrs. Truman's being on the payroll. When he became president, Truman said that neither Clare Boothe Luce nor Adam Clayton Powell would ever be invited to the White House while he was there, and they were not.

Truman was at his gregarious best when mingling in small social gatherings. While he was critical of the use of off-color language in the company of women, he enjoyed the broad, earthy humor so often found in meetings of veterans, farmers, or politicians. He delighted in their repartee, but his own sallies were seldom subtle or sophisticated. He could not tell a joke well, and when he tried to do so in his public speeches his listeners, if they laughed at all, did so out of respect for his high office more than from any genuine mirth.

During the 1948 campaign, his writers developed an anecdote for him to use in Gary, Indiana, and it went as follows:

> Not long ago a priest driving into Gary stopped and picked up a young hitchhiker. During their conversation the good Father asked the young man, "What takes you into Gary?" The youth replied, "I'm working for the Republican National Committee, and they are sending me into Gary to see what can be done to get Gary people to vote Republican."
>
> The kind priest was silent for a minute and then said, "Son, I've listened to confessions for over thirty years and that's the saddest one I've ever heard."
>
> "I agree with the Father."[48]

When Truman delivered the talk, he changed the dialogue slightly so that it read:

> Not long ago an *elderly man who was driving into Gary* . . . and the young man hesitated, *put his head down* and said. . . . The old man was silent for a while and then he said: "Son, I've listened to sad stories for *fifty* years and that's the saddest one I've heard yet."[49]

Truman then paused momentarily after the last word before adding his, "I agree."

Occasionally a joke went well because the audience was in a good mood and predisposed to laugh. Such an instance occurred when Truman spoke to the Jefferson-Jackson Day dinner on February 24, 1949. He was elated because of his recent election, and the audience likewise was exhilarated. Early in his prepared speech he told the story of Andrew Jackson's coffin:

> Once upon a time, there were a number of citizens who thought that Andrew Jackson ought to have a suitable coffin. At great expense, they went

to Syria and purchased a marble sarcophagus. A sarcophagus, as you know, is a tomb—a big marble coffin with a marble lid. These citizens then shipped this marble box to Washington, which was quite a job as it weighed four or five tons.

At last, they thought, a suitable resting place had been provided for Andrew Jackson. The only trouble with the project was that Andrew Jackson was not dead. [Laughter] Moreover, he wasn't ready to die. [Laughter] He did not intend to be hurried to the grave. Courteously but firmly he wrote to these well-meaning citizens, and said, "I must decline the intended honor." [Laughter]

And they never did get Old Hickory into that thing. You can still see it, if you're interested, out in front of the Smithsonian Institution.

I think that this little story has a moral in it. It is this: Before you offer to bury a good Democrat, you better be sure he is dead! [Laughter and applause][50]

Humor often depends on the way it is told, and particularly on the timing used by the speaker. Truman was not blessed with either the voice or the gift for mimicry that characterizes those who become truly great speakers. On the platform he was adequate rather than remarkable.

Truman's Voice and Gestures

It was inevitable that Truman's oratory would be compared to that of his predecessor. The comparison was unfortunate because the latter had long been praised for his eloquence and demeanor on the public platform. Matt Connelly, whom Truman had picked in 1941 to be on the staff of his War Investigating Committee, early recognized some of Truman's shortcomings at the rostrum and had tried to help him with this aspect in his several offices:

Well, when I first worked with Mr. Truman on the Truman Committee, the few minor experiences I had with him in speechmaking were pretty sad. He had a great tendency to want to get things over, and you'd give him a prepared speech and he couldn't wait until he got to the end of a sentence so that he could get started on the next one. As a result, the delivery was terrible. . . .

He made a speech at some kind of lawn party in Washington, and it was a pretty sad situation. When he became Vice President, one of the first things I wanted to do was to try to correct that little fault of his about rushing through a speech.[51]

There is no doubt that even before Truman got into the White House, his aides were trying to improve his platform effectiveness. In large part they tried to mold him into a prototype set by Roosevelt, but their efforts in that direction were not entirely successful. Roosevelt had proved himself a masterful radio speaker, and Connelly was among those who helped bring in Leonard Reinsch to coach Truman in his radio delivery during his campaign for the vice-presidency. Reinsch was from the Cox Broadcasting Company in Georgia and had worked on the technical side of speeches for Roosevelt, mainly in the selection and placement of microphones. Reinsch gave an account of his first meeting with Harry Truman:

> The first time I met with Senator Truman was to discuss the campaign of 1944 at his home in Independence. You recall that this was during the wartime and we had severe travel limitations . . . so I had secured, following the nomination [Truman's as vice-president in 1944], a transcript and also a transcription of a speech that Mr. Truman had made in Philadelphia, which ran 55 minutes. The delivery was very rapid to the point that sometimes the material was not intelligible. One of my first questions to the vice presidential candidate was, "Why did you go so fast at this speech in Philadelphia?"
> And he said, "Well, I didn't think it was very interesting, and I wanted to get it over with."[52]

It was obvious to all who were then trying to help candidate Truman that the first problem in his public speaking was to get him to slow down. He chose to give his speech accepting the vice-presidential nomination at his birthplace of Lamar, Missouri. In preparation for that event, he and Reinsch went to a Kansas City radio station owned by Truman's friend, Tom Evans. There Truman recorded the talk several times, and, with Reinsch as his tutor, listened to the playbacks. The pacing was slower but still faster than normal speech, so the two decided to put less and less material on each page hoping that the mechanical process of turning pages would decrease Truman's rate of reading. The technique helped but did not eliminate his tendency to race his words.

After Truman became president, the practice continued, and just a few sentences were put on each page in the hope that Truman would read more slowly and with better emphasis. Some observers noted, however, that it seemed he merely turned the pages faster. Reinsch was asked whether he thought it was true that the president flipped pages more rapidly:

> That is not entirely true because there was a marked slowdown. After he became President, we had several advantages in that we knew that the President would not be cut off the air; as Vice President we had to be very careful about the timing. There were several thoughts that were implanted in his mind as Vice President; one was that when he talked into the microphone the people that were hearing him were not assembled in a multitude of a million or five million. The audience was represented by three or four people in a home in a living room, seated around a radio console. . . . So I took little slips of paper which I would put in at various points throughout the speech which read "remember the living room" or "take it easy" or "slow down" or "easy does it." . . . I think this was some

help. He did not turn the pages faster; it is impossible to pace your delivery and turn the pages faster because you can't read that fast. This technique, of course, was abandoned later on, but it was very helpful at the time.[53]

Reinsch also called Truman's attention to words in his prepared addresses which might give him trouble in reading. Because of Truman's rapid rate, there was an ever-present danger that syllables would be omitted or necessary pauses overlooked. A radio report given on January 3, 1946, went through six drafts before Truman began practicing it aloud. In one draft, Reinsch selected six words as articulation danger spots: "particularly, generally, objective, provide, and production." Just as careless speakers often do, Truman might say, "pervide" or "perduction," and Reinsch wanted to be sure that the president got in every syllable and did not substitue "per" for "pro." Reinsch also wrote in his instructions for pauses, sometimes writing the word "pause," and sometimes suggesting it by using slanted marks— / or / /. Three marks / / / meant a very long pause within a paragraph. At one place, he penciled in the instruction "drop voice." Other written advice included "make it slow," "conversational style," or "friendly and easy here." In one sentence which read, "Time is runn*ing* out," Reinsch underlined the ing in an effort to keep Truman from his habit of substituting *en* for *ing*. Reinsch concluded his memo which accompanied his marked draft of this speech with some encouragement for the president:

> My carbon has been marked with a few suggestions. This speech is in *good* [emphasis in original] shape. You are doing a selling job! There is plenty of time and Easy does it!
>
> Leonard[54]

In 1945 and 1946, tape recorders had not been perfected, so Reinsch and Truman used a wire recorder which did not have the fidelity of later machines. They usually set up the recorder in the cabinet room, and sometimes they would listen to a recording while having a quick lunch. There is no hard evidence that Truman ever profited very much from the delivery suggestions given him, except that his pace, although always fast by normal standards, did become noticeably slower. Reinsch insisted, however, that the president appreciated and profited from his early help. Later Truman became far too busy to be bothered with what he considered trivia.

Timing in speech results from three factors: words per minute, duration of sounds, and length of pauses. Truman was able to lengthen his pauses, but he never got away from the clipped, staccato character of his sounds. Vowels were not prolonged as in the best oratorical tradition, and as a result his voice, thin and nasal in quality anyway, never developed the full resonance associated with great speakers. Although listener preferences vary and rate depends on several factors such as complexity of subject and size of audience, most experienced public speakers speak at a rate of about 125 words per minute. Franklin Roosevelt's normal reading rate was 127 words per minute, and some scholars estimate that Abraham Lincoln seldom spoke faster than 110 to 115 words per minute. Truman by comparison spoke much more rapidly and approached 150 words per minute even after his rate had been slowed by writers and advisers. In the peroration to his speech accepting the presidential nomination in 1948—an occasion when he was doing his best to slow down—his rate was slightly more than 138 words per minute. By that year, his secretary, Rose Conway, had devised a system of typing manuscripts so that natural pauses occurred at the end of a line, no matter whether the line contained only two or three words or reached to the edge of the page. Truman could read one line, regardless of how short, to its end, pause and then read the next line to its end. Thus the pauses tended to come out more naturally.

At a Gridiron dinner on December 15, 1945, Truman wrote out his speech on five-by-eight-inch White House stationery. After a typed copy was prepared for him, he gave it to Charlie Ross, with a penciled note: "In fear and trembling, 12/15/45."[55]

The process of coaching and use of recordings and playbacks helped produce noticeable changes in Truman's presentations. Yet as late as 1950 most of his staff recognized his need to deliver prepared speeches more slowly. Murphy suggested in a memo that President Truman should deliver manuscript and extempore speeches slowly and with full conviction.[56]

Although he professed not to care about the way in which he delivered his talks and did not try hard to perfect his presentations, Truman really was interested in his platform appearance. In the summer of 1947 after one speech which he knew he had delivered poorly, he told an aide; "This is quite a job for a farmer."[57]

His early ineptness as a public speaker led Truman and his advisers to experiment with several methods of delivery. He was the first American president to speak over public television, for that medium was in its infancy in 1947. By that time he had become convinced that he did not read well aloud, so he did not want to use manuscripts while speaking over the new medium. Therefore, he tried to speak extemporaneously while aides squatted with huge cue cards below the television camera. Actually, this practice worked rather well for him, but after viewing newsreels of his reading from script and then reading from cue cards for television, he told his staff that if he had to watch those pictures very often he would not even vote for himself.[58]

The extempore method did permit him to develop more freedom of action while speaking, although he was always somewhat inhibited because of his preference for standing directly behind the lectern. Moreover, his thick glasses prevented good strong eye contact if the crowd were large or distant from his position. In private conversations, his eyes came alive and were warm and animated. Then the twinkle or intensity could be seen as he looked directly into the eyes of his listeners, but this advantage was lost in most of his public addresses. His hands were not very expressive during his public talks, and critics frequently referred to the way he placed his hands about a foot apart squarely in front of his body as his "chopping wood gesture."

Truman's voice generally was considered monotonous and lacking in inspiration. His voice was not deep but rather nasal; it had little inflectional variety, and he often stumbled when he turned the pages of his manuscripts. The quality of his voice, although not rich in resonance, projected reasonably well. Whenever he spoke extemporaneously, he developed more vocal range and variation than he was able to use when reading. In reading he had a tendency to use upward inflections at the end of sentences, and this pattern limited his emphasis and communication. Whenever emphasis was attempted, it occurred because of volume and pitch, not pacing or pause. In extempore speech, he seemed more robust, vigorous, and had an enthusiasm lacking in the manuscripts.

Even Truman's critics agreed that his speaking showed tremendous improvement after his first year in the White House. In large part, the improvement came as a result of increased experience. The president, no matter who he is, cannot avoid giving speeches, and the expanded opportunities helped Truman gain more confidence and poise on the platform. Also, he benefited greatly from guidance and advice from persons chosen because of their expertise in written or oral communications. The advisers did not try to remake him or change his character, but they did try to write material in ways that would be compatible with his vocabulary and personality. Truman never became a strong platform interpreter of prepared manuscripts, but as demonstrated in 1948, he became especially effective in extemporaneous speaking. Professor A. Craig Baird, a contemporary and distinguished speech critic from the University of Iowa, summarized Truman's speech best by writing:

> No speaker of high rank, he [Truman], nevertheless, had a down-to-earth quality of voice, language, and ideas that millions of Americans recognized as like their own.[59]

Truman's characteristic hand movements during speeches were described by some as a "chopping wood gesture."

13

Truman—A Final Reckoning

Be not afraid of greatness: some are born great, some
achieve greatness, and some have greatness thrust upon
them.

WILLIAM SHAKESPEARE

THE seven and three-quarter years Harry Truman was president were spectacularly eventful ones. The period saw the epochal bombing of Hiroshima and Nagasaki, the beginnings of the United Nations, the founding of NATO, the Korean War, the dismissal of General Douglas MacArthur, the peacetime draft, the Berlin airlift, and critical strikes in the coal, steel, and railroad industries.

It was he who led in the development of a bipartisan foreign policy assuming responsibility for the economic and military stability of virtually the entire non-Communist world. The Truman Doctrine, as it was soon named, made its first appearance when as president he called for $400 million to aid Greece and Turkey stave off Communist pressures. In later economic phases of the doctrine $12.5 billion was spent in an ambitious effort to rescue Europe from almost certain bankruptcy and communism.

His domestic appeal arose from his forceful advocacy of broad programs, including public works, social security, full employment, labor legislation, fair employment of blacks, and integration of the armed forces. Indeed, it was mainly the troubled domestic scene that encouraged most observers to predict his defeat at the polls in 1948. A Republican Congress had been elected in 1946. Two years later, President Harry Truman chose to run for reelection and make this Congress his whipping boy. Public opinion polls and political experts were almost unanimous in predicting a Republican victory, but the stubborn fighter from Missouri refused to admit defeat. His "Give 'em Hell" tactics carried him through one of the most vigorous campaigns in history. He traveled 23,000 miles and made 272 speeches against that "awful, good-for-nothing

80th Congress'' and especially the Taft-Hartley Labor Act, which it had passed over his veto. The results in November showed that Truman had won reelection by more than two million popular votes. Often and with impish glee, he would display a headline which had appeared on an early election night edition of the *Chicago Tribune* announcing boldly but erroneously, ''Dewey Defeats Truman.'' He had reason to savor his triumph, for he had stood almost alone as a man with confidence in his party's victory.

In 1962 a group of eminent historians ranked the nation's thirty-three presidents and placed Harry S. Truman in the category ''near great.'' In that ''near great'' category, Truman joined Andrew Jackson, Theodore Roosevelt, and James K. Polk. During the time Truman was in office few would have predicted such an evaluation for him because seldom have presidents in their incumbency been so downgraded as was the sturdy midwesterner. During most of his years in Washington, he was regarded as unusually mediocre. Careful observers noted that he had the habit of surrounding himself with men of stature. People felt that he was honest and there was no credibility gap, but he was never a father figure. They liked him and admired his courage—on his desk was the famous motto, ''The Buck Stops Here.'' When he saw a need for a change he worked for it. To some he would always be a hick from Missouri whose ancestors had fought on the side of the Confederacy. He was not without his personal prejudices, but he tried hard to be president of all the people. Capable of stubborn enmity or unflinching loyalty, he was a man whose emotions often surfaced. To his foes he was a tough opponent who asked no quarter, and his associates knew him to be like Marc Antony, ''a plain blunt man that loves my friends.'' No one claimed that he was a great organizer or manipulator of men; instead people talked about his candor, his warmth and simplicity, and his willingness to come front and center. Years later they would recall fondly his outspoken blasts against critics. Today his name can enliven any conversation, and each year the collection of stories about him grows larger.

In his life and in his presidency, Truman had both successes and failures; he can be eulogized without being mythologized. Growing folklore is apt to paint him in colors brighter than life. His bluntness would plead for accuracy in accounts and recollections, On that scale alone, history must surely show that if this common man did not seek greatness he at least used it wisely when it was thrust upon him.

Chronology of President Truman's
Important Speeches and Messages*

1 9 4 5

April 16. Address before Joint Session of Congress. (Direction of the war and government will remain "unhampered and unchanged.")

May 28. Special Message to Congress on Unemployment Compensation. (Congress should take emergency action to widen coverage of unemployment compensation and should increase amount and duration of benefits.)

June 1. Special Message to Congress on Winning the War with Japan. (Review of efforts in winning the war with Germany and pledge to bring about unconditional surrender of Japan.)

June 19. Special Message to Congress on Succession to the Presidency. (Recommendation that Congress enact legislation placing the Speaker of the House of Representatives first in order of succession in case of inability of president or vice-president to function.)

July 2. Address to Senate Urging Ratification of the Charter of the United Nations.

August 6. Statement Announcing Use of the A-Bomb at Hiroshima. (We shall destroy Japan's power to make war.)

August 9. Radio Report to American People on Potsdam Conference. (The "Three Great Powers" are bound together in a determination to achieve a just and lasting peace.)

September 6. Special Message to Congress Presenting a 21-Point Program for the Reconversion Period. (Presents an outline for the Fair Deal.)

October 3. Special Message to Congress on St. Lawrence Seaway. (Recommendation that Congress speedily approve an agreement between the U.S. and Canada for the development of the Great Lakes–St. Lawrence Basin.)

October 3. Special Message to Congress on Atomic Energy. (Urges establishment of Atomic Energy Commission which should employ research knowledge and technology for benefit of society.)

October 23. Address to Joint Session of Congress on Universal Military Training. (Universal training is the only adequate answer we have to our problems in this troubled world.)

October 27. Address on Foreign Policy at Navy Day Celebration in New York City. (We shall refuse to recognize any government imposed upon any nation by the force of any foreign power.)

October 30. Radio Address to American People on Wages and Prices in the Reconver-

---

*The best single source for the speeches, statements, and other messages referred to in this abbreviated chronology is *The Public Papers of Harry S. Truman.* There is one volume for each of his presidential years, except for the year 1952 and the month of January, 1953, which are combined.

sion Period. (Congress must pass full employment legislation if we are to avoid unemployment, depression, and relief lines.)

November 19. Special Message to Congress Recommending a Comprehensive Health Program. (Millions of our citizens do not have full opportunity to achieve good health.)

December 19. Special Message to Congress Recommending Establishment of a Department of National Defense. (War and Navy Departments should be combined into a single department.)

1 9 4 6

January 3. Radio Address to American People on the Status of the Reconversion Program. (Progress is made, but price and rent controls must remain.)

January 21. Message to Congress on the State of the Union and on the Budget for 1947. (Review of foreign policy and domestic affairs; recommends legislation in specific fields: 1) price controls, 2) food subsidies, 3) extension of War Powers Act, 4) small business competition, 5) minimum wage, 6) agricultural programs, 7) resource development, 8) public works, 9) housing, 10) social security and health, 11) education, 12) federal government personnel, and 13) territories, insular possessions and District of Columbia; summarizes the federal budget.)

May 16. Statement Announcing Breakdown in Coal Strike Negotiations. (Negotiations between operators and miners have completely broken down.)

May 17. Statement by the President on Issuing Order Directing Possession and Operation of Railroads. (By executive order the Office of Defense Transportation temporarily will operate the country's railroads.)

May 24. Radio Address to American People on the Railroad Strike Emergency. (The welfare of the country must come first, and I have no alternative but to operate the trains by using every means within my power.)

May 25. Special Address to Congress Urging Legislation for Industrial Peace. (Midway through this speech Truman was interrupted, and he announced: "Word has just been received that the railroad strike has been settled, on terms proposed by the President.")

June 29. Radio Address to Nation on Price Controls. (I vetoed Price Control bill because as drafted it did not give adequate protection against inflation.)

October 14. Radio Report to American People on the Removal of Major Price Controls. (Lifting of price controls on livestock and meat does not mean the end of controls on rents, wages, and all prices.)

December 18. Statement Explaining U.S. Policy toward China. (We shall continue a realistic policy toward China but hope that the National Government will broaden its base to make it more representative of the Chinese people.)

1 9 4 7

January 6. Annual Message to Congress on State of the Union. (Year just passed was marred by labor-management strife, but the domestic economy is healthy; in foreign affairs, basic differences between us and the Soviet Union should not obscure the fact that the interests of both nations lie in establishing world peace.)

February 13. Statement Urging Extension of Authority to Ship Emergency Supplies to Europe. (Quick legislative action is needed if export programs for fuel and grain are to be kept from collapse.)

February 21. Special Message to Congress Requesting Appropriations for Aid to Liberated Countries. (We should try to provide basic essentials of life, such as medical supplies, food, and items which will aid in production of foodstuffs.)

March 6. Address on Foreign Economic Policy, Delivered at Baylor University. (Our foreign relations, political and economic, are indivisible.)

March 12. Special Message to Congress on Greece and Turkey: The Truman Doctrine. (It must be the policy of the U.S. to support free peoples who are resisting attempted subjugation by armed minorities or by outside pressures.)

April 17. Extempore Remarks at a Meeting with the American Society of Newspaper Editors. (Aid to Greece and Turkey is an outgrowth of events that have been building since the German surrender, and a truly bipartisan foreign policy has resulted.)

June 17. Commencement Address at Princeton University. (Universal military training represents the most democratic, most economical, and most effective method for maintaining national strength.)

June 20. Message to House of Representatives Explaining Veto of the Taft-Hartley Labor Bill. (The bill would increase strikes, restrict the area of voluntary agreements between labor and management, expose employers to hazards by which they would be hampered, would deprive workers of vital legal protection they now have, and the bill itself is burdensome and unworkable.)*

June 20. Radio Address to Nation on Veto of Taft-Hartley Bill. (Taft-Hartley Bill would increase industrial strife.)

June 29. Address before the National Association for the Advancement of Colored People. (We can no longer await the growth of a will to action in the slowest state or most backward community; the federal government must show the way to end discrimination in education, medical care, and jobs.)

September 25. Statement by President on the Marshall Plan. (Extremely grave food situation abroad, and the U.S. is taking measures to meet it.)

October 24. Radio Address to Nation on Special Session of Congress. (Congress must meet in order to consider problems of high prices at home and emergency aid abroad.)

November 17. Special Message to Congress on First Day of the Special Session. (I call for ten different legislative actions that will combat the problems of inflation in our domestic economy.)

December 19. Special Message to Congress on the Marshall Plan. (Interests of the U.S. are closely linked with European recovery, and proper aid will promote world peace; some self-denial will be necessary on the part of American citizens.)

1948

January 7. Annual Message to Congress on State of the Union. (Report of President's Commission on Civil Rights points way to corrective action by federal, state, and local governments; Alaska and Hawaii should be admitted to statehood; the nation lacks adequate health provisions; rent controls must be extended; price supports for farm commodities must be extended; price supports for farm commodities must be continued; U.S. can be effective for world peace only if it remains strong; Marshall Plan is strengthening the economy of Europe; our nation must continue measures to fight inflation; there should be no general tax cut.)

---

*On June 23, 1947, the Congress passed the bill over the president's veto.

February 2. Special Message to Congress on Civil Rights. (Recommends legislation for strengthening civil rights statutes, federal protection against lynching, protecting right to vote, establishing a Fair Employment Practices Commission, and providing for more self-government in District of Columbia and in territories and possessions.)

February 18. Special Message to Congress on Need for Assistance to China. (Proposed aid is necessary but will not substitute for action that must be taken by the Chinese government to improve economic conditions there.)

March 17. Special Address to Congress on Threat to Freedom of Europe. (There are times in world history when it is far wiser to act than to hesitate; recommendation that Congress speedily complete action on: 1) European Recovery Program, 2) enactment of universal military legislation, and 3) reenactment of selective service.)

May 14. Special Message to Congress on Agriculture. (Congress should pass permanent legislation for flexible price supports, expand the program for soil conservation, and take steps to increase consumption of agricultural products.)

May 24. Special Message to Congress on Social Security. (Congress must take steps to broaden the benefits provided by Social Security.)

June 12. Commencement Address at University of California. (Refusal of Soviet Union to work for world peace is the most bitter disappointment of our time.)

June 14. Address before Greater Los Angeles Press Club. (There are things Congress has not done that they should have done.)

July 15. Address in Philadelphia Accepting the Nomination of the Democratic National Convention. (I will recall Congress.)

July 27. Address to Special Session of the Eightieth Congress. (There must be quick legislative action to do two things: 1) check inflation and the rising cost of living, and 2) help meet the acute housing shortage.)

September 6. Labor Day Address in Cadillac Square, Detroit. (If you let the Republican administration reactionaries get complete control of this government, the position of labor will be so greatly weakened that living standards of the American workingman will go down.)

September 18. Address at Dexter, Iowa, on the Occasion of the National Plowing Match. (The big money Republican looks on agriculture and labor merely as expense items in a business venture.)

October 6. Address at Convention Hall in Philadelphia. (You will never get anything done about high prices by a Republican President or a Republican Congress.)

1 9 4 9

January 5. Annual Message to Congress on the State of the Union. (Congress should enact legislation for the following purposes: 1) to continue controls on consumer and bank credits, 2) to regulate speculation on commodity exchanges, 3) to provide for export controls, 4) to allocate authority in field of transportation, 5) to allocate materials in short supply, 6) to extend and strengthen rent controls, 7) to provide standby authority to impose price ceilings, and 8) to provide an immediate study of production facilities for such key materials as steel; furthermore, in order to strengthen the nation's economic stability, Congress should repeal the Taft-Hartley Act.)

January 20. Inaugural Address. (We must embark on a bold new program for making the benefits of our scientific advances and industrial progress available for improvement and growth of the underdeveloped areas.)

April 4. Address on the Occasion of the Signing of the North Atlantic Treaty Organization. (Through this agreement we can exercise our right of collective or individual self-defense against armed attack, in accordance with Article 51 of the United Nations Charter.)

April 22. Special Message to Congress on Nation's Health Needs. (As a nation we have not yet succeeded in making the benefits of scientific advances available to all who need them.)

June 7. Special Message to Congress Recommending Continuation of Economic Assistance to Korea. (The U.S. has a deep interest in the progress the Korean people are making toward establishment of a united, self-government, independent of foreign control.)

June 24. Special Message to Congress Recommending Point Four Legislation. (Development of underdeveloped nations will strengthen the United Nations and the fabric of world peace.)

July 13. Radio and Television Report to the American People on the State of the National Economy. (We are not in a depression, and we must expand programs in social security, health, education, and housing.)

July 25. Special Message to Congress on the Need for a Military Aid Program. (Free nations must have military aid if they are to protect themselves against aggression.)

August 22. Address in Miami at the Golden Jubilee Convention of the Veterans of Foreign Wars. (The Soviet Union has blocked every effort to free the world from fear of aggression; for that reason we have to join other friendly nations in forming regional defense pacts.)

1 9 5 0

January 4. Annual Message to Congress on the State of the Union. (Our national strength has moved us from the outer edge to the center of world affairs; the challenge from communism is more than a military challenge; our domestic economy will be strengthened if free collective bargaining is protected and encouraged; there is still an acute shortage of housing; social security and health programs must be broadened.)

March 3. Special Message to Congress on the Coal Strike. (The coal industry is a sick industry, and temporary seizure by the government must be authorized.)

April 6. Special Message to Congress on the Unemployment Insurance System. (My recommendations for extended coverage, higher benefits, and longer duration should be acted upon by the Congress.)

April 20. Address on Foreign Policy at a Luncheon of the American Society of Newspaper Editors. (Soviet actions in Berlin, in Czechoslovakia, in the Balkans, and in the Far East show that communist propaganda is but a cloak for imperialism.)

June 9. Commencement Address at the University of Missouri. (Nations of Western Europe, with Marshall Plan aid, are setting records of production; Point Four is a creative exercise full of promise for a better future.)

June 27. Statement by the President on the Situation in Korea. (I have ordered United States air and sea forces to give the Korean government troops cover and support; the attack on Korea makes it plain that communism has passed beyond the use of subversion to conquer independent nations and will now use armed invasion and war.)

July 19. Radio and Television Address to the American People on the Situation in Korea. (The attack in Korea has made it clear, beyond all doubt, that the international Communist movement is willing to use armed invasion to conquer independent nations.)

August 8. Special Message to Congress on the Internal Security of the United States. (Congress should pass legislation remedying certain defects in present laws concerning espionage and internal security, but we must be on guard against extremists who urge police state measures.)

September 1. Radio and Television Report to the American People on the Situation in Korea. (United Nations forces in Korea are in the front line of a world struggle between freedom and tyranny.)

December 15. Radio and Television Report to the American People on the National Emergency. (There is actual warfare in the Far East, but Europe and the rest of the world are also in very great danger; the same menace—the menace of Communist aggression—threatens Europe as well as Asia.)

1951

January 8. Annual Message to Congress on the State of the Union. (Aggression in Korea is part of the attempt of the Russian Communist dictatorship to take over the world; Congress will need to consider legislation to increase our productive capacity and keep our economy strong.)

April 11. Radio Report to the American People on Korea and on U.S. Policy in the Far East. (We do not want to see the conflict in Korea extended; a number of events have made it evident that General MacArthur did not agree with that policy; I have, therefore, considered it essential to relieve General MacArthur so that there would be no doubt or confusion as to the real purpose and aim of our policy.)

November 2. Memorandum of Disapproval of Bill Requiring Segregation in Certain Schools on Federal Property. (Basic purpose of the bill is meritorious, but because it would require certain schools to be segregated I will not sign it.)

November 7. Radio and Television Report to the American People on International Arms Reduction. (Armament reduction, to be acceptable, must include all types of weapons, must be accepted by all nations having substantial armed forces, and must be based on safeguards that will ensure compliance. Until these conditions are met, the United States will continue to build strong defenses in Europe and in other parts of the world.)

1952

January 9. Annual Message to Congress on the State of the Union. (Action of the United Nations forces in Korea have been a powerful deterrent to a third world war; the grim fact remains that the Soviet Union is increasing its armed might; throughout the world we must continue to strengthen the forces of freedom; at home we must move ahead on the defense program; inflation must be controlled; some sacrifices will have to be made; social insurance, education, and better health are not frills; we should keep working for improvement in labor-management legislation until we get a fair labor law.)

March 4. Address Broadcast from the Voice of America Floating Radio Transmitter *Courier.* (We have undertaken to answer Soviet propaganda with truth.)

March 6. Radio and Television Address to American People on the Mutual Security Program. (This program is vital if we are to block the plans of the Soviet rulers to dominate the world.)

March 24. Special Message to Congress on Aid for Refugees and Displaced Persons. (Help must be provided for persons who are escaping from Communist tyranny behind the iron curtain.)

April 8. Radio and Television Address to American People on the Need for Government Operation of the Steel Mills. (I am taking steps to keep steel production rolling; in this emergency, if our defense production fails our security is threatened.)

June 10. Special Address to Congress on the Steel Strike. (Need is to get the nation's steel mills back into production quickly; it is up to Congress to pass fair and effective legislation to deal with such labor emergencies.)

June 13. Commencement Address at Howard University. (Progress is being made on civil rights, but the matter cannot be left to the states alone.)

October 27. Statement by the President on the Decision to Withdraw U.S. Forces from Korea, 1947–1949. (Decision to withdraw occupation forces in 1949 was based on recommendations of the military staff, including those of General Eisenhower.)

December 19. Address at the National War College. (A strong military policy must be based on a sound domestic policy; by every means the United States is trying to restore peace in Korea; if Communist aggression there had been successful the United Nations would have been shattered; Point Four is working.)

1953

January 7. Annual Message to Congress on the State of the Union. (Review of nearly eight years of administration; domestic economy has flourished; in 1950 nation was forced into a rearmament program; progress has been made in civil rights, but the program is far from complete; the great question of avoiding a third world war is still the overriding question of our time; the world is divided by Soviet design; the United States through collective economic and political actions has been able to thwart much of the Soviet expansion; Europe is stronger economically as a result of the Marshall Plan; atomic power cannot be legislated out of existence; we face hard tasks and great dangers, but Americans will adjust to changing circumstances.)

January 15. The President's Farewell to the American People. (Review of dramatic events in the first months of Presidency; the beginning of the Cold War, including the Truman Doctrine, the Berlin Airlift, and military aid programs; instant action was taken to meet the threat in Korea; in domestic matters, the administration has seen more jobs created, incomes have risen, progress has been made on civil rights, and greater economic opportunities were developed; the president expresses humble gratitude to the millions of citizens who have helped him during his administration.)

Notes

1   Eloquence and Presidents

1. Papers of Harry S. Truman, Post-Presidential Files, 23 September 1952, the Harry S. Truman Library (hereafter referred to as HSTL).
2. Edward D. McKim, Oral History Transcript, pp. 22–23. HSTL.
3. *Kansas City Star,* 5 July 1965.
4. *Ibid.*
5. James Reston, "The Number One Voice," *Propaganda in War and Crisis,* ed. Daniel Lerner (New York: George W. Stewart, 1951), pp. 314–15.
6. Kenneth E. Boulding, "National Images and International Systems," *Journal of Conflict Resolutions* 3 (1959):122.
7. A thorough analysis of Woodrow Wilson as a speaker can be found in David McKean, "Woodrow Wilson," *History and Criticism of American Public Address,* ed. W. Norwood Brigance, vol. 2 (New York: McGraw-Hill, 1943).
8. Charles A. and Mary R. Beard, *America in Mid Passage,* vol. 2 (New York: Macmillan, 1939), pp. 947–49.
9. *Franklin Delano Roosevelt: A Memorial,* ed. Donald Porter Geddes (New York: Pitman, 1945), pp. 14–15.
10. Theodore C. Sorensen, *Kennedy* (New York: Harper & Row, 1965), pp. 240–48.
11. Wayne C. Minnick, *The Art of Persuasion* (Boston: Houghton Mifflin, 1957), p. 33.

2   Young Truman in Missouri

1. Hamlin Garland, *Main Travelled Roads* (New York: Macmillan, 1899), Preface.
2. *New York Herald,* 8 May 1884, p. 1.
3. *New York Herald,* 9 May 1884, p. 6.
4. *New York Times,* 8 May 1884, p. 2. After his retirement from the presidency, frequent proposals had been made in Congress to restore the military rank with its appropriate pay to Grant. Each proposal failed until the last session of Congress during Chester A. Arthur's administration. By then popular sympathy had risen for the former president, now dying from a painful throat cancer. Finally, just as Congress was ending its labors on March 4, 1885, the measure passed both the House and the Senate. Arthur, as the last act of his administration, signed the bill; his successor, Grover Cleveland, in the first act of his administration, appointed Grant to his former position. The money was badly needed, and the honor was a tonic to the dying soldier, who grew steadily weaker and passed away four and a half months later.
5. As quoted in Margaret Truman, *Harry S. Truman* (New York: William Morrow, 1973), pp. 256–57.
6. *Ibid.,* pp. 27–28.
7. Harry S. Truman, Memoirs, vol. 1, p. 113. These two volumes of memoirs, vol. 1—*Year of Decisions* and vol. 2—*Years of Trial and Hope,* were published by Doubleday, 1955 and 1956. They will be referred to so frequently that for brevity they are cited hereafter as Memoirs, with appropriate volume and page numbers.

8. Margaret Truman, *Harry S. Truman*, p. 46.

9. *Ibid.*, p. 50.

10. *New York Herald*, 8 May 1884, p. 7.

11. *New York Times*, 8 May 1884, p. 5.

12. *Ibid.*

13. Margaret Truman, *Harry S. Truman*, p. 46.

14. Truman, Memoirs, 1 p. 113.

15. Margaret Truman, *Harry S. Truman*, p. 49.

16. Charles F. Horne, ed. *Great Men and Famous Women* (New York: Selmar Hess, 1894).

17. *Ibid.*

18. *Ibid.* ("Question Book")

19. Merle Miller, *Plain Speaking: An Oral Biography of Harry S. Truman* (New York: Berkley Publishing, 1973).

20. *Ibid., passim.*

21. Truman, Memoirs, 1, p. 116.

22. Eugene E. White and Clair R. Henderlider, "What Harry S. Truman Told Us About His Speaking," *Quarterly Journal of Speech* 40 (February 1954): 39.

23. Cicero, *de Oratore* 2, 331.

24. Ralph Waldo Emerson, "The American Scholar," *The Works of Ralph Waldo Emerson. Nature, Addresses, and Lectures.* Vol. 1. Boston: Phillips, Sampson & Co., 1855. pp. 93–94.

25. Sinclair Lewis, *Babbit* (New York: Harcourt, Brace, 1922), p. 80.

26. As quoted in Jonathan Daniels, *The Man of Independence* (Port Washington, New York: Kennikat Press, 1950), p. 58.

27. As quoted in Frank McNaughton and Walter Hehmeyer, *This Man Truman* (New York: McGraw-Hill, 1945), p. 29.

28. Truman, Memoirs, 2, p. 200.

29. *A Study of the Presidential Vote: November 1948,* University of Michigan Institute for Social Research (Ann Arbor, 1948), p. 90.

30. William P. Helm, *Harry Truman: A Political Biography* (New York: Duell, Sloan & Pearce 1947), p. 12.

31. Truman, Memoirs, 1, p. 132.

32. Quoted by McNaughton and Hehmeyer, *This Man Truman*, p. 55.

33. *Ibid.*, p. 56.

3   The Truman Women

1. Merle Miller reported without documentation that President Truman expressed this opinion to him while the two were in Truman's office at the Truman Library in Independence in 1962. Merle Miller, *Plain Speaking: An Oral Biography of Harry S. Truman* (New York: Berkley Publishing, 1974), pp. 384–85.

2. Margaret Truman, *Harry S. Truman*, p. 48.

3. Truman, Memoirs, 1, p. 6. President Truman subsequently explained that he was referring to Alexander Wiley, Republican Senator from Wisconsin.

4. *Ibid.*, pp. 43–44.

5. *Ibid.*, p. 107.

6. *Ibid.*, p. 295.

7. Truman, *Memoirs*, 1, p. 63.

8. *Ibid.*

9. *Ibid.*, p. 331.

10. *Ibid.*, p. 370.

11. *Ibid.*, p. 206.

12. *Ibid.*, p. 107.

13. *Ibid.*, p. 294.

14. *Ibid.*, p. 402.

15. *Liberty*, 9 June 1945.

16. *Kansas City Star,* 17 July 1903.
17. *Kansas City Star,* 12 September 1948.
18. *Kansas City Star,* 6 March 1910.
19. Helen Worden Erskine, "The Riddle of Mrs. Truman," *Collier's,* 9 February 1952.
20. This anecdote is told in several biographies. See, for example, Bert Cochran, *Harry Truman and the Crisis Presidency* (New York: Funk & Wagnalls, 1973), p. 41.
21. *Ibid.*
22. Quoted by Marianne Means, *The Woman in the White House* (New York: Random House, 1963), p. 225.
23. Dean Acheson, *Present at the Creation* (New York: W. W. Norton, 1969), p. 150.
24. *Ibid.,* pp. 150–51.
25. *Life,* 27 (11 July 1949): 88–92.
26. Erskine, *"The Riddle of Mrs. Truman."*
27. *Newsweek,* 4 October 1948.
28. Marianne Means, *The Woman in the White House,* p. 219.
29. Truman, Memoirs, 1, p. 107.
30. *Washington Post,* 6 December 1950, p. 12b.
31. *Washington Post,* 9 December 1950, p. 1.
32. The close friend was Charles Ross, a high school classmate and long-time newspaperman associated with Harry Truman. Ross served as President Truman's press secretary for five years until his sudden death in his office at the White House the afternoon of Miss Truman's concert.
33. *Washington Post,* 9 December 1950, p. 1.
34. *Ibid.,* p. 8.
35. As quoted by Margaret Truman, *Harry S. Truman,* pp. 502–3.
36. *Ibid.,* p. 503.

4   Grass Roots Politician

1. William M. Reddig, *Tom's Town: Kansas City and the Pendergast Legend* (New York: J. B. Lippincott, 1947), pp. 33–35.
2. Daniels, *The Man of Independence,* p. 78.
3. Mary Ethel Noland, Oral History Transcript, HSTL.
4. Truman, Memoirs, 1, p. 125.
5. Harry S. Truman, Handwritten Autobiography, pp. 10–11, PSF, HSTL.
6. Henry P. Fry, "The Masonic History of Harry S. Truman," *Virginia Masonic Quarterly* (April 1949): p. 7.
7. Papers of Harry Vaughan, "My Masonic History," p. 2, HSTL.
8. Daniels, *The Man of Independence,* p. 108.
9. Tom Murphy, Oral History Transcript, HSTL.
10. Truman, Autobiography, p. 27, President's Speech File (hereafter referred to as PSF), HSTL.
11. See, for examples, Edgar Hinde, Oral History Transcript, p. 19, HSTL; Edward D. McKim, Oral History Transcript, p. 22, HSTL; Charles T. Curry, Oral History Transcript, p. 2, HSTL.
12. Private Papers of Jonathan Daniels, Interview with Harry S. Truman, 12 November 1949, HSTL.
13. Private Papers of Jonathan Daniels, Interview with Eddie Jacobson, 27 September 1949, HSTL.
14. Truman, Autobiography, pp. 25–26, PSF, HSTL.
15. *Ibid.,* pp. 27–28.
16. William Southern, *Independence Examiner,* 5 June 1922, p. 1.
17. Edward D. McKim, Oral History Transcript, pp. 22–23, HSTL.
18. *Independence Examiner,* 18 July 1922.
19. *Ibid.*
20. Hinde, Oral History Transcript, p. 19, HSTL.

21. McKim, Oral History Transcript, p. 3, HSTL.
22. *Independence Examiner,* 7 August 1922.
23. *Independence Examiner,* 21 October 1922.
24. *Kansas City Star,* 29 October 1922.
25. *Independence Examiner,* 6 November 1922.
26. *Kansas City Star,* 22 October 1922.
27. *Independence Examiner,* 8 November 1922.
28. *Blue Springs Herald,* 30 November 1923.
29. *Kansas City Times,* 25 June 1924.
30. Hinde, Oral History Transcript, p. 22, HSTL.
31. A similar evaluation was made by Thomas Joseph Heed. See, for example, Thomas Joseph Heed, "Prelude to Whistlestop: Harry S. Truman the Apprentice Campaigner" (Ph.D. diss., Teachers' College, Columbia University, 1975), p. 177.
32. Hinde, Oral History Transcript, p. 12, HSTL.
33. *Independence Examiner,* 5 November 1924.
34. Heed, *Prelude to Whistlestop,* pp. 241–43.
35. H. L. Mencken, *Baltimore Evening Sun,* 30 January 1933, p. 15.
36. Truman, Memoirs, 1, p. 141.
37. Statement to Kansas City Chamber of Commerce, 11 May 1932, PSF, Pre-Presidential File, Box 239. Folder on Addresses of Harry S. Truman, 1929–1931.
38. Speech to Kansas City County League of Young Democrats, PSF, Box 239.
39. Commencement Address to Raytown High School, 14 May 1931, PSF, Box 239.
40. *Ibid.*
41. *Ibid.*
42. *Ibid.* Punctuation in this handwritten manuscript is frequently erroneous or missing.
43. Address to Committee on Taxation and Governmental Reforms, Jefferson City, Mo., 28 November 1931. Papers of Harry S. Truman, Presiding Judge of the Jackson County Court 1927–1934, Folder on Speeches, HSTL.
44. Address to Club Presidents' Round Table, 7 October 1929, Papers of Harry S. Truman, Presiding Judge of the Jackson County Court 1927–1934. Folder on Speeches, HSTL.

5   *The Happiest Ten Years*

1. Truman, Autobiography, p. 34, HSTL.
2. *Ibid.,* p. 35.
3. Speech by the Honorable Joseph B. Shannon, Clayton Missouri, 30 July 1934. Papers of Harry S. Truman, Presiding Judge of the Jackson County Court, 1927–1934, Box 2, HSTL.
4. *St. Louis Post Dispatch,* 26 June 1934, p. 2c.
5. *Kansas City Times,* 9 August 1934, p. 1.
6. *St. Louis Post Dispatch,* 4 November 1934, pp. 1a and 2h.
7. Speech at Flat River, Missouri, 1 October 1934, PSF, Box 239, Folder: Election to U.S. Senate, 1934, HSTL.
8. Speech at Houston, Missouri, 5 October 1934, *Ibid.*
9. Truman, Autobiography, p. 36, HSTL.
10. *Kansas City Times,* January 1935.
11. Address over Station WGY Schenectady, New York, 20 March 1935, Papers of Harry S. Truman: Senatorial File, Box 163, HSTL.
12. Manuscript of address over National Broadcasting Company, Papers of Harry S. Truman: Senatorial File, Box 163, HSTL.
13. See, for example, his speech before the Grandmasters Conference, 22 February 1935, *Ibid.*
14. Draft of untitled speech for Masonic Lodge, Appleton City, Missouri, 22 November 1935, *Ibid.*
15. Manuscript of speech delivered in Neosho, Missouri, 30 July 1936, Papers of Harry S. Truman, Senatorial File, Box 163, HSTL.

16. *Kansas City Journal Post,* 12 September 1935.

17. Truman, Autobiography, p. 39, HSTL.

18. *Kansas City Star,* 31 January 1938.

19. Jonathan Daniels, *The Man of Independence,* p. 187.

20. *Congressional Record,* 7th Congress, 3d sess., pp. 1932–34.

21. *St. Louis Post Dispatch,* 16, 17 February 1938.

22. Letter from Senator Truman to President Roosevelt, 14 September 1940, PSF, Pre-Presidential Files, Box 238, Folder: Truman-Roosevelt Correspondence, HSTL.

23. Manuscript of speech delivered, 10 September 1935, Papers of Harry S. Truman, Senatorial File, Box 163, HSTL.

24. *Ibid.*

25. Truman, Autobiography, p. 47, HSTL.

26. *Ibid.,* p. 49.

27. Draft of speech by Senator Harry S. Truman over National Broadcasting Company, 24 April 1936, Papers of Harry S. Truman, Senatorial File, Box 163, HSTL.

28. *Congressional Record,* Vol. LXXXI, Part 5, 19 May 1937 to 17 June 1937, pp. 5271–73 *passim.*

29. Typewritten draft of manuscript, Papers of Harry S. Truman, Senatorial File, Box 163, Folder 2, HSTL.

30. *Ibid.*

31. *Ibid.*

32. *Ibid.* The underlined phrases are in Truman's handwriting.

33. *Ibid.*

34. *St. Louis Post Dispatch,* 16 June 1940.

35. *Kansas City Star,* 28 March 1940.

36. Based on an interview with Harry S. Truman, August 1959, described by Eugene Francis Schmidtlein in "Truman the Senator" (Ph.D. diss., University of Missouri, June 1962), p. 217.

37. *St. Louis Post Dispatch,* 12 April 1940.

38. Telegram from Stephen Early to R. H. Wadlow, PSF, Pre-Presidential Files, Box 238, Folder: Truman-Roosevelt Correspondence, HSTL.

39. *Kansas City Star,* 22 July 1940.

40. *Kansas City Times,* 26 October and 1 November, 1940.

41. Truman, Autobiography, pp. 43–44, HSTL.

42. Harry S. Truman to L. W. Matthews, 7 August 1941, Papers of Harry S. Truman, Senatorial Files, HSTL.

43. Letter from Mark W. Drehmer, Secretary of the Topeka Chamber of Commerce, 12 May 1941, Truman Papers, Senatorial File, HSTL.

44. Letter from Truman to Lou E. Holland, 4 February 1941, Truman Papers, Senatorial Files, HSTL.

45. Truman, Autobiography, p. 46, HSTL.

46. As quoted by Edward Alexander Rogge in "The Speechmaking of Harry S. Truman" (Ph.D. diss., University of Missouri, 1958), p. 201.

47. Roger Edward Willson, "The Truman Committee" (Ph.D. diss., Harvard University, 1966), p. 456.

6   Building a New Administration

1. Memorandum from Edwin W. Pauley to Jonathan Daniels, Appendix in Oral Interview with George E. Allen, 15 May 1969. HSTL.

2. As quoted in *New York Times,* 18 July 1944, p. 1.

3. Truman, Memoirs, 1, p. 190.

4. Truman, Autobiography, pp. 49–50, HSTL. In this handwritten autobiography the date is clearly *1940,* but President Truman must have been mistaken and meant to write *1944.*

5. Herbert Eaton, *Presidential Timber: A History of Nominating Conventions, 1868–1960* (London: The Free Press of Glencoe, Collier-Macmillan, 1964), p. 405.

6. Truman, Memoirs, 1, p. 192.

7. Edward J. Flynn, *You're the Boss* (New York: Viking Press, 1947), pp. 182–83.

8. Truman, Autobiography, pp. 58–59, HSTL. In the handwritten autobiography, a parenthetical phrase, "who was the Republican candidate," is printed above a caret immediately after the word *Governor,* paragraph 2.

9. *New York Times,* 24 September 1944, p. 36.

10. John Daly as recorded by Edward R. Murrow and Fred W. Friendly, "I Can Hear It Now—1933–1945," Columbia Masterworks Records ML 4905.

11. Truman, Memoirs, 1, p. 19.

12. *Ibid.,* p. 2.

13. Robert L. Riggs, *The New Republic,* 11 April 1955.

14. Truman, Memoirs, 1, p. 21.

15. William D. Leahy, *I Was There* (New York; Whittlesey House; McGraw-Hill, 1950), p. 348.

16. George E. Allen, *Presidents Who Have Known Me* (New York: Simon and Schuster, 1950), p. 165.

17. Judge Samuel I. Rosenman, Oral History Transcript, p. 19, HSTL.

18. Draft of speech to Congress, 16 April 1945, Papers of Harry S. Truman, President's Personal File (PPF hereafter), Box 248, HSTL.

19. Letter from Lois V. Adams, 16 April 1945, PPF, Box 247, HSTL.

20. Letter from Addison A. Wallace, 17 April 1945, PPF, Box 248, HSTL.

21. Letter from Gladys Dodge Alberti, 16 April 1945, PPF, Box 247, HSTL.

22. Letter from Walter Wismar, 16 April 1945, PPF, Box 248, HSTL.

23. Diary of Eben A. Ayers (hereinafter cited as Ayers Diary), entry for 16 April 1945. HSTL.

24. *Ibid.,* entry for 17 April 1945, HSTL.

25. Charles G. Ross, *The Writing of News* (New York: Henry Holt, 1911), p. 211.

26. Charles G. Ross in the *St. Louis Post Dispatch,* 15 April 1945.

27. As quoted in an interview with Mrs. Roy A. Roberts, widow of Charles Ross, reprinted in Ronald T. Farrar, *Reluctant Servant: The Story of Charles G. Ross* (Columbia, Missouri: University of Missouri Press, 1969), p. 156.

28. *New York Times,* 13 April 1945, p. 1.

29. William Hillman, ed., *Mr. President: The First Publication from the Personal Diaries, Private Letters, Papers and Revealing Interviews of Harry S. Truman* (New York: Farrar, Strauss, and Young, 1952), p. 112.

30. Cable from Harriman to Secretary of State Stettinius, *Foreign Relations of the United States, 1945,* 5 (Washington: Government Printing Office, 1967), p. 281.

31. Averell Harriman, *American and Russia in a Changing World* (New York: Doubleday, 1971), pp. 39–40.

32. Henry L. Stimson and McGeorge Bundy, *On Active Service in Peace and War* (New York: Harper, 1947), p. 609.

33. President Truman later wrote that near the close of this interview, Molotov said, "I've never been talked to like that in my life." President Truman then rejoined, "Carry out your agreements and you won't get talked to like that." Truman, *Memoirs,* 1, pp. 79–82. Charles Bohlen's account of the conference does not include this angry exchange. Cf. *Foreign Relations, 1945,* 5, pp. 256–58.

34. John Lewis Gaddis, *The United States and the Origins of the Cold War 1941–1947* (New York: Columbia University Press, 1972), p. 206.

7   Persuasion for Change

1. As quoted in *New York Times,* 24 June 1941.

2. Quoted in *The Forrestal Diaries,* ed. Walter Millis (New York: Viking Press, 1951), pp. 39–41.

3. See, for example, Robert Sherwood, *Roosevelt and Hopkins* (New York: Harper, 1948), pp. 887–914.

4. William D. Leahy, *I Was There* (New York: Whittlesey House, McGraw-Hill, 1950), pp. 388-93.

5. Ayers Diary, 6 July 1945, p. 112, HSTL.

6. In addition to memoirs from various American participants, other accounts of the Potsdam Conference are available. Excellent summaries and analyses can be found in the following: John Lewis Caddis, *The United States and the Origins of the Cold War, 1941-1947* (New York: Columbia University Press, 1972), pp. 230-43 *passim;* Barton J. Bernstein, ed., *Politics and Policies of the Truman Administration* (Chicago: Quadrangle Books, 1970), pp. 21-35; D. F. Fleming, *The Cold War and Its Origins, 1917-1960,* vol. 1 (New York: Doubleday, 1961), pp. 290-94.

7. *New York Times,* 10 August 1945.

8. *Ibid.* In retrospect, it is interesting to note Truman's selection of the word *Japs* rather than Japanese. In 1945 there was little American sensitivity to the emotional impact of this word. At the time to most persons it did not seem undignified or colloquial for the American president to use this pejorative term. Roosevent, too, used it frequently. There was then a great deal of popular hostility against Japan; Pearl Harbor was too recent and the war losses too hurtful.

9. Lane Cooper, trans., *The Rhetoric of Aristotle* (New York: D. Appleton-Century, 1932), pp. 8-9.

10. Hillman, *Mr. President,* p. 125.

11. James Byrnes, *Speaking Frankly* (New York: Harper, 1947), p. 104.

12. "Potsdam Decisions," *The Reviewing Stand,* 12 August 1945.

13. *Nippon Times* (English language edition), 12 August 1945, p. 1.

14. *Chicago Daily Tribune,* 11 August 1945, p. 6.

15. *Chicago Daily News,* 10 August 1945, p. 7.

16. Hillman, *Mr. President,* p. 125.

17. *Ibid.,* p. 122.

18. Quoted by Daniels, *The Man of Independence,* p. 266

19. *Foreign Relations of the United States,* Conference of Berlin, 2 (Washington: Government Printing Office, 1960), p. 1361.

20. This conversation with Stimson is apparently the one referred to by Churchill in his *Triumph and Tragedy* (Boston: Houghton Mifflin, 1953), p. 638. Also, see FDR, Conference on Berlin, 2, p. 225.

21. Byrnes, *Speaking Frankly,* pp. 205-09.

22. *Public Papers of Harry S. Truman, 1945* (Washington: Government Printing Office, 1961), p. 97.

23. Truman, *Memoirs,* 1, p. 419.

24. Cabell Phillips, "Truman at Seventy-Five," *The New York Times Magazine,* 3 May 1959.

25. See, for example, Henry L. Stimson, "The Decision to Use the Atomic Bomb," *Bulletin of the Atomic Scientists.* vol. 3 (February 1947): 37-66.

26. Karl T. Compton, "If the Atomic Bomb Had Not Been Used," *Atlantic Monthly,* (December 1946): 54-56.

27. Letter reprinted in *Bulletin of Atomic Scientists,* vol. 3 (February 1947).

28. Ayers Diary, 7 July 1945, p. 113, HSTL.

29. *Ibid.,* p. 188.

30. *Ibid.,* p. 189.

31. *Public Papers of President Harry S. Truman, 1945,* p. 434.

32. *Ibid.,* pp. 436-37.

33. Byrnes, *Speaking Frankly,* p. 107.

34. Will Lissner, *New York Times,* 28 October 1945.

35. *Ibid.*

36. *Chicago Daily Tribune,* 28 October 1945.

37. *Chicago Daily Tribune,* 29 October 1945.

38. *New York Times,* 29 October 1945.

39. *London Times,* 28 October 1945.

40. As reported in *New York Times,* 29 October 1945.

41. *Ibid.*
42. *Chicago Daily Tribune,* 30 October 1945.
43. Brooks Atkinson, *New York Times,* 29 October 1945.
44. *Public Opinion Quarterly,* 9 (Spring 1945): 103.

8   *The Truman Writers*

1. An indication of the extent of this controversy is shown in Victor Hugo Paltsits, *Washington's Farewell Address* (New York: New York Public Library, 1935), pp. 89–91.
2. Matthew Connelly, Oral History Transcript, p. 51, HSTL.
3. Ayers Diary, 17 April 1945, p. 45, HSTL.
4. *Ibid.,* p. 46.
5. Connelly, Oral History Transcript, p. 40, HSTL.
6. Ayers Diary, 1 May 1945, p. 51, HSTL.
7. Samuel Rosenman, Oral History Interview, pp. 19–20, HSTL.
8. *Ibid.,* pp. 24–25, HSTL.
9. Richard E. Neustadt, "Extending the Horizons of Democratic Liberalism," in *The Truman Years,* ed. J. Joseph Huthmacher (Hinsdale, Illinois: Dryden Press, 1972), p. 82.
10. Rosenman, Oral History Transcript, p. 20, HSTL.
11. *Ibid.,* p. 21.
12. *Ibid.,* p. 25.
13. President Truman's handwritten draft of this intended speech can be found in Box 28, Papers of Clark Clifford, PSF, HSTL.
14. Quoted from an interview with Clark Clifford reprinted in Patrick Anderson, *The Presidents' Men* (New York: Doubleday, 1968), p. 116. Cf., Rosenman, Oral History Transcript, p. 213, HSTL.
15. *Public Papers of Harry S. Truman, 1946,* p. 216.
16. Ayers Diary, 28 February 1946, HSTL.
17. David E. Lilienthal, *The Atomic Energy Years 1945–1950,* vol. 2 (New York: Harper & Row, 1964), p. 116. Hereinafter these works will be cited as Lilienthal Journals.
18. Cabell Phillips, *The Truman Presidency* (Toronto: Macmillan, 1966), pp. 119–20.
19. Ayers Diary, 8 December 1946, HSTL.
20. Lilienthal Journals, 2, p. 434.
21. Rosenman, Oral History Transcript, p. 30, HSTL.
22. Charles S. Murphy, Oral History Transcript, p. 15, HSTL.
23. *Ibid.,* p. 29.
24. *Ibid.,* p. 47.
25. John E. Hopkins, "An Investigation of the Speech and Statement Preparation Process During the Presidential Administration of Harry S. Truman 1945–1953, (Ph.D. diss., Ohio University, 1970), p. 45.
26. Ayers Diary, 26 April 1947, HSTL.
27. Report entitled, "Functions of the White House Map Room," undated, Truman Papers Folder, Elsey Papers, HSTL.
28. Note, June 15, 1945, Berlin Conference Folder, Elsey Papers, HSTL.
29. George M. Elsey, Oral History Transcript, pp. 343–44, HSTL.
30. Paper dated July 12, Foreign Relations—Russia, 1946, Folder 1, Elsey Papers, HSTL.
31. Memo in Elsey's handwriting, dated Wednesday, July 17, in Foreign Relations—Russia, 1946, Folder 1, Elsey Papers, HSTL.
32. Arthur Krock, *Memoirs: Sixty Years on the Firing Line* (New York: Funk and Wagnalls, 1968), p. 224.
33. George Elsey, Oral History Transcript, pp. 144–48, HSTL.
34. *Ibid.,* pp. 297–98.
35. *Public Papers of Harry S. Truman, 1947,* pp. 178–79.
36. George Elsey, Oral History Transcript, p. 162, HSTL.
37. This itinerary is drawn from the Elsey Papers, Box 24, Speech File, HSTL.

38. Folder: Biographical Material, Box 33, Papers of David D. Lloyd, HSTL.
39. David E. Bell, Oral History Transcript, p. 67. Also cf. p. 158, *Ibid.*, HSTL.
40. *Ibid.*, p. 94.
41. James L. Sundquist, Oral History Transcript, p. 6, HSTL.
42. Farewell Address Folder, Papers of Richard E. Neustadt, Box 1, HSTL.
43. Bell, Oral History Transcript, p. 198, HSTL.

9 Persuading the Congress

1. John Nance Garner is most often quoted as having said, "The vice presidency isn't worth a pitcher of warm spit." According to *Time* magazine, Garner actually said the office "isn't worth a pitcher of warm piss." After his retirement he complained that those "panty-waist writers wouldn't print it the way I said it." Cf. *Time,* (9 September 1974): 46.
2. *Boston Transcript,* November 1, 1924.
3. *Congressional Record,* 77th Cong., 1st sess., 3 January 1941, p. 7.
4. Steinberg, p. 175.
5. From a filmed interview of Speaker Rayburn by Martin Agronsky (NBC).
6. *Ibid.*
7. Joseph G. Feeney, Oral History Transcript, p. 53, HSTL.
8. As quoted in *U.S. News and World Report* (April 1 1949): 37.
9. For more detailed accounts of this involvement, cf. Stephen G. Xydis, *Greece and the Great Powers, 1944-1947* (Thessaloniki: Institute for Balkan Studies, 1963). Prelude to the Truman Doctrine.
10. Truman, Memoirs, 2, p. 105.
11. *Congressional Record,* 81st Cong., 2d sess., pp. 6476–78.
12. Truman, Memoirs, 1, p. 272.
13. *Congressional Record,* 79th Cong., 1st sess., pp. 164–65.
14. As quoted by Arthur Vandenberg, Jr., in a personal letter to him from Walter Lippman. Arthur H. Vandenberg, Jr., ed., *The Private Papers of Senator Vandenberg* (Boston: Houghton Mifflin, 1952), pp. xx–xxi.
15. Quoted by Undersecretary Acheson, who was present at the meeting. Dean Acheson, *Present at the Creation* (New York: W. W. Norton, 1969), p. 219.
16. *Congressional Record,* 80th Cong., 2d sess., p. 7801.
17 Alben W. Barkley, *That Reminds Me* (New York: Doubleday, 1954), p. 58.
18. *Ibid.*, p. 91.
19. Will Rogers in the *New York Times,* 28 June 1932, p. 16.
20. *New York World-Telegram,* 9 July 1948.
21. *New York Times,* 13 July 1948, p. 10.
22. *New York Times,* 15 July 1948, p. 4.
23. Barkley, *That Reminds Me,* p. 207.
24. *Ibid.*, p. 213.
25. Ayers Diary, 28 February 1949, HSTL.
26. Ayers Diary, 24 December 1947, HSTL.
27. *State Department Employee Loyalty Investigation,* Hearings before a Subcommittee of the Senate Committee on Foreign Relations, 81st Cong., 2d sess., p. 1760.
28. Quoted in Ayers Diary, 6 May 1949, HSTL.
29. See, for example, Jack L. Bell, Oral History Transcript, pp. 64–66, HSTL.
30. As quoted by Jules Abels, *Out of the Jaws of Victory* (New York: Henry Holt, 1959), p. 139.

10 Persuading the People

1. James E. Pollard, *"Truman and the Press,"* Journalism Quarterly, 28 (Fall 1951): 458.

2. For a more extended account of these briefing sessions, see Irving Perlmeter, Assistant Press Secretary, Oral History Transcript, pp. 5–7, HSTL.

3. Elmer Cornwell, *Presidential Leadership of Public Opinion* (Bloomington, Indiana: Indiana University Press, 1965), p. 306.

4. Douglass Cater, *The Fourth Branch of Government* (Boston: Houghton Mifflin, 1959), p. 42.

5. *Public Papers of Harry S. Truman, 1948*, p. 42.

6. *Public Papers of Harry S. Truman, 1950*, p. 153.

7. Walter Trohan of the *Chicago Tribune*, Oral History Transcript, pp. 101–2, HSTL.

8. *Public Papers of Harry S. Truman, 1950*, p. 727.

9. *Public Papers of Harry S. Truman, 1948*, p. 432.

10. *Ibid.*, p. 433.

11. Herbert Lee Williams, "Truman and the Press" (Ph.D. diss., University of Missouri, 1954), pp. 431–32.

12. *Ibid.*, p. 421.

13. *Public Papers of Harry S. Truman, 1950*, p. 159.

14. Ayers Diary, 16 February 1950, HSTL.

15. Personal letter to Carl W. McCasland, 1046 West 42nd St., Los Angeles, 29 December 1950, in Williams, "Truman and the Press," p. 443.

16. At the time he wrote the memo destined to play such a significant role in Truman's campaign strategy, James Rowe, A.B. Harvard (1931), LL.B. (1934), was serving as a member of the commission to reorganize the executive branch of the government.

17. Elsey, Oral History Transcript, pp. 414–15, HSTL.

18. *Ibid.*

19. Papers of James E. Webb, Director of the Budget, General File, Box 2, HSTL. Mrs. A. presumably is Mrs. Harriet Adkinson, Webb's personal secretary at the time.

20. Personal letter dated 13 June 1978, from James Rowe to the author.

21. Summarized from paper entitled, "Memorandum for the President," Papers of Clark M. Clifford, Political File, Box 21, pp. 1–19, HSTL.

22. *Ibid.*, pp. 32–33.

23. *Ibid.*, p. 34.

24. *Ibid.*, pp. 39–40.

25. *Congressional Record*, 80th Cong., 2d sess., 1948, XCIV, Part 1, pp. 65–66.

26. *New York Herald Tribune*, 8 January 1948.

27. For a survey of other press reactions, see *New York Herald Tribune*, 8 January 1948, and *Time* (19 January 1948).

28. Jack L. Bell, Oral History Transcript, pp. 64–66, HSTL.

29. Edward T. Folliard, Oral History Transcript, p. 11, HSTL.

30. *Public Papers of Harry S. Truman, 1948*, p. 348.

31. *New York Times*, 12 June 1948.

32. For these and responses from other cities, see Jack Redding's, *Inside the Democratic Party* (Indianapolis: Bobbs-Merrill, 1958), pp. 178–81.

33. *New York Times*, 13 June 1948.

34. *Public Papers of Harry S. Truman, 1948*, 328–29.

35. Robert L. Riggs, Chief, Washington Bureau, *Louisville Courier-Journal*, Oral History Transcript, pp. 30–31, HSTL.

36. Undated Memorandum from George Elsey to Clark Clifford, Clifford Papers, Political File, HSTL.

37. As quoted in Joseph C. Goulden, *Mencken's Last Campaign* (Washington: New Republic Book Company, 1976).

38. William L. Batt, Jr., Oral History Transcript, pp. 32–33, HSTL.

39. *Ibid.*, p. 18.

40. Leonard J. Reinsch, Oral History Transcript, pp. 32–33, HSTL.

41. Taken from tape recording made by the National Broadcasting Company: President Harry S. Truman's acceptance speech at the Democratic National Convention, 15 July 1948.

42. *Ibid.*

43. *Ibid.*
44. *Ibid.*
45. *Ibid.*
46. Ayers Diary, 10 July 1948.
47. William L. Batt, Jr., Oral History Transcript, pp. 14–17, HSTL.
48. Memorandum dated 29 June 1948, entitled, "Should the President Call the Congress Back?" Clifford Papers, Political File, HSTL.
49. Elsey Papers, Folder: Reconvening Second Session—80th Cong., dated 7 July 1948, Box 23, HSTL.
50. *Congressional Record,* House of Representatives, 27 July 1948, p. 9592.
51. As reported in the *New York World-Telegram,* 2 August 1948.
52. As reported in the *New York Herald-Tribune,* 12 August 1948.
53. President's Secretary's File, Speech File, HSTL.
54. Robert L. Riggs, Chief, Washington Bureau, *Louisville Courier-Journal,* Oral History Transcript, pp. 37–38, HSTL.
55. Oscar Ewing, Oral History Transcript, vol. 2, pp. 268–69, HSTL.
56. Telephone interview with Clifford on 13 June 1967, as quoted in Ross, *The Loneliest Campaign,* p. 183.
57. Richard H. Rovere, "Letter from a Campaign Train," *The New Yorker,* 9 October 1948, p. 72.
58. Elsey Papers, Box 24, HSTL.
59. Matthew Connelly, Oral History Transcript, p. 124, HSTL.
60. Elsey Papers, Speech File, Box 25, HSTL.
61. *Ibid.*
62. *Public Papers of Harry S. Truman, 1948,* p. 559.
63. Quoted in Abels, *Out of the Jaws of Victory,* p. 226.
64. Elsey Papers, Speech File, HSTL.
65. *Ibid.,* Box 25, HSTL.
66. *Ibid.,* San Marcos, Austin, and Temple Folder, HSTL.
67. Memorandum to Clifford from Stephen J. Spingarn, dated 16 September 1948, Elsey Papers, Speech File, Box 26, HSTL.
68. *Ibid.,* Folder: Campaign Speeches, HSTL.
69. Elsey Papers, Box 28, HSTL.
70. *Public Papers of Harry S. Truman, 1948,* p. 839.
71. Elsey Papers, Speech File, Box 26, HSTL.
72. *Public Papers of Harry S. Truman, 1948,* p. 883.
73. Richard H. Rovere, "Letter from a Campaign Train," *The New Yorker,* 16 October 1948, 79.
74. *New York World-Telegram,* 2 November 1948.
75. Elsey Papers, Folder: President's Speaking Tours, Speech File, HSTL.
76. *New York Herald-Tribune,* 4 November 1948.

11 Truman the Debater

1 Lucius D. Clay, *Decision in Germany* (New York: Doubleday,1950), p. 361.
2. Truman, *Memoirs,* 2, pp. 125–26.
3. *New York Times,* 1 July 1948.
4. *Public Papers of Harry S. Truman 1948,* p. 394.
5. *Ibid.,* p. 412.
6. *Ibid.,* p. 422.
7. *Ibid.*
8. *Ibid.,* p. 423.
9. *Ibid.,* p. 481.
10. *Ibid.*
11. *Ibid.,* pp. 481–82.

12. *Ibid.*, p. 944.

13. *Public Papers of Harry S. Truman 1949*, p. 214.

14. *Ibid.*, p. 241.

15. Truman, Memoirs, 2, p. 333.

16. John J. Muccio quoted in a conference sponsored by The Harry S. Truman Library Institute for National and International Affairs, Independence, Missouri, 1975. Cf. Francis H. Heller, ed., *The Korean War: A Twenty-Five Year Perspective.* (Lawrence, Kansas: Regents Press of Kansas, 1977), p. 11.

17. There are many excellent books and articles dealing with special aspects of the Korean War. A sample of these works might include the following. David Rees, *Korea: The Limited War* (New York: St. Martins, 1964); I. F. Stone, *The Hidden History of the Korean War* (New York: Monthly Review Press, 1952); Glenn D. Paige, *The Korean Decision, June 24-30, 1950* (New York: Free Press, 1968); John W. Spannier, *The Truman-MacArthur Controversy and the Korean War* (Cambridge: Harvard University Press, 1959); and Walter LaFeber, "Crossing the 38th: The Cold War in Microcosm," in *Reflections on the Cold War: A Quarter Century of American Foreign Policy*, Lynn H. Miller and Ronald W. Pruessen, eds. (Philadelphia: Temple University Press, 1974).

18. *Vital Speeches*, 17 (1 January 1951): 171.

19. Joseph P. Kennedy in a personal letter to the writer dated 3 January 1954.

20. *Ibid.*

21. *New York Times*, 16 December 1950.

22. *New York Times*, 17 December 1950.

23. *Ibid.*

24. *Ibid.*

25. *Ibid.*

26. *New York Times*, 6 January 1951.

27. The MacArthur episode is treated in biographies of Truman or MacArthur, in most general histories of the period, and in many special books or articles dealing with the event. Discussions of the controversy and its outcome can be found in each of the following books. Francis H. Heller, ed., *The Korean War* (Lawrence, Kansas: Regents Press of Kansas, 1977); Dean Acheson, *Present at the Creation: My Years in the State Department* (New York: W. W. Norton, 1969); Douglas MacArthur, *Reminiscences* (New York: McGraw-Hill, 1964); John W. Spannier, *The Truman-MacArthur Controversy and the Korean War* (Cambridge: Harvard University Press, 1959); and Charles A. Willoughby, *MacArthur 1941-1951* (New York: McGraw-Hill, 1954).

28. Quoted by John C. Miller, *Sam Adams: Pioneer in Propaganda* (Boston: Little, Brown, 1936), p. 24.

29. Oscar Ewing, Oral History Transcript, pp. 137–38, HSTL.

30. *Congressional Digest*, 28 (April 1949): 106.

12   *Truman at the Rostrum*

1. Lane Cooper, trans., *The Rhetoric of Aristotle* (New York: D. Appleton-Century, 1932), p. 7.

2. Quoted by the author from remarks made by Harriman during an Invitational Conference on the Administration of the Presidency under Harry S. Truman. The conference was sponsored by the Truman Library Institute and held in Kansas City, Missouri, 5 May through 7 May 1977.

3. Factual reports of the circumstances of Truman's meeting with MacArthur at Wake Island, 15 October 1950, can be found in any of the following: *New York Times*, 21 April 1951, dispatch by Anthony Leverio, White House correspondent; Cabell Phillips, *The Truman Presidency*, pp. 315–22; John J. Muccio, U.S. Ambassador to Korea, 1949–1952, Oral History Transcript; Edward T. Folliard, White House correspondent for the *Washington Post*, Oral History Transcript, HSTL.

4. Ayers Diary, 22 September 1951, HSTL.

5. *Public Papers of Harry S. Truman, 1948*, p. 477.

6. *Ibid.*, p. 587.

7. *Public Papers of Harry S. Truman, 1950,* pp. 109–10.

8. *Public Papers, 1952,* pp. 543–544.

9. *Public Papers, 1947,* p. 298.

10. *Public Papers, 1947,* pp. 4–5.

11. *Public Papers, 1947,* pp. 492–93.

12. *Public Papers, 1951,* p. 223.

13. *Public Papers, 1951,* p. 225.

14. *Ibid.,* pp. 225–26.

15. *Ibid.,* p. 227.

16. Edward T. Folliard, Oral History Transcript, pp. 17–18, HSTL.

17. President's Secretary's File, Speech File, longhand notes, Box 48, HSTL.

18. *Ibid.,* Box 46, HSTL.

19. *Ibid.*

20. President's Secretary's File, Speech File, longhand notes, Box 48, HSTL.

21. *Public Papers of Harry S. Truman, 1946,* p. 407.

22. *Ibid.,* p. 408. The word is not listed in the unabridged version of *Webster's New International Dictionary.*

23. *Ibid.*

24. Folliard, Oral History Transcript, p. 18, HSTL.

25. David E. Bell, Oral History Transcript, p. 40, HSTL.

26. Ayers Diary, 4 August 1950, HSTL.

27. Elsey Papers, Speech File, Box 25, HSTL.

28. Ayers Diary, 13 September, 1950, HSTL.

29. A personal letter to John T. O'Rourke, ed., *Washington Daily News,* in Herbert Lee Williams, "Truman and the Press" (Ph.D. diss., University of Missouri, 1954), p. 426, HSTL.

30. *Ibid.,* personal letter to Robert M. White, Mexico, Missouri, p. 429, HSTL.

31. Ayers Diary, 20 September 1947, HSTL.

32. *Ibid.,* 23 December 1950, HSTL.

33. *Ibid.,* 1 May 1945, HSTL.

34. *Ibid.,* p. 67, HSTL.

35. *Ibid.,* p. 87, HSTL.

36. Folliard, Oral History Transcript, p. 9, HSTL.

37. Ayers Diary, May 4, 1945, HSTL.

38. *Ibid.,* 22 February 1949.

39. *Ibid.,* p. 53, HSTL.

40. *Ibid.,* p. 70, HSTL.

41. *Ibid.,* 6 July 1948, HSTL.

42. *Ibid.,* 3 August 1951, HSTL.

43. *Ibid.,* 2 May 1945, HSTL.

44. *Ibid.,* p. 97, HSTL.

45. Remark made by Beth Campbell Short, correspondence secretary to the president (September, 1952–January, 1953), at Conference on the Administration of the Presidency under Harry S. Truman, May 1977.

46. Robert K. Walsh, Oral History Transcript, pp. 58–59, HSTL.

47. As related by Folliard, Oral History Transcript, HSTL.

48. Elsey Papers, Speech File, Box 29, HSTL.

49. *Ibid.*

50. President's Secretary's File, Box 48, 24 February 1949, HSTL.

51. Matthew Connelly, Oral History Interview, pp. 60–61, HSTL.

52. Oral History Interview with J. Leonard Reinsch, pp. 3–4, HSTL.

53. President's Secretary's File, Speech file, Box 46, HSTL.

54. *Ibid.*

55. Memorandum from Charles Murphy to President Truman, 13 September 1950, HSTL.

56. Ayers Diary, 20 June 1947, HSTL.

57. *Ibid.,* 28 October 1947, HSTL.

58. A. Craig Baird, *Representative American Speeches: 1951-1952* (New York: H. W. Wilson, 1952), p. 66.

Index